INDIGENOUS MOVEMENTS
AND THEIR CRITICS

INDIGENOUS MOVEMENTS AND THEIR CRITICS

PAN-MAYA ACTIVISM IN GUATEMALA

Kay B. Warren

PRINCETON UNIVERSITY PRESS

Copyright © 1998 by Princeton University Press
Published by Princeton University Press, 41 William Street,
Princeton, New Jersey 08540
In the United Kingdom: Princeton University Press,
Chichester, West Sussex
All Rights Reserved

Library of Congress Cataloging-in-Publication Data

Warren, Kay B.
Indigenous movements and their critics : Pan-Maya
activism in Guatemala / Kay B. Warren.
p.   cm.
Includes bibliographical references and index.
ISBN 0-691-05881-4 (cl : alk. paper). —
ISBN 0-691-05882-2 (pb : alk. paper)
1. Mayas—Guatemala—Government relations.   2. Indians of
Central America—Guatemala—Government relations.
3. Mayas—Guatemala—Ethnic identity.   4. Mayas—Guatemala—
Politics and government.   5. Guatemala—Politics and
government—1985–   I. Title.
F1465.3.G6W37   1998
972.81′004974152—DC21   98-3531

This book has been composed in Times Roman

The paper used in this publication meets the minimum
requirements of ANSI/NISO Z39.48-1992 (R 1997)
(*Permanence of Paper*).

http://pup.princeton.edu

Printed in the United States of America

10   9   8   7   6   5   4   3   2   1

10   9   8   7   6   5   4   3   2
(Pbk.)

**To the variety of paths to lasting peace
in Guatemala**

Contents

Preface

THIS BOOK BEGAN in the late 1980s as a reexamination of identity politics and racism twenty years after my original fieldwork in Guatemala. Right away, I knew this would not be a restudy in any classical sense because ethnic politics, Guatemala, "Indian" communities, cultural anthropology, and Kay Warren had changed so dramatically since my first trip in 1969. Analytically, there was no constant frame of reference.[1] On the ground, I really had no choice. The atmosphere of uncertainty and violence that stemmed from the 1978–1985 civil war between the army and guerrilla forces still permeated everyday life in Guatemala and in San Andrés Semetabaj, an agrarian community in the western highland department of Sololá, which had been the focus of my earlier work. Moreover, self-proclaimed pan-community Maya groups were springing up throughout the country. Maya academics and activists confronted Western scholars with pointed critiques of politics, research practices, and published findings on Maya culture. One could hardly use the old rationale—the strategic innocence—that anthropology meant speaking out for those who had no voice.

The public intellectuals in Pan-Mayanism and I share several threads of a transcultural history dating from the time of that first field research. At that point, nascent San Andrés activists in their early twenties (as I was) were just beginning to rebel quietly against their families. Their siblings were young children and toddlers. I knew the families of some of these restless youths, even their grandparents, and wrote about the insights and the frustrating impasse their parents had reached politically because indigenous activism was locally and religiously focused (Warren 1989). I would never have guessed that, along with successful careers in rural development and education, some of these questioning youths would become more, rather than less, active in indigenous cultural politics or that one toddler would become a nationally known linguist specializing in Maya languages. Given the localized arenas for intellectuals in marginalized indigenous communities, it did not occur to me that one day we would routinely share the podium at national and international conferences.

San Andrés was not the only site of restlessness in the early 1970s. Four hours away by bus, in the colonial city of Antigua, young foreigners converged on a fledgling research center, the Francisco Marroquín Linguistics Project (PLFM), where I volunteered on weekends in 1970 and 1971 to return something to the country I was studying.[2] The aspirations and contradictions of the project reflected the political subjectivity of my generation of activists. We were inspired and limited by the idealism of the 1960s, the call for volunteers by President Kennedy and Pope John XXIII, the civil rights movement, and the tragedy of Vietnam. Bob Gersony, a driven, self-educated Vietnam vet; Jo Froman, a midwestern philosophy B.A. studying Kaqchikel as part of her Peace Corps training; Tony Jackson, an Oxford-trained British volunteer; and Terry Kaufman, a well-known American research linguist—took over the center from a pair of tired American priests, who had run a language program for missionaries and used Mayas as passive informants for their studies. Soon thereafter three rounds of Peace Corps volunteers with M.A. or Ph.D. degrees in linguistics joined the rejuvenated project as instructors—this time to offer professional training to Mayas.[3]

Given the counterinsurgency climate of the time—the military was focusing on the containment of urban guerrillas through army check points on major roads, curfews, and the suspension of civil rights such as the freedom of assembly—the institution had no choice but to present itself as nonpolitical. Guatemalans in power generally regarded the field of linguistics, especially research on unwritten "native tongues," as a peripheral enterprise with no political significance. For its own part, the Linguistics Project aspired to be an integrator across rural communities and language divides and a conduit of ideas for national policy.

Rejecting the social hierarchies conventional to development assistance, the foreigners worked to create a novel institution "to vigorously promote the study and use of Indian languages in communication, education, and community development" (Froman et al. 1978, 103). Instead of intervening directly in communities, as was the norm for Peace Corps volunteers and missionaries, they decided to train Indians in skills not available in Guatemala and to encourage participants to make their own decisions about community projects. Through intensive course work, the students gained M.A.-level training from Terry Kaufman, Nora England, Will Norman, and others[4] and applied their lessons by producing studies and educational materials based on language practices in their home communities. After classes, the trainees, who came from all over the highlands (though not at that time from San Andrés), exchanged experiences and ideas among themselves in an environment highly sympathetic to indigenous issues.[5] The result was an extraordinarily wide construction of linguistics as a scholarly and activist field of knowledge.

The Mayas recruited for the project were not the indigenous professionals with secondary educations and professional degrees who had begun to form their own associations in the early 1970s. These emerging elites were felt to be highly antagonistic toward foreigners, too mobile and urban-oriented for community-focused work, and disdainful of those with less education. Nor were families with successful rural businesses in towns such as Tecpán or Totonicapán interested because the wages offered did not compete with what their children could generate in family enterprises.[6] Rather, the project recruited locally nominated Mayas between the ages of twenty and thirty-five with strong social ties with their home communities and no more than six years of education.[7] Apparently there was no pressure from the trainees to incorporate women and no early feminists among the foreign staff to press for their involvement. Later, when attempts were made to widen recruitment, the project encountered reticence from rural parents and husbands who did not want young women to live away from home.

In a country where most of the indigenous population worked as illiterate peasant agriculturalists, the goal was to build a self-governing institution through which Indians could produce bilingual dictionaries and collections of readings and take an active role in decisions regarding the use and future of the Maya languages spoken in their communities. Through three rounds of courses during the first six years, 138 full-time students were trained in Maya linguistics and a talented core group—including Narciso Cojtí and Martín Chacach, who later became national leaders—received on-the-job administrative training.

The founders created an inspired solution to the problem of generating funds for a Maya organization while avoiding dependence on institutions that might compromise the project's goals. They established a Spanish school for tourists, students, and international development volunteers, staffed by a nonindigenous administration and teachers.[8] Although the two wings of the project were administratively insulated from each other, the founders enjoyed the ironic inversion of the conventional division of labor at a time when Ladinos rarely worked for Mayas. By 1976 the Spanish school employed 120 instructors in three Guatemalan cities; by 1978 it had taught five thousand students.[9]

The *gringo* volunteers planned to leave a fully functional institution in Maya hands after five years, which they accomplished on schedule in January 1976. Over the last twenty-seven years, hundreds of Mayas have spent time training and later working as linguists and administrators at the project, studying with professional linguists in subsequent programs and research centers, and, more recently, taking and teaching university courses. Language issues have stood at the heart of the Maya movement and its political vision. The Linguistics Project, which stopped training new linguists in 1990 (Chacach 1997), never escaped the stigma of its initial association with foreigners. Other institutes, frequently with alumni from the project, gained prominence with the surge of Pan-Maya institution building in the late 1980s. Not surprisingly, linguistics was not the only route to Pan-Mayanism, though it is striking how many current activists have backgrounds in the field.

Pan-Maya oral histories, however, rarely dwell on the Francisco Marroquín Linguistics Project.[10] Rather they root the political fascination with language in Adrián Chávez's (1969) battle in 1945 to promote a specialized orthography (or alphabet)[11] for K'ichee' and his founding of the Academy for the Maya-Kíchè Language in 1960. Mayanists cite these events as evidence of early indigenous attempts to wrest control over language and representation from the government and North American evangelizers. Control (whether it be by well-meaning foreign idealists, government indigenous institutes, or missionaries) and the ranking of languages, cultures, and ethnicities (accepted as a transparent fact by many Guatemalans) have been continuing preoccupations of the Maya movement. Many regard 1987 as the watershed, when Mayanists took control for the first time of the national framing of indigenous language policy with the creation of the government-sponsored Academy for Maya Languages of Guatemala (ALMG) (López Raquec 1989; England 1996).

To better understand the transformations of the last thirty years—and the choices chroniclers make as they marshall the authority of their own experiences to narrate important transitions—I made repeated trips to Guatemala from 1989 through 1998, participated in international and national forums with Maya scholars, and began to publish essays dealing with different facets of Maya social criticism and ethnic revitalization. Yet, a larger project remained: to interrelate the convergent and divergent strands of cultural resurgence in rural communities and in the national movement for *reivindicación*. The Spanish term expresses the wide-ranging demands for vindication, recognition, recovery, and rights as indigenous peoples. This study draws on and expands the scope of my recent work on Maya definitions of self-determination in a world often, but not always, hostile to their efforts. As the title of this book indicates, indigenous movements do not come in the singular nor do they have unitary politics. Rather they are heterogeneous products of diverse antecedents—local, international, national—even as they attempt to forge unifying political programs.

The book also deals with the movement's critics—foreign and domestic, indigenous and nonindigenous—who see tactical mistakes, threats to their own achievements, or even danger in the movement's phrasing of cultural politics. The challenge for anthropology is to trace the interplay and impact of these critical voices without silencing the movement, speaking for its proponents, or romanticizing its politics. Throughout the book, this inquiry examines the political stakes of those who author and circulate the contested representations of Pan-Mayanism.

At various points, I subject the terms of my own investigation to the same questioning. Over and over again, the experience of writing this book convinced me there is simply *no neutral* position or language of analysis through which to author the story of ethnic resurgence. Finding an authorial subject position has involved uncovering the key moments—some of them not so noble—that capture the process through which I came to this awareness and the rhetorical strategies I use in this volume to convey these and other research findings to my readers. I remain convinced that one can produce a reflexive account without losing track of the demanding project of studying the cultural politics that inform the extraordinary transition in Guatemala from counterinsurgency warfare to unfinished democratic peace.

Given the controversial issues raised in this study of ethnic politics, readers may find themselves buffeted by antagonistic political positions on many consequential issues and troubled by ethnic organizing in the name of multiculturalism. As an anthropologist, I have found this to be a particularly difficult historical moment to write about ethnic revival because of the turbulence of ideas and events that surround identity politics in the United States and beyond. I have been astonished by the hostility provoked by my research on Pan-Mayanism. At an international conference in Princeton in 1995, the problem was not so much how I was approaching the issue, whether my framing was useful or not, but that I was studying it at all. In particular, I was condemned by a pair of senior American academics, a historian and a political scientist, for writing about this example of ethnic intensification as if it were constructive. In the heat of the moment, one critic accused the discipline of anthropology of being in the business of lending legitimacy to cultural difference and, thereby, contributing to the global crisis of ethnic violence. Although the charge is absurd—the discipline commands neither the power nor the uncritical agenda imputed to us here—one of the purposes of this book is to understand and respond to these and other critics in terms of this instance of ethnic organizing.

As we know, Americans are highly ambivalent about race- and ethnic-based politics and cultural pluralism at home. A growing backlash has been mobilized to challenge multiculturalism and multilingualism in the schools, disestablish affirmative action, and dismantle the welfare state's minority programming. The militia movement became a lightning rod for the expression of racial anger. In California, the passage of Proposition 187 focused anti-immigrant hostility on the families of Mexicans and other Latin Americans working in the state. The O.J. Simpson trial and the beating of Rodney King, which set the stage for its reception, revealed a tremendous gap between white and black attitudes on the intensity of racism in daily life. Media explanations of poverty have shifted toward the moral language of individual character and the biological language of inherited IQ. The Ebonics controversy and vote to disestablish bilingual education in California public schools, the funding of public-library acquisitions in diverse immigrant languages in New York, and the state supreme court ruling that the Arizona English-only policy for government affairs is unconstitutional illustrate the intricate politicization of language and cultural difference.

Internationally, the situation appears even more charged. Anti-immigrant politics and violence have spread across European democracies. Throughout the world, ethnic mobilization and nationalist movements have been cast as a primary source of post–Cold War violent conflict.[12] Groups that articulate their demands in ethnic terms are seen as dupes of cynical leaders seeking political power at any price. Because political demands for self-administration sometimes become territorial—calling for the subdivision of states and the collective mobilization of nationalist groups dispersed across different countries—distinctive situations of ethnic nationalism are lumped together as threats to the stability of existing nation-states. Epithets like "Balkanization" and "separatism" have been used by UN officials and academics to condemn politicized groups in multi-ethnic states.

Like all writers in politically charged circumstances, I hope for an engaged, proactive readership that will savor the story of an intricate struggle to build peace in an ethnically heterogeneous neighboring country—one intimately connected to the United States yet culturally distinctive in many ways. That I can see no distanced neutral position from which to consume this work means that it will be read in many ways.[13] In part this is the consequence of thick description ethnography, which rejects the voice-of-God expository style in favor of demonstrating the flux and multiplicity of viewpoints that make a difference in shaping social conflicts. In reality, there is no single route through the dilemmas of the moment.

Of course, I hope this study will rectify some basic misunderstandings for all—that, rather than being members of a dead culture, Mayas are as involved in the politics of the 1990s as any other activist group and that, once seen as peers, intellectuals in other societies have much to teach American academics and students about engagement in nationally important issues.

Acknowledgments _____

THERE ARE MANY individuals in Guatemala to whom I am indebted for time, insights, meals, a roof over my head, key questions, and the cultural histories this book recounts. None of them is responsible for my interpretations, interconnections, or final analysis although all offered contributions, large and small, accompanied by important analytical insights. Other collaborators shared ideas through research networks—anchored momentarily in Guatemala, Delhi, Campinas, Utrecht, Portrack, Santa Fe, Washington, Chicago, San Francisco, Princeton, and New York—through which this research gained its narrative form, to be tested later in lectures and seminars at Princeton, Brandeis, Harvard, Michigan, Johns Hopkins, NYU, Wisconsin, Pennsylvania, Chicago, and the Institute for Advanced Study. The reviewers of the manuscript for publication—Charles Hale, John Watanabe, Joanne Rappaport, Les Field, Michael Kearney, and R. McKenna Brown—offered enthusiastic evaluations followed by generous and challenging intellectual engagement with the work as a whole. Other colleagues—especially June Nash, Judith Maxwell, Vincanne Adams, Diane Nelson, Abigail Adams, Richard Adams, and Carlos Iván Degregori—offered insightful feedback on important aspects of the analysis. This is a better book for the critiques and urgings of my fellow Latin Americanists.

In San Andrés, a rural county (or *municipio*) of sixty-five hundred inhabitants in the western highland department of Sololá, I returned to the extended family networks I had known years before and learned the sorrowful news that some venerated elders, such as Don Emiliano Matzar, had died long ago. I began to catch up on regional history. Alfonso Ixim and Antonia Jab introduced me to the many people who coursed through their busy household seeking advice on how to organize cooperatives, cope with the legal requisites of bureaucratic transactions, resolve simmering family disputes, retell town history for class assignments, and seek protection for loved ones through Maya ceremonies. Alfonso also found time to talk about his changing vision of Maya culture and share drafts of his new writing project. Doña María Tul and Don Luis Ixim drew me into their kitchen to catch up on town affairs and, quite unexpectedly, to hear of the positive repercussions for their family of my first fieldwork in the early 1970s. Their adult sons, No'j and Javier—small children when I saw them last—now questioned my presence as a foreigner, one becoming a good friend and the other an evasive skeptic. Don Gustavo Ixim and I spent thoroughly enjoyable hours, as we had in the past, under a metal roof in the hammering rain, talking through the din about history, philosophy, politics, culture, language, and religion. More recently,

Alfonso, No'j, and Don Gustavo reviewed translated drafts of my San Andrés analysis, and we began a joint essay on the tremendous changes the
town has experienced over the last half-century.

In San Andrés the social arrangements that in the past had been so central
to public affairs—the dominance of local *Ladinos* (non-indigenous Guatemalans) in politics and plantation agriculture, despite the fact they made up
only a quarter of the town's population, and the importance of the Maya
hierarchy of religious and governing authorities to indigenous sociality—had
been displaced by other organizations and events after the mid-1970s. The
1976 earthquake flattened the town. In a few moments, the impressive colonial church with its beautiful high dome and adobe walls, freshly restored
after decades of saving and work, lay in ruins. Homes, businesses, and the
municipal center had to be rebuilt. Two years later, the nationwide counterinsurgency war overwhelmed local politics and forced Maya organizations
elsewhere, such as the Francisco Marroquín Linguistics Project, to disband
until the worst of the violence subsided in the mid-1980s. Subsequent generations of Maya leaders worked alongside, but not always with, the community elders who had been central to resisting earlier structures of ethnic
domination.

On my return it was good to see community groups such as Catholic
Action still striving, as they have since the 1950s, to promote public service.
The colonial church had been abandoned for a safer, newly constructed
building above town. As in the past, I followed countywide celebrations at
Holy Week and the November festival in honor of the patron saint. The
activities of young people, Maya officials, and local branches of national
organizations were choreographed in familiar ways, often, though, with
changes in political significance. At nightfall, the unpredictable rupture of
army sweeps—heavily armed soldiers in camouflage with blackened faces
who appeared from nowhere—made it clear that menacing state surveillance
continued as an aspect of everyday life. Through festivals, soccer matches,
funerals, a vicious dog bite, the flu, and visits to the seminary and convent
(both new to me), the public elementary school, the cooperative, and Catholic Action's still-expanding church, I became reacquainted with the town.
During my most recent trips, the teachers, administrators, and students at
Kikotem, the newly inaugurated Maya school, welcomed me into their classrooms. My thanks to the many people who took time to chat and let me join
their activities.

Inevitably, my revisit took me to a variety of urban centers (Guatemala
City, Antigua, Chimaltenango, and Quetzaltenango), back to Maya organizations and old friends I had known years before, and on to new institutions.
Seemingly overnight, Mayanists began to publish their own commentaries
and studies for wider publics. I am grateful to the national Mayanist leadership for sharing their social analyses and thoughts on cultural revitalization. I

learned a great deal from these intellectuals, who combine a passion for scholarship with a commitment to activism. I also had the pleasure of working with non-Mayas who contribute to these organizations.

During subsequent trips, my research moved on to unexpected issues to deal with the breadth and intensity of Maya activism: linguistics, history, education, literature, the media, state politics, and the international development community. What began as a story of one community's struggle to survive and rebuild after tidal waves of national violence became an account of national and community movements urging cultural resurgence. Perhaps inevitably, the project became so large that I have had to leave most of my discussion of Maya schools and women's leadership—but not gender—for another volume.

Over the years, Guatemalan public intellectuals have collaborated with their North American counterparts to organize joint panels for international meetings and encourage others to bring together researchers working on cultural issues. Demetrio Cojtí, Martín Chacach, Victor Montejo, Enrique Sam Colop, Irma Otzoy, and Marta Elena Casaús Arzú have been especially generous transnational colleagues at conferences in Guatemala and the United States and during visits to lecture and give seminars at Princeton University. As protagonists in the following chapters, their feedback on my research has been invaluable. Otilia Lux de Cotí, Geronimo Camposeco, Margarita López Raquec, Narciso Cojtí, Guillermina Herrera, Carol Smith, Edward Fischer (and many others named elsewhere in the acknowledgments) have enhanced these transnational exchanges with their participation. It has been stimulating to be included and a pleasure to work with these scholars on research related to the book.

In Guatemala I have visited many Pan-Mayanist organizations and workplaces and followed members of the PLFM, CEDIM, SPEM, COMG, CO-CADI, Cholsamaj, OKMA, PRONEBI, ALMG, CECMA, Rutzijol, U.S.-AID, UNICEF, the Ministry of Education, the Institute of Linguistics at Rafael Landívar University, and PRONADE as they changed offices, set up regional projects in other locales, organized conferences, participated in peace commissions, and contributed to panels on education, linguistics, and Maya Studies. In addition to those already named, I am especially grateful to Demetrio Rodríguez, Arnulfo Simón, Ernestina Reyes, Leopoldo Tzian, José Serech, Germán Curruchiche, Elsa Son, Gaspar Pedro Gonzáles, Estuardo Zapeta, Miguel Angel Velasco Bitzol, Ruperto Montejo, Celso Chaclán, and Akux Calí, among many others, for sustained discussions and background on the current movement.

In Antigua and Austin, Nora England (Ixkem), Waykan (José Gonzalo Benito Pérez), Pakal B'alam (José Obispo Rodríguez Guaján), Lolmay (Pedro Oscar García Matzar), Nik'te' (María Juliana Sis Iboy), Ajpub' (Pablo García Ixmatá), Saqijix (Candelaria Dominga López Ixcoy), Kab'lajuj Tijax (Martín Chacach), and Judith Maxwell (Ixq'anil) provided feedback on my emerging analyses and helped me understand the outlines of Maya linguistics, chronicles, and the complexities of language revitalization across the twenty-one Maya languages.

Like many scholars, I benefitted from the multifunctional Center for Regional Investigations of Mesoamerica (CIRMA) and am thankful to several generations of the staff and to the generosity of Christopher Lutz who has made this unique multicultural research center possible. I enjoyed stimulating conversations in Antigua, Guatemala City, and beyond with Tani Adams, Marcie Mersky, Katherine Langan, Christa Siebold-Little, Todd Little-Siebold, Brenda Rosenbaum, Liliana Goldin, Linda Asturias, Clara Arenas, Matilde González, Antonella Fabri, Anna Blume, Paola Ferrario, Susan Clay, Tracy Ehlers, Linda Green, Victor Perrera, Jim Handy, Susanne Jonas, John Ruthrauff, and Roger Plant. Helen Rivas, Elaine Elliot, and Flavia Ramírez helped me collect hard-to-find materials on Maya Studies and San Andrés history. Through SMART-Antigua, Margarita Asensio and Guisela Asensio facilitated the publication permissions for key illustrations. The late Linda Schele's workshops on Maya glyphs brought us together for remarkable exchanges of experiences. Few of these collaborators will be surprised to hear that the proceeds of this book will go to a variety of educational projects in Guatemala and the United States.

Colleagues at other universities and research centers, including Jean Jackson, David Maybury-Lewis, Michael Herzfeld, Arthur Kleinman, Jennifer Schirmer, Chris Tennant, Marilyn Moors, Jane Collier, Junji Koizumi, Arturo Escobar, Sonia Alvarez, Fred Myers, Faye Ginsburg, Tom Abercrombie, Mary Louise Pratt, Al Stepan, Val Daniel, Katherine Verdery, Lynn Stephen, Veena Das, Jean Lave, Dorothy Holland, Liisa Malkki, Steven Gregory, Vanessa Schwartz, Quetzil Castañeda, and the late Libbet Crandon were important sources of encouragement and feedback.

At Princeton University, Jim Boon, Larry Rosen, Gananath Obeyesekere, Rena Lederman, Hildred Geertz, Begoña Aretxaga, Jeff Himpele, Stephen Jackson, Michael Hanchard, Davida Wood, Darini Rajasingham, Yael Navaro, Wende Marshall, Rosann Fitzpatrick, Ranjini Obeyesekere, Toni Morrison, Natalie Davis, Henry Bienen, Arcadio Díaz, Miguel Centeno, Richard Falk, Jennifer Hochschild, Jeff Herbst, John Waterbury, and Wolfgang Danspeckgruber were formative and inspiring colleagues. I am particularly grateful for their responses to the early stages of this study. Carol Zanca kept the Anthropology Department on course throughout my tenure as chair and helped me balance research, teaching, and administration.

At the Institute for Advanced Study, where a lively and challenging interdisciplinary atmosphere inspired the final framing of the study, my thanks go to Clifford Geertz, Michael Walzer, Joan Scott, Albert Hirschman, and my postdoctoral colleagues at the School of Social Science. Our discussions reaffirmed my conviction that the best way to tell this history was through open-ended ethnographic essays that embrace an interactive style, concerned with indigenous genres and mine, to catch the uncertainty of Guatemala's political transition and Maya constructions of the self.

My gratitude for the financial support of this research and writing goes to the John Simon Guggenheim Foundation, Institute for Advanced Study, John D. and Catherine T. MacArthur Foundation, Wenner Gren Foundation, Liechtenstein Research Project on Self-Determination, Princeton Program in Latin American Studies, and the Humanities and Social Sciences Research Fund at Princeton.

At Princeton University Press, I am thankful to Mary Murrell, Madeleine Adams, Jan Lilly, Molan Chun Goldstein, and Lys Ann Shore, who saw the manuscript through production. Megan Peterson designed the illustrations. Gail Vielbig, Hilary Berger, and Wren Fournier were expert proofreaders. Gillett Griffin, Sonia Baur, Justin Kerr, Susanne Jonas, Beatriz Manz, and friends in San Andrés and OKMA helped track down photographs to round out my visual essay.

Finally, special appreciation goes to my family, most especially to Loy Carrington, who helped stretch early sabbatical salaries the whole year and, when she had the opportunity to visit Guatemala, told entrancing stories across language barriers in San Andrés and carried firewood through the streets of Antigua for the joy of evening fires. She has always made home and office places of mutual learning, collaboration, and inclusion.

Portions of the following essays have been reprinted in this volume with the publishers' permission. In framing the sustained argument for this analysis, however, I have felt free to rework these materials, to let the volume as a whole take new theoretical turns and address different literatures, and to update earlier work as the movement and the peace process unfolded.

"Transforming Memories and Histories: The Meanings of Ethnic Resurgence for Mayan Indians." In *Americas: New Interpretive Essays*, ed. Alfred Stepan (New York: Oxford University Press, Annenberg Foundation, and WGBH-Boston, 1992), 189–219.

"Interpreting *la Violencia* in Guatemala: Shapes of Kaqchikel Resistance and Silence." In *The Violence Within: Cultural and Political Opposition in Divided Nations*, ed. Kay B. Warren (Boulder: Westview Press, 1993), 25–56.

"Each Mind Is a World: Dilemmas of Feeling and Intention in a Kaqchikel Maya Community." In *Other Intentions: Culture and the Attribution of Inner States*, ed. Lawrence Rosen (Seattle: University of Washington Press and School of American Research, 1995), 47–67.

"Reading History as Resistance: Mayan Public Intellectuals in Guatemala." In *Maya Cultural Activism in Guatemala*, ed. Edward Fischer and
R. McKenna Brown (Austin: University of Texas Press, 1996), 89–106.

"Narrating Cultural Resurgence: Genre and Self-Representation for Pan-
Mayan Writers." In *Auto/Ethnography: Rewriting the Self and the Social*, ed.
Deborah Reed-Danahay (Oxford: Berg, 1997), 21–45.

"Indigenous Movements as a Challenge to a Unified Social Movements
Paradigm for Guatemala." In *Cultures of Politics/Politics of Cultures: Revisioning Latin American Social Movements*, ed. Sonia Alvarez, Evelina Dagnino, and Arturo Escobar (Boulder: Westview Press, 1998), 165–95.

"Enduring Tensions and Changing Identities: Mayan Family Struggles in
Guatemala." In *History in Person; Enduring Struggles and the Practice of
Identity*, ed. Dorothy Holland and Jean Lave (Santa Fe: School of American
Research, forthcoming).

Transcription of Maya Languages and Personal Names

IT IS CONVENTIONAL in academic books to note the wide variety of current practices for representing specific languages whose written forms are not standardized. Most authors decide to simplify diversity by introducing their version of a unified orthography for the ease of readers. By contrast, I have decided not to introduce artificial uniformity into a situation where alphabets are in fact political codes, guided by a history of intense controversy over ethnic politics and education.

In Guatemala minor written differences—for instance, Quiché, Kiche, and K'ichee' for the Maya language spoken by over a million people or *Popol Vuh*, *Pop Vuj*, and *Poopool Wuuj* for the sacred text often called the Maya bible—mark major philosophical and ideological cleavages. (As will become clear, the precise number of Maya languages and dialects is also politicized.) My practice is to use the form current with the group or individual in question—increasingly this is the official Academy for Maya Languages of Guatemala (ALMG) orthography (which itself is subject to refinement)—and to explain the controversies as appropriate. For Guatemalan readers, my use of these orthographies, which will continue to change and converge, marks this study from its inception as a product of a very particular moment in history.

Personal names are also changing as individuals involved in revitalization switch situationally to Maya names, often derived from ancient calendrics and chronicles, to complement their Spanish given names. There are also conventional Maya counterparts to Spanish first names in many communities. The names used in revitalization circles—where Raxche', Nik'te', and Ixkem displace Demetrio, María Juliana, and Nora—may or may not be known in one's home community. My practice follows the form individuals use for themselves in a given context. Many Mayanists use a single name in work groups or use their Maya and hispanic names together in publications, practices I also adopt.

In the past I was caught in the dilemma of using pseudonyms, and thus not being able to recognize fully the Maya contribution to my work, or using real names in an environment that remained politically uncertain. Mayas were also caught in these dilemmas. By 1997 the national movement had become public and very high profile, which allows me to identify individual protagonists. Nevertheless, it continues to be appropriate to use pseudonyms to protect the privacy of local leaders in San Andres.

For geographical names, I have retained the usage found on national maps. This, too, may change as under the peace accords some communities move to readopt the preinvasion pronunciation of hispanicized place names and others switch from colonial saints names to the earlier Maya names of their communities.

INDIGENOUS MOVEMENTS
AND THEIR CRITICS

Introduction

Democracy, Marginality, and Ethnic Resurgence

> The Mayanist movement is at once predominantly
> conservative on the cultural plane and
> predominantly innovative and revolutionary on the
> political and economic plane. For that reason, it is
> said that the Maya movement's path leads not only
> to Tikal (traditionalism) but also to New York and
> Tokyo (modernism).
>
> *Demetrio Cojtí Cuxil (1997a, 78)*

THIS BOOK PORTRAYS the ways in which Maya public intellectuals, as cultural nationalists and agents of globalization, have pursued projects for "self-determination" in Guatemala's climate of chronic political uncertainty. Doubtlessly, what has changed most since 1989 is the awareness among Maya activists that, as members of regional, national, and international networks, they can and need to advance their arguments for change in a range of overlapping arenas. In James Scott's terminology (1990), making public the "hidden transcripts" of resistance to the status quo has transformed the movement and pressured the wider society to respond to Guatemala's indigenous population in novel ways. The following chapters highlight the work of national and local intellectuals, who since the 1980s have authored key publications, engaged in educational activities in large areas of the country, and created many new institutions. The Maya movement for cultural resurgence, which came into public view in Guatemala in the late 1980s and early 1990s, is the realization of their activities.[1] This study is based on ten months of extensive discussions with movement participants in urban centers and small agrarian communities, many of whom I have known since the early 1970s. In addition, I attended a variety of meetings, workshops, and conferences from 1989 through 1998. The book examines the politics of Maya understandings of multiculturalism and Guatemalan racism and the politics of social scientific readings of this movement.

As an anthropologist with a grounding in interpretive and political anthropology, my approach examines the social construction of Pan-Maya politics and demonstrates the way elements of Maya culture (and many other cultural hybrids) inform that construction and are transformed in the process. The *movimiento maya*, as it is called, raises a series of important questions: What are the enduring contributions and limitations of a social movement that has pursued scholarly and educational routes to social change and nation building, in contrast to the mass mobilizations of the popular Left (or the troubled Zapatista rebellion in neighboring Chiapas)? What are the paradoxes and politics of the movement's "reverse orientalism," which categorically elevates the "self" and condemns the structurally dominant "other" as racist to promote solidarity and resistance? How do issues ideologically marginalized in this pan-ethnic movement—such as gender, class, religious diversity, diaspora, and the distinctiveness of local community—reassert themselves in the practice of the movement? These issues call for a consideration of the political contexts—Guatemala's historically weak civilian government, strong military, and highly successful grassroots Left—in which the movement has developed its vision of a multicultural state. The analysis touches on the ways in which nine years of on-again, off-again peace negotiations—which involved the Guatemalan National Revolutionary Unity (URNG) guerrilla coalition, the government, the military, and United Nations mediators—generated an opportunity from 1992 to 1996 for renewed discussions between the Maya movement and other politicized groups in the country. Quite unexpectedly, the peace process brought about a striking transformation in the terms of debate for indigenous issues in national politics. Most recently, Pan-Mayanism has experienced the contradictory pressures of international funders who in the name of neoliberalism pressure the government to trim bureaucracies and social services and in the name of peace offer very specific kinds of support for the strengthening of civil society and democracy.

Social theorists Chantal Mouffe and Ernesto Laclau argue that the urgent political work for this historical moment is the quest for "radical and plural democracy." They advocate diverse routes for individuals to pressure democracies for wider social, economic, and environmental justice. In the view of many analysts, this is a post-Marxist project, "given a profound crisis in socialism as a utopian horizon for a series of anticapitalist traditions, in Marxism as a doctrinal basis of support, and in the very idea of revolution as the founding act of a new society" (Rénique 1995, 178).[2] The dramatic collapse of state socialism and the apparent exhaustion of its appeal in much of the world painfully confirm the limits of ideologies that construct a political subject focused uniquely on the politics of class conflict.[3]

Yet these theorists would not free democracy from criticism, given liberal capitalism's crisis seen in the growing gap between the rich and poor and the persistence of systems of "rights [that] have been constituted on the very exclusion or subordination of rights" of others (Mouffe 1993, 70). The proliferation of social movements and backlash organizing in many countries signals the growing politicization of economic and jural tensions and reveals the multiplicity of concerns and identities salient to individuals in their daily lives.

Theorist Alberto Melucci (1989) sees a distinctive role for progressive movements in mass society because they operate outside conventional politics and create "submerged networks" that surface to focus public attention on nodal points of contention over social policy. Lacking the resources of larger formal institutions and political parties, many social movements specialize in symbolic challenges to the status quo that offer alternative interpretations of individual and collective experience. Their impact may be farther reaching than one would expect as they provoke reactions that render power visible and thus negotiable in unanticipated ways:

> By exaggerating or pushing to the limit the dominant discourse of power, the movements expose the self-contradictory nature of its "rationality" or, conversely, they show that what is labeled as "irrational" by the dominant apparatus is perhaps dramatically true. (Melucci 1989, 76)

For movements that seek to mobilize around indigenous identity in Latin America, the goal is to expose the contradictions inherent in political systems that embrace democratic egalitarianism yet, by promulgating mono-ethnic, monocultural, and monolingual images of the modern nation, epistemically exclude major sectors of their populations. The political mainstream has often cast radical assimilation as the logical way to resolve the "ethno-national" problem and insure national unity. To understand the distinctive subjectivity of political minorities, however,

> the ethno-national question must be seen . . . as containing a plurality of meanings that cannot be reduced to a single case. It contains ethnic identity, which is a weapon of revenge against centuries of discrimination and new forms of exploitation; it serves as an instrument for applying pressures in the political market; and it is a response to needs for personal and collective identity in highly complex societies. (Melucci 1989, 90)

Interestingly, while making analytical room for ethnic mobilizing in a wider celebration of working-class, ecological, and feminist movements, Melucci remains ambivalent about the practice of ethnic politics. In this he is not alone.

At the center of many observers' reservations about ethnic mobilizing are two expressed fears: that calls for self-determination inexorably lead to the destructive breakup of existing states and that ethnic violence is the sign of our times. Global preoccupations with self-determination intensified at the close of World War I and set the stage in colonial and postcolonial situations for the awkward balancing in the United Nations of state sovereignty with the right of "a people" to "freely determine their political status and freely pursue their economic, social and cultural development" (Resolution 1514, 1960).[4] The Declaration on the Granting of Independence to Colonial Peoples used this language to reaffirm the territorial rather than ethnic character of self-determination in post–World War II decolonization. The goal was to protect the territorial integrity and stability of new states in world regions, such as Africa, where European colonizers had frequently partitioned colonies without regard to the geographical distribution of indigenous inhabitants. Between 1948 and 1976, the process of decolonization resulted in the recognition of eighty new states and shifting political concerns at the United Nations.

The end of the Cold War in the late 1980s brought a new wave of state-shattering separatist political movements and the breakup of the Soviet Union and Yugoslavia. Clearly the normative assertions of international law were destined to be overtaken by the realities of fast-moving international politics. As Richard Falk observes,

> The right of self-determination has matured along three distinct, often overlapping, and sometimes uneven and confusing paths; those of morality, of politics, and of law. Indeed, the incorporation of self-determination into international law has consistently lagged behind advocacy based on aspiration and consideration of justice (the moral debate) and political movements and their results (the political experience). (1997, 51)

It is not by accident that indigenous groups[5] have remained at the margins of official debates over self-determination. Richard Falk argues that United Nations member states are particularly threatened by this new category of several thousand potential claimants residing in countries throughout the world. Furthermore, the geographic distribution of indigenous groups does not conform to the colonial units that were the archetypal candidates for decolonization in international law. He concludes that the international order has tactically overreacted to indigenous movements' use of the language of self-determination despite the fact that "it is widely appreciated that the goal of such claimants is "autonomy' in an economically, politically, and culturally meaningful form, rather than an effort to be a separate state in the international sense" (1997, 49).

In their quest for leverage and recognition, indigenous peoples as collective nonstate entities have asserted their claims in the language of state power, self-determination, and decolonization—even though they do not correspond to the United Nations state-centric paradigm for protagonists. A turning point occurred in 1971, when the United Nations decided that indigenous issues represented more than the domestic politics of member states and, thus, were the rightful provenance of international deliberation. Throughout the 1970s and 1980s, international groups worked to articulate a new agenda of legal norms in spite of the fact that indigenous groups had no direct power in the realm of international affairs (Wilmer 1993).[6]

Efforts were begun to reformulate the 1957 International Labor Organization (ILO) Convention 107 Concerning the Protection and Integration of Indigenous and Other Tribal and Semi-Tribal Populations in Independent Countries. Instead of paternalistically advocating conventional models of economic development, integration, and the assimilation of indigenous peoples into national life, the new document supported a paradigm of strengthening indigenous cultural rights, languages, schools, and autonomy in development priorities. Indigenous groups in the Americas considered the final product of these deliberations, ILO Convention 169 of 1989, as a breakthrough for their claims of greater autonomy in national affairs, though it would be years before states such as Guatemala affirmed the convention.

In a parallel effort, the United Nations Working Group on Indigenous Peoples was convened in 1982 to begin discussions of what was to become the Draft Universal Declaration of the Rights of Indigenous Peoples. Organizations with United Nations consultative status, indigenous groups from throughout the world, and observers from member states contributed to these deliberations. The draft declaration, first issued in 1989 and amplified in 1990, has raised international consciousness at the same time as it has met serious opposition from member states. In brief, it advocates the rights of indigenous groups to develop their own ethnic and cultural characteristics; to protect their cultural practices and ceremonial, historical, and archaeological sites; to practice their own spiritual traditions; to promote their own languages; to name themselves and their communities; to have a voice in legal and administrative proceedings with the assistance of interpreters if necessary; to control their own schools; to have access to the mass media; to gain recognition of their customary laws and land tenure systems; to receive restitution or compensation for lands that have been usurped; to enact a wide range of environmental protections; to actively participate in their own social and economic improvement with state support; to have autonomy in internal and local affairs including the ability to collect taxes; to gain direct representation in the political affairs of the state; and to exercise autonomy in international and local affairs. Along with many other indigenous groups, Mayas have been involved in the process of articulating these issues at UN conferences. A variety of organizations and alliances have turned to press for these concerns in Guatemala.

Indigenous movements have urged constitutional reforms to expand their recognition, rights, and autonomy at home. Although there has been growing international concern with minority rights, the application of substate self-determination to cultural minorities has been hotly debated since the 1960s. As Halperin and Scheffer (1992, 47) observe:

The full exercise of self-determination can lead to a number of outcomes, ranging from minority rights protection, to cultural or political autonomy, to independent statehood. The principle of self-determination is best viewed as entitling a people to choose its political allegiance, to influence the political order under which it lives, and to preserve its cultural, ethnic, historical, or territorial identity. Often, though not always, these objectives can be achieved with less than full independence.

For governments that seek to limit claimants within their borders and ethnic groups that seek cultural rights including regional self-administration, at issue is who merits legal recognition as "a people" rather than as "a population" that lacks the legal status to advance these claims. As other indigenous groups in the Americas, Pan-Maya activists in Guatemala point to the 1989 version of the International Labor Organization's convention for the protection of indigenous rights as the basis for their legitimacy as rights-bearing collectivities, given their historical, cultural, linguistic, and spiritual bonds. The word Pan-Mayas use for themselves in national and international forums is the Maya *pueblo*, meaning the Maya people, nation, community.

In the early 1990s, the United Nations Sub-Commission on the Prevention of Discrimination and Protection of Minorities, the Conference on Security and Cooperation in Europe (CSCE), and the European Commission for Democracy through Law (a consultative body of the Council of Europe) were active in articulating the legitimacy of minority rights within democratic pluralism, including the right to develop cultural identities, seek schooling in minority languages, and widen minority participation in public affairs. Maya activists have been frequent visitors to European forums on cultural rights and often marshall European policies to support their own case for national reform.[7] Thus, transnational United Nations working groups, European rights commissions, and activist nongovernmental organizations have become key participants in generating legal discourse, political leverage, and financial support for indigenous movements in the Americas.

Unlike other parts of the world, Latin America is often deemed fortunate because its conflicts have not generated collective ethnic violence as in Northern Ireland, the former Yugoslavia, the Middle East, Central Africa, South Asia, and Indonesia. Demographically, 90 percent of the indigenous population in the Americas—which totals approximately 36 million people—live in Mexico, Guatemala, Ecuador, Bolivia, and Peru. While Mexico has the largest number of indigenous citizens, more than 10.5 million, they represent only 12.4 percent of the national population. In the United States, the indigenous population of 2 million citizens makes up 0.8 percent of the national population. By contrast, there are indigenous majorities in Guatemala, where 5.4 million indigenous citizens make up 60.3 percent of the population, and in Bolivia, where 5 million indigenous citizens make up 71.2 percent of the population (Yashar 1996, 92).

As late as 1988, political scientists such as Crawford Young concluded that New World indigenous groups were too fragmented, assimilated, and marginalized to press for wider political goals. Jorge Castañeda's 1993 Latin American history of the Left's transformation from insurgency to reformist politics after the Cold War, published on the eve of the Zapatista rebellion in Mexico and the year before peace accords focused on indigenous rights in Guatemala, did not anticipate that room needed to be made at the bargaining table for indigenous activists in the rebuilding of their nations.[8]

Recent indigenous-rights movements, which have sprung up throughout the Americas from Hawaii and Canada to Chile and Brazil, demonstrate the limits of these judgments.[9] Indigenous groups point to incidents of ethnic violence; make political claims for reforms concerning land, schools, and legal systems in the language of universal rights; and work to "revitalize" and to "modernize" their cultures. They reject conventional ethnic divisions of labor that have been used historically to naturalize their poverty. National constitutions have been rewritten and in several instances rural regions have won important measures of autonomy.[10]

Political scientist Deborah Yashar asks a key question: "What are the conditions under which strong ethnic identities are compatible with, and supportive of, democracy?" (1996, 87). She argues that the current moment of politicized resurgence in the Americas is tied to the democratic opening that occurred in many Latin American states in the 1980s and 1990s and was accompanied by neoliberal economic reforms that endangered many rural communities' subsistence (Yashar 1996; forthcoming). As authoritarian governments were pushed by international organizations to liberalize their regimes, hold elections, and honor basic civil rights, indigenous groups emerged publicly to press for concerns that had no legal channel in the repressive years before. As we will see, Yashar's state-focused explanation fits the contemporary Guatemalan case very well and, furthermore, raises the important issue of which state-formulated policies generate ethnic responses and how governments attempt to channel identity politics for their own ends. The top-down model, however, begs the issue of the multiple sources of social agendas in indigenous Guatemala and the cultural and organizational controversies through which early activists, despite the fact their actions were not deemed "political" by the state or "movements" by others, built social forms that crossed several generations of local activists before taking their current Pan-Maya form.

Critics[11] of indigenous movements in Latin America question the validity of these politics by arguing there is no clear demarcation between indigenous populations and the *mestizo* mainstream.[12] In many cases, there is no

transcendent concept of an indigenous people but rather many micro-eth-
nicities and community identifications. That indigenous individuals and communities shed localized identities situationally or permanently, that much
purportedly indigenous culture is Hispanic, and that nonindigenous society
sometimes appropriates indigenous rituals and aesthetics provide further evidence of culture flows and hybridity. Any attempt to argue in overarching
terms is deemed artificial both for indigenous and nonindigenous populations. For very different reasons, both the Left and the Right in Guatemala
have sought to deconstruct and destabilize the ethnic argument.

Situating Pan-Mayanism in the context of Guatemala's political transition,
the history of ethnic formations and politics, and in a range of distinctive
frameworks for analysis—particularly the literatures on rights, revitalization,
the invention of culture, ethnic nationalism, social movements, and anthropologies of the state[13]—are cross-cutting themes in these essays.

Maya Activists and the Movement

Pan-Mayanism does not represent an ivory-tower enterprise, given that virtually all activists come from rural backgrounds. The movement rejects Guatemala's melting pot ideology, which has compelled indigenous people "to
pass" as nonindigenous Ladinos if they seek employment outside their home
communities or pursue education and economic mobility. An ethnic formation in which passing becomes possible, if not coerced along certain social
frontiers, is in part the legacy of the early Spanish colonial order, which in
the sixteenth century generated a hybrid category of Spanish-speaking Indians, called Ladinos, who contrasted most sharply with those of European
backgrounds, the Spaniards and their New World offspring, the Creoles.

Though the content of this category was variable in time and space, most
colonial Ladinos were Hispanicized indigenous people living outside their
communities, or people of mixed parentage, that is, mestizos. For a while,
particular kinds of mestizos were defined by an elaborate colonial system of
castas, but the resulting categories imploded as ever finer distinctions were
advocated for different proportions of indigenous, Spanish, and African
blood. In contrast to other areas of Latin America, by the eighteenth century,
the term *Ladino* displaced *mestizo* in Guatemala, and both Ladinos and indigenous populations remained impoverished and politically marginalized in
the colonial social order (Lutz 1982, C. Smith 1990b).

Revisionist histories, such as Carol Smith's insightful hypothesis (1990b),
argue that the distinction between Ladino and indigenous groups became
polarized and rigidified so that Ladino came to signify *non*-indigenous in
culture and descent late in the nineteenth century.[14] The liberal government
of Creole elite Justo Rufino Barrios (1871–85) created an export economy

based on the cultivation of coffee on large plantations. To harness indigenous workers for the labor-intensive harvest, the Barrios regime promoted the resettlement of Ladinos into the western highlands, where indigenous communities predominated. They were introduced as a structurally privileged class of labor recruiters, money lenders, liquor merchants, and state officials who represented the economic interests of the Creole elites who controlled national politics and economics. Thus, it was through a process of state intervention that the Ladino-indigenous contrast took on its characteristic contemporary form as a mutually exclusive and hierarchical class-like distinction and the Creole elite came to transcend everyday ethnic politics (C. Smith 1990b, 84–87). The actors in Guatemala's current social formation interweave and contest images of racial, ethnic, and cultural difference in a variety of ways.

Pan-Mayanism challenges the legacy of colonial and nineteenth-century state formations, which repeatedly used forced-labor policies that associated *indígenas* with heavy manual labor and small rural communities while conferring advantages on Creoles, mestizos, and Ladinos based on their fluency in the national language and culture. The twentieth-century image of Guatemala as a Spanish-speaking Ladino country, proud of its cosmopolitan Latin American culture, becomes another historical construction the movement seeks to interrogate.

Ironically, Pan-Mayanism is composed primarily of individuals for whom ethnic passing into the dominant mainstream to escape invidious racism and discrimination would be feasible, given that they are educated, fluent in Spanish, and economically mobile. Rather than becoming urban Ladinos— an open possibility in this hierarchical ethnic formation and one that many recent bicultural migrants have pursued—activists have turned to the difficult project of promoting the resurgence of "Maya culture." Who are the activists in this movement? What is their agenda? How do they see their political goals in a world that is highly ambivalent about ethnic mobilization and in a political system in which they are widely criticized? With its particular blend of conservatism and radicalism, how does the Maya movement destabilize the Right/Left polarities of Guatemalan politics and perhaps lead us as American readers to reimagine very different political situations closer to home?

In discussing Pan-Mayanism here, I have sometimes found myself struggling not to succumb to a portrayal of "Maya culture" as a static pre-Columbian essence; that is, treating the impressive persistence of preconquest knowledge and practices as "real" Maya culture and the rest as a distant colonial imposition or a recent extemporaneous add-on. Rather, this book attempts to do justice to the various syntheses of Maya culture, elements of which have long and short histories, and their appropriation and recombination by local communities, religious confessions, social movements, and political groups in opposition to a variety of others. The following chapters explore ways to write about the rolling distinctiveness that is Maya—the continued practice of embracing and rejecting all sorts of intersecting ideas and identities—in a multicultural world and state.

The history of anthropological approaches to Maya culture is deep and distinguished. Mesoamerican Studies, whose scholars have chosen more often to focus on the Yucatan and Chiapas, in Mexico, rather than on Guatemala, offers different kinds of inspiration. Evon Z. Vogt (1969), Nancy Farriss (1984), and Victoria Bricker (1981) have pursued striking continuities in the deep structures of Maya worldview and belief despite or, better put, to spite colonialism. William Hanks (1997) sees sixteenth-century Spanish colonial resettlement and missionization policies as subtly but fundamentally reconfiguring Maya language and culture and, thus, creating a paradigm shift to colonially inflected cultural distinctiveness. Quetzil Castañeda (1996) shows how the archaeological invention of an essentialized Maya civilization in the twentieth century through the foreign reconstruction of sites such as Chichén Itzá in the Yucatan has been appropriated in myriad ways by anthropologists, tourists, local entrepreneurs, and Maya intellectuals. Gary Gossen (1994) and June Nash (1995) are struck by the reemergence of indigenous identity and cultural themes with great historical depth in rural communities and the Zapatista rebellion in Chiapas. There is a cumulative argument here for multiple, often conflicting sources of Maya culture.

The goal of this analysis is not to document an invariant culture—though notable elements of the current mix have long histories—or to count only those elements we imagine as separate from the colonial process as "real" (read authentic) Maya culture. (If culture takes on the attributes of "property" that belongs uniquely to a group, then European colonialism has inevitably led to clouded titles.) Rather, in my view, Maya culture represents the meaningful selective mix of practices and knowledge, drawn on and resynthesized at this historical juncture by groups who see indigenous identity as highly salient to self-representation and as a vehicle for political change. Their assertions are actively challenged by other groups. Through the process of public debate and private meeting, the significance of being Maya has altered in important ways.

The Maya movement currently works to promote the revitalization of Maya culture for the 60 percent of the national population that they count as indigenous in background.[15] Even at the lower "official" 1994 census number of 43 percent, there are 3.6 million Mayas out of a national population of 8.3 million inhabitants. One-third of the country's departments (primarily in the northwestern highlands) have indigenous majorities that range from 60.5 percent to 97.2 percent; one-third have roughly balanced numbers of indigenous and nonindigenous inhabitants; and one-third (primarily in the southeastern sections of the country) have nonindigenous majorities of 66.4 percent to 99.2 percent (Cojtí Cuxil 1997a: 29–30). According to R. Adams

(1997), the twentieth century has witnessed a consolidation of stronger indigenous majorities in regions where their numbers are already high. (See figures 1 and 2 to compare Maya language regions versus the administrative regions of the country.)

Given the resemblance of local culture in communities throughout the western highlands, the movement is attempting to cultivate common cause across the twenty-some historically related Maya language groups in the country.[16] The largest four language communities (K'ichee', Mam, Kaqchikel, and Q'eqchii') number between 350,000 and 1 million speakers each and comprise almost 80 percent of the Maya-speaking population (see figure 3 for language demographics). Vital to the image of unity is the Maya language tree, generated by historical linguists and widely circulated in movement publications to demonstrate that diverse languages in the present are legacies of a common past (see figure 4).

Mayanists hope that the ideology of "unity within diversity" will bring Mayas powerfully into the mainstream to readdress Guatemala's serious development dilemmas.[17] They propose a multicultural (*pluricultural*) model for participatory democracy. This model recognizes multiple national cultures rather than the overarching Hispanic standard for nationalism that predominates in Latin America. This mandate defines collective cultural, linguistic, and political rights for Maya citizens and legitimizes their claims for cultural and political space in the country's educational, judicial, and administrative systems (COMG 1991; Cojtí Cuxil 1994; 1995; 1996a). This political vision works within an idealized paradigm of regionalized language diversity, although Mayanists are well aware of the importance of more localized identities for many indigenous people and the many internal diasporas, ancient and modern, that complicate regionalization. That the regional language map is at odds with the national administrative division of Guatemala into departments has many ramifications for both parties. That, despite their regionalization, languages are not neatly territorial in everyday life raises important issues for Pan-Maya identity construction and language revitalization. In the highlands, their speakers are geographically mobile, bilingual across Maya languages, and/or across Spanish and indigenous languages, or for some youths monolingual in Spanish.

A set of interrelated theses guides this analysis. First, the movement's emphasis on self-determination (*autodeterminación*) is part of a historically constituted language for agency that needs to be studied in the context of transnational institutions and Maya histories of social criticism, community formation, and international involvement. The language itself and the stress on constituting oneself as "a people" are the products of the elaboration of rights discourse through organizations such as the United Nations, which finds itself caught in a field of competing interests, given its role as the international custodian of state sovereignty.

Second, this analysis argues that the particular cultural forms and social

SOURCES: N. Cojtí (1988), England and Elliot (1990), and England (1996)

FIGURE ONE. MAYA LANGUAGE MAP OF GUATEMALA
In Guatemala, the maps on these two pages are at war with each other. Mayanists use the language map to assert that language diversity and indigenous identity are regional issues. The state insists on the primacy of the administrative division of the country into departments (*departamentos*), which ignore language divides, and counties (*municipios*), which perpetuate Maya political fragmentation and localized dialects. The Maya movement imagines various strategies for reconciling the maps, while as of 1997 the government refused to consider representations of the nation that might set a framework for regionalized self-administration.

FIGURE TWO. POLITICAL-ADMINISTRATIVE DIVISIONS OF THE COUNTRY

Language Demographics

Language	Number of Speakers	Departments	Number of Municipios
K'ichee'	1,000,000	Sololá, Totonicapán, Quetzaltenango, El Quiché, Baja Verapaz, Alta Verapaz, Suchitepéquez, Retalhuleu.	73
Mam	687,000	Quetzaltenango, Huehuetenango, & San Marcos	56
Kaqchikel	405,000	Guatemala, Sacatepéquez, Chimaltenango, Sololá, Suchitepéquez, Escuintla, & Baja Verapaz	47
Q'eqchii'	361,000	Alta Verapaz, El Petén, Izabal, El Quiché	14
Q'anjob'al	112,000	Huehuetenango	4
Tz'utujiil	85,000	Sololá & Suchitepéquez	7
Ixhil	71,000	El Quiché	3
Ch'orti'	52,000	Chiquimula & Zacapa	5
Poqomchii'	50,000	Alta Verapaz, Baja Verapaz, & El Quiché	7
Popti' (Jakalteko)	32,000	Huehuetenango	6
Poqomaab'	32,000	Guatemala, Jalapa, & Escuintla	6
Chuj	29,000	Huehuetenango	3
Sakapulteko	21,000	El Quiché	
Akateko	20,000	Huehuetenango	2
Awakateko	16,000	Huehuetenango	
Mopan	5,000	El Petén	4
Sipakapense	3,000	San Marcos	
Itzaj	3,000	El Peten	6
Teko	2,500	Huehuetenango	2 (plus 2 in Mexico)
Uspanteko	2,000	El Quiché	1

SOURCE: Oxlajuuj Keej Maya' Ajtz'iib' *Maya' Chii'* (1993: 10–19); England (1996).

FIGURE THREE. LANGUAGE DEMOGRAPHICS
Approximately twenty Maya languages are spoken in the country depending upon how the difference between dialects and languages is negotiated by speech communities and by linguists. Language communities vary from over a million to a few thousand. The leadership of the Maya movement has been drawn primarily from Kaqchikel and K'ichee' speakers who come from communities closer to urban centers and continuing educational opportunities than do other groups. However, many national Mayanist organizations—from the Academy for Maya Languages of Guatemala (ALMG) to Oxlajuuj Keej Maya' Ajtz'iib' (OKMA)—self-consciously seek representation of as many language communities as possible in their organizations.

Historical Development of Mayan Languages

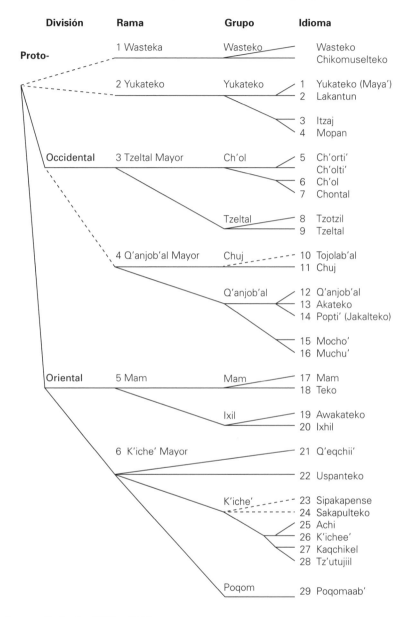

División	Rama	Grupo	Idioma

Proto-

1 Wasteka — Wasteko — Wasteko / Chikomuselteko

2 Yukateko — Yukateko — 1 Yukateko (Maya') / 2 Lakantun / 3 Itzaj / 4 Mopan

Occidental — 3 Tzeltal Mayor — Ch'ol — 5 Ch'orti' / Ch'olti' / 6 Ch'ol / 7 Chontal — Tzeltal — 8 Tzotzil / 9 Tzeltal

4 Q'anjob'al Mayor — Chuj — 10 Tojolab'al / 11 Chuj — Q'anjob'al — 12 Q'anjob'al / 13 Akateko / 14 Popti' (Jakalteko) — 15 Mocho' / 16 Muchu'

Oriental — 5 Mam — Mam — 17 Mam / 18 Teko — Ixil — 19 Awakateko / 20 Ixhil

6 K'iche' Mayor — 21 Q'eqchii' / 22 Uspanteko — K'iche' — 23 Sipakapense / 24 Sakapulteko / 25 Achi / 26 K'ichee' / 27 Kaqchikel / 28 Tz'utujiil — Poqom — 29 Poqomaab'

Source: England and Elliot (1990)

Figure Four. Maya Language Tree for Mesoamerica

Mayanists use this genealogical tree, based on reconstructions by historical linguists, to represent the common linguistic and cultural origins 4,000 years ago of the diverse current indigenous linguistic communities in Mexico, Guatemala, and Belize. Themes of cultural continuity and diversity within unity are hallmarks of the movement which proposes a transcendent level of Maya identification to unify the struggle against racism, cultural and political marginalization, and poverty.

relationships through which Mayas assert their cultural claims are integral aspects of self-determination. This book illustrates the genres, media, forums, and social organizations through which Pan-Mayanism has developed its concept of identity politics.

Third, ironically but not unexpectedly in this world of diasporas, the production of cultural distinctiveness through the movement's interdisciplinary field of Maya Studies involves important instances of transnational appropriation, blurring, and polyculturalism. The flow of culture across borders becomes apparent when one traces the production and practice of Maya history, linguistics, education, and collective rights.[18] This analysis illustrates these appropriations as they are forged into a language of ethnic distinctiveness. Culture, history, politics, and academic research combine to make the Maya movement a related yet different process from ethnic nationalism and multiculturalism elsewhere in the world.

Given these concerns, it is important to trace the internal debates and evolving language of the movement, the politics of its production of knowledge, and the ways social relations mediate participation instead of attributing the dynamics of the movement solely to the material interests of its leaders. Clearly power takes both cultural and material forms in the movement. How and why are these intellectuals authenticating certain visions of Maya culture and discrediting others? What novel resources are they making available to potential participants? This analysis argues that Maya struggles for self-determination may be muted if they are viewed solely in terms of universalizing schemes, whether they be the language of minority cultural rights or the historical materialist language of oppression and class conflict.[19] So it is crucial to follow the movement in practice, to trace the circulation and consumption of ideas and, just as importantly, to understand the ways local populations adopt or resist the rethinking of indigenous identity.

It would be inaccurate to dismiss this cultural revival as parochial, primordial, or detrimental to modern politics. Mayas are highly aware of global identity politics, even more so since the surge of indigenous organizing in the Americas and Rigoberta Menchú's award of the 1992 Nobel Prize for Peace (Menchú and Comité de Unidad Campesina 1992; 1993). As the chapters on public intellectuals and Maya Studies demonstrate, Mayanists bring to the international process of ethnic intensification their own experiences, ideologies, dreams of socioeconomic mobility, and evolving politics.

Self-Definition and the Other

At the onset of the analysis, it is important to confront the politicized irony of a non-Maya talking about Maya self-determination. Recent scholarship from a number of academic fields has questioned the disinterested position of the social scientist. Subaltern studies has examined the history of European representations of the "other" and has shown that the imagery of civilized versus barbarian became an integral aspect of the Western colonizing project.[20] African-American, feminist, Latino/a, and lesbian and gay scholars have confronted researchers and policymakers who assume the powers of objective science yet in their studies of contemporary society marginalize and stigmatize nondominant viewpoints.[21] In a related development, ethnic studies and postorientalist critics have questioned the agendas of anthropology and area studies to the extent that these fields focus on cultural difference when the compelling issue in other societies may be widespread disenchantment with the status quo. They also fault scholars for assuming the unity and superiority of Western culture and liberal democracy rather than examining the deep divisions and tensions within American society.[22] Politicizing "who speaks for whom" is a central issue inside and outside movements that seek recognition, greater cultural autonomy, and political influence.

Political essentialists commonly argue that group membership is a prerequisite for the legitimacy of the analyst's voice. Authors must physically and experientially represent the group if they are to write authoritatively of Maya, Latin American, women's, or working-class experiences. This assertion is accompanied by critiques of dominant scholarship as disempowering in practice as well as in theory. These critics argue for the decentralization of the production of knowledge in order to reveal respected canons as politically vested constructions, and for alternative readings of social reality to reveal hidden structures of power.

Yet, after exposing the exclusionary character of so-called objective neutrality, anthropologists such as Renato Rosaldo (1989), literary critics such as Gayatri Spivak (1988), and activists such as Gloria Anzaldúa (1990) have gone on to destabilize images of the *essentialist social critic* as a unitary subject. They note the multiplicity of social cleavages, identities, and cross-cutting identifications imputed and practiced by all subjects—insiders and outsiders alike.

If one is at all convinced by these arguments, then it is increasingly clear that knowing the world and producing knowledge involve the interplay of continually shifting positions and perspectives. This is evident even when the language of racism (or other ideologies of categorical difference such as class) creates hierarchies of discrimination that obscure other powerful threads of identification, loyalty, and enmity, such as gender or religion. As James Clifford (1988) and Donna Haraway (1989) assert, shedding the image of the unitary critic and protagonist calls for an airing of the ways in which all research is situated and partial. The challenge becomes including the analyst within the framing of that which is to be researched.

Questioning the politics of "who speaks for whom" will always be important for insiders and outsiders alike. It raises the issue of representation in both senses: who claims the authority to craft representations of ongoing social and political realities and who gains the position to represent others in public affairs? But an intersubjective question also needs to be posed: "who speaks with whom"; that is, how do individuals and groups selectively engage and influence each other, often across politicized cleavages? In forging the Maya movement, activists have developed shifting and provocative answers to both questions.

Current dialogues—sometimes affirming and other times discordant—involve Maya, U.S., European, and Latin American writers and activists working on a range of academic, anticolonial, indigenous, and class-inflected projects. This book discusses Maya social critiques and their appropriations of voices these intellectuals label the "other." *Kaxlan* (pronounced kash-LAN; originally used in Mesoamerica by indigenous people to distinguish Castilian-speakers and now often extended in practice to "foreigners" or "outsiders")[23] is a term Mayanists employ for the "other." The K'iche' term—which has been adopted by Mayanists across language groups (and displaces words like the Kaqchikel *mo's*)—often carries a pejorative tone. Its prime referent is the Ladino, the twentieth-century "outsider" and hated racist within national society. In everyday affairs, the word marks "otherness" in more benign ways: the Kaqchikel word for bread is *"kaxlan* tortillas" (*kaxlan wëy*). Although there is an abundant vocabulary for foreigners— *gringos,*[24] *canches* (blonds), and various nationalities—*kaxlan* is the term with political bite in Mayanist circles.

Kaxlan contrasts with a range of expressions for the indigenous "we": language-specific expressions for "our people" (*qawinaq* in Kaqchikel), the nationalist *Mayab'* or *Maya'* for all Mayas, and the encompassing *pueblos originarios* and *naciones nativas del continente*, terms adopted from indigenous activism elsewhere in the Americas.[25] It also contrasts with the community-specific names people have for themselves—Trixanos in San Andrés, for example—which for many living in the countryside continue to be the most intense axis of cultural distinction.

In practice, *kaxlan*—not to speak of its contrast—is a highly charged but heterogeneous construction. Otherness has been situationally essentialized *and* diversified as Maya intellectuals engage those who have become the useful other, the ambivalent other, the racist other, or the class-movement other. This analysis traces the flow of ideas between Mayanists and diverse others as these exchanges relate to Maya quests for "autonomy" and "self-determination."

Pan-Maya strategies involve confrontational challenges to others who would presume to speak for Mayas *and* a great deal of joint antiracism work with non-Mayas. At a major national forum, the annual Maya Workshop (*Taller Maya*), linguist Enrique Sam Colop questioned North American researchers' ethics and politics, noting how little research is repatriated to Maya communities and wondering about investigators' hidden motivations and political interests (Sam Colop 1990; England 1990). Skepticism drives Maya intellectuals to extend the notion *kaxlan* to international researchers. The term is a biting one because it merges the foreign researcher with the national racist, whether the researcher is a human-rights advocate, evangelizer, or ambitious academic. In this context, essentialist constructions are generalized to all non-Mayas: All are colonizers, the categorical "other" with interests inevitably suspect.

Maya skepticism of the ethics of foreign researchers coexists with their recognition of the utility of foreign research for Maya nation building. Mayanists are interested in foreign scholarship that supports Maya revitalization and are strategic in their appropriations of Western essentialism for their own ends.[26] They encourage studies that address the vitality of Maya culture and trace continuities in language, culture, and religion from pre-Columbian times to the present (COCADI 1989). Maya resistance to domination and Ladino racism are other high-priority projects. Their own research agendas include continuity and resistance along with special emphasis on discrimination in education, academic research, national history, the media, and the tourism industry.

Mayanists are quick to discard anthropological scholarship when it portrays the hegemony of Ladino culture as inevitable. In repatriating foreign scholarship of Maya culture, they have selectively promoted the translation of classical ethnographies for portrayals of Maya rituals of great antiquity that were the center of community life until recently (La Farge and Byers 1997). The appropriation of foreign scholarship—the movement of signs across space and systems of meaning, as Gupta and Ferguson would put it (1992)—is being used by Mayas to reject older patterns of identity-destroying assimilation. The movement seeks to break the association of Maya identity with abject poverty and Ladino oppression, and to make room for new combinations of ethnicity, work, religion, public culture, higher standards of living, and democratic political participation.

International involvements have been accompanied by the *intra*national intensification of ethnic difference. This is no accident. Critiques of the 1992 Columbus quincentenary brought prominent indigenous leaders and activists from the Americas together in a variety of international forums, where they discussed, both on and off the record, distinctive national struggles and ethnic nation-building.[27] Community leaders in highland agrarian towns agree that the antiquincentenary campaign was a turning point in their political consciousness and demands.

In Guatemala, the state continues to be a central player in the forging of ethnicities. Maya cultural intensification was incubated in the brutal repression of the military-guerrilla warfare of 1978–1985. Tens of thousands of

Guatemalans were killed; hundreds of thousands were forced to flee as political refugees to the United States, Mexico, and Europe. The western highlands, where Guatemala's Maya population is concentrated, received the
most punishing militarization. The war threw a spotlight on the dangers the
military imputed to cultural difference and the vulnerability of Maya leaders.

As the war intensified, some Mayas thought in more explicit terms of a
social movement based on the revitalization of Maya culture. Members of
pro-Maya groups personally experienced the repression directed toward indigenous leaders and witnessed the marginalization of Maya concerns during
the civil war. The few who gained access to national universities, where they
were exposed to a variety of political voices, most vocally those on the Left,
kept low profiles while also writing theses that critiqued racism and envi-
sioned a Maya-specific politics. A handful received scholarships to study in
Europe or the United States. By the late 1980s, members of these different
networks had reemerged into public to create a wide variety of research
centers and national forums for cultural rights. The current movement has
been propelled by leaders in their forties and fifties, many of whom participated in the nascent movement in their twenties, and is fueled by younger
teachers, development workers, and students.

Rethinking the Role of Public Intellectuals

Maya intellectuals have used a Benedict Anderson (1991) strategy—including the production of all sorts of print media supplemented with cassette
tapes and videos—for building a sense of identification that transcends face-
to-face community. This bicultural, multilingual effort extols literacy in a
country where rural illiteracy rates are extraordinarily high. Activists write in
both Spanish and Maya. They emphasize the capacity of indigenous languages to engage all spheres of contemporary life and a Whorfian sense of
language as the generative source of cultural distinctiveness. That the prime
movers of Pan-Mayanism are public intellectuals continues to generate controversy—in part because of their transgression of conventional ethnic hierarchies but also, I would argue, because of the ambivalence with which
intellectuals are held in the West.

Even if one defines public intellectuals as educated observers who craft
social criticism to stimulate the public rethinking of important conflicts, it is
clear that American experiences are far from universal. Russell Jacoby
(1987) narrates the recent social history of public intellectuals in the United
States as a reflection of very specific generational and historical circumstances that nurtured and later compromised their creativity. During the in-
terwar years, young writers found their way to the intense countercultural
circles of bohemian New York, where they developed their ideas in dialogue

with each other and their readers. In his view, the post–World War II expansion of American universities crushed free thinking by offering employment security and professional status to the next generation of independent minds in exchange for conformity to specialized disciplinary power structures. As a result, wide-ranging critical voices were coopted into a comfortable professional class, judged not by wider publics but by their inward-focused academic elders.

One can agree with Jacoby's provocative questioning of the intellectual and the university without joining in his lament of the death of social criticism with the transformation of free-spirited urban writing into suburban conformity. To confront the prejudices of this singular history, it would be important to appreciate the diverse American settings in which people find a public voice as producers of knowledge and as vocal audiences in communities, social movements, regional politics, and education. Some community historians are known only in their neighborhoods; others build alternative imagined communities through the print media. The prominence of local and national intellectuals—none of whom would make Jacoby's list of notables—in civil rights, ethnic, feminist, gay rights, ecological, religious, and community-based movements (and their political backlash) has been a vital part of the social history of our country since the 1960s. Many of these critics have come to challenge the mainstream from the margins; others have been recruited by contending currents of the mainstream. Some speak and write as independent or anonymous movement intellectuals, others as part of the academy where they have transformed disciplinary canons and founded controversial interdisciplinary fields.

Nevertheless, Jacoby's Foucauldian insight remains: American universities demand that their junior faculty submit to a punishing six- to ten-year apprenticeship before they are eligible for the grueling "up or out" tenure decision. The current academic model, the discipline of disciplines, has not inevitably generated scholarship cut off from wider social controversy but its complex conventions certainly reward certain paths of research and discourage other routes. Nor are academics free from the pressures of the national political economy. Recently, the erosion of tenure with the growing recruitment of less expensive part-time faculty who will never qualify for job security demonstrates that the neoliberal pressures on governments to cut public spending affect the metropole as well as the "Third World."

A comprehensive social history of public intellectuals in Latin America, Africa, and other post-colonial regions of world remains to be written. In focusing on the impact of the end of the Cold War on socialist intellectuals, James Petras and Morris Morley (1992) echo Jacoby's lament of the compromise of independent critical voices. They reserve special condemnation for the "retreat of the intellectuals," especially ex-Marxists who in this view have betrayed their long-standing alliance with the working-class struggle that seeks to confront capitalism and imperialism through revolutionary politics, trade unions, and student movements. In the 1970s and 1980s, the shift in Latin America from revolutionary to liberal democratic politics and from organic to institutional intellectuals resulted, in their view, from the slaughter of political activists by repressive military dictatorships and from the support by North American and European funders of research institutes with post-Marxist agendas. The new research program is a familiar one:

> The first wave of external funding supported critique of the economic model and publicized human rights' violations of the military dictatorships. The second supported the study of new social movements, while the third bankrolled studies of the democratization process and the debt. . . . The studies of the dictatorship focused on its politically repressive feature and not on its economic and military ties to Western European and North American elites. State violence was analyzed in terms of human rights' violations, not as expressions of class domination—as part of the class struggle, as class violence. From these studies the political alternatives that emerged were posed as a conflict between liberal democracy and military dictatorship. (1992, 160)

The audience for this sponsored research was not local activists and militants but rather other research institutes, foreign funders, and the international conference circuit.

For Petras and Morely, the repudiation of Marxist orthodoxy by social observers has led to the mischaracterization of Latin America's transition from military dictatorships to civilian regimes as "democratization." Rather they note that this shift has often brought a reconstitution of state authoritarianism, limited arenas for democratic processes, and the intensification of class conflict and poverty.[28]

One response to pointed questions about the interconnection of political economy and intellectual agendas involves the ethnographic study of the ways political issues are contested in specific situations. Given anthropology's concern with multiple lines of coalition and conflict, this approach would leave open the possibility of a more heterogeneous history of public intellectuals than Petras and Morely would advocate, operating from different political positions. To what extent are issues of democratization and class conflict debated by public intellectuals and social movements? How do social critics see the application of their research to wider social struggles? How have national universities, think tanks, and foreign funders directed intellectual agendas? How have they been influenced by social movements that have diversified the significance of democratization past the classical realm of electoral politics?

It is important to note that while facing similar economic pressures, American and Latin American universities play different roles in the lives of critics. In Latin America, private universities have long trained national elites, the professional classes, and powerful mainstream nationalist intellectuals. By contrast, it is not uncommon to hear students at flagship public universities express special pride in their institutions' contributions to radical critiques of the status quo. In times of crisis, students have experienced terrible repression for their advocacy. Characteristically, underfunded universities have not been able to offer more than token salaries to their professors or minimal support for undergraduate studies. At public institutions, where students attempt to arrange studies around their work schedules and growing family responsibilities, graduation rates may be as low as 5 percent.[29]

Even at high-status institutions, urban intellectuals cannot support themselves as university professors. Rather they typically combine part-time teaching at several institutions with research projects, writing for the press, and consulting for politically engaged think tanks and international NGOs. Relatively few have Ph.Ds. They support their families with continually shifting jobs and publish books as they complete the *licenciatura*, the undergraduate degree equivalent to M.A.-level studies in the United States. In countries such as Guatemala, it is common to see well-published intellectuals in their forties or fifties who have gained national prominence as political and cultural leaders and who still yearn to find the time to finish their undergraduate theses.[30]

Maya intellectuals have their own social history and organizational involvements in rural communities and urban forums. University trained Mayanists have followed the Latin American route of multiple jobs and wider public exposure rather than the specialized North American university career path. Despite the resulting financial and time pressures, this work pattern has allowed Maya professionals from a variety of fields—education, law, health, social work, and linguistics—the freedom to engage in transdisciplinary research, to reject the disciplinary norms and intense politics of Guatemalan universities, and to create their own discipline of Maya Studies. The effect of this distinctive pattern of professionalization on the critical posture of the Maya movement and the relation of its university-trained critics to grassroots intellectuals are major issues for this ethnographic analysis.

The 1990s has been an important period for rethinking the relation of public intellectual to society. Latin Americanists and Africanists, such as Florencia Mallon (1995), Claudio Lomnitz-Adler (1992), Steven Feierman (1990), and James Ferguson (1994), have framed a striking agenda for the study of the ways public intellectuals (among other specialists) affirm and dispute power structures in their countries. Through revisionist readings of Gramsci, they have fostered a reappraisal of who counts as an intellectual and a reconsideration of the roles community and regional intellectuals play in anticolonial and nation-building movements.

Local intellectuals may lack formal credentials but they are recognized communally as producers of authoritative knowledge and interpreters of social reality. As anthropologist Steven Feierman (1990, 18) observes, "intellectuals are defined by their place within an ensemble of social relations" and their influence becomes apparent through their "directive, organizational, and educative" activities as elders, leaders, teachers, priests, healers, mediators, officials, and so forth.

At issue are the ways individuals continually rework ideas and practices drawn from various sources to authorize "communities of shared discourse" and conventionalize the specifics of their power structures. Since community-building inevitably takes place in a world of conflicting possibilities, it is important to trace the way leaders dispute other political visions, and their alliances marginalize specific categories of people. The overarching goal of this new political anthropology is to demonstrate the dynamic way that ideas, practices, discourses, and alliances are used to shape paths of action and to constrict alternatives across important political transitions (Feierman 1990, 33, 237).

Anthropologists Claudio Lomnitz-Adler (1992) and James Ferguson (1994) warn that the knowledge produced by intellectuals and development professionals most often serves the interests of regional and national elites and state hegemony—that their primary function, whether explicit or intrinsic, is to naturalize taken-for-granted social hierarchies. This approach documents the cooptation of regional intellectuals and demonstrates telling parallels between political views and elite positions in regional and national class systems. The formulation, however, leaves little room for Feierman's community-based anticolonial struggle in Tanzania or concern with the particular ideas that arise from dispersed centers of social criticism elsewhere. Nor does Ferguson's powerful analysis—which convincingly demonstrates how development discourse and the exercise of bureaucratic power have depoliticized large areas of public life in Lesotho—leave much room for social movements that attempt to repoliticize inequality, as has been the case in Guatemala.

Historian Florencia Mallon contributes a particularly insightful synthesis of these approaches and their preoccupations. As meaning makers in a world of competing discourses and unequal access to knowledge and power, she sees local leaders as working to "reproduce and rearticulate memory, to connect community discourses about local identity to constantly shifting patterns of power, solidarity, and consensus" (Mallon 1995, 12). The duality of their roles is striking. Public intellectuals can take on the work of "counterhegemonic heroes" who create new possibilities in community life and press for the recognition of local struggles in wider political affairs, or they can be "enforcers" who normalize state-centric politics and prejudices in local affairs (1995, 317). In practice, one could imagine many instances in which these roles would be blurred.

In Mallon's study of postcolonial Mexico, local intellectuals shaped the understanding of wider conflicts through their pivotal involvements in nine-teenth-century agrarian movements that used the discourses of rights and democracy to articulate a variety of contending social visions for the nation. Despite their active role in social movements that shaped national agendas from below, politically engaged communities were left behind after the 1855 Liberal revolution as national elites and complicit local intellectuals across the political spectrum consolidated their powers and used demeaning imag-ery—the backward, violent Indian who lacked political judgment—to mar-ginalize these communities as incapable of direct political participation in the wider affairs of the nation (1995, 287–324).

Mallon's concern with the innovative and complicit role of intellectuals on all levels and for the emancipatory and marginalizing use of the discourses of rights and democracy raises important questions for contemporary Gua-temala. If only for a moment, the peace process has opened the door to greater direct involvement of Mayas from a variety of political positions in national efforts to reimagine the state. In debate are the terms in which urban and rural worlds are included or excluded in this process of democratization. To address this issue, one must engage the widest possible range of intellec-tuals, from the first generation of university-trained Mayas to traditionalist consensus builders and community activists in rural communities. The pre-sent study pursues the diverse practices of Maya public intellectuals, the substance of their critiques of hierarchy, and the variety of their social posi-tions in a political system under conflicting pressures to change and in which they have many antagonists.

Culture Makers and the Maya Movement

The move away from cultures as bounded entities and fixed authenticities toward a focus on culture makers—who draw on a range of cultural forms to make new claims on memory and history—has helped anthropologists widen their understandings of contemporary ethnicity and cultural re-surgence.[31] Transcultural forms of political critique and collective pride have become important for local resistance in such countries as South Africa, Northern Ireland, Brazil, and the United States.[32] In Guatemala, the produc-tion of cultural representations in a variety of media is used quite self-con-sciously by public intellectuals to support struggles for social change.

As I have suggested, this is not a one-way flow of culture but an interplay of local, national, and international cultures, movements, and individual rela-tionships. Because much of this book concerns the convergent and divergent character of this interplay, it does not make sense to begin the narrative with local communities and build linearly toward national and international "levels" of resurgence. Many events central to this inquiry are at once local, national, and international in their manifestations, repercussions, and author-ship. The Maya diaspora—which has a long history but intensified during the violence of the late 1970s and 1980s—crosscuts these analytical divisions.

The chapters in this book will tack back and forth between urban-centric and rural-centric views of culture, politics, and social change. My analysis resists a totalizing account of the movement in favor of an ethnographic focus on specific public intellectuals, the personal stakes of their cultural activism, and key events and texts that illustrate the movement's language of social criticism and practice of revitalization. I refer to the activities of other Pan-Maya organizations, some of them inaccessible to foreigners, and to scholarship on other regions of the country to underscore the partiality of any framing—including this one, which foregrounds Kaqchikel-Mayas—in the face of the variety of experiences of being Maya in Guatemala and beyond.

Chapters one and two introduce the advocates of Pan-Mayanism, their goals, and the movement's critics. The analysis situates the movement in the contrasting politics of class-based social movements in Guatemala. Chapter one asks why the grassroots *popular* Left, which sees itself as a powerful umbrella movement fighting oppression, was initially so disparaging of those who identified with "cultural" struggles for social change. Indigenous reac-tions to the 1991 Second Continental Meeting on Indigenous, Black, and Popular Resistance reveal the accomplishments and unfinished business of the *popular* Left in the early 1990s. The analysis examines a variety of critiques of Pan-Mayanism, illustrates the appropriation of post-modernism and cultural studies by journalist Mario Roberto Morales in scathing attacks on the movement's leadership, and discusses Mayanist Demetrio Cojtí Cu-xil's use of the language of collective rights in reply to his critics during the peace process.

Pan-Mayanism and its antagonists have been engaged in a "racism versus class conflict" debate about the persistence of unequal life chances for the country's citizens. These understandings generate distinctive priorities for social policy and distinctive images of the nation. Beyond these differences, however, there are also rising social tensions in an uncertain economy with the emergence of parallel middle classes of Maya salaried *profesionales* in rural towns and urban bureaucracies who compete with Ladinos for jobs.

Chapter two focuses on Guatemala's peace process, which to the surprise of many provided an important opening for indigenous issues in national politics. The analysis reviews the resulting 1995 Accord on Identity and the Rights of Indigenous Peoples and discusses the first round of the implemen-tation process in 1997. The analysis pursues the theme of ethnic tensions unleashed by "multicultural, ethnically plural, and multilingual" visions of the nation and demonstrates important moments of convergence in the class-based *popular* and Pan-Mayanist political programs during the negotiations to end Guatemala's thirty years of militarized strife. Following chapter two, a section of photographs represents the movement in context.

In a flashback, chapter three examines the highly critical face-to-face dialogues Maya intellectuals had with North American and European researchers—including the present author—in the late 1980s. Mayanists assert that, just as the disempowering structures of international research need to be displaced, so do the basic frames of reference international scholars have used for identity: "ethnicity" and "minority" politics. This chapter considers the ways Mayanists practice their strategic essentialism as a political tactic. The ethnographic analysis finds that the diverse Maya reactions to foreign scholarship reflected important differences in the backgrounds and aspirations of intellectuals in the movement.

Chapters four and five discuss what was still suppressed in public discussions in 1989: memories of the terrifying experience of being caught between military and guerrilla forces during the worst of the civil war.[33] Violence devastated many communities in the western highlands; in San Andrés it provoked a local revitalization of earlier streams of Maya culture. Chapter four shows how, as dominant religious paradigms seemed to falter under the political and psychological pressures of the counterinsurgency war, local Maya leaders turned to traditionalist beliefs of transforming selves—which they had previously vilified and discarded—to describe the existential dilemmas of growing violence in the countryside and its corrosive impact on families and community affairs.

Given widespread killings and repression, Mayanists could not safely deal with political violence in their own public writings in the early 1990s— clearly they did more in the relative safety of their own meetings. By contrast, Maya refugees writing from exile, such as Victor Montejo and his collaborators, were able to publish powerful testimonies of military massacres and explore the difficult issue of Maya complicity in state violence. Chapter five offers close readings of these testimonial narratives and argues they can be read as striking autoethnographies and ethnographies of the state. Testimonies have gained new public import with the signing of the peace accords, the archbishop's program to gather testimonies as part of the postwar healing process, and the 1997 establishment of a national truth commission. The brutal murder of Bishop Juan José Gerardi in 1998 after his announcement of the impending release of the church's final report underscores the fragility of peace in a country unaccustomed to the free expression of criticisms of government and military repression.

Chapters six and seven illustrate the Pan-Maya fascination with projects that question the authoritativeness of national histories and imagine alternative accounts. Chapter six offers a close reading of Enrique Sam Colop's social critiques, published in 1991 and distributed on the eve of the Columbus quincentenary through national and international channels, which sought to expose the historical roots and perniciousness of racism. Implicitly, his commentaries make important arguments about the normalization of violence in contemporary society. The analysis argues that, given the hazards of producing social commentary in Guatemala in the early 1990s, Mayanist authors created veiled political critiques in the idiom of history. They counted on the active participation of readers to see the relevance of their critiques for the current situation. The analysis examines Sam Colop's selective appropriation and reworking of insights from diverse international sources of social criticism. It also traces Sam Colop's postwar transformation into a public intellectual who as a regular columnist now debates politics in the national press.

Chapter seven provides a detailed ethnography of reading by following the members of a Maya linguistics research team, *Oxlajuuj Keej Maya' Ajtz'iib'* (OKMA), as they participated in an informal group that studied chronicles of culture, history, and colonialism written by Mayas more than five hundred years ago at the time of the Spanish invasion. Their readings demonstrate the rich linguistic, cosmological, and hermeneutical knowledge indigenous intellectuals are able to bring to sixteenth-century chronicles. Most compelling for the Maya readers are the historical echoes in the annals of current personal and political dilemmas. In practice, their search for reflections of a distinctive pre-Columbian past still vibrant today, faces colonial ruptures and evidence of expanding Hispanic hegemony, which upset but, for them, never completely erase narratives of continuity.[34]

Chapters eight and nine deal with the counterpoint to Pan-Maya standardization by examining indigenous struggles from the vantage point of agrarian communities, such as San Andrés. While Mayanists have been active in rural towns as educators teaching literacy in Maya languages, calendrics, and religion, these same communities have pursued their own agendas, often with other social ideologies and organizational forms. The ethnographic analysis in chapter eight illustrates the history of community intellectuals and local Maya preoccupations with effective leadership, the erosion of moral authority, and the problem of integrating alienated youths into an encompassing sense of common purpose. A reexamination of older religious narratives shows that, rather than being a new issue, the fear of youthful alienation is a fundamental concern born of beliefs in an intrinsic limit to the knowability of other selves.

Chapter nine offers an intimate political biography of a prominent Kaqchikel-Maya family that has produced antiracism activists in a variety of organizations over the last three generations. The constant has been social activism, first in local and regional affairs and most recently in national arenas. But their tactics, their sense of indigenous identity, religious commitments, and ways of moralizing cultural continuity have put members of this extended family at odds with each other at important junctures. This chapter argues that the ideological diversity of the Maya movement is not solely a product of regional language differences, decentralized community loyalties, or emerging class cleavages. Additionally, Maya cultural constructions of the person, structures of kinship relations, and the political experiences of different historical generations contribute to diverse definitions of antiracism activism and critiques of Pan-Mayanism. These final two chapters examine the impact on local politics of the practice of cultural standardization by competing religious and development groups, and ask if the Maya movement will consolidate its power by displacing or embracing local variants of indigenous multiculturalism.

The emerging model is still in flux. Mayanists are actively using the language of rights and cultural relativity to press their demands on the Guatemalan state. Activists face the paradox of having to assert claims in a universalistic language that does not recognize the cultural specificity of their concerns.[35] On the one hand, Mayanist intellectuals have long debated alternative models—some hierarchical and theocratic and others egalitarian and ecumenical—for a new society composed of regionalized indigenous languages and peoples (*naciones*). On the other hand, Mayanists are actively experimenting with decentralized private Maya schools and community councils that privilege the authority of elders and local decision making. How these various arenas of "self-determination" will relate to Guatemala's political future as a multi-ethnic state remains to be seen. It is clear that the movement has been successful in causing many Mayas and increasing numbers of Ladinos to rethink who they are. Less certain is whether, given highly partisan congressional politics and the frustrating pace of change in the national political system, the movement will in the future advocate a territorialized and perhaps religiously informed image of a unified nation or continue to pursue a tactic of state reform and institutional decentralization in which there are many ways of being Maya.

This book seeks to contribute a heretofore missing interpretive dimension to literatures on marginalization, democracy, and new social movements—literatures that in Latin America have most often focused on the class-based politics of the *popular* Left.[36] Sonia Alvarez, Evelina Dagnino, and Arturo Escobar (1998) recognized this shortcoming in previous work and convened an international network of scholars to work on the cultural and political dimensions of social movements. The present effort feeds directly into this project and attempts to make the case for an ethnographic approach to the cultural production and practices of political movements.

The interpretive political approach taken in this study asks about the ways in which "Maya culture"—conceived of as a fluid and diverse practice—both informs the definition of what is political and influences the internal dynamics of the movement.[37] The analysis traces a movement that, in addition to its quest for indigenous rights and a multicultural transformation of the state, seeks to stabilize and standardize core elements of Mayaness that, they argue, survived Spanish colonization and the birth of the modern state. The movement seeks to communicate its message through a revitalization of traditionalist social forms, such as councils of elders, and through pan-community institutions that have been denied Mayas, their own schools, publishing houses, multilingual court systems, administrative systems, universities, and international forums.

This transregional ethnographic approach stands in creative tension with the more urban-centric, textual, and mass media–focused approaches to nation building in cultural studies. As ethnography has been influenced by postmodernism, the field of cultural studies is beginning to pursue ethnographic issues and to see the importance of research on the dispersed sites of cultural production. Moreover, I hope this study will be of interest to anthropologists, comparative sociologists, political scientists, and activists concerned with identity formation, cultural rights, and narratives of self-determination in a polycultural world of frequent diasporas and globalized economies, where autonomy is a striking if ironic quest.

One

Pan-Mayanism and Its Critics on Left and Right

> There is the difficulty of defining anticolonialism,
> in concept and practice, when the ideological
> context is triply colonial: the Marxist-Leninism of
> the armed left, the doctrine of National Security of
> the terrorist state, and the outrage of liberalism that
> sees only consumption and production.
> *Demetrio Cojtí Cuxil (1997a, 95)*

IN 1991, the Second Continental Meeting for Indigenous, Black, and Popular Resistance was convened in a huge, echoey cement-block hall at the dusty fairgrounds just outside Guatemala's second city, Quetzaltenango.[1] Throughout this week-long international congress,[2] covered by three hundred journalists, the Latin American grassroots Left asserted that diverse political struggles—including those for labor, indigenous, Afro-Latin American, women's, and human rights—could be successfully encompassed by the reigning grassroots paradigm, which called for the organization of the masses by sectors.[3]

Representing fifty-one ethnic groups from twenty-five countries in the Americas, 259 delegates with voice and vote participated in small work groups and plenary sessions. As one participant assured me, all had impeccable political credentials. Their numbers were swelled by sympathetic spectators, some 125 guests and 362 observers, primarily from Latin America and Europe. An estimated thirty thousand community activists in grassroots organizations[4]—many of whom were impoverished rural women who did not participate in the congress itself—marched for more than three hours through the city's streets in the final public demonstration of support for the grassroots Left and the goals of the congress.

One could not fault the courage of those attending the meetings, which took place in a highly militarized Guatemala, where the murderous repression of political activists as "subversives" continued in the early 1990s. Three decades of military rulers gave way after 1985 to a series of civilian governments, which struggled with the legacy of a highly militarized nation-state. After the failure of the Guatemalan National Revolutionary Unity (URNG) guerrilla alliance to topple the state in the 1980s, grassroots organizations with strong ties to the Left—among them the Committee for Campesino Unity (CUC), National Coordinator for Guatemalan Widows (CONAVIGUA), Mutual Support Group (GAM), Council of Ethnic Communities Runujel Junam (CERJ), Highland Campesino Committee (CCDA), and National Council for Guatemala's Displaced (CONDEG)—rededicated themselves to pressing for influential roles in national politics. Aided by Majawil Q'ij's promotion of Maya concerns, these key elements of Guatemala's *popular* Left found themselves well represented at the congress, with thirty delegates in the national delegation of thirty-five.[5] The remaining spots were filled by hurried invitations of "independent" Mayas.

Rigoberta Menchú, whose nomination for the Nobel Prize was enthusiastically endorsed at the meeting, facilitated the complex politics of choreographing groups of activists from very different national situations, so they moved toward consensus on movement politics in the post–Cold War world. She also sought to guarantee the safety of the participants through the international surveillance generated by her press conferences and the supportive presence of Danielle Mitterrand, wife of the French president. By all accounts, Menchú's tactics were successful in heading off government reprisals against the Guatemalan participants.

Through its leadership and working documents, the congress argued for a unified theory of oppression, the continued relevance of economic class as the master inequity, and the capitalist world in the guise of Western neoliberalism as the prime engine of oppression. In their post-revolutionary discussions of colonialism, neocolonialism, and self-determination, the *popular* movement portrayed itself as the vital political umbrella:

Self-determination, whether it be political independence, confederation, or autonomy, is realized in accordance with the ways peoples/communities (*pueblos*) practice different forms and styles of organization. Autonomy does not signify the rupture of a state but rather its transformation, since it continues to exercise sovereignty. Autonomy is self-government; it represents the struggle against the centralist state. A *popular* [grassroots Left] government is necessary to make the economic transformation of the state possible.

Therefore, the unity of all oppressed and exploited sectors is vital for the attainment of autonomous self-determination. Moreover, it is necessary to be attentive to hegemonic sectors' attempts to divide the movement by encouraging traditional and reductionist ethnic positions. . . .

The popular movement as a whole is the best guarantee indigenous peoples have for their struggle to rescue sovereignty, maintain their connection with the earth and nature, and preserve the spirituality of their culture's communities. The transformation of their position should have *popular* content, and oppose imperialism and its domestic agents. (Segundo Encuentro 1992, 37)

Some indigenous participants, however, found political and personal dilemmas in this framing of social conflict and possibilities for change.

The Second Continental Meeting achieved only partial success in channeling cultural dissent. Nationally prominent Mayanist leaders shared complaints in conversations between sessions: they had been invited as observers only at the last minute and found themselves marginalized by the rigid structure of the meetings, which in their view allowed only two official representatives of Pan-Maya organizations in the national delegation. Demetrio Cojtí Cuxil, among others, saw these problems as indicative of larger differences that had become apparent at Guatemala's democratic opening in 1985:

> *Popular*-Maya organizations were not considered part of the Pan-Maya movement because they did not demand indigenous rights. Rather they demanded social rights, especially fundamental ones such as the right to life and physical integrity. They had been embroiled in a fight against the government and army and allied with groups that organized against repression and impunity. From this standpoint, their struggle was heroic and persecution bloody. Their involvement in social struggle[6] was evident at the Second Continental Meeting—they cheered in support of Cuba and condemned the United States. Since they manipulated the indigenous issue and very few indigenous delegates came from other countries, Mayanists rejected these meetings. The Left's colonialism was evident at the final march, headed by leftist Ladinos followed by platoons of illiterate peasant Indians making up the body of the march. (1997a, 106–7)

Cojtí questioned, at that point, whether the international Left's public concern with indigenous issues was designed largely for external consumption, and, consequently, whether international funders might fail to understand differences between class-based and national or ethnic movements (1997a, 84, 137).

Indeed there were indigenous *populares* in the Guatemalan delegation. Yet, the personal and political stakes of grassroots activism created special tensions for these insiders, as American anthropologist Charles Hale explains:

> Indians who identify as *populares* generally have chosen to emphasize the demands that unify them with subordinate Mestizos. This does not imply a "loss" of Indian identity ("culture loss" is a problematic term in any case) but it does tend to involve either a shift in priorities away from demands specific to Indian cultural roots, or to a difficult commitment to struggle for those demands from within a predominately non-Indian political movement. (1994b, 36)

Some indigenous Guatemalans have made their peace with the grassroots model and have pursued long careers of activism. Others have found elements of the *popular* movement unresponsive to their personal politics.

Despite these shortcomings, around the edges of the official program, Mayanists met privately with indigenous representatives from other countries, and, after the congress, a group went out of town to Zunil's famous thermal baths for a private retreat. This was not the first time indigenous leaders from across the Americas created opportunities to discuss common concerns and compare strategies. Rather it was another moment in what some have termed "the Indian awakening in Latin America."[7]

Skeptics of the congress suggested that the grassroots Left included "indigenous" in the conference title and documentation largely for pragmatic reasons; that is, to tap into the anti-quincentenary fervor throughout the Americas in order to reassert the viability of leftist movements in the years immediately after the Cold War. Although *popular* politics may have needed renewed support elsewhere in Latin America, the Guatemalan activism continued to be diverse, highly successful, and championed by the international solidarity groups in the face of continuing repression in the 1980s and early 1990s. The *popular* movement organized many local and national groups that worked with cultivators, migrant laborers, students, urban workers, widows, families of the disappeared, and refugees. The struggle of labor versus capital informed the insurgency and diverse leftist movements with their own histories of organizing specific sectors of the population in Guatemala.

This chapter and the next argue that over the last forty years, the movement of oppositional politics away from the class-antagonism paradigm toward a more heterogeneous politics of social movements has been complicated by widespread intolerance of indigenous activism and its distinctive political agenda.[8] What characterizes this ambivalence? How are critiques of indigenous mobilization deployed by a variety of political interests? How has this adversarial environment influenced the relation between Pan-Mayanism and the *popular* movement? Let me start with the dissenters at the Second Continental Meeting, those indigenous leaders who were alienated by an international congress intended to include their interests.

The Development of a Pan-Maya Movement in Guatemala

Since the mid 1980s, educated Mayas have worked to create a social movement focused on the cultural revitalization and unification across language divides of indigenous Guatemalans, who most observers now agree make up a marginalized majority of the national population. The Pan-Maya movement seeks recognition of cultural diversity within the nation-state, a greater role for indigenous politics in national culture, a reassessment of economic inequities, and a wider distribution of cultural resources such as education and literacy in indigenous languages. The movement's commitment to education—both for its leadership and for the families in rural communities—represents a compelling change, given an educational system in which 70 percent of the public schools offer only four years of classes and 92 percent of the population over fifteen years of age has never finished the conventional six years of primary education (Herrera 1987, 13).

Through the movement, Maya academics, development workers, linguists, social scientists, lawyers, and publishers have become public intellectuals and contributors to research centers that produce materials for a variety of educational and political projects. These combinations of cultural identity and profession rarely existed before the early 1970s, when being Maya often meant working as an impoverished peasant agriculturalist, land-starved wage laborer, or market vendor. Most Mayanist professionals have been schooled in Guatemala; a handful have studied in the United States or Europe.

Through Maya Studies, the interdisciplinary academic field created by the movement, these intellectuals have formulated counterhistories denouncing the racism of national histories, searing critiques of foreign research practices and scholarship, textbooks to promote Maya language retention, challenges to Western models of development, and political psychology to counteract internalized racism. They condemn colonialism and racism as an ongoing situation rather than a moment of sociogenesis that occurred five centuries ago at the Spanish invasion.

Mayanists assert there is a culturally specific indigenous way of knowing: a subject position no one else can occupy and political interests no one else has to defend. The essentialism is tactical and situational: they advance this position to claim unique authority as social critics. Their goal is clear: to undermine the authoritativeness of non-Maya, or *kaxlan,* accounts—be they Guatemalan Ladinos or foreigners—which, until the recent indigenous activism and resistance surfaced, monopolized the representation of Maya culture and national history.

The early years of the movement were focused on issues of cultural origin and self-definition—"Who are we if we are not the negative stereotypes we have been taught?" As one activist put it, Indians were like street children who did not know their parents and therefore could not plan for the future. Echoing these sentiments, a recent poster produced by the Committee for the Decade of the Maya People pictured a mystical volcano ringed by a lake with a Maya couple embracing the four sacred colors of corn in the foreground. The accompanying text read: "Only when a people accepts its history and assumes its identity do they have the right to define their future."[9] In the late 1980s and early 1990s, Maya Studies publications by Demetrio Rodríguez Guaján (see Raxche' 1989), Demetrio Cojtí Cuxil (1991a), and Enrique Sam Colop (1991) were preoccupied with these issues.

Since those early years, however, Mayanists have refocused their debates more squarely on questions of the best direction for Maya nation building. Cojtí Cuxil (1994; 1995) has elaborated the movement's explicit demands on the state for major reforms in administration, language policy, the military, economics, education, communication, and respect for Maya ceremonial centers. Víctor Rancanoj (1994) has used Maya hermeneutics to generate a revisionist history of precolonial society and to argue for the renewal of earlier models of authority and leadership in the new social order Mayanists hope to establish. The issue at hand for Mayanist leaders is the longer-term planning of their agendas—done in twenty-year increments to reflect the Maya shape of time and their base-twenty mathematics—rather than the year-to-year planning called for by development funders who follow UN models.

The production and circulation of Maya Studies is not an esoteric urban enterprise, given that virtually all participants in the movement come from rural backgrounds. Some have stayed in their home communities working as farmers, school teachers, or extension agents in development organizations. Often, they are regional and grassroots leaders in the agricultural cooperative movement, religious groups, or local development efforts. Others have relocated to urban centers to pursue professional training and higher education, working as professors, bookstore owners, publishers, social workers, administrators, teachers, and professionals for NGOs, UNICEF, and government development programs. On weekends, during vacations, and for major events, professionals often return to their home communities, where many maintain their own immediate families and work on local development projects.

It would be short-sighted to dismiss this cultural revival as primordial or marginal to modern politics. Social analysts such as Eric Hobsbawm and Terence Ranger (1983) have pointed to the reemergence of tradition precisely at times of discontinuity. Anthony F. C. Wallace's early historical work (1972) and James Clifford's postmodernism (1988) have taught us that revitalization is a process of political articulation and cultural hybridizing, not an inevitable nostalgic escape to the past. Clifford Geertz (1973), Ernest Gellner (1983), Richard Fox (1990a), Partha Chatterjee (1993), and others have noted the important role public intellectuals play in social movements and raised questions about the class composition, culture, and politics of nationalist movements. Chantal Mouffe (1993) has warned against essentialism, against the positing of unitary constructions of identity politics.

Contested Views of the Pan-Maya Movement

As one celebrated Pan-Maya leader put it: "This wave is not carved in granite; rather, it defines a certain tendency. There is great variation within the Maya movement. Some are more radical in Maya religion, others in language, others in politics." It is difficult to characterize a movement as institutionally diverse, polycentric, and dynamic as this one. On the revitalization and education fronts, however, Mayanists have given priority to the following projects:

(1) Language revitalization, literacy training in Maya languages, and local language committees.[10]

(2) The revitalization of Maya chronicles of culture, history, and resistance to the Spanish invasion—such as the *Popol Vuj* and the *Annals of the Kaqchikels*, which are read as sacred cosmological texts and indigenous histories. There is great fascination with the Maya shape of time; that is, with Maya calendrics and numerics, the great precision of ancient eclipse predictions, and the complex religious associations with historical astronomy. Activists have studied glyphic texts, many of them dynastic histories, with art historians and linguists. Another striking characteristic of the movement is its historical consciousness—its multiculturalist sense of the ways Mayas were written out of national history and its urgency to imagine new histories.[11]

(3) The production of culturally inclusive school texts and teacher training materials for use in intercultural school programs. Activists have been successful in creating Maya elementary and secondary schools in some communities as a viable alternative to national schools.[12]

(4) The revitalization of Maya leadership norms, specifically community councils of elders, midwives, and Maya shaman-priests.[13]

(5) The dissemination of an internationally recognized discourse of indigenous rights, focusing on recognition and self-determination. The movement envisions a radical transformation of Guatemalan politics to accommodate a *pluricultural* nation with decentralized state services.[14] The movement has sought to make candidates for national office more accountable to indigenous voters by holding public candidate forums before elections.[15]

Projects that flow from these priorities currently operate throughout the western highlands, where most of the country's indigenous population resides. Although the movement has received support for particular projects from diverse sources—including the European Union, European NGOs, various United Nations entities such as UNICEF, U.S. foundations, U.S.-AID, the Guatemalan government, and national universities[16]—it has also attracted intense skepticism. In the 1990s, Pan-Mayanism's detractors increasingly made their opinions known through the mass media. Open criticism has spurred Mayanists to use the media to disseminate their ideas and generated continued reassessments of the usefulness of dialogues across social movements.

Almost from its inception, the Pan-Maya movement was disparaged on the Right and Left in Guatemala and beyond. Critics, including Latin Americanists at U.S. universities, were quick to dismiss the movement in the 1980s, despite the paucity of information on its goals or activities. U.S.-AID and Guatemalan business elites hoped to undermine the movement, which, although market-oriented, stresses collective rights to development resources. The Summer Institute of Linguistics, a U.S.-based missionizing organization also known as the Wycliffe Bible Translators, repeatedly clashed with the movement over language issues and control over the production and distribution of publications in indigenous languages. Ladino intellectuals, many of whom were deeply invested in anti-imperialist struggles, militantly opposed ethnic organizing. Local Ladinos generated their own charges of reverse racism and rekindled fears of Indian rebellion.[17] European and Latin American development professionals working in UN-sponsored human rights projects also expressed serious reservations about the movement.

Regardless of their politics, detractors of Pan-Mayanism have tended to draw from a common pool of images:

(1) The movement is accused of separatism, ethnic polarization, and the potential for violence by citing international examples of ethnic nationalism.

(2) The movement is accused of violating the local grounding of indigenous identity in place and community. The attempt to create a transcendent sense of "Mayaness" is seen as an unauthentic act culturally and a manipulative act politically.

(3) The movement is seen as not appropriate for the country because some regions are populated predominately by a single indigenous language group, some regions are mixed with different proportions of indigenous groups and Ladinos, and other regions are predominately nonindigenous. Return refugee communities are commonly an amalgamation of groups, which after help from human rights groups with *popular* leanings may identify themselves as *campesinos*, not Mayas or indigenous.

(4) That Ladino culture includes indigenous elements, Maya culture is Ladinoized, and all of Guatemala has been drawn into the globalization of consumer products and popular culture is further seen as erasing the relevance of ethnic-based organizing in favor of blendings in the name of *mestizaje* and hybridity.

(5) Building on language as a key basis of revitalization, activists are criticized for allegedly stressing language group endogamy and seeking to prohibit marriage across language groups.

(6) Pan-Maya leaders and urban participants are seen as neither indigenous nor Ladino—but rather as a third ethnicity—because they do not farm the land with wide-bladed hoes, and thus are seen as not rightfully representing their people.

In addition to the foregoing, criticism from the *popular* Left and U.S. Left has added the following issues:

(1) The movement is condemned for idealizing Maya community life and focusing on cultural issues rather than dealing with more urgent, material concerns such

as poverty and access to land for farmers. Given the rapidly growing rural population and the skewed ownership of farmlands, which leave many agriculturalists virtually landless, employment and poverty issues should take first priority.

(2) The movement, which initially decided not to label itself "political" and avoids the term "activist," is devalued as dodging the real politics of Guatemala.

(3) The measure of success of a social movement centers on its ability to achieve mass mobilizations and public protests. Pan-Mayanism, with its focus on language, culture, education, and scholarship, is judged as not passing this basic test to demonstrate its mass appeal or effect.

Mayanists dispute these criticisms, which they see as tactical mischaracterizations designed to disempower the movement and attack the intentions and legitimacy of its leadership.[18] From their point of view, the Right and Left in Guatemala have either wanted to absorb Mayas or use them as shock troops, as facades for particular political agendas.[19] Although they are willing to work with organizations of diverse political tendencies, Mayanists remain convinced of the distinctiveness of their vision, which they find neither translatable into nor reducible to the agendas of other groups.

In the 1990s, critiques of Pan-Mayanism have received intensive coverage in Guatemalan newspapers. The pressure was relentless, especially in 1994, 1995, and 1996, with weekly opinion pieces by well-known commentators across the political spectrum. Political debates that used to be fought in the university are now aired to wider audiences in the press. Among the most prolific and controversial of these journalists is Mario Roberto Morales, who has written for *Siglo Veintiuno*, *Prensa Libre*, and *Crónica*. A long-standing literary intellectual in Guatemala who sees himself as a leftist, Morales is currently finishing his Ph.D. in literature at the University of Pittsburgh. His tactic—mimicked with varying degrees of sophistication by other journalists, including many on the Right—uses strategies from cultural studies to deconstruct and delegitimize Pan-Mayanism.

Morales is committed to attacking "Maya fundamentalism" as an elite construction promulgated by intellectuals who do not represent the masses of impoverished "*indios*"[20] because they are far removed from community leaders. In his words: "This does not mean that indigenous revindications are invalid. I am against Pan-Mayanism as a construction, not against indigenous rights. They are two distinct issues."[21] Although his graduate-school advisers may not know this, Morales has cleverly appropriated a method many associate with the cultural Left in the United States to provide the Right and other readers with political ammunition in Guatemala. Pan-Mayanist leaders see his columns—along with the work of Miguel Angel Asturias (1977), Severo Martínez Peláez (1985), and other newspaper commentators—as key sources of "intellectual racism" in the country.

With a lively cynical postmodern tone, Morales employs images of globalized popular culture, hybridity, mimesis, culturally fabricated otherness, and *mestizaje* to argue against the existence of "the Maya" in Guatemala.[22] In a similar vein, he takes on structuralist models of power and racial hegemony for his newspaper readers:

> Where—in the analyses of the radicalized Maya intellectuals, the Ladino Indianphiles or even the Ladinoists—are the kids who walk around with tape players on their shoulders listening to heavy metal, with Reebok shoes, punk haircuts, and t-shirts that say "Save the Tropical Rainforest," and who have last names like Tujab, Quexel or Ujpan? Anthropologists don't like to get into these new identities because they stand outside their schemes. They prefer to continue thinking of Guatemala as a country where there are Indians and Ladinos or Mayas and *mestizos* and where the good guys in the film are the Indians and the bad guys are the Ladinos, so one has to help the Indians because they are the victims. (*Siglo Veintiuno*, Jan. 7, 1996)[23]
>
> . . . Evidence indicates that what dominates now are hybrid identities—impure (Indians with Reeboks or Pierre Cardin, depending on whether they work washing cars or for international organizations), negotiable, plural, and mediated by the laws of the market.
>
> . . . I want to show that the idea that racism exists only in ladinoness—that for discrimination to exist it has to be generated from a position of power, and, since indigenes don't have power, they are not racists—is only an idea in the realm of pure formal logic. Moreover, it is demagoguery if power is understood only as the structural power of the state apparatus and if other forms of power—which allow discrimination against Ladinos in areas of labor contracting by indigenous bourgeois exporters—are ignored. Racism presupposes genetic superiority, and here there is too much mixing (*mestizaje*) and hybrid identity for anyone to feel sufficiently certain, when he shakes his genealogical tree, that a conqueror or conquered won't fall from it. (*Crónica*, July 19, 1996)

There cannot be racism, Morales suggests, unless the races are distinctive and hierarchies unambiguous. In his writings, the postmodern insights of decentralized power, multiple identities, cultural and biological hybridities, and transnational cultural flows render the Ladino/indigenous split and the language of ethnic subordination a two-dimensional caricature of the national situation.

Morales has devised provocative, contemporary arguments, elements with which many cultural observers would find themselves in agreement, at least in theory. Latin America is a dynamic, fluid cultural field in which plural identities are being continually reconstituted and in which international mass media and consumer products are taken-for-granted aspects of life in even remote areas. There is little doubt that changes that accompany globalization have complicated older ethnic divisions of labor. Despite these probing insights, however, many social analysts fault the deconstructive impulse as a mental exercise that makes invidious ethnic discrimination and poverty dissolve before one's eyes—but, of course, only on paper.

For his part, Morales sidesteps extreme deconstructionism by appropriating the critiques of capitalism generated by cultural studies. He asserts that, far from being a local creation, international funders promote Pan-Mayanism as part of their agenda to expand global markets, exploit cheap labor, and champion exotic others for tourist consumption:

> It is clear that the market does not annul ethnic prejudice or discrimination. But what it does is to convert them into merchandise, into tourist attractions. And, thus, as fat and thin sell their humanity, considered defective, to the cinemagraphic market, marginal, subaltern, Indian cultures rapidly become "othernesses," sold to tourism as part of the New Age wave, with its esoterics for tourists in a hurry. In this scheme, the ideological construction of Mayanism [*mayismo*] is nothing more than a product for the academic funders' market, on the one hand, and, on the other, a basis for the game of democracy and for the tourist market. All of which is fine. But it should be branded as such because if Mayanism wants to sell itself to us as a superior fundamentalism, we won't buy it. (*Siglo Veintiuno* July 7, 1996)

Morales designs his columns to incite Mayanists and to delight their opponents. Mayanists find his mockery deeply offensive because it demeans their movement and their cultural nationalist project and dehumanizes Mayas as objects for consumption. Cultural difference becomes oddity and spectacle— "as fat and thin sell their humanity, considered defective, to the cinemagraphic market." Capitalist orientalism, which profits by creating exotic commodities for this market, allows no exit. The role cast for Mayas of inescapable "otherness" shows how they have already lost the struggle for self-determination to the globalizing forces of incorporation. In this view, no one avoids complicity with the market: tourism, academics, human-rights advocates, international cooperation—and by extension Morales's writing and mine—are all industries that for their own reasons support the Pan-Maya "boom":

> Human rights, women's rights, those for children, Indians, and gays are the issues for which there is now international money. So projects to develop these areas constitute the nucleus and the motive for the formation, cohesion, and legitimation of groups and associations which seek to describe themselves as new social movements. These movements do not present demands for socialist or capitalist modernity, but rather a (postmodern) revindication of specific groups, which do not question the capitalist system but only suggest reforms of it and within it. . . . Thus, money from international cooperation is the principal motor of Mayanism and the boom in indigenous movements. Also for the peace signing. In other words, western paternalism, through its act of contrition, incorporates (not separates) the marginal subject and the subaltern in the globalizing scheme. (*Siglo Veintiuno*, July 22, 1996).

Once again, one might well agree, certainly in principle, with the importance of interrogating the interests of foreign support for social movements
and international development initiatives. However Morales's reductionism
and polemicism become apparent when he argues that cultural resurgence is
all play-acting by Ladinoized Maya intellectuals serving as opportunistic fa-
cilitators for those seeking to widen their markets. In practice, Mayanists
have complicated views of the foreign funding of their work in publishing
and education. Moreover, the leadership is highly critical of tourism that
returns nothing to local communities and perpetuates images of timeless
Maya culture.

My problem with Morales's argument lies not with his desire to question
the personal motivations of Mayanists, the importance of global markets and
powers in national affairs, or the parallels of tourism, anthropology, and
human rights solidarity. Rather I find that his framing simply avoids serious
engagement with the social practices, the everyday significance of the market, and the national and local politics to which this movement reacts as it
struggles for rights that have been denied much of the national population.
Displacing agency to the international market has important political uses. If
Pan-Mayanism and rights struggles are understood as foreign impositions,
then Morales has freed the country from the need to examine and transform
its own policies and institutions. Significantly, Morales's views attracted
other commentators at significant political moments in the 1990s when public debates intensified during the UN-mediated peace negotiations between
the Guatemalan government and the URNG guerrillas and, after it became
clear the accords would pass, during the ongoing discussions of what should
be implemented and what should be politically sidelined.

Interestingly, Morales parts ways with many of his fellow commentators
when it comes to Guatemala's potential for ethnic violence. As adversaries
of multicultural reforms, many conservative Ladino commentators opposed
the ratification of the International Labor Organization (ILO) Convention
169 (which recognizes the legitimacy of indigenous rights in a variety of
spheres)[24] and specifically denounced the peace negotiation's Accord on
Identity and the Rights of Indigenous Peoples. Mario Alberto Carrera and
Julio César Toriello, for example, invoked images of atrocities in the
Balkans and Nazi Germany to claim that the recognition of indigenous rights
would fuel ethnic conflict in Guatemala. Carrera (*Gráfico*, May 9 and 11,
1995, Apr. 27, 1996) argued that segregation, polarizing leadership, and uncertainties over the implementation of the accords and models of nation
would lead to protests and instability. As secretary of the Guatemalan Academy of Language and corresponding member of the Royal Spanish Academy, he worried about the place of the Spanish language—the "roots" and
"marrow" of national culture—in a society where the Academy for Maya
Languages of Guatemala (ALMG), a government-sponsored entity run by

Mayanists from each language community in the country, intends to play a central role in language policy.

Toriello (*Siglo Veintiuno*, May 6, 1995) argued that the accords created a new minority—composed of Ladinos, mestizos, and European immigrants—who would not enjoy equal treatment before the law because of the imposition of new cultural rights (such as the recognition of indigenous languages and culturally specific styles of decision-making), which, he asserts, conflict with established rights. Both journalists express alarm over land conflicts, which have only become more serious over time, and the new demands inspired by the accords. These lines of criticism most likely narrowed the scope of the final identity accords.

Although Morales has occasionally expressed reservations about indigenous rights as "special" group rights, he believes that the market, not the threat of ethnic conflict, will prevail:

> The false claim (which I often made before) about the existence of a threat of ethnic war, if the disadvantageous position of indigenous Guatemalans is not remedied by the powers of the state on down, is not certain. It's enough to travel through the countryside to become aware that the laws of the market have brought indigenes into global postmodernity. They are making the best capital available from their culture for investment in tourism and their best merchandise for export. In this context an ethnic war does not have protagonists. (*Crónica*, July 19, 1996)

As an active figure in Guatemala's intense literary circles and professor at the University of San Carlos, Morales has long been a critical observer of capitalism. He supported the Rebel Armed Forces (FAR) guerrillas at the age of nineteen in 1966 as a *"militante de base."* After the western branch of the FAR fractured in 1976 and the Organization of People in Arms (ORPA) consolidated in 1979, he followed a splinter group, the MRP. His disenchantment with the URNG—which became the umbrella organization for the insurgency and, later, a chief protagonist in the peace process—dates from a period when he lived in Nicaragua and was jailed and psychologically tortured after what he describes as false accusations were made about him by Guatemalan guerrillas to the Sandinistas (*Siglo Veintiuno*, Oct. 29, 1995). After years in exile, he returned to Guatemala in 1992 as a cosmopolitan intellectual, cultural promoter, and journalist.

He sees himself as a left-leaning public intellectual critical of the URNG, the PAN political party currently in power, and Pan-Mayanism. Various elements of the Left seem painfully eager to reframe his changing politics as an instance of post–Cold War leftist self-criticism.[25] His deconstruction of Maya identity echoes the modernist argument of the well-known communist intellectual in exile, Severo Martínez Peláez (1985), who wrote that Maya culture died with the conquest and that today's indigenous culture is only a refraction of colonial constructions of the other.[26] In her provocative analysis of

Martínez Peláez, Carol Smith (1991) notes how easily Ladino racism moves across the political spectrum between Left and Right.[27]

Unfortunately for this historical moment of Maya resurgence, Ladino columnists from the intellectual Left were very quiet in print in the mid-1990s. Their public unwillingness to engage the authors of this anti-indigenous hostility, to probe Ladino identity and entitlements, or to offer more complex readings of Maya resurgence has meant that judgments of the movement have tended to be ethnically polarized in the mass media.[28]

Mayanists have not been defenseless or unselfcritical in this war of words. Demetrio Cojtí writes for *Siglo Veintiuno* and *El Regional*, Estuardo Zapeta contributes regularly on a range of subjects to *Siglo Veintiuno*, Miguel Angel Velasco Bitzol contributes to *La República* as a member of CECMA, Rigoberto Quemé Chay writes for *El Regional*, novelist Gaspar Pedro Gonzáles offers cultural analysis in the magazine *Tinamit*, and Enrique Sam Colop began regular columns for *Prensa Libre* in 1996. Many of these writers contribute to the national bimonthly news supplement *Iximulew*, which has a circulation of 50,000 copies and is edited by Velasco Bitzol at CECMA with the help of Germán Churruchich, Demetrio Rodríguez, Martín Chacach, and Obdulio Son. This is a highly educated, well-published group of Maya intellectuals.[29] Cojtí, Sam, and Gonzáles are elder statesmen of the movement and have written widely in their own right. Maya viewpoints on public debates have an additional route of circulation through *Rutzijol*, which republishes bimonthly collections of national news about Mayas from a variety of political perspectives and includes its own collective editorial responses to current political issues and coverage of Maya events.

Guatemala's most important Maya intellectual, Cojtí, used the commentary genre in a leading newspaper, *Siglo Veintiuno*, to make high-profile interventions during the negotiations of the identity accord. His commentaries dismissed polemical attacks on Mayanists as "marxists, racists, radicals, bigots, purists, etc." and focused instead on collective rights and models of the State.

In the last weeks, we have read various newspaper articles that attack and reject Maya demands for the restructuring the State and for an ethnic reordering to allow the recognition of regional autonomy. We are referring to assertions, among others, found in articles by Mr. Sandoval, Lionel Toriello, Marta Altolaguirre, Mario David García, Eduardo Evertsz, etc. These writers are not totally opposed to Maya demands, since the majority accept that the poverty Mayas suffer must be combatted and some support demands for participation in wider spheres of the State. But almost no one accepts the shift toward a State with autonomous units. . . .

. . . Maya people recognize rights at the level of collective rights which have as their subject the community/people (*pueblo*). If individual rights were sufficient, they would not be participating in the Maya movement, which involves cooperation among social classes. Its object is to defend the interests of the Maya community and not of a particular social class. (Feb. 16, 1995)

For Cojtí, constitutionally derived individual equality does not confront the problem of hierarchical relations between Maya and nonindigenous communities.

In 1996 the hostility of Ladino columnists escalated. As mainstream institutional editorials began to echo the biting language of partisan columnists, the directors of Mayanist organizations met privately to decide whether they should respond in print. With the exception of young Zapeta, who thrives on direct engagement with all parties, they decided not to publish direct counterattacks and, instead, to continue the process of interpreting the relation between Pan-Mayanism and Guatemalan politics for the public.[30] For their part, highly regarded progressive Ladino intellectuals, who have long histories of *popular* support, grew alarmed by the crescendo of hostility and worried that it would only fuel ethnic antagonism and complicate dialogues for social reconstruction after the peace accords. Ladino intellectuals began to meet privately to explore their personal views of identity and cultural difference and to pursue opportunities for off-the-record dialogues with Maya leaders.

That these concerns are more than academic is clear from the ethnic tensions in Quetzaltenango, the country's second-largest city. In 1996 opponents of Rigoberto Quemé Chay, the first Maya mayor elected in recent history, pursued a vitriolic anti-Maya campaign, which publicized its cause in racist graffiti throughout the city. Mayas, who make up just over half the urban population, went on alert. The *Prensa Libre* editorial, with a very telling title—*Indians? Ladinos?—No! Only Guatemalans*—took the incident very seriously:

> In fact, Guatemala has lived in constant confrontation during the last four decades, and now, as the end of internal armed conflict nears, we speak of the beginning of a period of peace. It would be lamentable if a new conflict began, this time racial, which could have greater consequences than the revolutionary war promoted by the extreme Left (Sept. 2, 1996).

In this moment of transition, debates about Pan-Mayanism serve as a veiled language for resistance to Maya socioeconomic mobility.

Cultural Capital and the Emergence of a Parallel Middle Class

Implicit in many of the criticisms of Pan-Mayanism is a Guatemalan version of the "racism versus class conflict" debate about the real sources of unequal life chances in ethnically plural, class-stratified societies. Rather than seeing class and ethnicity as politically and culturally interactive, critics from a variety of positions on the Left have long argued that Mayanists are making the wrong choice in stressing their cultural identity and ethnic discrimination as the country's core social issues.

One can also see in these debates a reproduction of the material/cultural cleavage that continues to trouble the social sciences despite all the paradigm blurring over the last several decades. In this instance, material conditions are portrayed as more autonomous, real, and basic than anything else. To reforms outside the grammar of land and labor, the classic reply from the international Left is "but what about exploitation?" through which critics seek to convey a materialist urgency that trumps cultural issues, no matter how worthy. The fundamentals of the material world—in this construction, land, labor, economic class structures, and ethnicity itself—are not infrequently conceptualized by *popular* movements as if they were transparent realities, free from cultural and social mediation. There is little sense that in practice material demands are politically advanced selective constructions, conveyed in fields of social relations created by *popular* organizations that also inform their significance. The alternative framing I want to advance would confront the cultural issues (and political interests) infused in the construction of materialist politics as well as the materialist concerns (and political interests) infused in cultural framings of politics.

The problem of culture and class remains a challenge for all poststructural analysts, especially given the legacy of structuralist frameworks such as historical materialism, internal colonialism, and world systems theory in Latin American Studies. Most analysts would agree that classes are not theoretical abstractions—they are culturally and materially fashioned in particular situations, as are other forms of stratification. High theory aside, class is not a separable domain but rather in practice a multidimensional form of stratification, often gendered, racialized, and saturated with cultural difference.

For instance, as a result of the genocidal civil war in Guatemala, impoverished rural widows became a distinctive political-economic class—the result of Maya family structure, agrarian sexual divisions of labor, and the violent repression that killed their husbands and left these women without a subsistence base. Courageously, CONAVIGUA, the *popular* movement's rural widows' organization, brought women from this gendered class together for crucial psychological, political, and material support. The constructed nature of this identification does not diminish the vital way CONAVIGUA came to meet the needs of women and children who were scarred by the war's violence.

Thus, the political recognition of a particular "class-based" identity—by mobilizing groups around certain foundational representations of social reality—is also a process of construction. Inevitably, this political process is fraught with many of the same dilemmas, such as the standardization and displacement of local culture, that critics attach to the Pan-Maya movement.

When Mayanist leaders assert that "class conflict is *not* our issue" but rather all forms of contemporary colonialism and racism are, one sees the heterodoxy and originality of the movement. What they mean here is that "class struggle" is not their unitary framework. They seek to build a cross-class movement—a new sort of Maya solidarity—that would include middle-class professionals and business people as well as cultivators, students, teachers, development workers, and rural shopkeepers. In fact, urban migration for employment or physical safety and novel organizational involvements mean that members of many extended families routinely have multiple class/ethnic identifications, localized in different ways in rural and urban space.

Recognizing the interplay of cultural and material issues allows us to ask important questions of social movements, whatever their politics. How do activists structure the production and circulation of the political vision crucial to their movement? How in practice do other participants consume this imagery and generate their own social meanings in the process? Movements may seek to change access to all sorts of resources, both to attract participants and to pursue their political goals. The creation and redistribution of "cultural capital"—which in this setting includes all sorts of media, education, knowledge of the past and present, languages with which to interrogate the status quo, cosmological knowledge, models of community authority, experience with organizational cultures, and skills to communicate across language communities and through various technologies—involves differential access to resources that make a material *and* cultural difference in peoples' lives.

In this context, scholars of social movements might consider the utility of an anthropological notion of "cultural capital."[31] Unfortunately for the case at hand, analysts have conventionally understood cultural capital to be a monopoly of the mainstream. In an early psychological approach, Oscar Lewis's notion of the "culture of poverty" (1966) condemns capitalism but also faults the underclasses for the poverty of their lived culture, which meant their lack of idealized mainstream norms (many of which, in fact and in practice, ironically elude the middle class).[32] From a sociological perspective, Pierre Bourdieu (1977, 1984, 1986) presents a formulation of cultural capital and status hierarchies as singular ladders with high-status culture at the apex. For him, cultural capital is embodied in individuals through family socialization and schooling while being objectified in material objects and the media. In bourgeois society, there is a clear, if sometimes mystified, relation between economic capital and cultural capital (1986:242–43, 246).

More recently, Philippe Bourgois (1995) has urged that the notion of cultural capital be historicized and made interactive by noting how inner-city entrepreneurs in the United States mobilize their own cultural and social capital in highly segregated social settings. He remains astutely aware of the political and economic contexts in which this occurs. But although Bourgois acknowledges the local deployment of different kinds of cultural capital, he largely dismisses their salience for or impact on the wider society.

Such approaches—especially when they are generalized by their later interpreters—tend to portray cultures as bounded groups and communities rather than to pursue, as Michael Kearney (1996) urges, the transnationalism and polyculturalism that individuals in marginalized communities have used to manipulate status hierarchies and widen their access to resources at the center and the margins. Along these lines, I would argue for a concept of cultural capital that (a) identifies the ways in which specific cultural formations in their larger contexts give distinctive shapes to the cultural capital they find relevant, (b) recognizes the circulation and distribution of nonmaterial and nonquantifiable cultural resources as an additional issue for social movements, and (c) draws our attention to the changing forms of capitalist production—in this moment of transnational intensification, the global flows of knowledge, information, and people—which make certain media and transculturalism especially important and powerful.

Note that in the Pan-Mayanist case there is no simple link between cultural capital and economic capital; rather, specific links need to be problematized in particular situations.[33] In fact, many Mayanists have access to a great deal of cultural capital—from fluency in indigenous languages and shamanism to the high-tech tools of the electronic age—yet the overwhelming majority live in modest economic circumstances. At work, they have been quick to push development donors for access to computer technology for their research and publication efforts. Specialized software now facilitates the publication of educational materials and research on Maya linguistics, pre-Columbian Maya calendrics, historical astronomy, and glyph texts. Public intellectuals have mastered the conventions of national and international meetings as public forums for their work. Tactically, Mayanists have internationalized and hybridized Maya culture to intensify and repoliticize the difference between indigenous and Ladino communities at home.[34]

When Mayanists make charges of widespread racism in Guatemala instead of focusing on class conflict, they seek radically to reframe who is accountable to social criticism. For them, Ladino peasants, urban migrants, and the working classes are complicit along with elites in the reproduction of prejudices that have destructive effects in everyday life. A wide array of "public" institutions is also implicated. The signal problem for social action—as the labor/capital analysts would have it—is not limited to Guatemala's tiny economic elite, which, shockingly, owns 75 percent of the country's agricultural land. It is additionally the more diffuse persistence of racism in national culture, where indigenous illiteracy rates run twice as high as Ladino rates[35] and where everyday life and the media are untroubled by open discussions of indigenous people as not rightful participants in civil society and as not ready for jobs, education, or elective office because of their ethnic inferiority.

Education and nontraditional jobs are major issues for Maya families, given highland demographic pressures, which make it clear to many youths that their futures will likely take them away from their parents' wide-bladed hoes and three-stone cooking hearths.[36] Class tensions, however, are racialized in Guatemala for Ladinos who resent the mobility of Mayas and their demands for political space.[37] Many leaders have had firsthand experiences of resentment to Maya mobility.

Doubtless, one source of the negative feelings toward Mayanist leaders is the growing competition between the parallel middle classes for professional and office employment in urban areas.[38] Middle-class Ladino intellectuals with social-science degrees now face a new source of direct competition for development work as institutions are caught in neoliberal economic pressures to downsize development, academic, and state bureaucracies. Interestingly, while Maya professionals are aware of job competition, they argue that indigenous professionals bring to these positions specialized fluency in indigenous languages and cosmological knowledge, which few Ladinos invest time in learning.

What especially puzzles Maya intellectuals is the ambivalence—which they see as hypocrisy—of some international scholars, human rights advocates, and development workers toward their achievements in the face of so many barriers.[39] Here they would argue that there are diverse ways of being Maya.

Two

Coalitions and the Peace Process

ON DECEMBER 29, 1996, huge crowds gathered in Guatemala City's central square and cheered representatives of the government, military, and guerrillas as they signed the "Accord for a Firm and Lasting Peace." The counterinsurgency war had finally ended, twelve years after the worst of the conflict. In the end, Guatemala's difficult peace negotiations spanned four presidencies, a coup, and many restructurings of the negotiating bodies.[1] While the peace accord represents only the first step in what will be a demanding process of reconciliation and reconstruction, it nevertheless reflects an extraordinary political achievement. One key element of the behind-the-scenes peace process was the involvement of *popular* Left and Mayanist groups, who saw this as a unique opportunity to push for the demilitarization and democratization of the country. Their input not only redefined Guatemalan political culture but also facilitated a rethinking by both groups of their characteristic analyses of inequality. The surprise was that these and other civilian groups gained access to the peace process at all (Cojtí Cuxil 1997c).

How was a peace accord achieved in a situation where low-intensity warfare had continued to undercut democracy for more than a decade? How did indigenous issues become central to the peace process when neither of the negotiating parties had a history of commitment to multiculturalism? To answer these questions, it is necessary to retrace the peace process, understand the novel indigenous coalitions it activated, and consider the wide array of national and international actors who found the creation of a more open democracy, however imperfect, an important alternative to military control.

The Seeming Intractability of Conflict

Tidal waves of warfare in the late 1970s and 1980s took a devastating toll on Guatemala, especially in the western highlands, where most of the country's indigenous citizens live. An estimated 70,000 to 100,000 people were killed; half a million people out of a national population of 8 million became internal refugees; 150,000 fled to Mexico as political and economic refugees; and 200,000 found their way to other countries, such as the United States.[2] This was the worst of a series of national crises during the three decades of authoritarian regimes that plagued the country after 1954.

Even after the reduction of mass violence and the turn to civilian rule with the election of President Vinicio Cerezo in 1985, the military had few incentives to negotiate with the Guatemalan National Revolutionary Unity (URNG) guerrilla coalition, which sought an end to armed conflict. It had long been clear that the insurgents would not be able to topple the state and establish a revolutionary socialist government. Their numbers were small—dwindling in 1996 to several thousand rural guerrillas facing an army of forty thousand soldiers—and civilian support had been brutally suppressed. Despite its best efforts, however, the army was unable to extinguish the insurgency or capture its leadership—in contrast to Peru, where the Shining Path guerrilla movement had been vanquished with the capture of its leader, Abimael Guzmán, by special forces in 1991. The military resisted peace in Guatemala because it would inevitably bring military downsizing and restrict the army's power to script presidential decision making and national policy. Furthermore, negotiations might yet give communist insurgents the victory they had been denied on the field of battle.

Peace negotiations dragged on with few tangible results. The guerrillas searched for political leverage where at first glance it appeared they had very little. The military seemed hesitant to engage a process that could only strip them of their substantial coercive power, and the government struggled with its image as a human-rights violator with little credibility in international circles. Interestingly, in 1997 the minister of defense, Brig. Gen. Balconi Turcios, argued that despite these impediments an inner group coalesced early in the negotiations. The challenge was to find a way out of intractable disagreements that had plagued the process between 1987, when President Cerezo created the National Commission for Reconciliation as a forum for civilian discussions of peace, and 1993, when negotiations between the principal antagonists began in earnest, only to be interrupted by a coup.[3]

By the early 1990s, many Guatemalans felt the time was right for a negotiated peace. After Rigoberta Menchú was awarded the Nobel Peace Prize, international attention turned to human-rights abuses, indigenous issues, and Guatemala's unresolved politics. The *popular* movement captured the high moral ground by drawing public attention to the tragedies of hundreds of thousands of refugees, forced military recruitment, and clandestine cemeteries.

Members of the Pan-Maya movement, which gained prominence in the late 1980s, saw cultural stakes in the peace process. It was a chance for them to gain recognition of cultural and collective rights and to argue for a state in which Maya communities would have "decision-making power over their own destiny." Their arguments for Maya recognition and self-determination echoed those articulated by indigenous groups working through the United Nations:

> All people have the right to take part freely in the cultural life of the community, to enjoy the arts and participate in scientific progress and its benefits. The dignity and rights recognized by the Universal Declaration of Human Rights imply the recognition of the person as a social being, affiliated with a community, ethnic group, nation, or state and at the same time as a *distinctive* social being in terms of language, religion, culture, or other pluralizing or diversifying conditions. (ALMG 1997, 1, emphasis mine)

For them, the issue was how to set the framework for asserting commonalities and legitimizing distinctiveness.[4]

Guatemala's economic elite, which had supported authoritarian rule in the past, came to see the pariah status of the country as a liability for their business dealings, especially in the emerging world of global assembly lines, the European Union, and transnational investment opportunities. After years of U.S. sanctions for human rights abuses and European support of grassroots organizing, Guatemala could not reenter the community of nations without a definitive peace. While politically leery of other Guatemalan sectors on many issues, the business community came to recognize the economic interests involved in a move to a more open society.

Finally, the civilian population wanted some sense of closure so that it could turn to other pressing social problems. Citizens had been exhausted by the militarization of daily life; the displacement of so many families from their home communities; the burden of war taxes extorted by underpaid soldiers, guerrillas, and criminals alike; and the fate of family members who had been kidnapped and tortured and had "disappeared" to unknown fates. Without ending the civil war and demobilizing armed forces on both sides, how would Guatemala cope with the legacies of violence, endemic poverty, and unemployment, a rapidly growing population, escalating street crime, and the growing use of the country as a transshipment point for international drug cartels?

The power of crosscutting coalitions among politically disparate groups became clear in 1993 when President Serrano Elías attempted a Fujimoristyle[5] authoritarian takeover of his own government, instituted media censorship, and attempted to disband Congress, the Supreme Court, and the Constitution. A surprising alliance of business elites, union groups, students, and indigenous leaders convinced the military that such a regime would lack international and national legitimacy. The takeover's failure demonstrated the powerful fluidity of interests and factions in Guatemala and the growing citizen involvement in national politics. The momentum for democratic change was propelled by the overwhelming rejection of the coup by national and international groups.

The peace process quickly gained momentum in 1994 with a reorganization that designated the United Nations as the moderator between antagonists, established the Assembly of Civil Society as the forum for indirect civilian input, and created the Group of Friends (including Colombia, Mexico, Venezuela, Spain, Norway, and the United States) to support the process internationally.

Guatemala was surrounded by countries that had recently found ways to end internal wars. Nicaragua and El Salvador, for example, had reincorporated guerrilla forces into civil society and the political party system. In fact, the negotiation of El Salvador's peace accords in 1990–92, brokered by the United Nations, paved the way for Guatemala. This history also provided an important lesson: to be successful, negotiations might well benefit from constructing a mandate beyond the immediate concern of demobilizing armed groups. Some observers felt the El Salvador process had not gone far enough. A fuller agenda of issues might provide the opportunity to bring wider democratic reforms and address the root causes of violence.[6]

Many Guatemalans found it ironic and disconcerting that antagonistic armed forces with little experience in democracy were negotiating the fate of the nation in distant, secretive talks in Europe and Mexico. In response to these tensions, the Assembly of Civil Society set up consultative discussions with civilian leaders from a variety of social sectors to provide advisory documents for the peace process. The assembly brought together representatives of groups with very different politics and created space for debates and alternative proposals. Maya activists worked through the Coordinator of Organizations of the Maya People of Guatemala (COPMAGUA), which commissioned position papers from different groups and worked toward a consensus on key issues in order to influence the assembly.[7] In this way, *popular* and Maya groups, among others, gained institutionalized representation and the opportunity to organize their own parallel meetings in a process that might otherwise have thoroughly marginalized civilian input.

As a result of pressures, compromise, and consensus-building, indigenous rights gained a forum in the negotiations. Grassroots *popular* groups— whose high-profile leaders captured support from their Latin American counterparts, European and North American solidarity movements, international Catholic activists, and liberal Protestant groups—had promulgated human rights discourse in their early days of labor organizing and more recently in responding to military repression. To these concerns, Pan-Mayanists added the issue of cultural rights and self-determination, which they advocated through the Council of Maya Organizations of Guatemala (COMG), an umbrella group founded in the late 1980s.[8] Pan-Mayanists drew support from discussions at the United Nations on the rights of politically marginalized indigenous groups.[9] The European Economic Community and northern European NGOs directly supported projects of cultural reaffirmation in the name of social justice.

In the end, the peace process generated a separate Accord on Identity and

the Rights of Indigenous Peoples,[10] signed on March 31, 1995, by the government, military, and URNG high command and put into force at the con-
clusion of the peace process a year later.[11] (See appendix one for a detailed
summary of the four sections of the accords.) The identity accords called on
the government to pursue the following commitments and reforms:

> Recognition of Guatemala's indigenous people as descendants of an ancient people
> who speak diverse, historically related languages and share a distinctive culture
> and cosmology. Non-Maya Xinca and Garifuna communities are accorded
> equivalent status.
>
> Recognition of the legitimacy of using indigenous languages in schools, social
> services, official communications, and court proceedings.
>
> Recognition and protection of Maya spirituality and spiritual guides and the con-
> servation of ceremonial centers and archaeological sites as indigenous heritage,
> which should involve Mayas in their administration.
>
> Commitment to education reform, specifically the integration of Maya materials
> and educational methods, the involvement of families in all areas of education,
> and the promotion of intercultural programs for all children.
>
> Indigenous representation in administrative bodies on all levels, the regionalization
> of government structures, and the recognition of localized customary law and
> community decision-making powers in education, health, and economic
> development.
>
> Recognition of communal lands and the reform of the legal system so Maya inter-
> ests are adequately represented in the adjudication of land disputes. The distribu-
> tion of state lands to communities with insufficient land.

Despite these achievements, Mayanists hold that the accord process was
seriously compromised by secrecy, limited Maya input, and disregard of indigenous norms of consultation with communities and elders. Of great concern is the fact that the final document dealt only obliquely with collective
rights. Major issues such as the recognition of regional autonomy, historic
land rights, and the officialization of Maya leadership norms were deemed
irreconcilable and dropped. In practice, governmental "promises to promote"
the various legislative reforms outlined in the accords left many loopholes
and ambiguities in a political system where antireform forces are experienced and well-organized. Other central issues were eliminated from the
agenda when they were transferred for discussion to negotiations for the
accord on socioeconomic issues. What could one expect, asked editorialists
in *Rutzijol*,[12] given that the formal negotiations were between guerrilla
leaders and government representatives?

Nevertheless, the decision to make indigenous rights a separate stage in
the peace negotiations—which, after all, were explicitly convened to demo-
bilize guerrilla and counterinsurgency forces and establish the framework for
political peace—signified a breakthrough for the movement. After summa-

rizing critiques of the assembly's process, Mayanist representative José Serech reported that some Maya groups nevertheless concluded: "The accord widens and opens space in all levels of national life . . . space that until our time has been historically reserved by the colonizers and their descendants. It is a formal instrument to combat racism" (Serech 1995, 7). The document calls for an explicit public acknowledgment of the fierce discrimination Guatemala's indigenous majority has endured on the basis of their distinctive origin, culture, and language. As a consequence, the document argues, indigenous Guatemalans have often been unable to exercise their rights or gain effective political representation.

Much of the accord's language (see Saqb'ichil/COPMAGUA 1995 and appendix one) focuses on the state's *recognition* of indigenous languages, cosmology, spirituality, dress, customary law, and sacred places of worship. For its part, the government repeatedly promises to work with the legislature to promote constitutional reforms to make Guatemala a "multiethnic, culturally plural, and multilingual" nation-state where ethnic discrimination will be prohibited. The government also commits itself to seek institutional reforms in the courts, make sexual harassment a crime, and decentralize and regionalize the school system.

Implementation of the identity accords has involved the creation of joint governmental-Maya commissions to make policy recommendations for constitutional and legislative change on highly contentious issues for the country and the movement. Their stress on consensus decision making through frequent meetings and public forums has been extraordinarily demanding of time and energy for Mayanists who see this as a unique opportunity to forge coalitions around controversial issues. Some Ladinos have found their participation a consciousness-raising experience, especially when the hearings broke through the accepted compartmentalization of Guatemalan life to reveal hidden injustices.

For instance, during the 1997 Second Congress on Maya Studies, Frederico Fahsen, a member of the European-identified elite, epigrapher, and member of the Commission on Sacred Sites, described his group's daunting responsibility to produce in a period of only ten months a comprehensive survey of the country's Maya religious centers, some regionally and nationally famous and others the locus of devotion for particular communities, families, and individuals. In public hearings, the commission, which has also involved Mayanist leaders such as Narciso Cojtí, listened to accounts of the efflorescence of Maya spirituality during the violence and painful reports of current religious repression, including the destruction of mountaintop altars by evangelicals, the looting of tombs and archaeological sites for the international market in pre-Columbian artifacts, the blocking of diviners' access to traditional ceremonial centers by property owners, and the hostility of Catholic Action and charismatic groups toward practitioners of Maya spirituality, whom they denigrate as witches (*brujos*). Fahsen found these instances of intolerance deeply disturbing, both because of their obvious injustice and because, as a member of the elite, he had been shielded from awareness of these social tensions. On a more optimistic note, he described the recent efforts of some communities to promote the reconciliation of Catholic Action catechists and Maya spiritual guides (*ajq'ijab*).

The peace process has been marked by a shift in Mayanist discourse on sacred cosmology and nation away from a theocratic model, advocated by some activists, in which Maya religion and priests would rule supreme. The emerging ecumenical recognition of Maya spirituality and spiritual guides leaves room for a variety of relations with other religious groups, a multiplicity of individual religious practices, a diffuse understanding of Maya cosmology as cross-cutting conventional religious divisions, and secular Mayas whose activism is religiously disinterested. As a result, striking esoteric Maya ceremonies conventionally used to convene public events have been shortened and made more accessible across language divides, while many families continue Mayanist healing and devotional activities along with Catholic masses to celebrate their children's graduations.

Another fruit of the peace process has been the Commission on Officialization, organized by the Academy for Maya Languages of Guatemala. Building on the academy's national network of community language committees, the commission convened consultative workshops in each of the country's linguistic communities in July 1997 and a month later held a three-day national congress in the capital to discuss national policy issues (ALMG 1997). Respected elders of the movement, such as Alfredo Tay Coyoy and Martín Chacach, chaired the work groups and encouraged local representatives to air concerns about the role of their own community languages in national policy. All agreed that the fact that Spanish remains the only official language in the country fuels discrimination against the indigenous majority.

One basic goal of this commission is to achieve formal acknowledgment of the multilingual character of the nation through a listing of the country's indigenous languages in the Guatemalan constitution; another is to begin the process of standardizing a written version of each language to take the place of the many ad hoc alphabets currently in use. Participants agreed on the importance of urging government recognition of each regional language group. Yet, it is also evident that community-specific language loyalties within regions raise tricky issues for the selection of a single oral dialect to be transformed into the standard written form for each language, a necessary precursor in the view of Mayanists to a national language policy and the production of administrative and educational materials in Maya languages.

Here knowledge is power in the sense that the movement looks to the expertise of professional linguists to transcend community-centrism by making scientific determinations of the most appropriate dialect. According to

Mayanists, the choice of dialect for standardization can be made on several grounds, including which of the many dialects in a given language community incorporates the widest range of early Maya language forms, whether there is regional consensus about a high-prestige dialect, or whether it would be more effective to invent a transcendent dialect that combines features of various spoken versions. In the quest for standardization, scientific knowledge is playing a key role in the historical reconstruction of tradition and the mediation of what otherwise might be endless disputes between actual communities based on loyalty to place and ancestors.

Yet, on another level, officialization is seen as an overtly political act that compels difficult choices. The most pressing issue is how many of the twenty-three languages, including non-Maya Garífuna and Xinca, need to be officialized in the practice of state politics and administration. Some activists want all languages to operate on a par with Spanish in national and regional affairs. While this might be appealing in terms of its immediate fairness, many worry that financial constraints—such as the required translation of official documents and proceedings into so many languages—would undermine any real chance that the new policy would be implemented.

Others believe that a *lingua franca*, most likely the numerically dominant K'ichee', would be the best national choice complemented by the use of regional languages for public services, local schools, courts, and administration. There is consensus that government jobs in education, health, public administration, and the courts should be allocated to those who are fluent in regional languages, whether they are Mayas or Ladinos. This vision produces a clear indigenous alternative to Spanish as the transcendent medium for intergroup and official communication. Debates over the best model for officialization are likely to continue through the commission process and into any call for constitutional and legislative reforms.

Mayanists are active in other aspects of the peace process, including the commissions on participation, land issues in indigenous communities, and the truth commission, whose work is phased in at different points during the implementation process. For instance, Otilia Lux de Cotí, a prominent educator, accepted an appointment to the Commission on Historical Clarification, which in August 1997 assumed the controversial task of reconciling the de facto amnesty granted to the soldiers on both sides as part of the peace process with the pressing need urged by many organizations and citizens to document the human rights abuses during the war. At issue are ways to promote reconciliation and healing, to avoid the escalation of old conflicts into new brutality, and to dismantle the mechanisms of terror that engulfed the country for so long. With a high-profile mandate and fifty thousand complaints filed at the truth commission's inauguration, the question remains how it will operate with limited staff and government funds. Members are under enormous pressure from the *popular* Left to defy the limits on their formal mandate—which severely limits their ability to name protagonists of violence or seek prosecution of human rights violators. From the Right they are urged to document that the guerrillas were just as violent in their treatment of civilians as the army. From the Catholic Church, which has gathered tens of thousands of personal testimonies of violence through the Project for the Recuperation of Historic Memory (REMHI), they are under pressure to respond to community needs (Oficina de Derechos Humanos del Arzobispado 1997).

Negotiating these political white waters will be extraordinarily challenging, as we have learned from the South African truth commission. In that instance, the legal process has revealed much about the authors of violence and the daily functioning of the state terror apparatus under apartheid. Yet, the truth commission has embittered civilian victims who in order to testify have rekindled terrifying memories of abuse only to be denied the concrete personal support they anticipated.

In addition to their participation on commissions, Mayanist organizations (such as CEDIM and COCADI) and *popular* organizations (such as the Rigoberta Menchú Foundation) have directed their energies toward rights education. Foreigners, including Europeans, Latin Americans, and North Americans, have worked through the United Nations Mission for the Verification of the Peace Accords (MINUGUA) to teach community groups about their identities and rights as recognized by the accords. MINUGUA also works to verify cases of discrimination with respect to cultural, political, and civil rights. They have also supported research on Maya customary law and programs for bilingual legal translators to assist Mayas in court proceedings. Given the rocky history of recent constitutional reforms, the limited numbers of Mayas in Congress, the absence of governmental norms for local consultation, and the chronic lack of budgetary support to enact legislation, however, serious problems remain concerning the implementation and verification of peace-process reforms.[13]

The movement is working to widen its public appeal and put pressure the government through publications such as the Mayanist newspaper *Iximulew*, a bimonthly supplement in *Siglo Veintiuno* newspapers, which offers news reports, interviews, and editorials on civic and political participation, the impact of the accords, Maya involvements in the construction of peace, Maya women, Maya and Ladino debates on the significance of their respective identities, language issues, and constitutional reform.

With the identity accords, Cojtí Cuxil and other leaders pressed on with the task of explaining the Mayanist vision of rights as a remedy for ethnic discrimination:

Almost all the constitutions of Guatemala . . . have established norms which state that all people "should be treated as human beings, should not be discriminated against for any reason," "all human beings are free and equal in dignity before the law," and "discrimination is totally prohibited for reasons of race, religion, sex, origin, or nationality," etc. These norms are excellent when individual rights are discussed . . . but discriminatory when collective rights are treated specifically in terms of ethnic group or community. By dealing with them as equal, community differences are ignored or absorbed.

Ethnic discrimination consists of not recognizing, respecting, and promoting the cultural differences that indigenous communities present in all areas: religion, linguistics, organization, economics, politics, etc. Discrimination is created by disqualifying and inferiorizing people and then by blocking, persecuting, and eliminating indigenous issues and indigenes. . . . But this should change. Thus, in the Indigenous Accord, among the government's obligations is to present to the legislature a plan for standardizing ethnic discrimination as a crime. (*El Periódico* Nov. 13, 1996)

Like the U.S. civil rights struggles in the 1960s, many of the Guatemalan reforms outlined in the indigenous accords are highly controversial. To be successful the accords will have to generate legal reforms, institutional change, wider indigenous representation in national life, and more effective legal means for settling conflicting interests. Such accomplishments will require coalition-building among the existing political parties. Political parties, such as Ríos Montt's rightist party, the Guatemalan Republican Front (FRG), are well-practiced in the art of politically derailing reforms. Former URNG guerrillas have moved ahead to create their own party—in addition to the *popular* Left's New Guatemala Democratic Front (FDNG)—one that may or may not focus on the revolutionary Left's historic concern with class-based politics at the expense of the new indigenous agenda. Work will also have to be done to convince nonindigenous Guatemalans that these reforms will benefit the country as a whole. Finally, the funding of cultural reforms will be a controversial issue in a neo-liberal climate where the government is cutting jobs and privatizing government functions and where some economists anticipate that the economy is heading for a recession and others note that, despite robust national economic growth, low inflation, and exchange rate stability in 1997, the purchasing power of the working classes was seriously compromised by rising transportation costs, stagnant employment, and eroding public services (MINUGUA 1998). Some organizations, such as MINUGUA, have reoriented their attention to monitoring the socioeconomic accords, which will also prove highly controversial in their implementation, especially as they are seen to "universally" affect citizens. Apparently, despite years of effort, the Pan-Maya movement has yet to convince Guatemalans that racism is an issue that affects all citizens.

The first eight months of the implementation process did not focus on indigenous issues. Rather, national priorities concentrated on the more urgent tasks of dismantling civil patrols, disarming and reintegrating the guerrilla combatants, downsizing the army, and removing land mines from the countryside. Attention has turned to the problems faced by internal and international refugees—many of whom find their families dispersed and their homes and lands occupied by others. The cause célèbre for grassroots activism has been to challenge what many perceive to be a dangerously comprehensive amnesty program, the impunity enjoyed by those in power given a weak judicial system, and the need to have an effective truth commission. Community involvement in teacher selection in local schools has proven to be highly controversial, given the resistance of teacher unions. Land issues have also been highly politicized. Clearly the changes advocated in the accords will create new dilemmas and provoke organized political resistance along many fronts. By 1997 Mayanist leaders found themselves active in a wider range of organizations and political settings than ever before. Within Saqb'ichil/COPMAGUA and the indigenous accord commissions, consensus decision-making and community consultation have been incorporated as Maya models of democratic participation. Important decisions on controversial issues have come from these bodies. Funders (such as U.S.-AID, which had been quite critical of Pan-Mayanism) have responded with renewed educational initiatives, including four hundred college scholarships for Mayas studying bilingual education and legal interpreting.

Yet there have also been mismatches between peace-accord organizations and international funders. The fast-paced time table for accord implementation disadvantages groups that are not centrally organized and already decisive about their immediate goals. International funders (such as the World Bank, which has earmarked $1.9 billion for democratization initiatives in Guatemala) have sometimes found Maya group process illusive and hard to fathom because it does not conform to the organizational discipline expected of participants in transnational development networks. Funders on this scale appear not to be interested in peace implementation as a coalitional group process in which discussions and consultations raise important debates, group membership is fluid, and the mechanisms for reaching authoritative decisions situationally dependent.

Many observers agree that the "best-organized groups" with clear-cut agendas, concrete projects, and track records of working with outside experts to generate concrete proposals have made the most headway and reaped the greatest rewards in the implementation process. Thus, while individual Pan-Maya and *popular* organizations with Maya-identified agendas have been highly successful in gaining support for their own efforts, especially with educational and community-focused projects, the coalition of representatives of politically diverse Maya organizations created through the accord process appears to have played less of a role than groups working in other areas of the accord process.

Without the Mayanist movement, the peace-process reforms might have remained little more than a political gesture in the negotiation process, an opportunity for the guerrillas to show they could be responsive to Maya civilians and activists in the *popular* movement, and for the government to appear inclusive and universalistic to the international community. With a decade of organizational experience and their own effective ties to international donors, the European Union, UNICEF, and the UN, however, Pan-Mayanists have already begun projects that flow from the indigenous accords. They are working most actively to promote Maya schools as forums through which children might gain education supportive of indigenous culture and language. Additionally, they continue to publish a wide variety of educational texts for the schools and scholarship on indigenous issues, and to press for legal recognition of indigenous customary norms and the authority of elders in rural communities. Currently, Mayanist leaders are advising the government on strategies for decentralization that, consonant with neoliberal reforms, would allow decision-making powers to devolve regionally and locally. Here is where Mayanists hope to reintroduce the issue of autonomy, which was lost in the accord process. Demetrio Cojtí Cuxil argues:

> Isn't it possible to conceive of Guatemala as a free association of Maya and *mestizo* communities which undertake common objectives but preserve their respective integrity and identity? Mayanists consider this federal form of political organization an ideal that is still not feasible, and therefore accept the location of their project for national liberation within the framework of the pyramidal State. . . . In this model, the ethnic diversity and autonomy of each ethnic group would not be complete, but would function at the intermediate level of government. Autonomous regions or microregions would be formed from counties [*municipios*] composed of the speakers of the same language. (Cojtí Cuxil, in *Siglo Veintiuno*, Feb. 16, 1995)
>
> There can be no other choice than that the central state apparatus carries out the supraethnic functions that concern all individual and collective members of society (such as national defense, diplomatic relations, common standards), while the particular ethnic region could and should exercise administrative and legislative powers in areas that directly affect its existence and well being (education, culture, social work, police, health, etc.). (Cojtí Cuxil, in *Siglo Veintiuno*, Aug. 28, 1994)

Officially, the government is committed to legislative and institutional change to create the new multiethnic, multicultural, and multilingual vision of Guatemala in the years 1998–2000.[14] It is estimated that the implementation of peace in Guatemala will cost $953 million, with the indigenous accords requiring about $88 million, of which $60 million, almost 70 percent, will need to go to educational reform (Colmenares 1997, 31). Clearly, indigenous groups did not wait for the official phasing in of the accords; rather, they began networking internationally and organizing locally in the mid 1990s to pursue their agenda for peace and a more inclusive national society.

Defining Common Purpose across Cleavages

The peace process has demonstrated that the divide between the Pan-Maya and *popular* movements, which some commentators have portrayed as unbreachable or irreconcilable because of ideological or class differences, is, in fact, bridged quite frequently by individuals who are active in both camps or who borrow ideas from other groups for their own uses. Thus, in practice there are many instances of cross-fertilization and frequent moments of common purpose between the movements.

In responding to *popular* critiques, Mayanists have sharpened their class analysis. They see Ladino poverty as an important issue that needs to be addressed, and they recognize that the racism of the Ladino underclass is economically fueled. In their reflections on the multiple meanings of racism, they have drawn on Ladino scholars such as Carlos Guzmán Böckler and Jean-Loup Herbert (1995) who used "internal colonialism" to conceptualize domination and discussed the unstable nature of Ladino identity.[15] They also have turned recently to Marta Elena Casaús Arzú's (1992) powerful social history of Guatemala's oligarchy. Of special interest is her lineage-by-lineage documentation of the reproduction since the sixteenth century of Guatemala's microelite through class endogamy, marriage alliances between lineages that controlled vast private resources and public powers, and the racist ideology of "blood purity" (*limpieza de sangre*). In fact, many of these elite lineages see themselves as whites who stand totally apart from and above the indigenous/Ladino divide; none regard themselves as having indigenous blood. These lineages have historically controlled banking, commerce, government, the Catholic church, and high culture in Guatemala.

For their part, many intellectuals on the Left have changed their views on indigenous issues over the years and moved away from total assimilation as the only future for indigenous communities.[16] Mayanists have long admired the courageous work of *popular* human rights activists who publicized human rights abuses at great risk to themselves. They certainly agreed on the importance of demilitarizing civilian life and disbanding civil patrols, which functioned as prime movers in the government's counterinsurgency policy and which parents feared would socialize their sons into violence, corruption, and disrespect for the moral authority of their families.

There have been other important experiments—some more promising than others—in institution building across the Pan-Mayanist/*popular* divide. When the *popular* Left created a coalitional political party, the New Guatemala Democratic Front (FDNG or el Frente) in 1995, well-known *popular* leaders won six congressional seats. The party, however, was not seen by Mayanists as autonomous from the URNG guerrillas and, thus, had limited appeal across the *popular*/Mayanist divide. Only some are convinced that el

Frente will shed its leftist roots, push for the implementation of Pan-Maya-nist reforms over other priorities, or develop wider electoral appeal. Nev-ertheless, many felt and continue to feel the time is not yet ripe for a Maya political party.

In another experiment before the 1995 elections, a low-key group called K'amalb'e was formed to begin discussions about developing a "Maya way of electoral politics" (*vía maya de política electoral*). The idea was to create not a political party but rather a dialogue in which indigenous leaders from *popular* groups and the Pan-Maya movement would be more than tokens and Ladinos would listen to their concerns. The group has also been inter-ested in informing public opinion on the practice of Maya culture. These discussions appear to have generated new lines of collaboration across old political divisions.[17]

From the time of the Second Continental Meeting in 1991 to the present, Mayas active in the grassroots Left have become increasingly engaged in cultural and ethnic issues, leaving some of their Ladino colleagues wonder-ing about the impact on the Left of Maya resurgence and the possibility of new Maya alignments across old political cleavages. Maya members of the Committee for Campesino Unity (CUC), for example, created a splinter or-ganization, the National Indigenous and Campesino Coordinator (CONIC) to focus their efforts more squarely on indigenous land struggles. In recent years, Mayas from a variety of political backgrounds have begun to evoke Ruwach'ulew (the Earth/the World) or Qate' Ruwach'ulew (our Mother the Earth or Mother Nature) to mark their political discussions culturally. Build-ing on the early work of Mayanist groups like COCADI, activist organiza-tions use an indigenous ecological discourse in overlapping ways to inter-connect Maya cosmology, agricultural rituals, strategies for socioeconomic change, land issues, and rights struggles.

As of 1996 and 1997, some Ladino leaders believe that indigenous *popu-lares* could go either way: toward a cross-movement alliance that would either include Ladinos or perhaps lead in an independent direction with other Mayas. Maya *popular* leaders—some of whom have grown weary of the hierarchies of command in the traditional Left—will be a critical fulcrum point in this process. The militancy of the demobilizing URNG guerrillas who appear to insist on the preeminence of a Ladinoized class-conflict line has only heightened the tensions around the issue of realignments.

The missing Ladino voice, one which would publicly condemn Ladino racism and affirm Maya cultural existence, was added to the calculus in August 1996. Casaús Arzú, the analyst of elite hegemony and a member of one of the country's most eminent families, returned to Guatemala after years of exile for her radical politics in the 1970s. For her, this is a crucial historical juncture, an opportunity for Ladino-Maya dialogues to work to-ward intercultural understanding and the dismantling of racism. She has collaborated with Demetrio Cojtí Cuxil and others to promote these exchanges. During the First Congress for Maya Studies in August 1996, she spoke with great urgency in an interview for the country's major newsmagazine *Crónica*:

> The emergence of the Maya movement plays a very important role not only in its capacity to propose change, but also by forcing us, as Ladinos, to think: How do we create our nation from this diversity? . . . There are indigenous leaders, like Cojtí, whose project is one of an inclusive political nation [*nación política*], with multiculturalism and ethnic diversity, in which economic and political power are shared. I ask myself and Ladino intellectuals: What kind of a nation do we have? What frame of reference do we use to debate this? (*Crónica*, Sept. 16, 1996, 40)

Casaús Arzú argues that Guatemala must avoid perpetuating either the *"nación étnica,"* in which Ladinos continue to rule a homogeneous national culture, or the *"nación étnica maya,"* in which Mayas seek a separate nation. Instead, her goal is the *"nación política,"* which would recognize cultural difference and tackle racism but rule out the formation of separate ethnic nations. In her mind, continuing dialogues are absolutely crucial to avoid future violence:

> In the face of Maya emergence or rebirth, a certain fear has arisen among Ladinos. First, since we have never reaffirmed our identity, we do not strengthen our Ladino culture, and, besides, we never think in terms of the nation since, as the hegemonic class, the Nation-State used to be ours. To the extent another ethnic group formulates a different project in much more inclusive terms, Ladinos go into a panic, manifested in these predictions of an ethnic war, but also in a greater interest in discussing Ladino identity. During my stay in Guatemala I have encountered this desire among some groups. . . .
>
> I have been surprised to find the belief among Ladinos that there could be an ethnic confrontation, or the basis for one, right around the corner. I have heard this among the military and among leftist intellectuals with connections to the Maya movement. The elites in power think less about this than I thought they would. I believe that it is historic irresponsibility to promote these fears, first, because not even the minimal conditions for this possibility exist, and second, because we have not even signed the peace treaty and we are already talking of another war. We cannot forget that those who feed this myth may provoke a slaughter over some totally subjective incident, just like what happened with the myth of the Jew and the holocaust. (*Crónica*, Aug. 16, 1996, 39, 40)

In effect, Casaús Arzú offers a reply to Morales that seeks to render problematic Ladino culture and Ladinos' vested interest, however inchoate, in the status quo ante of nation. She reminds her readers that fears are not raw, spontaneous emotion but rather are orchestrated and given narrative form by parties with specific political interests. The implementation of the accords will offer opportunities to rethink national culture and to mobilize around the politics of fear. Renewed interest in intercultural programs and dialogues throughout Guatemalan society is an attempt to bridge these gaps in a potentially volatile situation.

Do the recent lines of dialogue, collaboration, and self-examination between the Pan-Maya and *popular* movements mean there will be a new unified paradigm, a new synthesis of social movements? Will the early division of labor between collective cultural rights and education, on the one hand, and human rights abuses and agrarian issues, on the other, continue after the accords? The notion of a variety of social movements that pursue their own projects and coalitional opportunities is closer to some European, South Asian, and South African notions of social activism than to the unified paradigm approach that guided the Guatemalan *popular* movement through years of repression and the beginnings of a transition to a yet unfinished democracy.[18]

The issue of forging wider unities and identifications, how these would be labeled, and at whose expense they will be established has been very much on the minds of radical democracy theorists such as Chantal Mouffe, Ernesto Laclau, and David Trend, who see constructive possibilities in adversarial relations.[19] However, the definition of what is "progressive" in these movements is highly contested in Guatemala, given alternative framings of community and participation. Interestingly, there is still great intellectual nostalgia for the past in much of this political theorizing. As in the *popular* movement, it is marked by the dream of a radical and plural democracy as an enduring project of the Left rather than a novel set of struggles that are the legacies of many different histories.

At this point, the Pan-Maya movement maintains its own language for transcendence—one that would promote ethnic politics as the highest measure by seeking an institutionalized voice for Mayas and structural reforms in power relations. In practice, the impulse toward separatism has been moderated by alliances with other groups to transform state and society fundamentally: to change conventional social procedures, renegotiate the terms by which people live, and transform the cognitive structures that shape meanings and identities (see Trend 1996, 105, 110, 161). In their own ways these are thoroughly revolutionary changes, without, however, seeking to topple the state. The failure of several waves of guerrilla opposition in the past decades has convinced most Guatemalans—including Mayanists who witnessed many deaths in their own communities and lost friends who joined the guerrillas—that nonviolent paths to social change are the only feasible option.

I would agree with Michael Kearney's provocative analysis (1996, 181) that "post-peasant" politics takes on an ethnic as opposed to a class character for very specific reasons. In the Guatemalan instance, the boundaries of peasant-like communities have been torn by violence and a land base insufficient for the growing population since the early 1970s. Secondary education and special continuing education opportunities, which often called young adults away from their home communities, increased the internal differentiation of rural communities. Individuals have been recruited by organizations with strong national and international ties: development projects, religious groups, educational programs, and political groups. Increased geographical mobility means that young Guatemalans commonly work in a variety of nonagrarian occupations in towns and cities not only in Guatemala but also in the United States. Yet both societies are ambivalent about indigenous workers.

With its blend of tradition and novelty, Pan-Mayanism offers a language for common identification in the face of fragmentation and dislocation, designs for transcommunity affiliation, and nonmanual job opportunities.[20] The movement is especially attuned to the dilemmas facing post-peasants who have managed to *superarse*, to get ahead, as many agrarian parents wish for their children. In prizing Maya culture, the movement has given educated Mayas a continuing stake in the future of their home communities. With its emphasis on community councils, the movement seeks to include those for whom agrarian life remains central. Maya cosmology—its agrarian ontology, sacred cycles, social preoccupations, and syncretic aesthetics—has been selectively used by a variety of interests as a marker of the intimacy of community in the countryside and as a common moral language for transcommunity movements.[21] Thus, these ethnic "post-peasants" continue to reaffirm religious meaning and cultural distinctiveness through an idiom that reflects their Maya-agrarian roots.[22]

As the last two chapters have sought to demonstrate, Guatemala as a culturally heterogeneous society does not fit Bourdieu's European model of bourgeois society with its singular ladder of class, maintained through the accumulation of cultural capital, which in important ways is unself-consciously transferred across generations. Rather, in all its dilemmas and unfinished business, Guatemala resonates with images of a globalized, postindustrial world of multiple interacting sites of cultural capital, political urgency, and hybrid forms of stratification, mobility, and cultural distinctiveness.[23]

Crónica *semanal*

AÑO IX, NÚMERO 436 ● Guatemala, del 26 de julio al 1 de agosto de 1996 ● Q10.80, IVA incluido.

Un análisis del movimiento que busca reconstituir y refundir antiguos elementos culturales en una renovada identidad

RENACIMIENTO MAYA

SALA CARDOZA ❦ EL ARTE DE LOS CUERPOS PINTADOS ❦ EL FESTIVAL DE AVIÑON ❦ LOS AYCINENA ❦ LIBROS PROHIBIDOS DE GRANDES AUTORES ❦ ESPIONAJE BAJO EL MAR

Source: *Crónica* (July 26 to August 1, 1996)

Maya Rebirth in the Media

Maya resurgence and the controversies it generates have gained wide attention in the media and brought Maya intellectuals into the mainstream as newspaper columnists. In feature articles that contrast the views of Mayanists, their allies, and critics, the press has presented virtual debates on cultural rights, the authenticity of Maya culture, and the danger of ethnic tensions. The cover of *Crónica,* Guatemala's equivalent of *Newsweek,* beckoned readers in 1996 to detailed coverage of Pan-Mayanism with images of an ancient text overflowing with untranslated glyphs and cosmological figures, a classic-era jade mask, and a realist woman in miniature from an unrelated, very contemporary article on body painting.

Cholsamaj	ALMG	Second Maya Studies Congress
COMG		Saqb'ichil-COPMAGUA
Rutzijol/Saqb'e	COCADI	OKMA
CECMA	IXIMULEW	CNEM
CEDIM		
Rajpopi' Mayab'	CONIC	PLFM

MAYA ORGANIZATIONS

For their identifying logos, Maya activist forums use glyphs that represent prehispanic writers, calendrical day names, creation myths, and cosmological directions. This sampling includes *(from left to right, top to bottom)* the Maya publisher Cholsamaj, the Academy for Maya Languages of Guatemala (ALMG), the Second Maya Studies Congress, the Coordinator of Maya Organizations (COMG), the Coordination of Organizations of the Maya People of Guatemala (Saqb'ichil-COPMAGUA), the news publisher Rutzijol, the Kaqchikel Coordinator of Integral Development (COCADI), the Oxlajuuj Keej Maya' Ajtz'iib' (OKMA) linguistics group, the Center for Studies of Mayan Culture (CECMA), *Siglo Veintiuno*'s Maya-edited news supplement *Iximulew,* the National Council for Maya Education (CNEM), the Center of Mayan Documentation and Investigation (CEDIM), the Rajpopi' Mayab' aj Kaqche' center for Maya spirituality, the National Coordinator of Indigenous and Campesino Organizations (CONIC), and the Francisco Marroquín Linguistics Project (PLFM).

URL

CIRMA

Ministry of Education

FLACSO
GUATEMALA

European Community

REAL EMBAJADA DE NORUEGA
NORAD

Redd Barna

IWGIA

unicef
1946 – 1996
FONDO DE LAS NACIONES UNIDAS PARA LA INFANCIA

OAS

USAID

THEIR SUPPORTERS AND CRITICS

Important national supporters of Mayanist initiatives include the Rafael Landívar University (URL) Institute of Linguistics, the Center for Regional Investigations of Mesoamerica (CIRMA), the Ministry of Education, and the Latin American Faculty of Social Science (FLACSO) think tank. Pan-Mayanist publications routinely cite the logos of their international funders, which range from the European Community and northern European development funders such as NORAD, Redd Barna, and IWGIA-Denmark, to UNICEF, the Organization of American States (OAS), and the U.S. Agency for International Development (U.S.-AID). While an obsession with calendrics and cosmology is often imputed to Maya civilization, it is striking how often their supporters' logos incorporate historical markers and global imagery as well. Obdulio Son Chay and Pakal B'alam José Rodríguez (1994) offer a Mayanist analysis of glyphs and logos across cultures.

ARMY BASES AND CIVILIAN RECRUITMENT
While repressive military governments dominated public life in the 1960s and 1970s, clashes between the military and guerrillas escalated into full-scale warfare between 1978 and 1984. *Above,* army installations such as the "helmet-and-boots" base at Sololá deployed detachments to root out subversives and their civilian supporters and to monitor local populations.

Below, reservists practiced maneuvers. Forced military recruitment brought young rural Mayas into the army. During the worst of the war in 1981, the army organized civilians into poorly armed self-defense patrols to watch over their own communities and inform the army of suspicious activities.

CONTINUING SURVEILLANCE

Although the peace accords led to the demobilization of guerrilla groups and local civil patrols and the downsizing of the army by a third, military patrols continue to be a feature of everyday life in urban centers.

Source: Montejo (1992)

A CHILD'S VIEW OF MILITARY VIOLENCE
This eight-year-old boy remembered the violence of an army massacre in the Jacaltenango region of Huehuetenango from the relative safety of a refugee camp in Chiapas, Mexico, where his family sought refuge after the 1982 destruction of their community. Mayanists in exile have written ethnographic testimonies to the human costs of the war.

LOW-INTENSITY PEACE OF THE LATE 1980s AND EARLY 1990s

Announcements posted on the walls of municipal buildings in San Andrés called on civilians to participate in a polio vaccination campaign and to denounce the guerrillas, in this case members of the Guerrilla Army of the Poor (EGP), "who bring people sadness, hatred, and destruction."

Below, one of the subtle markers of fluctuating levels of repression was the availability of publications on political issues at book fairs such as this one in Antigua.

ORIGINAL PHOTO: Sonia Baur

SOURCE: Segundo Encuentro Continental (1991)

THE SECOND CONTINENTAL MEETING FOR INDIGENOUS, BLACK, AND POPULAR RESISTANCE
Delegates from the multifaceted *popular*-Left in the Americas met in war-torn Guatemala in 1991 to articulate a common agenda for post–Cold War organizing. The
conference slogan "Sing, Rise Up America, Voice of So Many Origins" decorated the
dais during the plenary sessions.

Below, publicity from the meeting pictured the Americas supported by a diversified
working class. Although the grassroots-Left critiqued racism and colonialism on the
eve of the Columbus quincentenary, Pan-Mayanists felt excluded by the focus on class
politics at the expense of cultural rights, ethnic organizing, and cross-class alliances.

PUBLIC INTELLECTUALS ACROSS POLITICAL DIVIDES
Maya Studies conferences in 1996 and 1997 served as forums to publicize the evolving agenda of the Maya movement, discuss research from Pan-Mayan and
popular-Left centers, and engage the movement's critics in public debate. Maya
public intellectuals, such as journalist Estuardo Zapeta, truth commission member
Otilia Lux de Cotí, anthropologist Margarita López Raquec, Quetzaltenango mayor
Rigoberto Quemé Chay, sociologist Amanda Pop, educator José Serech, and educator María Alicia Telón de Xulú *(pictured here top to bottom)* represent a variety
of organizations and positions on cultural and ethnic politics.

PAN-MAYA LEADERS
(Left to right, top to bottom) Among the many nationally prominent activists are publisher Raxche' Demetrio Rodríguez Guaján, movement theoretician Waqi' Q'anil Demetrio Cojtí Cuxil, journalist Miguel Angel Velasco Bitzol, anthropologist Victor Montejo, linguist Narciso Cojtí, lawyer Enrique Sam Colop, novelist Gaspar Pedro González, former vice-minister of education Manuel Salazar, and educator Ernestina Reyes de Ramos.

Non-Maya Supporters and Critics
(Left to right, top to bottom) Pan-Mayanism's high-profile Guatemalan supporters include public intellectuals such as historian Marta Elena Casaús Arzú, cultural patrimony commission member Frederico Fahsen, and university dean Guillermina Herrera Peña. Spanish anthropologist Santiago Bastos, literary critic Arturo Arias, and American anthropologist Richard Adams have questioned Pan-Mayanism's relation to other forms of indigenous activism. Journalist Mario Roberto Morales has denounced the Maya movement in a series of widely circulated editorial columns. Supporters and critics alike have been active in Mayanist conferences, in private meetings, and in print.

SOURCE: *New York Times*

CELEBRATING PEACE

On December 29, 1996, the final peace accords were signed by representatives of the government, army, guerrillas, and the United Nations, which played a key role in brokering the agreement. Crowds gathered and groups, such as the *popular*-Left Committee for Peasant Unity (CUC) which had been brutally repressed during the 1980s, joined the celebration.

Facing page, diverse groups decorated the capital's main square with their banners to applaud the formal end to war. Saqb'ichil-COPMAGUA brought Mayas together across the Pan-Maya and *popular*-Left divide to channel civilian input into the negotiations through the Assembly of Civil Society. Other group banners pictured here include the Movement for Women Weavers of History and the National Coordinator of Indians and Campesinos (CONIC), a *popular*-Left organization focusing on Maya land struggles.

SAQB'ICHIL COPMAGUA

Ies da la Bienvenida a los Pueblos Maya Garifuna Xinka en el compromiso de de construir el Estado Pluricultural plurilingüe

La Paz es tu oportunidad de dar felicidad

MUJERES Y HOMBRES ORGANICEMONOS PARA EL CUMPLIMIENTO DE LOS ACUERDOS DE PAZ

MOVIMIENTO DE MUJERES TEJEDORAS DE LA HISTORIA

VIVA·LOS·ACUERDOS·DE·PAZ VIVA·LA·LUCHA·MAYA·Y·CAMPESINA C·O·N·I·C

SOURCE: Susanne Jonas

With the signing of the peace accords, the United Nations mission in Guatemala (MINUGUA) among many other national groups sent volunteers, such as this German and Italian team in San Andrés, to review the Accord on the Identity and Rights of Indigenous People with community groups.

As part of the peace-accord implementation, local representatives of the country's marginalized language groups met in August 1997 to consider whether to seek the official recognition on a par with Spanish of all twenty Maya languages in the courts, schools, and electoral politics or, more realistically, to emphasize the four numerically dominant languages in affairs of state. The commission also discussed regional roles for Maya languages and the prospect of adopting a Maya *lingua franca,* such as K'ichee', in place of Spanish for transregional communication.

Breakthroughs in the reading of ancient Maya glyph texts—which build on comparative linguistics as well as on local knowledge—prompted Maya professionals, shaman associations, and community groups to invite American art historian Linda Schele to Guatemala for workshops and training sessions until her untimely death in 1998.

Composed of professional Maya linguists and an American collaborator, Oxlajuuj Keej Maya' Ajtz'iib' (OKMA) trains technical linguists, publishes widely on Maya linguistics, and produces a range of language and culture materials for adult education.

The new generation of linguists being trained by OKMA is likely to be employed in a variety of policy frontiers, given current moves to officially recognize Maya languages.

The Maya press Cholsamaj publishes school texts, literacy materials, resource books on revitalization, Maya-centric studies of identity politics and the state, and translations of repatriated foreign research on Maya culture.

MAYA LINGUISTICS AND PUBLISHING

San Andrés Ladino and Indian Families in the 1970s

Despite visual evidence of *mestizaje* in many families, ethnic hierarchy was fortified by a regional network of intermarrying Ladino families that owned major stores, large extensions of land planted in wheat and corn, and dairy herds in addition to their virtual monopoly on salaried teaching and office positions. Advanced schooling and better job opportunities drew the younger generation of these families to urban centers. When the civil war engulfed the town at the end of the decade, many Ladinos relocated to the capital and sold their lands.

Below, Indians, as they were then called, generally earned subsistence wages as day laborers on farms and road crews. Families cultivated their own small plots and engaged in businesses such as bread baking, brick making, and running corner shops. At that point, few indigenous leaders in the town had as much as three years of education, and there were no Maya teachers in the schools.

In 1971, an elder carved an airplane and took a group of cousins and friends, ready with their backpacks, on an imaginary trip to Guatemala City during which he told traditionalist morality tales of transforming selves, pacts with the devil, and the Lord of the Wilds.

Source: PLFM (1994)

Community elders and the national Maya movement alike worry that Maya children will ignore their ancestry and become half-Maya half-Ladino, as pictured in this Mayanist drawing of a young girl.

In the early 1990s, two brothers watched transformer cartoons, Florida-produced *Sábado Gigante,* Mexican cowboy movies, and reruns of *MacGyver* on TV at home.

San Andrés Children at Play in the 1970s and 1990s

WORKPLACES AND MARKETS
In San Andrés, Mayas have long cultivated corn and beans for their own consumption and worked as day laborers on regional plantations. Cash crops have shifted from wheat for highland bakeries to broccoli, cauliflower, and snow peas for international frozen-food markets. Some women still weave, although to be viable their household production must adjust to the ever-changing aesthetic preferences of a global market. Here women assemble hand-woven fabrics for a small German NGO whose European sales generate employment for the women and help support an infant nutrition program and Maya school.

Literate Mayas now regionally compete with Ladinos for positions as retail clerks, office workers, teachers, and extension agents in branch offices of development organizations. Municipal development money generated local employment to pave streets and build the town's first modern open-air market in the late 1980s. Workers in the building trades commute to construction jobs in the nearby tourist center of Panajachel and add luxuries such as electricity and modern plumbing to rural homes for the Maya middle class.

In the old days, public life in San Andrés was organized by the indigenous civil-religious hierarchy, which hosted processions by the saint societies and administered local affairs as long as they did not impinge on Ladino concerns. By the mid 1970s, it appeared that Catholic Action and evangelical groups had successfully torn down traditionalist authority and marginalized shamanic practices.

More recently, the Maya movement has sought to enhance the stature of community elders, promote Maya spirituality, and organize shamans.

THE COLLAPSE OF TRADITIONALIST RELIGION IN THE 1970s AND ITS REBIRTH AS MAYA SPIRITUALITY IN THE 1980s

LOCAL REVITALIZATION EFFORTS

The terror of being caught between the army and guerrillas during the war actually spurred a resurgence of traditionalist beliefs in transforming selves. At the close of the 1980s, Catholic Action briefly experimented with cultural events, such as these reenactments of traditionalist rituals by community youths for audiences entranced by the performances. The goal of youth programming was to arrest the loss of ethnic identification and compete with rapidly growing evangelical congregations for the next generation of believers.

President Ramiro de León Carpio, conference organizer Germán Churuchiche Otzoy, minister of education Alfredo Tay Coyoy, Nobel prize winner Rigoberta Menchú, and other dignitaries marked the political importance of education reform at the plenary session of the congress.

Maya teachers, school administrators, NGO educators, and development professionals exchanged experiences and tactics in a variety of school environments during three days of conference workshops. The Maya movement has reevaluated bilingual education programs in the public schools, critiqued racist stereotypes in school texts, run training sessions for teachers to disseminate new techniques and materials, and supported the local development of independent Maya schools.

Maya priests ritually blessed the work of the congress yet found themselves marginalized when they tried to offer their views of Maya education alongside the experts.

THE FIRST MAYA EDUCATION CONGRESS IN 1994

Maya Schools in Rural Communities

Faced with a slow-to-change educational bureaucracy, resistive teachers unions, and high dropout rates, Pan-Mayanists have begun to create private Maya schools that teach in regional languages and Spanish. Kikotem in San Andrés offers preschool, kindergarten, first through third grades, and an evening program for adults who want to complete high school.

Below, children visit the mayor's office during a field trip and hear from the acting mayor about his duties. The school stresses experiential learning and respect for Maya cultural norms.

TRANSCULTURAL DIALOGUES

Though much of the fieldwork for this book focused on urban-based organizations, research also drew me back to the Kaqchikel community of San Andrés for interviews across the generations, to the rare books collection at the University of Pennsylvania to see the handwritten seventeenth-century *Annals of the Kaqchikels* with visitors Marta Elena Casaús Arzú and Demetrio Cojtí, and on to the Princeton anthropology department, where I invited Martín Chacach to lecture on the Maya school texts produced by his research group through the Rafael Landívar University.

Three

In Dialogue: Maya Skeptics and One Anthropologist

ON RETURNING TO GUATEMALA in 1989, I soon realized that the politics of anthropological research had dramatically changed and foreign researchers were accountable to Maya critics in ways we had not been before. Knowing it was extremely important for North American scholars to present their research to Maya audiences, I eagerly if somewhat anxiously accepted invitations to lecture to Maya anthropologists and linguists in two different settings. My topic was a tactical compromise: the issue central to understanding social change at that point was the counterinsurgency war, a topic too dangerous for open forums. Rather, I decided to present a critique of North American scholarship on Maya ethnicity and to discuss comparative findings from my ethnographic research with Susan Bourque on indigenous communities in Peru.[1]

The lecture, given in Spanish, was entitled "Indian Identity in Guatemala and Peru: A Critique of the Concept of Ladinoization." I suspected Maya scholars would welcome my critique of *ladinización*—a linear model of cultural assimilation that suggests economic mobility will inevitably lead Mayas to become the ethnic other by "passing" as Ladinos outside their home communities. The possibility of an ethnic system where passing was common and situational had always drawn the fascination of North American scholars, perhaps because our biologized ideology of difference pretends that racial identity remains stable and dichotomous rather than mutable and heterogeneous. For their part, Pan-Maya scholars repudiate as academic ethnocide the concept of Ladinoization, which they associate with the early work of Richard Adams and with Guatemalan Ladino scholars promoting historical-materialist perspectives.[2] At the talk, I hoped my critique of North American literature and description of an alternative nonlinear model of change, which underscored grassroots agency, would establish common ground for continuing discussion.

I began the lecture with a critical reading of North American anthropology, unavailable to most Mayas because it is published in English.[3] Here I considered my role to be translator and critic, interested in revealing the political ironies of alternative formulations. The "four fallacies of Indianness," as I termed the review, will strike a familiar cord for scholars working elsewhere, given these are theory-driven models of ethnicity. To ground this

abstract discussion empirically, the second part of the talk involved an examination of conflicting local and state definitions of identity in Peru. The Peruvian case study illustrated individual and community activism in the face of
domination by presenting instances of local resistance to national reforms
that threatened rural development strategies and changing forms of self-identification. I hoped the Peruvian contrast would allow issues to surface without politically charging the discussion and leave room for audiences to offer
their own observations and analyses.

I received strikingly different responses from the two Maya audiences of
scholar-activists. Their dissimilar idioms of skepticism reflect important di-
versities that have emerged within the Pan-Maya movement. The responses
flow from a long history of Maya-foreign dialogues, which have generated
critiques of the ethics and politics of Western research. The goal of this
chapter is to show how ethnicity is problematic for both North American and
Mayanist anthropologies, how Maya intellectuals are forcing ethical and political self-consciousness on the part of foreign researchers, and how our
research projects inevitably stand in creative tension with each other.[4] Let me
begin with a synopsis of the lecture.

The Four Fallacies of "Indianness"

*The first common fallacy in North American formulations of Mesoamerican
ethnicity involves the assertion that "Indianness" is the product of a singular historical period.* Variants of this argument highlight different moments
of ethnogenesis. One essentializing line of reasoning holds that Indianness is
the pre-Hispanic cultural core that persists in contemporary practices such as
shamanic divining and the authority of Maya elders.[5] A contrasting formulation asserts Indianness is the product of sixteenth-century ethnic divisions of
labor. The template for the colonial master/indigenous laborer relationship
was created when indigenous populations were forcefully resettled into *reducción* settlements for missionization and the organization of saint societies. Through the forced-labor policies of the *encomienda* and *repartimiento*, Spanish colonizers commanded laborers for their plantations and
public works from Maya settlements at little or no pay.[6] Still another version
of ethnogenesis singles out the nineteenth century, when commercial expansion for international markets and liberal nationalist ideology justified new
forced labor policies, endangered Maya communal landholdings, and promoted export-oriented commercial production at the expense of small-scale
plantation agriculture. These dislocations created a class of impoverished
landless Mayas, dependent for economic survival on cash earnings from uncertain seasonal migration as agricultural laborers.[7]

Although each of these frameworks makes its contribution, the problem
with ethnogenesis models—with singular moments of origin—is their focus

on isolating particular determinants of ethnicity and their failure to see identity formation as a continuing process.

A second common fallacy argues that change in culturally plural systems inevitably means "culture loss."[8] The assumption is that cultural distinctiveness is culture, and national society is somehow the opposite of "the cultural." This reasoning parallels the common Western view that Third World societies are distinctively cultural, while the West has moved beyond these particularities through its economic and scientific rationality. Unfortunately, the categorical distinction cultural versus rational often obscures the global interplay of politics and cultures and mutes the contested and ideological aspects of dominant cultures—whether "national culture" in Guatemala or "Western culture" in and outside the Third World.

Another version of this fallacy holds that ethnicity means a hegemonic worldview—some sort of traditionalism—or nothing.[9] In this case, an individual's choice is either to embrace or reject a given construction of ethnicity. This is the perspective of much research on Mesoamerica. It renders Catholic or Evangelical Mayas, for instance, as unauthentic Mayas and suggests that the real choice for Mayas is between community-focused traditionalism or becoming Ladinos. Yet, the construction of polar, mutually exclusive choices—Indian or Ladino—ignores overwhelming evidence that individuals and communities continually rework identities, and traditionalist constructions of *costumbre* have promoted diversity rather than uniformity among Mayas.[10]

A third fallacy holds that ethnicity will wither away with the emergence of individualism and the transformation of agrarian class relations that accompany capitalist development. Modernization theorists phrase the argument in terms of growing freedom for entrepreneurship and democratic participation with the decline of collective traditionalism.[11] The withering of ethnicity is also a neo-Marxist prediction for those who see ethnicity as a barrier to the class-based politicization of newly proletarianized populations, or for those who view culture as derivative of economic relations. The modern market economy, in its homogenizing quest for consumers as well as wage laborers, is portrayed as inevitably undermining ethnic identities.[12] This is seen as a necessary if painful process, revealing underlying class conflicts that demand structural change. In this case, cultural distinctiveness is dismissed as an impediment, the product of colonial domination, which perpetuates false consciousness of the systemic character of oppression for agrarian underclasses.[13]

Finally, a fourth fallacy holds that the substance of ethnic identity is derived from defensive and oppositional reactions to the dominant culture. In its extreme form, the culturalist reply to economic determinism becomes another top-down formulation in which dominant Ladino culture is portrayed as creating the frame of reference to which Mayas can only react by defining themselves as the devalued opposite.[14] Thus, Mayas value work in the fields,

in contrast to those who despise manual labor. Mayas are pictured as isolated, in contrast to the ethnic other who seeks wider influence through personal contacts; they seek prestige through community service, in contrast to
Ladinos who do so through material accumulation.[15]

In this paradigm, Mayas react as prisoners of a grammar of ethnic dichotomies. The dominant group's ethnicity and ideology is portrayed as uncontested, unproblematic, and self-authored. The only direction for change is
conformity as individuals pass as Ladinos, leaving undisturbed the structural
hierarchy of the two groups.

One can see why Pan-Mayanist scholars such as Demetrio Cojtí Cuxil,
Irma Otzoy, Enrique Sam Colop, and Victor Montejo associate foreign research with the inevitability of Ladinoization, a theme repeated across very
different theoretical positions (see Otzoy 1988). After critiquing these
models of ethnicity, I suggested that new research might work to refine an
alternative constructionist formulation of identity. Such a perspective would
make a dynamic notion of culture central to the study of ethnic politics and
change.

The Constructionist Alternative

The case I made was for an interactive view of identity as a collage of
conflicting meanings, simultaneously advanced by different actors in social
systems. In this process-oriented formulation, ethnicity becomes the practice,
representation, negotiation, resistance, and appropriation of identity for all
parties.[16] Due to powerful economic, cultural, and political constraints on
individual and collective action, identity formation is not a free market of
personal options for self-definition. Rather, a whole host of groups are in the
identity production business, perpetuating invidious stereotypes in the media,
social policy, and national culture. The issue is how differences are politically constructed, opposed, and manipulated and how tensions simultaneously play out between the experience and representation of ethnicity for
individuals, communities, national society, state authorities, and trans-state
groups.

Analysts can make the terms of domination and subordination problematic
by showing how power is exercised and subverted in different situations.[17]
Moreover, nation-states and emerging regional associations have become issues of anthropological study, not as monolithic abstractions but as systems
of cultural production with their own conflicting ideologies and agendas.[18] In
short, this approach advocates the study of cultural process: the intimate
"how" rather than merely the anonymous "why" of change which has preoccupied modernization theorists and historical materialists.

The constructionist approach notes that the Guatemalan categories *indio, indígena*, *natural*, or *maya* may be contrasted with *ladino*. But over recent history, the meanings of "self" and "other" in this scheme has been tremendously variable. From this viewpoint, there is no Maya or Ladino except as identities are constructed, contested, negotiated, imposed, imputed, resisted, and redefined in action.[19] Other identities are always salient: for instance, in rural San Andrés there is a constant interplay of ethnicity, generation, birth order, gender, religion, education, land ownership, and family history. The process of identity formation is never-ending because identity never quite coalesces. Even the Maya-Ladino contrast is challenged by the diversification of contemporary Maya identities arising from pan-Maya ethnic nationalism, the diaspora of political and economic refugees, and the waves of successful evangelizers across ethnic divides.[20]

Constructionist views do not inevitably ignore the importance of economic and political transformations, as historical materialists have long complained. For their part, constructionists object to overly generalized models used to project the impact of changing political economies on local cultures. By contrast, it makes more sense to suggest that a different periodicity may prevail for the history of Maya communities, a different shape to ethnic time, rather than to assume their historical experience is entirely determined by international economic transformations accompanying the expansion of foreign investment and commercial agriculture for world markets. We can only know this, of course, by understanding Maya constructions of time and history (see chapters five, six, and eight). Although interested in resurgence and intensification, this view argues against any exclusive moment of ethnogenesis, stressing culture as continually reworked understandings of the world. In this sense, culture is not simply "lost" but transformed, displaced, resynthesized.

Thus, ethnicity and cultural difference are not assumed to give way to class or individualism in a linear narrative of progress toward a utopian future, as in liberal democratic or socialist visions. First of all, notions of "class" and "individual" have been culturally constructed in a variety of ways by Maya communities. Moreover, "ethnicity" appears to be very much a product of the modern world; it is not just a temporary holdover from the traditional past, as is evident in Canada, Iraq, Israel, Northern Ireland, South Africa, Sri Lanka, Yugoslavia, and Rwanda. If anything, it has become clear that nationalism and ethnicity are explosive political combinations, which, though their mix is incredibly various, often appear to influence each others' constructions. Studies of nationalism and ethnicity pose challenges to contemporary social science precisely because both are modern struggles with identity and otherness.[21]

Finally, the constructionist view argues against theories of meaning that focus on distilling a unified master worldview, identifying core symbols with definitive meanings, interpreting texts divorced from their use and contexts, or assuming meanings are always packaged in structuralist contrasts. As has been argued for Native American identities, narratives of cultural struggle carry many potential messages and, thus, their significance can alter dramatically as a counterpoint to the experience and lessons drawn from changing circumstances.[22] It is in the dilemmas and struggles of particular communities that we understand the significance of narratives of ethnicity. Ethnicity, like race, is continually reinvented and reimposed.[23]

Maya Studies Replies

The lectures in which I presented this overview were given at the Maya Studies Permanent Seminar (SPEM) and the Center for Regional Investigations of Mesoamerica (CIRMA). The Maya responses were very different: participants at the Maya Studies seminar enthusiastically challenged North American anthropology; at the CIRMA lecture, the Mayas (in contrast to others) were virtually silent at the public event, though, of course, not afterward. The Maya Studies seminar was attended by university-trained students and professionals, conversant in academic give-and-take. Their response was a complex counterpoint to my presentation: while I described constructionist transformations of ethnicity, they wanted to talk about anthropology as colonialism. This led to lively discussions of the politics of anthropological analysis. Clearly Mayas were in control of this medium and its conventions and were certainly in command of defining the visitor. They effectively subdued my constructionist approach with their own categorical political critique of foreigners as neocolonial academics.

One of the most interesting parts of the seminar was the closing remark by Professor Demetrio Cojtí Cuxil, the dean of Maya public intellectuals, then teaching at San Carlos University in addition to holding his continuing position at UNICEF. He argued forcefully that the appropriate role for North American anthropologists should be one of helping to identify continuities in Maya culture, the timeless characteristics that make Mayas Maya. This prescription stood in stark contrast to what I had just concluded in my review of North American formulations of ethnicity and descriptions of Peruvian communities: that being Quechua in Peru or Maya in Guatemala reflected whatever the populations were doing; that there was no essential Quechua or Maya; no constant core, but rather, in the face of discrimination, a complex, ever-changing self-authorship, which sometimes reweaves and sometimes rejects the past.

I made my empirical case by analyzing Quechua culture on the western slopes of the Andes in Peru. Local populations there have extended ancient social networks linking families across Andean ecological zones to newer migration routes leading to coastal cities. Urban Peruvian life is associated with non-Indian nationals, with *mestizos*[24] who look to national society for their cultural identity. The conundrum for Andean populations is how to participate in national *and* rural arenas.

In practice, urban migrants have used their social networks to maintain footholds in traditionalist communities where agriculture and animal husbandry predominate, along with Quechua religion and collective commitments to land and work. Depending on economic and family situations, participants in rural-urban networks position themselves to exchange resources: agricultural surpluses, access to cash earnings, higher education, housing, job opportunities, day care, and moral support.[25]

Have Quechua populations *lost* their ethnicity with migration and urban involvements? No. In this case it would be more appropriate to argue they have found a new idiom to express their sense of self: regionality. These populations call themselves "*serranos*" (people of the sierra), in contrast to their coastal kin, or "*costeños*" (people of the urban coast). Here they have attempted to evade the ethnic grammar of being *indios* (as indigenous Peruvians are called), *mestizos*, or *cholos* (a depreciating term for people in between).[26]

Identity transformation has been integral to the formation of rural-urban networks and populist development strategies. As a consequence, urbanites consider fresh migrants from the same locale and cultural background as kin. Women and men have internalized these understandings, moving among junctures on their networks depending on job openings and moral obligations. Their parents and grandparents may find themselves ill-at-ease on the urban coast, overwhelmed by the alien environment and grateful when they are designated as valuable rural outposts. In the capital, community heritage is often converted into common regional heritage. New allegiances allow strangers, who find themselves in the same squatter settlement, to remember common Andean origins as they become neighbors, swap urban survival skills, and share political concerns.

I ended the lecture at this point by observing how different Guatemala is, where similar paths of migration have been accompanied by very different experiences of identity formation.

I was thrilled by the long and animated discussions at the Maya Studies seminar—no doubt by my apparent survival in a forum of politicized Maya intellectuals, including much of the national leadership—and energized by the intensity of the audience.

Though the second presentation was more polished and included more information on Maya culture from my 1970s research in San Andrés, the response to it was further complicated by the setting and format. The audience at CIRMA was overwhelmingly foreign, full of visiting anthropologists, linguists, geographers, and language students. The Mayas were teachers in the summer Kaqchikel language and culture program, organized by Judith

Maxwell and McKenna Brown for North American students; some were working with linguist Nora England on research projects. I worried as the Mayas remained quiet during the busy question-and-discussion period; I knew they would have their own thoughts. Finally, with white-hot intensity, the young linguist Ruperto Montejo blurted: "What are you doing here in Guatemala? What benefit does your research have for the Mayas of San Andrés?" Although I then responded to these issues in detail—explaining my history of local support in San Andrés—I knew the Mayas had been inhibited and frustrated by the lecture format on someone else's turf. Furthermore, there were no Maya professionals, such as Demetrio Cojtí Cuxil, to empower younger students, who, in the case of these applied linguists, had little exposure to university lectures and seminars.

Later that night I talked to a friend among the Mayas, who said the lecture had indeed provoked much private discussion. Basically the Mayas were saying: "Even though her politics sound fine, how can we know who this anthropologist is? How can we know she is who she presents herself to be?" I was devastated, hurt, and angry, since I had spent a good deal of time with several of the young linguists as they worked on other projects during the previous five months.

That night I got quite drunk as I wrote my field notes. I felt I had been absorbed by a variant of the transforming-selves notion of personhood in Maya culture—which holds that the self is not stable or fully knowable. It appeared that I had been apprehended in a way that offered little chance for escape. How could I prove I was just myself, that there was nothing menacing to unmask?[27] Somehow this construction—though one that Mayas extend to each other in their home communities (for details, see chapters four and eight)—was much more difficult for me to shake off than being categorized as a North American academic colonizer at the earlier seminar.[28]

I talked to my applied-linguist contact again the next day and asked if there was anything to do about the suspicions. I suggested we meet again, just the group of Mayas and myself, to discuss the lecture and any related issues. These informal meetings were very useful. I found that the applied linguists wanted basic definitions of "identity" and other anthropological concepts. They also wanted to know more about doing research and how they might go about accomplishing community studies for their own concerns. Finally, they wanted to know about resources, specifically, how one might get small amounts of money to pay for travel, housing, tapes, and tape recorders to do more work in their communities. We also talked about research dissemination, a problem I also faced with my work in San Andrés. Could one set up tape libraries? How would people use these tapes? What anthropological training would be useful for researchers? What research projects would Mayas pursue?

Clearly, there were important intra-ethnic differences in education, in-

come, and rural versus urban residence between these two research networks. In effect, they epitomize different facets of the movement. That the
applied linguists at CIRMA were especially interested in taping oral narratives of an older generation—which was dying without passing on its
knowledge of *costumbre*—reflects how rooted their identities were in specific places and communities. These youths represent those Pan-Mayanists
who work in local development organizations, rural schools, or in positions
as intermediaries between local communities and national organizations.
Some planned to pursue university educations after completing high school;
others anticipated work with a variety of rurally anchored organizations.
They saw Maya university students and professionals, who are much more
likely to work in urban settings, as gaining greater support and recognition
for research projects. For their part, Pan-Mayanist professionals, academics,
and university students who attend Maya Studies Permanent Seminars and
publish in the seminar's series are seeking to build a more abstract and
translocal ethnicity, one not as intimately tied to place, community history,
and particular families.[29] In practice these networks are not exclusive bodies;
rather, members of both networks commingle and collaborate at frequent
conferences, workshops, and celebrations. Events such as the Maya Workshop, an annual conference that focuses on language and cultural issues, are
purposefully hosted in different rural locales to crosscut such divisions and
widen local access.

Notably, both audiences had similar messages for their invited visitor. Foreign anthropologists, no matter how supportive of Maya rights, have returned relatively little of their research to the communities studied. This is
one aspect of colonialism that Pan-Mayanists criticize in North American
academics. Why do foreign anthropologists study us? What do they do with
their findings?[30] Repatriating research is particularly important because the
traditionalist archive, the specialized knower or *k'amöl b'ey*, has disappeared
in many communities, and *costumbre* is being revitalized by various groups
with their own political agendas (see chapters seven and eight).[31] Yet here
again, a revealing contrast appears in the different groups' definition of the
"community" to which research and resources should be returned. For these
applied linguists, the issue was as local and personal as it was translocal. By
contrast, community for university-trained public intellectuals is not the old
municipio (the county with its commercial center and outlying hamlets) but
the nationwide commitment to the Mayaness they are striving to build. As
will become clear in later chapters, however, the intimacy of localized identity remains personally compelling for many national leaders.

One irony that stood out after these lectures was that North American
anthropology is exploring constructionist perspectives on ethnicity at the
very moment Mayas were articulating a nationalist essentialism. Demetrio
Cojtí Cuxil wanted me to do what I could not: be a cultural archaeologist or

ethnohistorian who finds continuities and, whatever their current significance, argues that they are the Maya culture core. How odd, I thought at the
time, that one would trust a North American's judgment. On this issue, the
ethnic projects of Maya and North American anthropologies seemed difficult
to reconcile.

On further reflection, however, I believe I initially failed to appreciate the
complexity of Maya motivations for their essentialist arguments. For
Mayas—who are in actuality creating all sorts of novel ethnicities and levels
of identity, and are highly aware of their choices in this construction—essentialism is a powerful rejection of the Ladino definition of Mayas as the
negative or weaker other. Thus, Maya scholars are challenging my fourth
fallacy with an essentialist alternative to seeing ethnicity as a self-denigrat-
ing reaction to domination. Maya languages, calendrics, shaman-priests, and
conceptions of moral authority antedate the Spanish conquest; they are examples of Maya cultural genius that were not effaced with Spanish and
Ladino domination or the passage of time. Maya scholars contend they must
be revalued and revitalized before the past slips beyond the grasp of
memory.

It would be a great mistake, however, to see this essentialism as the ultimate resolution to the problem of asserting the viability of Maya identity.[32] It
certainly is not the solution for Pan-Mayanists who, as emerging intellectual
elites, are actively fighting discrimination in education, employment, politics, and social life. Other dimensions of Maya identity and roles for foreign
anthropologists have been articulated at recent conferences in the United
States and Latin America.[33] Increasingly, Mayas are calling on foreign anthropologists and historians to document Maya resistance to racism and
domination. Like essentialism, resistance highlights a sense of identity independent of the dominant culture's definitions. In this instance, Mayas want to
document a heroic rather than complicit sense of their relation to the racism
that attempts to subdue them.

Resistance is another way to deny that change represents a linear erosion
of distinctiveness through assimilation. Maya resistance challenges narratives on both the Right and Left that speak of the definitive "conquest" of
indigenous populations in 1524, or the "reconquest" of Maya populations
during the genocidal violence of 1978–85. On the one hand—like descendants of other populations in the Americas who were displaced, involuntarily
brought over as slaves, or marginalized in the colonial process—Pan-Mayanists challenged plans for the national 1992 commemoration of the five hun-
dredth anniversary of the "discovery" of the New World. Many were astounded as huge crosses were erected by Catholic churches along major
highways to celebrate five hundred years of evangelization. Mayas wondered
what there was to celebrate: certainly not their own conquest, population
collapse through smallpox and influenza epidemics, forced resettlement and

conversions by colonial authorities, and brutal exploitation as forced laborers for the colonial economy.

On the other hand, Mayanists urge attention be paid to the human-rights abuses that accompanied the militarization of the Guatemalan countryside in the late seventies and forced displaced populations to face continual persecution, flee the country, or resettle in military-controlled "development poles." They do not, however, want this national violence portrayed as a definitive "reconquest" of the Mayas.[34] In their critiques of the language of conquest and reconquest, Pan-Mayanists contest disempowering narratives that obliterate Maya culture and resistance to domination. Perhaps, they argued in the early days of the movement, there is a possible convergence of Maya and North American anthropologies with the goal of documenting resistance as well as essentialist continuities.

The Ethics and Politics of Foreign Fieldwork

What is to be learned—for all parties—from discussions of the ethical ambiguities, paradoxes, and clashes of doing social research across cultures in Guatemala? One must begin by acknowledging that the current issues, pressures, and debates were not initiated by American anthropologists and linguists; rather, a self-directed network of Maya linguists, anthropologists, and students has extended and transformed the academic Left's earlier anti-imperialist critiques of foreign scholarship.[35] Pan-Mayanists see social science as profoundly political by definition and consequently doubt the motives and intentions of foreign researchers who act as if their verbal support for indigenous issues should be accepted at face value.

Along with the many other issues on its agenda, the Maya Workshop has been an important forum for evaluating foreign scholarship in Guatemala. Its meetings were first organized in the late seventies by North American linguists who modeled the presentations after academic conferences in the United States and gave most of the technical papers themselves, with their Maya research assistants in the audience. Through the years, Maya linguists and students, many of whom where trained at the Francisco Marroquín Linguistics Project (PLFM), became increasingly active on the panels. After a minirevolt in the late seventies, Maya linguists gained a voice in the organization of the meetings, the designation of panel topics, and the presentation of research papers (cf. England and Elliot 1990). Since then the balance of foreigners and Mayas has varied with another challenge to the power structure in 1989. Over the years, Pan-Mayanists—including professionals, students, and lay people—have come to share their research and cultural concerns through these meetings. Panels range from highly technical linguistics to debates about Maya cultural politics. A mix of science and politics is common, although the mix has, from time to time, become highly contested.

In June 1989, one of the panels dealt with the role of foreign linguists in the study of Maya languages. The foreigners were peppered with hostile responses from Maya members of the audience, and a decision was made to solicit anonymous written "questions for foreign linguists" (see appendix one for the compilation). The template for interrogating the politics of all foreign researchers had been formalized. (Although I was unaware of it at the time, my CIRMA lecture, in fact, occurred shortly after this workshop.) Underlying the "questions for foreign linguists" were serious doubts about interests, motivations, and intentions of foreign researchers; reservations about the benefits of research; and pointed observations about the continuing political asymmetry of research practices. This challenge to the status quo of research practices was mounted to shift the balance of power in what were still perceived as foreign-dominated meetings. The questions were infused with Maya political analyses and understandings of foreign researchers as "the other," coupled with the sense that some of these critiques were relevant for indigenous organizations as well.

Implicit in the language of veiled allegations is a backdrop of Maya preoccupations with built-in limits to the possibility of knowing other selves and their intentions, the capacity of certain persons to transform themselves (or be transformed), the consequent problems of deception and betrayal, and the unmasking of people who are not what they seem to be. These ancient themes and very current preoccupations, given the violence and political instability of the country over the last decades, will be explored throughout this book. Are foreign linguists and other researchers what they seem to be? Or are they something else? This signature engagement of the world saturates Maya critiques of foreign researchers, skepticism of their own social relations, and a savvy postmodernist politics.

What Mayas see so clearly is that linguistics and anthropology are not neutral sciences or nonpolitical ways of knowing. Rather they are practices that raise political questions for all involved—for the foreign researchers and Mayas involved in intercultural organizations alike. Hidden sources of control are central. Is research being done as an *explicit* strategy to foster the control of Maya populations by others—by the interests of internal and external colonialism, other governments, or proselytizing religions? This questioning aims at the unmasking of the *implicit* politics in research. Clearly if researchers are aware and responsive—something that would appear to be the case from their stated desires to be involved in "dialogues," "service," and "help" for Maya interests—then there is a terrible inconsistency between sentiments and actions, specifically the failure to publish in Spanish or return something to the language communities foreign researchers have studied. Finally, inscribed in these questions are traces of a contemporary Maya notion of alternative politics. The dream is that foreign researchers would give up some of their autonomy, working on an equal footing with Maya research groups, and that their research proposals would be subject (in some yet to be specified way) to regulation by Maya linguists.

Pan-Mayanists note the diverse politics of foreign researchers, with linguists as a revealing example. At one end of the spectrum lies the Summer Institute of Linguistics (SIL), also known as the Wycliffe Bible Translators, a global force in foreign applied linguistics. The SIL studies Maya languages and culture with the goal of translating the Bible in order to foster the conversion of Mayas to evangelical Protestantism. Theirs is not disinterested science but rather, according to this critique, part of a power structure bent on alienating Mayas from their own communities, religions, and forms of authority. The struggle for a unified alphabet for the twenty-one Maya languages by the Academy for Maya Languages of Guatemala (ALMG) is one manifestation of the clash between Pan-Mayanists, who have formulated a standardized national system of transcription, and the SIL, which favors unique community-focused alphabets developed for Bible translation and religious education projects.

Pan-Mayanists locate foreign linguists who believe there is no reason to justify their scientific research interests to local populations at the other end of the spectrum. Theirs is purely academic, theory-driven research concerned with the structure of human languages not the lives of their speakers. Naturally, many linguists fall between these poles and see themselves as obligated to take the emerging Maya critiques seriously, to reexamine the politics implicit in their own practices.

The 1989 Maya Workshop questions are highly relevant for cultural anthropologists. Like linguists, anthropologists are a fragmented collection of researchers with diverse backgrounds, political commitments, and religious beliefs. We are part-time field workers, career-driven professionals, teachers of a range of courses, human-rights advocates, activists on our own fronts, and so on. There is no SIL that I know of for anthropology. Many North American social scientists working in Mesoamerica pride themselves on being interested rather than disinterested researchers. Yet this is not universally true. Some, though this is rarer in Guatemala, see themselves as doing scientific work that calls for noninvolvement in order to avoid influencing the situation they are studying—something this book argues is impossible given the intertwined histories of the countries and the global flows of culture and economics that touch even the most remote communities.

Generally, anthropologists pursue more sustained periods of fieldwork in local communities than linguists, who typically, though not always, work with informants for shorter periods, use surveys collected by others, or bring native speakers to urban research centers. Because of the nature of field work, cultural anthropologists owe more to local communities. For many anthropologists, the Maya Workshop questions raise questions about our long-overdue debts to those we study.

In an article published in a widely read U.S. academic newsletter, Luis Enrique Sam Colop (1990)—a Maya leader who at the time was completing his dissertation for a doctorate in linguistics at SUNY-Buffalo—singled out aspects of the Maya Workshop he felt have special relevance for anthropologists. For Sam Colop, evidence abounds that foreign anthropologists evade their accountability to the people they study. He identifies the following ethical failures:

(1) Foreign scholars who do not consult with the community where they are going to work about their projects and who rarely present a final report of the study to the community.

(2) The existence of a large body of knowledge about the sociocultural history of Maya communities gathered and compiled by foreigners that is not available to them, leaving local communities ignorant of what foreign scholars have said about their language, culture, or community.

(3) Some foreigners who hide religious or proselytizing agendas behind their academic status and who interfere in Maya decision making and others who by not opposing these actions seem to approve them.

(4) Foreign researchers who seem only concerned with fulfilling their university or institutional requirements or with gathering data for publication and who take the service of the community for granted. (Sam Colop 1990)

Because "foreign" means non-Maya, these issues should be important for Ladinos as well as for scholars from outside the country. In Sam Colop's accounting and the Maya Workshop's questions, we see the reasoning behind the cryptic question *What are you doing in Guatemala to benefit the Maya people?* The political asymmetry of fieldwork is clear: researchers assume local cooperation and assistance with their work but they do not see themselves in a wider net of obligations as a result.

The Maya Workshop discussion was concerned with reciprocity and the empowerment of local communities so that they can pass on external research plans, see the results, and benefit in concrete ways from their cooperation with external researchers. Sam Colop shared the apprehension that researchers who misrepresent their religious motivations for work in support of evangelization have the potential to disrupt emergent Maya unity.

Foreign anthropologists will need to find ways of responding to scholar-activists skeptical of the intentions and practice of their discipline. One way is to build Maya skepticism and the field worker's dialogical (rather than omniscient) ways of knowing into anthropological representations of Maya culture. Another way is to share early drafts of ongoing projects with Maya researchers as colleagues (something I have learned to do as part of my research methodology).

Maya scholars do not want to be portrayed as informants who produce the raw material for more abstract Western analysis but as theorizers and producers of questioning critiques that build on their own experience and on earlier critiques of anthropology's neocolonialism (see Raxche' 1989; Stavenhagen 1971). As colleagues, they can be heard in their own right as lecturers invited to our universities, as is increasingly the practice at some schools. Access to advanced professional training for international scholars can be widened, as has been accomplished by anthropologists and linguists at the University of California at Davis, the University of Iowa, SUNY-Buffalo, the University of Texas, SUNY-Albany, and the University of Connecticut among others.

Maya and North American scholars have worked collaboratively at research centers, on scholarly panels at major conferences, and in networks producing edited volumes (cf. England and Elliot 1990, Brown and Fischer 1996, Universidad Rafael Landívar, Instituto de Lingüística 1997). It is likely, however, that anthropologists who respond to these ethical challenges will find themselves caught in dilemmas created by the politics of the Maya project. For example, negotiating tensions between local revitalization and Pan-Mayanism may prove complicated for field workers with long histories of local involvement. For linguists, the counterpart dilemma is the call for research that demonstrates the unity of Maya languages and casts doubts on the motives of researchers who would see substantial differences between dialects. In effect, dialect divergence is understood by Pan-Mayanists as standing for cultural cleavages that may be used to subdivide and thus control Maya populations. Ethics and politics are inextricably intertwined on all sides.

Implications of the Culturalist Critique

In the United States, cultural critics, feminists, black studies scholars, anthropologists, postorientalists, and others interested in cultural diversity have been working on issues closely related to the concerns of these Maya critics. To take these critiques from the margins to the metropole, Gayatri Spivak and Joan Dyan[36] suggest that we teach about sanctioned ignorance and cultural diversity in our college courses, unveiling the assumptions and politics of what one does not have to know to be an educated American. Anthropologists have long done this by actively teaching and writing against the prevailing American belief that the poor in other countries are passive victims or pawns, so busy with the daily struggle to survive that they do not care about politics, morality, international relations, their own country's development paradoxes, or scholarship. We have also taught across the grain by documenting the diversity and complexity of other cultural systems and their struggles against racism and other forms of discrimination. Many of us see this as a reflexive and global issue: we need to explore sanctioned ignorance and cultural diversity within the United States as well as outside our porous borders.

Maya challenges to North American social science, however, engage still other issues: the politics of the production of knowledge. They urge us to undermine the dichotomies of the researcher/object of research by participating in efforts to decentralize the production of scholarship about and for Mayas. They want to participate in the ethical process of judging research, its plans and outcomes.

It is unlikely that Maya and North American research and writing projects will be totally convergent. That would be a highly ironic consequence of the move to decentralize the production of knowledge. My prediction is that we will see an international proliferation of cultural and national anthropologies in the future. Foreign academics can decide to collaborate individually and institutionally in this process, depending on their assessments of particular situations and on whether their input is welcomed at all. To do so will involve acknowledging differences in the motivations, politics, and goals of inquiry. It will also involve a reexamination of our canons of validation for what counts as anthropological research. Is the center the only place where cultural studies are to be validated and resources allocated? Can we contribute to other forms of decentralization and transnationalism?

Finally, we can explore our own narrative forms for presenting anthropological findings so that analysis becomes something other than dominant truth telling about other cultures. Some anthropologists invite Mayas to write introductions to the translation of their works for Latin American audiences. Others are experimenting with ways of structuring texts so Mayas interrupt the analysis with their distinctive forms of narrative, commentary, and skepticism. Maya culture (and our own) can be portrayed as complex fields of debated representations not unified essentialisms or reflections of someone else's imposed colonialism. Anthropologists can challenge the singular power of their readings of culture by showing that these are but one of many possibilities, and that our "otherness" is interpreted and monitored by the very people who give us access to their cultural worlds. In short, we can show that our analyses have histories, modes of production, and politics.

Personally, I have encountered moments of revealing and troubling tension in this process. For instance, when I gave a cassette of rituals I taped eighteen years before to various groups in San Andrés for their local projects in 1989, I felt that I was parting with a treasure that belonged to me. I experienced this even though I knew at the time the reaction was inappropriate. Or, when faced with an identity crisis after my CIRMA lecture (after all the while thinking theirs was where the identity dilemmas lay), I had to reconsider my professional ethics and politics. Am I, as an anthropologist, who I seem to be? Or, finally, the importance of puzzling through particularly anxious moments at joint academic panels in the early 1990s when I found myself sweating through Maya responses to my discussions of their writings on revitalization. This was much more than a concern about political correctness, for in this flux of resurgence and nationalism there is no stable "correct" position, though there are many problematic ones. Mixed audiences—whether in Antigua at CIRMA, in Chicago at American Anthropological Association meetings, or in Guatemala City at the post-peace accords conference I am currently preparing for—surface conflicting expectations and political dilemmas for anthropologists who value engagement rather than detachment. Tensions have also led to moments of common purpose beyond the struggle for cultural recognition and rights, as when this feminist anthropologist and her Maya colleagues have talked about challenging established canons, ways of knowing, and structures of academic authoritativeness that seemed so immutable in the past.

Four

Civil War: Enemies Without and Within

BETWEEN 1978 AND 1985, the western highlands of Guatemala were engulfed in intense internal warfare, *la violencia*[1] as it was called in the countryside. This was the worst of a series of crises during the decades of authoritarian regimes and military-dominated democracies that plagued the country after the mid-1960s.[2] Like "the troubles" in Northern Ireland or the *intifada* in Israel, *la violencia* gives a shape to memories and to later experiences of repression.

The effects of *la violencia* in the western highlands ranged from the total destruction of some four hundred hamlets and municipal centers to periodic sweeps, repression, and selective killings in other settlements. Mass evangelical conversions were common as communities attempted to distance themselves from "political" groups. Coerced participation in community-based civil patrols (*patrullas de autodefensa civil*) became universal in the early 1980s. In some instances, however, highland communities experienced serious economic devastation with only scattered casualties or were relatively unaffected.[3] In one case, people are said to have discovered their own country's experience by watching the movie *El Norte*.[4]

Explicitly, *la violencia* was a confrontation between military and guerrilla forces. From the military's point of view, it was a battle against communism, against an armed and dangerous menace within.[5] Guerrilla terror needed to be met with counterterror. The counterinsurgency war began with the successful routing of guerrilla forces in eastern Guatemala in the 1960s. In the late 1970s and early 1980s, during the regimes of General Lucas García (1978–82) and General Ríos Montt (1982–83), the situation intensified as guerrilla groups mounted attacks on military installations, took over towns, and threatened major landowners in the western highlands.

Guerrillas extended and unified their operations through an umbrella movement known as the Guatemalan National Revolutionary Unity (URNG). Many Mayas expressed their frustration with party politics and the lack of government support for rural needs by joining activist networks such as the Committee for Campesino Unity (CUC), which organized highly successful farm-worker strikes.[6] From the guerrillas' point of view, this was an armed struggle to challenge the legitimacy of the state and the exploitation of Guatemalan peasants by wealthy landowners and export-oriented commercial elites. They recruited combatants from the countryside and sought support from peasant populations. In their terms, this was a war of liberation to resolve brutally conflicting class interests in a country with the lowest physical quality-of-life index in Central America and the third lowest, after Haiti and Bolivia, in all Latin America (Painter 1987, 3). In the western highlands of Guatemala, however, the relation of landowner to peasant, or officer to foot soldier, was lived out in a world of ethnic difference.

What were the implications of ethnic difference for this war of liberation and counterinsurgency? First, during *la violencia*, unresolved tensions in Guatemalan racism were inflamed and manipulated. Although it would be a mistake to reduce ethnic difference to agrarian class relations,[7] colonial and modern plantation economies were built on social ideologies and national development strategies that harnessed the labor of impoverished Mayas and kept them poor.[8] Philosophies of racial inferiority, which justified an ethnic division of labor delegating manual labor to Mayas and nonmanual labor to Spaniards (and later to their cultural offspring, the Ladinos), lies at the heart of the 470-year history of plantation economics. The guerrillas sought to radicalize the poor in class terms, while the army decided to punish them so they would not collaborate with or join the opposition.

Second, *la violencia* was understood by virtually all sides as a conflict with strong ethnic overtones. Many Mayas felt that the government used the counterinsurgency war as an excuse to destroy Maya populations.[9] Both their desire for wider political participation and their distinctiveness in language and community were seen as political threats by rightist political groups and the military. The painful irony that foot soldiers for this counterinsurgency effort were overwhelmingly Maya was not lost on rural populations.

Third, *la violencia* was to have a great impact on interethnic relations in many communities. The war served as a vehicle for the expression and intensification of ethnic distrust along two axes. Ladino hacienda owners became targets for assassination by guerrilla groups. Mayas, on the other hand, feared the special connections local Ladinos had with military authorities through the system of civilian-military cooperation set up in 1938.[10] Most populations assumed that military officers would automatically side with those who were identified as members of national culture—that is, with the Ladinos. In addition, Maya strangers from other language groups—who were easily identifiable in their community-specific indigenous clothes— were feared as army collaborators and spies.

Fourth, rather than leading to a suppression of ethnicity as happened in El Salvador in the 1930s as a result of *la matanza*,[11] *la violencia* sparked a wave of cultural resurgence in communities and provoked wider concerns with cultural identity among university students.

Studies of *la violencia* by North American, European, and Latin American scholars have been heavily influenced by international human-rights discourse, with its goal of documenting the abuses of power and the violation

of basic rights by states and their antagonists. The human-rights move-
ment—through groups such as Amnesty International, Americas Watch, the
Guatemalan Human Rights Commission, the Network in Solidarity with the
People of Guatemala (NISGUA), the Washington Office on Latin America
(WOLA), Cultural Survival, and the United Nations Mission to Guatemala
(MINUGUA)—sought to publicize the protagonists and victims of violence
and promote domestic human-rights monitoring to pressure governments to
release detainees and curb military and police abuses.[12] In fact, the activities
of NGOs have been crucial to the implementation of the UN's Universal
Declaration of Human Rights and related covenants. These organizations
convey their findings to international audiences in particular sorts of realist
narratives, which document, measure, and interpret the impact of violence on
local communities. As these two chapters argue, human rights narratives are
but one of a variety of ways Mayas have used to express the consequences
of war for their lives.

After it became relatively safe to return to Guatemala in the late 1980s,
the goal of anthropological research was to show the impact of *la violencia*
on Maya communities and to explore the internalization of violence, which
in some cases has led to chronic killings and death squads within communities. To understand the conflict, anthropologists sought to reveal patterns in
the killings, the escalating, personal character of intracommunity violence,
and the social characteristics of the perpetrators and the victims of violence.
In Carmack's pathbreaking collection, *The Harvest of Violence* (1988b), ethnographers who had done earlier work on highland communities pursued
these issues.

What have these various streams of scholarship discovered in their examinations of Guatemalan violence? McClintock (1985) documented the nature
of state violence and U.S. military advising and found a transnational pattern
of repression. Counterinsurgency techniques employed in Guatemala in the
early 1960s were later used in Vietnam in the late 1960s and then reincorporated into Guatemala in the 1970s and 1980s. He presents convincing evidence that rightist death squads operating out of the capital with the goal of
eliminating the opposition—whether political candidates, union leaders, or
students—were not independent vigilante groups but were tied closely to the
police and military and at times directly to the office of the president. With
Ramiro de León Carpio's assumption to the presidency in 1993, there was
pressure to disestablish the direct sponsorship of death squads at the highest
level and worries that government-mandated covert groups would simply
reappear under other names. More recent revelations—through Jennifer Har-
bary's militancy, Richard Nuccio's decision to divulge details of CIA involvement with Guatemalan officers, and the declassification of training
manuals for counterinsurgency warfare from the U.S. School of the Amer-

icas—make it clear that the United States continued its history of sub-rosa involvement in Guatemalan affairs during the war.

In rural areas, the militarization of civilian life took the form of setting up military bases and posting armed detachments (*destacamentos*) near rural towns as well as creating community-based civil self-defense patrols, organized to "protect" towns from outsiders and, much more importantly, to help monitor local populations. Under the presidency of General Ríos Montt, the patrols were installed in 1982 as a counterinsurgency measure; by 1985, under General Mejía Víctores, the military estimated that 1 million rural Guatemalans were involved in patrolling their communities (Simon 1986, 26).

Finally, current studies analyze the political and economic impacts of *la violencia* on rural communities in the western highlands, where most of the warfare occurred. The conflict did not have the same intensity in all parts of the highlands. Zones of major guerrilla activity, such as the Ixil Triangle in the Department of El Quiché, were the most heavily militarized, although bases and civil patrols were set up throughout the highlands. To resettle populations dispersed by the violence, the government created thirty-three model villages (*polos de desarrollo*), which left civilian populations directly under military control (Manz 1988).

For the better part of a decade, many anthropologists felt it was too dangerous to pursue these issues in print, a judgment that was reinforced by the political killing of a Guatemalan anthropologist in 1991. Nevertheless, researchers began to address Maya constructions of violence, regional experiences of guerrilla mobilization and militarization, refugee experiences in and outside the country, and the structure and ideology of the Guatemalan military. Carmack's collection (1988b) documents the social fragmentation that accompanied the militarization of civil life. David Stoll (1993) argues that rural populations in the Ixil Triangle adopted tactical neutrality in order to avoid engagement with either side. Another line of research has emerged on how Maya populations expressed and communicated their anguish in the face of military and guerrilla violence. Maya political commentators and anthropologists living in exile—such as Menchú (1984, 1985), Montejo (1987), and Montejo and Akab' (1992)—have offered powerful eyewitness accounts of military violence. Ricardo Falla (1994), George Lovell (1995), and Richard Wilson (1995) produced detailed regional studies. Linda Green (1998) and Antonella Fabri (1994) described the psychological fragmentation and lasting effects of violence on women and on urban refugees. Jennifer Schirmer (1996, 1997a, 1997b, 1998) has focused on military counterinsurgency strategies, engagement with human rights discourse, and tactics for downsizing during the peace process. Anthropologists and historians, such as Carol Smith (1990a), Robert Carmack (1995), Richard Wilson (1995), and

Robert Carlsen (1997), put the civil war in wider historical and cultural perspective.

This chapter focuses on the cultural construction of terror in the late 1980s—that is, on how Mayas looked back at the militarization of civilian life and the tortures, disappearances, and killings that became a daily occurrence during the civil war. I gathered the ethnographic materials for this analysis over five months of fieldwork in San Andrés in the spring and fall of 1989 and during shorter visits in the early 1990s.[13] While violence had deescalated by the late 1980s, life was still highly monitored, and communities were still shell shocked.

This chapter presents people's accounts of their experiences of *la violencia* and the issues that became central to their attempts to cope with a world suddenly turned upside down by the clash of army and guerrilla forces. As I talked with townspeople I had known in the early seventies, it became clear that eyewitness stories of violent events allowed these people to express the horror of widespread killings and repression. But first-person accounts were not the only medium through which Mayas expressed their feelings. Local leaders, who ironically had struggled to destroy the institutional bases of Maya *costumbre* in the 1960s and 1970s, began to revitalize elements of traditionalist culture—specifically, narratives about the capacity of certain people to transform themselves into supernatural beings. Renewed interest in these narratives stemmed from their resonance with the frightening existential dilemmas Maya families faced during the violence. For most, surviving counterinsurgency warfare involved embracing silence and living with chronic ambiguity and uncertainty. I close the chapter with a reflection on the role of the anthropologist in the study of cultures of terror.

San Andrés: Local Issues before *la Violencia*

In the 1970s, San Andrés was a community with fifteen hundred people living in the county seat and another four thousand in outlying hamlets and marginal plantations. Like other agrarian communities, the people cultivated corn—the staple for tortillas—and beans for subsistence. The town also had a history of producing wheat, milk, and cheese for regional markets; agricultural laborers for coastal plantations that grew coffee beans, cotton, and corn; and construction workers, agricultural surpluses, and weavings for the neighboring tourist center of Panajachel. Before the establishment of the regional cooperative in the 1960s, most Trixanos, as locals call themselves, worked seasonally on coastal plantations in exchange for minimal wages and access to agricultural land on which to grow corn. In the off-season families returned to San Andrés to cultivate whatever land they had. Others worked for local landowners during labor-intensive parts of the agricultural cycle, though local plantations supported very few permanent workers. When the agricultural cooperative began offering extension services and credits for seed and fertilizer, local yields increased dramatically, which allowed farmers to concentrate their efforts on their own tiny landholdings instead of facing the risky prospect of contracting as migratory laborers on the south coast. The highly successful agricultural cooperative gained regional fame.

San Andrés was also known for the vitality of Catholic Action, the revitalization movement that sought to convert traditionalist Maya-Catholics to sacramental orthodoxy. In the 1960s, the new group challenged the local system of Maya self-rule, established early in the colonial period, which included the saint societies, councils of elders, and the unified civil-religious administration of the Maya community. By 1975 the worst fears of the traditionalist elders of the town had been realized: a religious revolution had occurred. The traditionalist civil-religious hierarchy collapsed because of strong opposition from the younger generations. Catholic Action—along with two Protestant congregations, the Assembly of God and the Central American Mission—had successfully undermined local Maya participation in the saint societies. No longer was service in the saint societies obligatory for gaining access to outlying communal fields. The moral and economic powers of the traditionalist gerontocracy dissipated with the victory over traditionalism. The ancestors' *costumbre*—their religious practices and underlying views of the nature of the world and society—appeared to be all but dead in the town. But appearances can be deceiving.

Representations of *la Violencia* in San Andrés

People in San Andrés first experienced the terror of *la violencia* in the late 1970s. They had heard of troubles in other areas, then bodies began to appear in the Department of Sololá. During our discussions in the late 1980s, people cryptically recalled their encounters with death and terror:

> There was great fear. People frequently appeared along the highways, dead, dumped. You didn't know what town they were from.

> During *la violencia*, bodies were left dumped on the roadsides—those from another town here, those from here in another town. Now they bury them.

The immediacy of horror was evoked by tortured and abandoned bodies, corpses out of place in a country where one's home community is a crucial part of a person's cultural identity. The maimed bodies of strangers foretold what might happen closer to home. For each body out of place, a family somewhere else worried about a brother, son, or daughter who had vanished. They were called *desaparecidos*, those who had been disappeared. Styles of violence changed from making the public a witness to death, when mutilated bodies were purposely dumped beside major roads in the late 1970s, during the Lucas García regime, to the hidden burials and clandestine cemeteries of the early 1980s, during Ríos Montt's presidency. But the fact of torture and *desaparecidos* continued.

"*Por miedo,*" out of fear, people stayed in their homes. Kidnappings occurred most often in outlying hamlets, said to be closer to the routes taken by guerrillas as they moved from the coastal regions south of Lake Atitlán to the more active areas north of the lake near Chichicastenango. Some victims vanished and were never seen again; others wandered back, frightened and mistreated, after being held for several days. Some surprised mourning relatives, writing months later to explain that they had been kidnapped and forced to join the army. After losing their male protectors, splintered families fled their distant villages for the municipal center and shelter from dangerous army sweeps. But San Andrés was fortunate; it did not suffer the displacements or massacres of local populations that occurred to the north and west.[14]

The economic effects in San Andrés, however, were substantial. European and North American tourism to Lake Atitlán evaporated[15]; "even the long-haired hippies left," one Trixano dryly observed. So there was little demand for handwoven fabric, agricultural surpluses for restaurants, or construction workers for new hotels down the hill. Trixanos were very aware of the town's dependence on the neighboring tourist center of Panajachel, which absorbed excess labor and generated additional income for agriculturalists and weavers, even though tourists rarely climbed the steep hill to San Andrés itself.

Most important, agriculturalists dreaded going to their fields because the movements of individuals were closely monitored and army patrols were unpredictable. Herbs, mushrooms, and other foodstuffs gathered from the mountainsides to be used in cooking disappeared for two years when defoliants were used to clear underbrush where guerrillas might be hiding in the mountains north of the town near the more active areas. Trips to neighboring periodic markets were also dangerous because heavily armed soldiers continually stopped and searched trucks and buses at mobile checkpoints.

With the exception of religious groups, local organizations were forced to stop functioning when the military stigmatized public meetings as political and, later, when the national government declared a state of siege, banned public assemblies, and suspended all civil rights. Cooperatives, which served as key sources of credit for agriculture and housing, ceased functioning for several years during the height of war in the early 1980s.

It was clear to me as I interviewed people and followed public events in the spring and fall of 1989 that the counterinsurgency–guerrilla war left deeper marks: *la violencia* came up in every conversation, in every meeting or event. Like the 1976 earthquake, which leveled the town, the intensity of violence from 1978 to 1985 was used by many Mayas as a temporal marker—before *la violencia*, after *la violencia*, during *la violencia*.[16] Yet, as one person put it, "the truth is that the violence always continues, is always part of our lives."[17]

At the same time there was great reluctance to discuss *la violencia* in any detail. "It's best to avoid the subject," one man explained, "because there might be informers" (*orejas*, literally ears). So people usually responded to questions from anthropologists and others with the generalizations: "The violence wasn't so intense here." "It didn't have great force."[18] It is as if denial and a low profile would bring protection from a world that merited greater distrust than ever. The first legacy of *la violencia* was silence and denial.

In the late 1970s and early 1980s, the climate in San Andrés was one of tremendous uncertainty. When people talked about *la violencia*, they described constant anxiety:

> You didn't have security in anything. There was terror at night, great insecurity. You didn't know which group might come to get you. There was fear of both sides. No one had tranquility. We say, "He who owes nothing, fears nothing." We stayed in our homes.

> You couldn't work well in the fields. To do so was to run a great risk because who knows who you would find yourself with, right? The order of the day was violence. So people tried to get work closer to town.

Most described the situation as something rural communities were caught in but not of their making. One Trixano summed up the prevailing local views with these observations:

> Not even we know much [about the roots of the violence]. There were confrontations between the military and the subversives, but we never knew anyone from the subversives. With the climate of insecurity, we couldn't do anything, just continue with our work. The reality is that the clash of these two organizations affected everyone.

At the same time, Mayas found an explanation for the genocidal intensity of the violence in the deep fear Ladinos have of the Maya other:

> There has always been a clash of classes here in Guatemala. Many have thought that someday the Indian would rise up. But many people misconstrued this, and their fear caused panic. Of course they were against the Indians, thinking one day they would rebel. They thought the Indians would exploit the existing opposition to the state. They believed Indians were participants or were in the leadership. This is why they tried to eliminate, to kill the indigenous leadership.

The language was often veiled or oblique, often condensed into fragmentary observations with unspecified agents. The listener was expected to fill in the obvious: that Mayas were involved in the opposition and that the government was trying to eliminate the Maya leadership. Those unable to deal with strategic ambiguities were by definition strangers with whom it was not wise to share information.

Rural people predicted a difficult future for national governments if current problems were not dealt with adequately. For those who elaborated their views to me, the language of underdevelopment, class relations, and development projects—an interesting combination of rhetoric from the cooperative movement, progressive political parties, and historical-materialist denunciations— captured rural claims on national society. Development-oriented Trixanos argued for economic assistance, access to the banking system for business loans, infrastructure, health, and peace so people could work without being disturbed. One activist in development projects concluded:

> If they can offer opportunities, there will be stability and they won't have a revolution. If they don't, there will be future instability. The powerful receive support; the wealthy exporters have everything. They don't give peasants access to loans. To avoid future problems, we need financial access, roads, schools, progress for the environment, health, water, and help with diseases that are not known in other countries.

Most Trixanos I talked to, however, did not see the tension as existing between exporters and peasants; rather, they cast the conflict in ethnic terms as one between indigenous populations and Ladino nationals.

The rebels were greatly weakened by the counterinsurgency war as the 1980s wore on. The Organization of the People in Arms (ORPA) was active in the Sololá-Chimaltenango region. Apparently ORPA saw itself as a special cadre—a secretive, militant opposition composed of radicalized Ladinos and Mayas, without the primary goal of mass mobilization and education.[19] In the face of clearly superior military forces, most people did not feel the guerrillas would be able to bring about the changes they sought. For some, the army won the war; for others, everyone ran out of steam in the mid-1980s. For still others, the guerrillas were not strong enough to protect Mayas from military reprisals no matter how true the opposition critique rang. For many, the time was ripe for other kinds of political organizing. No one felt the underlying problems had been resolved.

Some people nevertheless had a romanticized image of the rebels operating on the other side of Lake Atitlán:

> They swept down into other towns, coming out of nowhere. They were great orators, speaking in Maya. They raised people's consciousness, talking about the high costs of everything and why are we working for the benefit of the monied. Then they disappeared. The guerrillas are like supernaturals; they are special people. It was exciting to actually see them.

Their leaders were called fair-haired (*canches*), which apparently referred to their uncertain origin—though there was no evidence of foreign troops in their ranks.

People talked about the pervasiveness of surveillance and monitoring during the violence. The word they used was the Spanish *control*. Buses and trucks were summarily stopped at roadblocks and passengers searched at gun point for evidence they were involved with the guerrillas. It was dangerous to be carrying a Walkman or cassette tapes—favorite items for Maya youths—or the traditional black-and-white knit bag (*morral*) worn by the Maya men of a more politicized Chichicastenango. In effect, it was risky to be too modern or too traditional.

On a local level, people's comings and goings and connections with others were reported to the military by local military commissioners. Civil patrols were in charge of protecting the town, monitoring movements, and reporting them to the commissioner. People restricted their travels because they did not want others to misinterpret their actions and conclude they participated in clandestine groups during absences from town. Leaders of local organizations lived in the greatest fear. For San Andrés, as in many communities, there were said to be lists of local leaders—teachers, bilingual instructors, catechists, and officers of the cooperatives. As one person put it: "One had to be very careful. If you were thought to be against the government, you were put on the list, and that was that." To be on a list meant one was a marked person likely to be targeted for abduction and murder as a subversive. By definition, being a leader in the cooperative or a catechist in Catholic Action was suspect. Organizations that at one time had been promoted by the government to "integrate" Mayas into national society, channel their politics, and keep them from being radicalized were now considered dangerous and subversive by rightist political parties and the military.[20]

Even worship services—where men sat on one side, women on the other, and little children roamed freely—were closely watched, as one catechist explained:

> They were monitoring us a lot, oh yes. One day my brother, Don Antonio, was preaching in the afternoon. Because of the violence, we met earlier than usual so people could return to their homes before nightfall. A hand appeared at the window of the auditorium with a tape recorder, recording what he said. Just imagine! These were heavily armed men. A girl saw the hand and the tape recorder and realized someone was there. She wrote a quick note so that my brother would understand what was happening—so he could finish right there or explain in Spanish so he would be understood. She sent a little child up front to deliver the note, and he immediately switched to Spanish so that everyone would know. Shortly afterwards the men left; there were several. When the men left, we began to sing tranquilly

there. The next day we went to see the footprints. They were the large prints of combat boots.

The switch to Spanish signaled two audiences. On the one hand, the congregation knew something was up; on the other hand, the strangers would have no trouble understanding the worship service and its nonpolitical nature. The code switching made the meeting more accessible to outsiders, whether they were from other indigenous groups or were Ladinos.

Respected adults in San Andrés were contacted by people in the countryside who wanted advice about what to do in the climate of uncertainty and with whom to ally themselves. Most leaders chose to curtail visits and remain in town because they knew their movements outside town would be known immediately and closely studied. Over and over again, I heard their apprehension that social contacts with friends and strangers alike were plagued with uncertainty. One elder said: "The problem was that you never knew what kind of people would turn up, who you were talking to." The town leadership felt increasingly insecure and in 1980 began to close local agencies such as the housing cooperative, which remained dormant for three years in the early 1980s. As one administrator explained: "We did it because we were concerned about working in the cooperative, because the truth is one never knew who might come by."

The situation of agrarian and housing cooperatives was particularly difficult. Their ideology was suspect because cooperativism was transformed into communism in the army's mind and the political loyalties of community leaders were in doubt. Local populations felt it would be suicidal to challenge the military's projection of these political labels and fears onto local organizations. People were unable to pay their loans, and no one—including the banks—wanted accumulations of money. The robbery and burning of the regional bank in the state capital of Sololá, less than an hour away by bus, underscored the point. People still faced great financial hardships in 1984, when the cooperative was reopened. One agriculturalist offered this explanation of why it was impossible to repay loans: "Even in 1984, people couldn't harvest their crops because of *la violencia*—they still couldn't work outside town. It wasn't safe; they didn't go to the fields." Going out to the fields could always be misinterpreted as sneaking off to a clandestine meeting.

The burning of the San Andrés municipal offices in 1981 was a turning point for the community. As Don Gustavo narrated:

> The times were dangerous. We heard about assaults below town. When I returned, there were three Sololatecos in the street by the Assembly of God church. Sololatecos at this hour here! What were these people looking for? So they were spies, they were Sololatecos, others from Chichicastenango. What were they doing here? I went home to eat dinner with my wife. Then we went to church—it was Thursday. We were there for two hours, and three Sololatecos were in the corner of

the hall listening. They were monitoring us, imagine. People left and we went down to the park. There were four men with binoculars. We went right back home and I was about to go to sleep when I heard the first shots. So it began, there it began, over here it began, over there. It began close to us. They had a machine gun here.

So they went to the mayor's office. Don Paco Anleu was the mayor. They went to his home:

"Well, father," they said, but with nasty words, "open the door now, yes!"

They had machine guns there. Luckily, miraculously, they didn't find him. They say he hid under the bed and, when they entered, his wife cowered behind the door.

The machine gun was right near us. They fired it in the air. Everyone on this side of town said, "Too bad, they've killed Don Gustavo, they've killed him. So sad."

The town center had been invaded at nine o'clock at night by an estimated force of two hundred armed people who opened fire throughout the settlement with rifles, small arms, and grenades. Everyone was terrified and hid the best they could in their cornstalk and adobe homes.

The invaders set fire to the municipal offices and a nearby shop and looted the cooperative's general store of supplies, including new machetes and four typewriters. They argued about whether to set fire to a huge storehouse of fertilizer at the cooperative, but were persuaded by one of the invaders that this would hurt the wrong people. They tried, it is said, to break down the doors of four carefully selected houses—all belonging to prominent Ladinos with businesses and substantial landholdings. The families fled their homes, fearing for their lives, and left the town for good soon thereafter. The invaders disappeared in the middle of the night and, surprisingly, no one was killed.

One interpretation holds that the army attacked the town, demonstrating the anarchy of the moment:

Ironically, the Ladinos were chased away by the army. They must have felt the other side would hurt them, and if the military was out of control, there was no choice but to move to the city and, like many others, escape. So they left their lands rented.

But most people believe it was not "*los palos*" (the sticks, as the army was called by Guatemalans) but the guerrillas coming to punish.

The next day the most feared section of the armed forces, the *judiciales*, came to investigate. They called people to the plaza and interrogated them:

"Why didn't you intervene? Why didn't you come after the intruders with sticks? Why were Ladinos the only ones sought out by the subversives? All of you must be involved."

People realized that to proclaim their innocence or to point out that they had no arms with which to confront the invaders would only single speakers out for retribution. Finally, the military left. Thereafter life was increasingly militarized in San Andrés. A military outpost was established nearby; all adult men were forced to serve on civilian patrols; and the public telephone office, with its one line to the outside, was closed.

Ladinos, who had watched Mayas demand a greater voice in town affairs throughout the 1970s, were very distrustful. They felt the guerrillas had come to kill prominent Ladinos, to destroy what they saw as "the society, the leadership" of the town. In fact, most Ladino families had already begun to relocate. The younger generations of many old families had moved to the capital in the early 1970s to prepare their sons and daughters for urban businesses and professions. Others migrated after the 1976 earthquake heavily damaged most homes and businesses in the town. The burning of the municipality completed the cycle, resulting in a town without powerful Ladinos. Over time, Mayas successfully consolidated their control over local politics, development organizations, and the cooperatives in addition to the religious groups they had always run. Ladino land went on the market, and those Mayas who had the money acquired additional parcels; others planned to organize cooperative projects to solicit credits for land purchases. This was a dramatic change from the commanding position Ladinos held in the town only a generation ago when they owned all the major businesses and plantations.[21] The dream for Maya families was to acquire a parcel—even a small one—of the lands their fathers had formerly worked as day laborers for a pittance. Thus, one night of terror marked the culmination of a longer process of Ladino out-migration and the beginning of what amounted to a localized agrarian reform.

The other event central to the way townspeople represented *la violencia* was the murder of a local teacher who worked in a distant village. As one community member related:

> One day it happened, according to the news we finally got. Every morning he went off to school; he lived nearby and walked to the village. As he went along, he was watched. On his way that day, masked men intercepted him. I don't know if they had uniforms. They kidnapped him. This was five years ago. We didn't get any news of this then. The next day the school sent us a message saying that he hadn't shown up at school. We didn't do anything; we couldn't. His father tried to find out what happened, but he didn't learn anything. Shortly thereafter, they kidnapped another man who was also a bilingual promoter. They kidnapped him because he taught. For a time the teacher's wife went to the military post, but they didn't help her. They said, "There's no evidence he's dead. Maybe he's alive." But they kidnapped him.

Once again, however, there is a deeper message in this story. As one person explained:

I believe some took advantage of the situation, some people who had personal differences. They used the opportunity to complain about others. There was much violence and many deaths because of this. It's possible this is what happened to the teacher. He was a good man, didn't even drink. It's possible that where he worked, someone didn't like him or that someone didn't like his being a teacher. So finally something happened, the day came. Because of envy, there were personal differences over something, or perhaps it was simply that he wasn't from the village where he taught.

In these two examples, we see the double-edged nature of *la violencia*. At the same time Maya agricultural communities were caught in a frightening national crisis over which they had no control, it was increasingly apparent that both the army and the guerrillas depended on local contacts for information. Thus, part of the world out of control, part of the insecurity and violence Trixanos suffered, was locally authored:

> What was most frightening was the army because they killed without finding out if in reality a person was involved in this politics. The most painful thing was that many died because of vengeance, because of envy. Just because a person was there, someone got bothered because he was doing all right. So he would go and say, "This man is with the guerrillas." And the army or the judicial police would come and, without checking if the person was involved . . . [shrug]

The internalization of violence and collaboration were the second and third legacies of *la violencia*.

One Trixano illustrated the connection in the following terms: "In one of the villages, a certain *señor*, they say, was collaborating with the guerrillas. The soldiers grabbed him, but they let him go—in exchange for whom, who knows?" Thus, noncombatants in the countryside became an integral part of the war. They could act on personal animosities and envy by denouncing fellow townspeople to either side. Vengeance in this situation became tantamount to a death sentence. In San Andrés, the process was felt to be driven by ethnic and individualized hatred; in other towns, existing factions or emerging power brokers turned on each other, which lead to widespread killings[22] Communities also had to face the inevitability of young soldiers returning after army duty. The youths had been indoctrinated throughout their service not to trust their communities or families, and, while seeing the painful dilemma of these lonely youths, community members decided to keep their distance:

> They don't say anything. If you ask, they don't say anything. The army has given them orders that they can never talk about army strategy. They keep it a secret. They served, they served. They left, they left. They have this in their heart. Sometimes they say a bit, "Once in the war, this went on, this happened." Nothing more.

They keep the secret. They are afraid. They had lots of experience because they weren't in the bases, they were in detachments where they had confrontations with the guerrillas. They saw their friends killed and they wanted perhaps to kill people in defense. Only one talked to us, he's not from here but from Godines. He saw the horrific things that happened in Nebaj, in the Ixil Triangle. What cruelty! When they killed people, it was because they were filled with anger because their fellow soldiers had been cut down in battle . . . soldiers blown to pieces. It's the same anger the others have. And when they catch a guerrilla, they take him apart piece by piece.

San Andrés was not a space of innocence corrupted by external forces in the late 1970s. Nor, luckily, was it a community in which preexisting factionalism escalated into self-destruction. A definitive explanation of why some communities were massacred by the armed forces and others were passed by or why some communities internalized violence by creating their own death squads and others did not is beyond the scope of the present analysis. One would have to look at a combination of factors: the military's classification of regions as more or less prone to subversion, guerrilla groups' decisions about their own regional involvements, local histories of factionalism and conflict, the ability of corrupt power brokers to take advantage of the situation for their own benefit, and local tactics to resist the violence through a number of low profile strategies.[23]

In San Andrés, local experiences were undoubtedly influenced by structural dimensions of the wider conflict. First, the military did not consider this a major zone for confrontations with the armed opposition, although it was far from inactive. Second, guerrillas tended to concentrate their armed rebellion in regions that were more remote and offered easier sanctuary than the largely deforested agricultural area immediately surrounding the lake. Third, people from the municipal center of San Andrés had come to terms with local religious factionalism in very specific ways. Religious congregations had long been a major force in local Maya politics. The civil-religious hierarchy/Catholic Action cleavage, which had troubled the town for years, was resolved without re-creating opposing factions when the traditionalist saint societies collapsed before *la violencia*. Catholic Action and the evangelicals continued to have marked religious differences, but key members of the most powerful congregations had a twenty-year track record of supporting each other and fighting discrimination against Mayas in the cooperative, the elementary school, and the municipal government. Luckily, these religious cleavages, which apparently channeled conflict in other rural communities, did not become the focus of internal tensions in San Andrés.

A dimension of heightened distrust during the *violencia* was the ethnic division. *La violencia* hastened but did not determine the breakdown of the old bi-ethnic community and the establishment of greater Maya local control. Although the fruits of the guerrilla invasion of San Andrés were not immediately available, because of the suppression of local economic and political organizations, it was clear to many that additional lands and new powers might become available. Despite the central importance of structural factors, they offer only a partial explanation of why violence did not escalate within the community of San Andrés. Significantly, they fail to convey how Trixanos portray the tragedy of local engagement.

Specters of Violence: Transforming Realist Representations

La violencia conjured up many ghosts. Mayas in San Andrés gave these phantasms very specific tensions to voice in stories they told of transforming beings. In 1989 I was surprised by the notice Catholic Action catechists gave these accounts, which for me were surrealist representations that echoed the magical realism found elsewhere in Latin America. Although the catechists were highly critical of aspects of traditionalist religion judged to be incompatible with Catholic orthodoxy, they insisted the events in these traditionalist stories really occurred: "This is really true; this really happened, Kay. My niece saw a woman as she was transforming herself." Why, I wondered, are those who appeared to have rejected traditionalist beliefs so intrigued with these narratives at this historical juncture?

In San Andrés gifted individuals gain a reputation for telling old tales late at night at wakes, after the formal part of the *velorio* is concluded and people struggle to stay awake for the all-night vigil with the body. Fathers used to recount highly entertaining magical realist narratives to their children after the evening meal, and both parents discussed the moral of the story with their children. Today they are shared among generations when extended families relax at home on Sundays and talk about what the town was like in the old days. Narratives are designed to be interactive, calling for audience laughter, questions, and comments during the telling.

Outsiders have demeaned this genre as "folklore." But oral mythistories are used by a variety of interests to convey moral education, social commentary, and political analysis. The genre reveals recent social history and traces of much older indigenous cosmology, also evident in pre-Columbian Mesoamerican sculpture, literature, and textiles.[24]

Let me present one of the shape-changer narratives I taped that spring.[25] An apt title for this story would be "Peel Off, Flesh, Come Back On."[26]

> This story happened here in San Andrés. . . . In the times of our grandparents, our fathers, there were many beliefs about spirits like the *rajaw a'q'a* [also called the *dueño de la noche* or in this translation "master of the night"]. . . . These masters of the night have the freedom to walk about at dark. They have this freedom the

same as we do during the day. We have our work during the day, but when the night comes we rest. Now these people, for they are people, come out at night.

It is said that sometimes in a married couple, the woman turns out bad for the man. . . . At first when the man [in this story] was married, the woman was just fine. No one was even aware that she was a master of the night, because, while the couple is still young, it seems the masters of the night do not dedicate themselves to this work. But then when they get to be more than forty years old, this is when they begin. Perhaps it's the destiny they have.

So this is what happened to the woman. The husband saw his wife every morning, all day, really sick. Totally sick with her head tied in a kerchief, with a shawl covering her. All of her body ached. The husband said, "Well what's wrong? You're always like this; I always see you with this thing."

"Yes, my body hurts, my head hurts. All my bones ache."

"Ah, you should prepare a sweatbath (*temescal*) so perhaps you can get better there." Because in the past, the cure, the medicine was the sweatbath. So one sweated out all the sickness in this oven.

"That's fine," the woman replied obediently. Except the woman knew why she was in pain all the time.

Well, the man kept thinking, thinking, thinking: "What could be happening to my woman because she wasn't like this before? But now I only see her sick and exhausted." The man was always thinking of the woman at work. Sometimes the woman came to leave him lunch, but she was always covered up, always sick.

"You came," he said, "How's your illness?"

"I can't shake it," she replied.

So this happened to the man. Time passed during which his woman wasn't dying nor was she getting any better. But one day the man thought about how much he loved his wife. Well, they went to bed, it was time. But the man stayed awake for a moment. The woman had a mystery. She had the power to make him fall into a deep sleep when she wanted to go out because she was a master of the night. The man did what he could to stay awake. Oh no, after trying so hard, in the end he didn't feel a thing. He was deeply asleep. This happened at midnight. The man stayed asleep but with the thought that he wanted to see if his woman really laid down to sleep with him or if she went out. The man thought something was happening. Well, when he finally woke up, the woman wasn't there. In her place, she left a long grinding stone in the blanket there beside the man because they slept together in the same bed.

"There he is alone, there he is alone," she said to herself. Yet he felt the weight, saying, "What is this?" He lit a pine-pitch stick. Hah, here was the grinding stone. "Hah! This woman, she is doing something; she's involved me with this thing." And throughout the town he heard the noise of dogs barking. Ahhhhh, so it really was his wife who was going around disturbing the dogs. Then the man was wide-awake, wide-awake, wide-awake! One o'clock in the morning went by, then two, then three. It was three thirty when he smelled a terrible odor. I don't know how the odor got into the house. Then once again he was lost in his dreams. That meant the woman entered without his being aware because he was asleep again. At five o'clock in the morning, the woman got up.

"You're there," he said.

"Of course," she said. "Get up, your tortillas are ready."

Oh, but the man didn't say anything more to her. He thought, "With me you are not going to do this. With good reason you continue to be ill."

Can you imagine why she continued to be in pain? The tremendous beating people gave her. People got out of bed when the dogs barked, so she always took her blows. For this reason she was in pain all the time: because of the blows she received there in the town and because people get up to look for the animal she became. Well, this happened. The man knew that this thing transformed itself. I don't know if it was in the form of a ram, a goat, or a dog. "Go on, you just wait, woman," he said to himself.

The next night she went out, and the man was ready to keep track of her return. But beforehand the man went to consult with a diviner. What was he to do to make sure the woman would fall into his hands? He consulted with an *ajq'ij*, a diviner priest of the day. The diviner said, "This is what you are going to do. You are going to get pinches of tobacco, with this plant that they call rosemary, and with fifty stems of cypress. But they should be hidden so you won't fall asleep again. Put them under your pillow so with this power you will discover when she gets up. She can't make you fall asleep." The man took all these things with him.

The woman didn't go out that night. She said to her husband, "Go to bed," and she embraced him. But the man didn't trust the woman now because he knew why she left the stone there. Well, the next night came, and she didn't go out. He felt the cloth. Then the third night, she began to stir again. But the man acted as though he were asleep. She threw the blanket over him. . . . The man was playing dead. The woman got up. Like this, she left the blanket draped over the man's head. The husband was very, very alert. She entered the kitchen again to take out the grinding stone and leave it beside the man. Awake, the man thought, "Good, now I'm going to see what this woman is doing." Clearly, the woman had decided that night she was going out. He didn't fall asleep again. "Now I'm going out," she said to herself. She went to the kitchen. And the man got up and remained low to the ground.

She opened the door and was transforming herself when her husband saw her. She was transforming herself, but she was there with four legs. Her hands and arms served like another pair of legs, with four legs, like this. She was talking, talking, talking. But what was she saying? Now she was there half-changed, and the part below was what was left. The lower part with her feet was still human. It was as if the upper part were a ram. Now she had the upper body of a ram. But yes, she spoke. Then she was saying, "Peel off flesh, peel off flesh." Peel off means all of her body was coming off. When the man looked again, she was an animal. And off she went. What remained in a heap was the woman's body—that is to say, her flesh. . . . She was an animal, a ram, a male goat. When the man saw her, the animal leapt twice and went off. It leapt over the wall. The man's hair stood on end: "And this woman!" *Eshhhhh*, she went, and her route was marked by the noise of barking dogs. "There goes my woman," says the man. [Laughter.] "Oh, my woman," said the man, so sad. He went over to see the body of the woman, all the flesh there. What am I going to do with this? Well, the *ajq'ij* diviner says it will return at three in the morning or three thirty because at four the local patrol goes out. The patrol of the spirits, as they say. . . .

The man was playing dead under the blanket, waiting for his woman. He heard the noise of the dogs, he heard that something was coming. And her body, her flesh was already there. A long-haired ram entered. Then it leapt twice and said, "Come up, flesh, come on up." First it was peel off, peel off. As it leapt, it took the form of a skeleton. It wanted to become a person once again. "Come up, flesh, come on up," it said. Little by little the flesh rose up, and it became a woman. And the man in bed was playing dead. The woman entered, complaining, complaining, complaining as she came. Why? Because of the blows she received once again. Because people come out to look for it. Because this happens. She came in and the man turned over, as when one tires of sleeping on one side. The man was awake, and the woman embraced her husband. [Here the storyteller grimaced and laughed.] And the man with his hair on end was thinking, "This is a male goat." [Laughter.] "Tomorrow you're going to drop off my lunch," he said, "How are you? How's your illness?"

"I'm sick, I'm sick," she said.

"Well," the man thought again, "This woman doesn't suit me; she's doing me bad."

The next night she went out again in the same form, in the same way. She transformed herself with the same words. And what happened? She left a mound of flesh again.

"Well, I'm going to teach this woman a lesson. Why does she mock me? She looks me in the face, but she's really a spirit. That's not a woman." He began to say things, very nasty things about his woman. "Well, today I'm going to prepare ten pounds of salt. I'm going to be the assassin of this flesh. I'm going to salt this flesh."

The woman went off again, leaving her flesh there. Aaaaand the dogs were barking. He began to put salt on her flesh. Salt burns. What happened to the flesh? It dried out right then. It no longer had life. . . . "I'm going to watch over this flesh to see what happens when she comes." Then, after the woman was finished, she leapt twice and said, "Come on up, flesh, come on." But the flesh was dead, it was dry. She began to cry. She leapt up, left, and went off, and since that time the ram has never returned.

So ends the narrative. Edward M. Bruner (1986) is correct in suggesting that we may fail to do interpretive justice to narratives if we examine them only as autonomous texts. Rather, we need to situate them in ways that demonstrate their historical contingency and show how they are redeployed in novel ways in changing circumstances. Texts become significant as people bring them into tension with ever-changing contexts. Because narrator, audience, text, and context shape each other, we need to be concerned with how Trixano storytellers and their audiences understand this narrative, just as it is important to confront our own preoccupations.

After hearing "Peel Off, Flesh, Come Back On," North American listeners often ask about the significance of the gender imagery in this story: a man's anger and violence toward a woman, and a woman's desire for autonomy but apparent lack of control over the consequences of her actions.[27] These themes resonate with the highly contested gender politics in our own society.[28] Yet, to understand Trixanos' interest in this narrative, it is important to find out whether the theme of gender politics is salient for them and, if so, what it represents for Trixano storytellers and their audiences.[29] As it turns out, gender in this instance resonates with the problematic nature of authority and cultural continuity. I would suggest that the narrative gendering of these issues during the civil war allowed Trixanos to explore the intimacy of violence as they confronted a host of paradoxes and anxieties in their daily lives.

What I found most striking in 1989 was the interplay of contingent issues—which spoke to the political climate of the 1980s—and endemic tensions—which Trixanos constructed as characteristic features of their community. This convergence of tensions, neither of which could be reduced to the other, may explain the attraction and power of these narratives for people who otherwise presented themselves as having rejected traditionalist *costumbre*. Gender, however, was not the initial Trixano preoccupation in discussions of the narrative.

Transforming Selves, Mesoamerican Cosmology, and Contemporary Existential Dilemmas

For the storytellers I talked to, the captivating aspect of "Peel Off, Flesh, Come Back On" was the capacity of some, but not all people to transform themselves. The masters of the night are special beings who have human and animal transformations. Their identities are not generally known by others. During the day they present themselves as conventional people, but at night they usher in another order in which spiritual forms dominate reality. This story catches transformation at its midpoint, dwelling on metamorphosis at the transitional, most abhorrent moment for Trixanos, when the woman is half human and half magical animal.

This depiction of the nature of the self is in fact a variation on a theme common throughout Mesoamerica: people have the capacity to transform themselves into animals and have animal counterparts. Scholars have traced these beliefs to pre-Columbian cultures in central Mexico and to the interplay of Mesoamerican and Spanish understandings and misunderstandings of indigenous cultures (Foster 1944; Musgrave-Portilla 1982; Tranfo 1979). Called *nagualismo* (the phenomena of transforming shamans) and *tonalismo* (the phenomena of companion animals or guardian spirits) in the literature, these conceptions are discussed by many anthropologists as part of a system of multiple souls.[30] In the pre-Columbian past, gods, charismatic leaders, and shamans had the capacity to transform themselves for good and evil. When the Spaniards colonized Mesoamerica in the sixteenth century, they brought their own beliefs in pacts with the devil and in transforming wizards (called *hechiceros* or *brujos*), which influenced missionaries' teachings and reactions to indigenous religion. The imagery available to today's storytellers, then, represents an amalgamation of sixteenth-century pre-Columbian Mesoamerican and Spanish beliefs.

In contemporary scholarship, Mesoamerican notions of these shape changers focus on the capacity of certain individuals to become spiritual animals at night, usually with malicious intent, frightening people or selectively pursuing those who are ill or who stand out as nonconventional consumers in their communities. Alternatively, they bring illness to other towns. In some cases, individuals seek their powers through battles and pacts with the devil or with the supernatural master of the mountain (*rajaw juyu*).[31]

Many Mesoamerican communities also believe individuals have companion animals or "animal co-essences," whose form may be divined shortly after birth, may become clear in dreams, or may never be known to the individual. Generally, animal co-essences live lives parallel to their human counterparts and share their fate in life and death. In certain cases, parts of inner souls wander from human bodies at night during sleep or when a person is sick, has sexual intercourse, feels strong emotions, or dies. In some communities, the ancestors can punish individuals by knocking out part of an individual's inner soul and freeing their animal counterparts from the safety of their special sanctuaries. In other places, only powerful elders and healers have animal spirits they can use to bring disease to individuals as a punishment for social transgressions. In cases of illness, healers diagnose the cause and direct social confessions, which counteract the illness.[32]

The Mayas of San Andrés, as with many populations in the southern regions of Mesoamerica, have syncretized their own blend of these issues and believe that only certain individuals transform themselves into animals. Apparently, the existence of companion animals has coalesced with beliefs about unstable selves. Masters of the night have an inner compulsion to wander at night, as in the narrative just presented. Other spiritual forms, called *rajaw kab'il*, go out at night with the specific purpose of bringing sickness to neighboring towns. Still other individuals gain their animal form when they are transformed by the *rajaw juyu*—the master of the mountain—who lives in a plantation inferno inside the sacred mountain.

When I listened to stories such as "Peel Off, Flesh, Come Back On" after hearing Maya accounts of the violence in the town, I was struck by the ways these constructions resonated with each other. When I asked the storytellers, both community leaders, if there was any connection, the answer was yes, with an elaboration of intersecting themes. The significance of the narrative for them was that the man, who had assumed he knew his wife after so many years of living together, discovered that he did not. She was really a *rajaw a'q'a*, an awful animal who had power over him, and a spiritual essence that violated their marriage and disrupted the town. Unlike normal humans, the animal-spirits are seen as unfeeling, *sin vergüenza* (without remorse), and driven to do what they must. There is a built-in antagonism between towns-people and the masters of the night; people's anger is felt to be natural and justified when they encounter animals out of place at night. A male goat should not be seen walking down the road alone at night, so it must be a *rajaw a'q'a*. In other narratives, people are shocked when they learn that the lone animal they had beaten as it wandered the streets is really a neighbor and that the neighbor is really a spiritual animal.

I would assert that for Kaqchikel Mayas, these accounts described a world parallel to their situation in the late 1970s and 1980s—one of betrayal and existential dilemmas:

> We held everything inside, in our hearts. But when we got to the religious meet-ings, we could only talk about religion. Preach, preach with a heart so full but you could not say anything. Everyone had so much on their minds but we could not talk about what was inside us.
>
> Some people would say, "How are you? How are we doing? How is this going?" They wanted to get something out of us. But we ignored this because it was not a good thing. Because one could not trust his own brother. He could be a spy. You couldn't know who he would talk to. There were cases here in Guatemala where you couldn't talk with your own wife—if the wife sided with the guerrillas or with the army. If the children were with the guerrillas and the father with the army. How would I be able to talk to someone in the kitchen, if I didn't know who it was? This was very ugly. Even among brothers, one wouldn't know if someone had been paid. Because money does all sorts of things.
>
> "Hide these men and we'll give you something."
>
> So if you start to say something is happening because of the guerrillas, what if there is someone there who has been paid off? Or if one begins to talk of the army, there could be someone paid off by the other family. We don't have to talk about these things. We don't know who is listening.

It is notable in the transforming-selves stories that the metaphor of be-trayal is often gendered as female. Masters of the night are frequently de-picted as women. The indigenous individuals who the master of the mountain punishes for sleeping with Ladinos are inevitably women. In both instances they have betrayed the authority of the males—fathers, brothers, and husbands—in their families. For Mayas, women are powerful metonymic representations of community because they are felt to be central to the continuity of Maya culture in their roles as the bearers of the next generation and the socializers of the children in Kaqchikel-Maya language. They stand for the essentialist construction of Kaqchikel-Maya identity—that there is an intrinsic uniqueness to being Kaqchikel—in the face of rapid social change. As Maya men often put it (and even the urban ethnic nationalists assert this), it is more important for women to wear traditional dress than for men, who in many communities have adopted Ladinoized clothing, because women perpetuate indigenous culture.

Without the moral weight of their role, women are felt to have the potential to do great social harm by secretly becoming sexually involved with men other than their husbands. They are said to do so out of their own weakness in a world in which men are easily tempted by, if not actively pursuing, other women. Trixanos describe the likely outcome of a woman's infidelity as dangerously escalating family betrayals because suspicious husbands may seek vengeance by pursuing their own sexual affairs. The viability of the family and, by extension, of the community is threatened by anger and distrust, which are unleashed by challenges to male authority. Strikingly, these portrayals capture the ultimate fragility of authority in a world in which men are supposed to be the unquestioned heads of their households.

When storytellers explained "Peel Off, Flesh, Come Back On" and people told me of the violence, they described similar existential dilemmas. In communities in which people had lived together for generations, suddenly one did not know who was who. Some people were not who they appeared to be, but no one knew for certain who all the betrayers were. Trixanos feared *la violencia* would divide sons from fathers and wives from husbands as it unleashed different political sympathies, nascent envy, and distrust. For Kaqchikel Mayas in San Andrés, "Peel Off, Flesh, Come Back On" and other related stories were revitalized as alternative phrasings of contemporary dilemmas: Although we live together in the same community, can I really know who you are? Can I know your loyalties when appearances may be deceiving and alliances shifting? Can I trust you with my thoughts; can I know yours? How can we know if our children or siblings are betraying us politically or our wives are betraying us personally, culturally, sexually? Stories of the *rajaw a'q'a* express skepticism about social relations, loyalties, and the capacity to know those with whom one lives. Perhaps the storytellers chose this veiled language, rather than a more explicit formulation, because mistrust during the civil war had its own corrosive powers in a situation in which one needed to count on others for cues in order to survive the shifting political currents.

La violencia did not originate the idea of clashes of interest, envy, and vengeance, or the ability of some to transform themselves into secret allies of others. But it did intensify and channel conflict, bringing the coercive powers of the state and its political opposition into everyday life and raising the stakes of social criticism and political action. Realist narratives of the capricious powers of particular soldiers, investigators, and rebels have become integral to the town's sense of its own history. The master-of-the-night stories are old and familiar languages of skepticism, which act to individualize betrayal rather than treating it as a collective act on the part of existing Maya factions in the community. Perhaps here in the realm of representation we have identified another factor that mitigated the internalization of violence in San Andrés.

Shapes of Anguish

La violencia claimed many more victims than merely those who suffered physical harm.[33] The first dimension of anguish was the silence imposed on rural populations who witnessed brutality and death but found themselves operating in a culture of terror in which they had to rephrase experiences into denials: "*Aquí no tuvo mayor fuerza la violencia.*" Silence in this case was a denial of involvement that communicated the irony of no escape. In San Andrés, silence was subverted with continual public allusions to *la violencia*, by the compelling desire to signal the influence of this period on the life of the town. It is as if people could not dismiss what they felt they had to deny.

Another dimension of anguish is represented as the arbitrariness of power, be it the military that largely controlled this region or the guerrillas when they were most active. Uncertainty and anxiety weighed heavily on Trixanos. There was no way of knowing if one might become a target of surveillance, when one might be singled out for detention, and what might be considered evidence of subversive or collaborationist intentions. One did not know what would trigger the wrath of the judicial police, whether guerrillas were moving from strategies of recruitment to punitive actions, whether one's name might be on a list or whose list it might be on, or whether a trip to the fields or the market would result in being caught in someone's sweep. In these representations of *la violencia*, the sources of discord were externalized to the world outside the community. Trixanos were rendered more passive than they actually were in this language of uncertainty:

This was so heavy, so heavy. You were disturbed, you wanted to have some way of defending yourself. The feeling emerged—it wasn't fear but anger. Why do they come persecuting if one is free of faults, if one works honorably? You felt bad, well we all did. Grief but also anger.

In practice, Trixanos recounted small but astute efforts to protect themselves from the powers that be: they carried heavy loads of firewood on their backs, for example, with tumplines stretched across their foreheads to communicate they were indeed hardworking peasants with an innocent reason to be out in the countryside. They switched languages from Kaqchikel to Spanish so strangers from other Maya language groups and Ladinos could understand the nonpolitical nature of religious meetings. And sometimes a quick-witted young girl and innocent milling children saved the day.[34]

Trixanos also represented violence as an internal matter. It was the product of ethnic hatred that denied Mayas their humanity, of interpersonal tensions experienced as angry *envidia*, and of betrayals for gain and vengeance in a situation of sustained crisis. This was another dimension of anguish, the existential dilemma expressed in the master-of-the-night stories. In practice it meant the blurring of the distinction between those one did not trust and those one might have trusted. Religious groups tried to counter the pressures of social fragmentation, as they had in the past, with expressions of solidarity and common purpose. However, the militarization of civilian life, with the creation of civilian patrols in 1982, forced all males to stand at the intersection of local and national violence. All had to face the double bind of being drafted officially "to protect and defend the town from outsiders" but, in fact, to monitor the activities of their own townspeople and families and report suspicious behavior to military authorities outside the town. In San Andrés, people tried to disengage themselves and to trivialize the duties of the patrols, which disintegrated soon after the 1985 election of the first civilian president in twenty years, Vinicio Cerezo.[35]

When referring to the perpetrators of violence, Trixanos learned to speak with carefully crafted ambiguity:

> "*They* burned buses and shot the drivers and their assistants."
> "*They* killed the teacher."
> "*They* kidnapped people in a nearby town."
> "*They* aren't bothering people right now."

There was most notably the illusion of safety for the speaker in the ambiguity of "they" during the lingering war, because one did not have to reveal one's analysis or political sympathies. Armed groups were often described as having taken pains to mislead people about who they really were and by disguising their identities when they went out to kidnap or rob. The culture of terror created a divided reality, one that balked at crediting any particular explanation of a violent act as definitive, even though people often suspected what had happened.

Uncertainty, divided realities, and strategic ambiguities continued for years. In the late 1980s, buses were being robbed near San Andrés on the back road through Godines to the Pan American Highway. Maybe the guerrillas were exacting a war tax. Maybe army soldiers were supplementing their incomes. Or perhaps it was *delincuentes* (highway robbers, thieves, and muggers) who, like those with festering animosities and envy in the towns, were taking advantage of the moment. As one woman recounted when describing how her bus had been intercepted, passengers searched, and some robbed by people in disguise: "You can look at their boots to really know, but we are so poor that it doesn't matter." In fact, the woman was a successful professional.

Postscript 1991

As Begoña Aretxaga pointed out to me in our comparative discussion of the violence in Northern Ireland and Guatemala, anthropologists are not exempt from the cultures of terror we live in and describe. Thus, it is important to stand back and reexamine my anthropological narrative of violence as a cultural form and a product of the fieldwork encounter. In significant ways, this analysis reproduces some of the same phenomena I encountered in my fieldwork: Like the Trixanos, I found myself caught in the paradox of having witnessed something I could not communicate fully. I recognize that there are limits to my abilities to translate between cultures, and there were horrors I knew about but could not recount. Anthropology's dilemmas are intensified when we study situations in which human rights are being violated. For many Latin Americanists, social research requires analysts to address inequalities, local culture, and human-rights abuses. Our contribution is to give voice to those who are muted by cultural difference and marginalization,[36] and to explore the interconnectedness of U.S. and Latin American political realities.[37] We also maintain personal moral commitments to the people with whom we work.

Flowing as they do from the paradoxes of our limitations and responsibilities, our analyses will embody some of the same silences, uncertainties, and ambiguities we document. Our accounts are products of dialogues, whether or not they result from formal interviews.[38] Sometimes we are chosen to witness the past; sometimes we are warned off; sometimes we are closed out; sometimes we are caught in an army sweep. Does our presence as outsiders—no matter how familiar—cause people to shift to a politically ambiguous language or to exaggerate uncertainty? Perhaps, although I found silences and ambiguities pervasive in public meetings, conversations over meals, local histories written for other audiences, accounts of discussions between people out of town, and the press.[39] Are the silences we document in part the result of people's distrust of us as another kind of outsider? Certainly, although Trixanos described their own encounters with others' silence and their own desire to break through to find out what happened—

especially in other, more militarized zones. While we cannot recapture the immediacy of *la violencia* as it was initially experienced in the late 1970s and early 1980s, we can work to understand the violence of memories only partially revealed and partially revealable.

Postscript 1993

Time has moved on and people throughout Guatemala speak more openly, though often not publicly of the violence. And so I was told by people in San Andrés that a troubling secret can now be revealed in print. Just out of town, the military established a clandestine cemetery during *la violencia*. One Trixano who had viewed the site in the early 1980s, described his discovery in the following words in 1989:

> There was a clandestine cemetery here, just up this hill. They brought people from Sololá, from various places, from Chichicastenango. They brought them here to bury them. Right up here, it was all overgrown, there were just trees there. I saw this cemetery. I was still a civil patroller, for two years. So one day the army detachment, which was stationed here, left town. Normally they didn't let people see this place. But when they inaugurated the military base in Sololá, the detachment and all the civil patrollers from here joined the celebration. Twenty-five of us were left in the town with instructions to call if anything came up.
>
> "So make sure you check the place and if you see a group—as always."
>
> "Fine."
>
> A couple of us decided to climb the hill where people were killed. We went. There were all these holes, squared-off, two meters square, below the thicket and trees. A pine tree stood there with its trunk all burned. That's where they tied them, they burned them, they tortured them. There were fragments of buttons, pieces of sweaters, parts of shoes, socks, sombreros there. That's where all the graves were in quantity. People came from Sololá, they were taken from there and brought here. Who knew? The same happened here with some neighbors. The soldiers would go to the houses around the detachment:
>
> "Loan us your wide-bladed hoes."
>
> They would take the people, these poor people prisoner. They dug the graves and when they finished they were killed here. It was a sad place.
>
> This was during the Ríos Montt presidency.
>
> "Yes," the president said, "now there won't be bodies on the roadsides. We have to create courts to see if a person is guilty or not."
>
> These were special courts. So there were courts. But here in San Andrés there were clandestine cemeteries. It was awful, Kay. It could have been us.

Five

Narrating Survival through Eyewitness Testimony

> We know that while intellectual debates wear
> themselves out with sterile rhetoric about how to
> understand "the other," indigenous people continue
> to live the most horrendous injustices which have
> been perpetuated across the centuries.
> *Victor Montejo*[1]

THE PUBLIC INTELLECTUALS involved in Guatemala's Pan-Maya movement critique the ethics and politics of foreign anthropology and openly reject interview-based research and the ethnographic genre for their own writings. They also distance themselves from autobiographical portrayals of cultural resurgence by arguing that the movement is a collective effort. For activists, this repudiation marks the rejection of divisive individualism in favor of a transcendent Maya identity for the indigenous majority of the national population.

As the movement developed an institutional base throughout the highlands in the late 1980s and early 1990s,[2] its leadership created a variety of genres of self-representation for different audiences: daybooks based on Maya and Gregorian calendrics, school texts, point-of-view columns for editorial pages, collections of Maya fables, conference proceedings, essays on Guatemalan racism, novels, testimonies, translations, poetry, linguistic research, reports to development organizations, social commentary, university theses, and statements asserting cultural rights. As resurgence has gained momentum, these works have been published and distributed by Maya presses, national newspapers, magazines, international development funders, universities, the Ministry of Education, and other organizations inside and outside the country.

Drawing inspiration from Mary Louise Pratt (1992), George Yúdice (1996), Doris Sommer (1991), Marc Zimmerman (1995a, 1995b), Jonathan Boyarin (1993), Joanne Rappaport (1994), and anthropologists working on Maya resurgence, the following chapters offer an illustrative survey of the writings of Maya intellectuals with an eye to the ways that politically marginalized groups represent themselves, interrogate power structures, and imagine alternative futures. I am interested in the ways in which Maya activists produce, circulate, read, and appropriate literature that now reaches hundreds of local communities through schools and nonformal education activities and by means of workshops, audio- and videotapes, publications, radio programs, and the press. These materials find an additional axis of transcultural circulation through organizations and publications supporting international human-rights struggles and through international meetings and courses in Latin American Studies in American and European universities.

This chapter discusses the prose of Victor Montejo, one of Pan-Mayanism's most prominent writers in exile. After fleeing Guatemala at the age of thirty in 1982, Montejo worked at Bucknell University, earned a masters degree at the State University of New York at Albany and a doctorate at the University of Connecticut at Storrs. He taught at Bucknell University and the University of Montana before joining the faculty at the University of California at Davis, where he is now associate professor of Native American Studies.

To use Mary Louise Pratt's insightful phrasing, Montejo has created "intercultural texts"—giving authority to subaltern voices through the *testimonio* genre—in order to describe the violence and existential dilemmas of living in Guatemala.[3] *Testimonios*, which have been widely used in Latin America to personalize the denunciation of state violence and to demonstrate subaltern resistance,[4] gain their narrative power from the metaphor of witnessing. On the one hand, they represent eye-witness experiences, however mediated, of injustice and violence; on the other hand, they involve the act of witnesses presenting evidence for judgment in the court of public opinion. Zimmerman (1995b, 12) notes that the literary *testimonio* involves

> generally linear first person narration of socially and collectively significant experiences, in which the narrative voice is that of a typical or extraordinary witness or protagonist who metonymically represents other individuals or groups that have lived through other, similar situations or the circumstances which induce them. By virtue of its collective representativeness, *testimonio* is, overtly or not, an intertextual dialogue of voices, reproducing but also creatively reordering historical events in a way which impresses as representative and true and which projects a vision of life and society in need of transformation.

Yúdice (1996, 16–17) adds that testimonial writing is a form of situated knowledge that, in heterogeneous ways, involves

> the rejection of the master narratives and thus implies a different subject of discourse, one that does not conceive of itself as universal and as searching for universal truth but, rather, as seeking emancipation and survival within specific and local circumstances. . . . Truth is summoned in the cause of denouncing a present situation of exploitation and oppression or in exorcising and setting aright official history.

The Guatemala of Montejo's testimony is not the tourist paradise of colorful weavings and isolated peasant villages awaiting Western development but rather a world of "'contact zones,' social spaces where disparate cultures meet, clash, grapple with each other, often in highly asymmetrical relations of domination and subordination" (Pratt 1992, 4).

Montejo's intercultural texts are both familiar and rebellious. They ignore the ethnographic conventions of anthropology that call on authors, sooner or later, to establish professional authority through abstraction, generalization, depersonalized narrative voices, and the theoretical justification of worthy research.[5] His books are also transgressive in light of Mayanist arguments against the autobiographical and ethnographic genres for the promotion of resurgence. Finally, while *testimonios* are most often autobiographical narratives edited by outsiders as acts of international solidarity, Montejo is an insider, a Jacaltec Maya who fled the extreme of rural violence in 1982 and met with other refugees, who in the compilation *Brevísima Relación Testimonial* became peers working on a project of common concern:[6]

> As an insider, my efforts are centered on the issue of how I (a native) can tell my collective story (of expropriation and exile) and, at the same time, elicit a strong commitment from anthropologists to promote issues such as social justice, self-determination, and human rights in the politics of native people. One of the most persistent struggles of modern Mayas is to get rid of their five century old denigrating images and colonial "representations." Thus, indigenous people have always complained that anthropologists do not listen to them, that instead they have represented native people with the anthropologist's preferred images: "primitives," "minorities," "backward," or just "informants." We Mayas find it difficult to deal with the academic world because if we tell the "experts" what is Maya, they are reluctant to listen; instead they find it more scientific (comfortable) to tell us what it is to be Maya, or to define Maya culture. This is not to say that we possess the sole "truth," but as our culture is at stake, we regret that our views are not taken seriously. . . . My aim has always been to make the sufferings of refugees more visible and to bring attention to their struggles to liberate themselves from continuous oppression and persecution. Mayas are again speaking for themselves and rupturing those barriers that have silenced us and positioned us in such unequal social relations. (1993a: 16–17)

As a Maya, a refugee, and an anthropologist, Montejo is aware of his own multiple accountability to readers with inherently conflicting politics and positionings. As an insider/outsider who studies displaced communities, Montejo must answer Abu-Lughod's question: "What happens when the 'other' that the anthropologist is studying is simultaneously constructed as, at least partially, a self?" (1991, 140).

Montejo has become an important interpreter of indigenous culture and Guatemalan politics during and after the counterinsurgency-guerrilla war. He argues that, just as the sixteenth-century Spaniards feared an indigenous uprising and used violence preemptively, so the Guatemalan army undertook a scorched-earth policy in the early 1980s to undermine any incipient alliances between indigenous communities and the revolutionary movement, then expanding into the western highlands (1993a). Montejo's writings, which have been published in Spanish, English, Jacaltec, and Italian, circulate in the United States, Latin America, and Europe. His published works include *El Kanil: Man of Lightning* (1984), *Testimony: Death of a Guatemalan Village* (1987), the collection with Q'anil Akab' *Brevísima Relación Testimonial de la Continua Destrucción del Mayab' (Guatemala)* (1992), *The Bird Who Cleans the World* (1992a), and *Sculpted Stones* (1995). Some of these works are extraordinarily painful accounts of state terrorism in Guatemala. Others are bilingual compilations of Maya fables from Montejo's home community, Jacaltenango in the state of Huehuetenango, and poetry that recounts his journey from rural Guatemala to exile.

As it was for past generations,[7] Maya writers involved in projects of revitalization are seeking a way to engage the terms of violence and racism and create space for something beyond extreme fragmentation. In the repressive environment of the late 1980s, the challenge was to represent the formative experience of cultural difference in a multiethnic society without being labeled subversive. Through the early 1990s, writers in Guatemala were forced by death squads and state repression to veil their analyses and maintain extreme public caution when discussing politics.[8] Mayanist writers such as Demetrio Cojtí Cuxil, Enrique Sam Colop, and Demetrio Rodriguez Guaján and organizations such as the Kaqchikel Coordinator for Integral Development (Coordinadora Kaqchikel de Desarrollo Integral or COCADI) and the Maya press Cholsamaj showed great courage when they published on social issues in Guatemala. Those in exile were the first Mayanists explicitly to chronicle memories of violent displacement during the civil war.

I Rigoberta Menchú: An Indian Woman in Guatemala (1984) is the most famous and controversial of the Guatemalan testimonial literature. In 1997, Menchú herself expressed serious misgivings about the work. As Elizabeth Burgos-Debray reveals in the preface, this is a highly mediated work, compiled by a Paris-trained Venezuelan anthropologist (formerly married to Regis Debray) who had a well-defined political agenda. Burgos-Debray did not know Guatemala well and spent only limited time with Rigoberta Menchú. The text was further edited by Committee for Campesino Unity (CUC) leaders in exile in France and Mexico (Thorn 1996). Yet, critics such as Doris Sommer (1991), have argued that the protagonist was an active participant in the literary process with political goals that shaped the product ethnographically and politically.[9] Used widely by solidarity organizers in the United States and Europe "to embody and represent revolutionary possibility and hope in her country"[10] (Zimmerman 1995b, 71), the work has overshadowed the writings of Mayanists living in exile, who have composed powerful personal testimonies, worked with Maya refugees in Chiapas, and advocated cultural revitalization rather than revolution.[11] In the post–Cold War era, with the transition to civilian governments and the signing of the peace accords, it is particularly important to hear other voices and grammars of dissent.

Moments of Resistance and Complicity

Victor Montejo's writings take readers on a personal journey of violence, displacement, and cultural renewal. From the safety and free speech of exile in the 1980s, he was able to criticize state terrorism directly. In the United States, one of his goals was consciousness raising, to reach North American and international audiences so they would understand the human cost of authoritarian military regimes. To this end, Montejo has lectured widely and participated in many forums on Maya culture.

In the face of anticommunist rhetoric used by conservatives in the United States and by Latin American governments to garner support for counterinsurgency warfare in the 1970s and 1980s, human rights activists worked to convince American citizens that the Guatemalan state had a cynical agenda that targeted armed guerrillas and unarmed civilian populations who were deprived of their fundamental human rights.[12] The Universal Declaration of Human Rights, a 1948 resolution passed by the United Nations General Assembly, set out the general framework for these rights. The 1966 International Human Rights Covenants on Civil and Political Rights and on Economic, Social, and Cultural Rights elaborated what are called second- and third-generation rights.[13] The basic internally recognized civil and political rights established in 1948 include:

Article 3. Everyone has the right to life, liberty and security of person.

Article 5. No one shall be subjected to torture or to cruel, inhuman or degrading treatment or punishment.

Article 9. No one shall be subjected to arbitrary arrest, detention or exile.

Article 10. Everyone is entitled to full equality to a fair and public hearing by an independent and impartial tribunal, in the determination of his rights and obligations and of any criminal charge against him.

Article 11. Everyone charged with a penal offence has the right to be presumed innocent until proved guilty according to law in a public trial at which he has had all the guarantees necessary for his defence.

Article 19. Everyone has the right to freedom of opinion and expression; this right includes freedom to hold opinions without interference and to seek, receive and impart information and ideas through any media and regardless of frontiers.

Article 20. Everyone has the right to freedom of peaceful assembly and association (Donnelly 1993, 166–67).

Groups like Americas Watch, Amnesty International, the Washington Office on Latin America, the British Parliamentary Human Rights Group, and Physicians for Human Rights achieved some success in pressuring the U.S. government to cut foreign spending that directly financed state violence in Guatemala.[14] Another goal was to make Americans aware of continuing human-rights abuses and the unfinished business of refugee return, clandestine cemeteries, demilitarization, and peace negotiations after the war deescalated in the late 1980s.[15] For his part, Montejo has participated in the Commission on Human Rights of the American Anthropological Association and continues to speak out on rights issues throughout the United States.

Over a period of several months at the end of 1982 and beginning of 1983, Montejo drafted his own story of state violence and survival, *Testimony: Death of a Guatemalan Village* (1987), while he stayed with relatives living in the Guadalupe Victoria refugee camp on the Mexico-Chiapas frontier. At that time, he visited neighboring camps in search of people he knew from his Kuchumatan homeland in northwestern Guatemala. He finished the book in the United States (Montejo 1992b, 1–2).

Testimony tells of the September 9, 1982, massacre of San José Tzalalá,[16] the village where Montejo had been in charge of the elementary school for ten years. Montejo initially presents the massacre as the consequence of a terrible mistake, one that made the cost of joining the newly organized civil self-defense patrols (PACs) to hunt guerrillas the same as suicidal noncompliance with the policy of citizen involvement in the counterinsurgency war. When the army first came to Tzalalá to set up the patrols, wives and mothers protested the extra work and danger for their men, who dared not resist directly for fear of being jailed for not following orders. Later the men argued, to no avail, for the alternative of joint work on community improvement projects (1992b, 29).

Under President Ríos Montt's policy, the men and youths of Tzalalá were forced in groups of eighty to one hundred to hunt from six o'clock at night to six o'clock in the morning for guerrillas. They used clubs, stones, slingshots, machetes, and one ancient rifle as weapons against the insurgents. In Montejo's testimony, the contrast of their makeshift arms with the army's sophisticated Galil rifles and machine guns only underscores the hierarchy of human value implicit in the conflict. To demonstrate they could kill, the army commander—who like his subordinates remains nameless in this testimony—compelled the men collectively to beat to death two of their neighbors on the pretext they had clandestine revolvers. Ten days after this brutal initiation, the villagers on patrol duty made the mistake of attacking a well-armed military patrol, dressed in unfamiliar fatigues.

Montejo recreates the tragedy from his vantage point at the schoolhouse: the eager shouts of patrollers who spotted the armed strangers they assumed to be guerrillas, the terrible sounds of machine-gun fire and grenade explosions, and the distant confusion that soon overtook the schoolhouse. Barring the doors and windows and yelling for the children to hide under their desks and pray, Montejo tried to protect and calm his terrified students.

Montejo uses an intimate first-person narrative to capture the immediacy of the unfolding massacre. His furtive glances through the slats of the schoolhouse windows allowed him only partial experience and knowledge in the face of chaotic uncertainty. To portray the horror of families caught directly in the cross-fire, he introduces Doña Malcal, who saw the violent encounter firsthand and tells of her only son's frantic search for his father, only to be shot. The soldiers did not even let Doña Malcal comfort her terribly wounded son as he struggled to breathe: "[The soldier] pushed us out of the house, and I had to leave my son behind. That is why I am here now like a ghost, while my heart remains with my son, who by now is almost certainly dead" (1987, 34).

In this realist account, Montejo becomes a narrator-witness, a Maya outsider who is not a member of this indigenous community but rather a commuter on foot from a nearby town. After fantasizing an escape, he realized he would not. Given his authority and fluency in Spanish, he was needed to mediate between the villagers and the army and to negotiate a deadly clash of interpretations. As the sergeant rounded up the surviving patrollers, some of whom were bleeding with shattered bones, anxious wives called out and begged Montejo to intercede. He found the commanding officer and cautiously explained:

> "I am the schoolmaster in this village and have come to let you know that the people you're holding captive are members of the civil patrol. By accident they mistook you for guerrillas."
>
> "Don't come to me with those stories. These sons of bitches are guerrillas. That's why they attacked us, and I am going to execute every damn one of them."
>
> I went on, unperturbed, "Up there by the chapel the rest of the men are waiting to clear up the situation for you."
>
> "With me you have nothing to clear up. Everything is already clear. They've wounded one of my soldiers, and all of you will have to pay for it. What more do you want to know?" (1987, 25).

The narrative anxiously reveals the nature of brute power: the soldiers toyed with understanding the situation (or not) as they sacked the town, assaulted pregnant women, rounded up the townspeople, and torched their homes. After the roundup, the officer in charge reviewed the captives' identity cards against a list of alleged guerrilla collaborators someone had anonymously denounced "for reasons of revenge or other personal reasons" (1987, 35–36). In a gesture, it becomes clear to the reader that the violent confrontation was no chance encounter.

Arbitrarily, some victims were sent to the school-turned-torture-chamber, where specialists unmercifully beat them to extract the names of accomplices. The identity papers of others were impatiently returned to them. Montejo's fate changed dramatically when one of the accused, for no real reason, named him as a guerrilla collaborator. After defending himself by keeping calm in the face of physical threats and arguing his case of mistaken identity, Montejo was released from detention only to discover the interrogators had slipped a noose around his neck. After being marked guilty as charged, even his friends shrank away from him in fear.

In a flashback, Montejo's account shows how quickly state violence fractured the community *before* the massacre, turning neighbor against neighbor as the army commanders indoctrinated the subsistence farmers:

> "We promised not to release anyone who fell into our hands," replied one of the heads of the civil patrol. "Not even if it's our own father or brother."
>
> This was the first time the civil defenders had begun speaking in these terms. . . . The defender was repeating to his own neighbor what the military had drummed into his head: Destroy, kill, even if it includes your own family. This military doctrine had gradually undermined the foundations of an indigenous culture, causing the Indian to act against his own will and best interests and destroying what is most sacred in his ancient Maya legacy: love and respect for one's own neighbor, which translates into a policy of mutual support (1987, 63).

Moreover, the counterinsurgency war used indigenous troops—"alienated Mayas," "all of dark complexion and ill-educated"—to kill their own people on the distant command of the elite officers, who remain remote physically and culturally in this testimony. Since, in the army's minds "to be poor was to be a guerrilla" (1987, 56), due process required nothing more in Tzalalá than to execute the six accused captives in front of their families. The commander of the foot soldiers would only be promoted for killing so many "guerrillas." Ironically, these counterinsurgency troops were called *kaibiles*, after the indigenous warriors who resisted the Spanish invasion force in the sixteenth century.

Montejo narrates the tragedy of Maya participation in the death of the village. He recreates the process of indoctrination, never complete but compelling to some patrollers and soldiers, which exploited internal cleavages in communities, the poverty of foot soldiers, the reward structure for career officers, and the cynicism of the armed forces that from the president down were structured to compel Mayas to kill Mayas in the early 1980s.

At the end of the narrative, Montejo takes his readers along as he was dragged to the army base in his hometown Jacaltenango for further questioning, since "he seems to know so much." There is the hint of class antagonism here: How is it that a Maya can be so articulate and direct in his explanations in the midst of more powerful soldiers who speak broken Spanish? Perhaps

Montejo finds a noose around his neck not so much because he was falsely accused by a neighbor fearing death but rather because his interrogators wanted to negate the capacity the schoolmaster had earned (and been given by villagers) to mediate between the community and the armed forces.

For Montejo, the horror in Jalcaltenango at the army installation is the coexistence of a space of mass torture and murder, institutionalized and normalized, within his hometown. This is a public secret, kept by signs that say "Forbidden Zone—No Trespassing" where the freshly incinerated bodies of torture victims were dumped.[17] Yet this move is also his salvation because his family was now to intercede on his behalf and press for his release. The Juan Bosch hell is run by drunken soldiers whose monstrous and capricious actions at night were only underscored by the moments of kindness in the morning. During his captivity, Montejo was grateful for gestures of humanity: a young officer who offered him a blanket and plastic poncho to sleep on as he huddled his first night wondering when his torture would resume, and, as he awaited his fate in the morning, others who brought a cup of corn *atole*, coffee from his wife, which meant there was hope for outside intervention, and a Bible, which, as he read the Psalms of David, brought him equanimity. One soldier even coached him not to "betray any fear or let them catch you shaking" (1987, 92) at his next interrogation. But it is clear to the reader that state terrorism meant that no one could really be trusted and no gesture was transparent. Nevertheless, Montejo insists throughout his accounts on seeing the soldiers as individuals and as victims at the same time as he exposes the collective cruelty of the torture center.

Throughout the interrogation, Montejo was convinced that his own demeanor and actions could make a difference. If he only controlled his expression and stayed vigilant, his captors might not initiate the process that would inevitably consummate in personal extinction, in the torture and screams Montejo heard all around him. Prayers to the Virgin and dreams of his brother, whom soldiers had killed the year before and who reappeared to Montejo as a spiritual guardian, gave him hope. He was determined to show no fear or anxiety and to maintain straight-forward innocence when questioned.

In the end, he had to accept an unbearable bargain to win even conditional freedom. Montejo promised the base commander to report names of people he heard were involved with the guerrillas and to return to the base each day for continued questioning at the officers' whim. This, of course, was an unstable solution because someday he would have to accuse others and perpetuate this unending cycle of complicity. Hearing that a civil patrol had harassed his family and his name had appeared on a death list, Montejo decided to flee with his family to the United States, where he had contacts from his earlier writings on Maya culture (1987, 115).

Refugee Testimonies of Ethnography

While composing his own story at the end of 1982 and the beginning of 1983, Montejo began talking to other refugees in the Chiapas camps about their experiences of violence. In conjunction with his dissertation research, he returned to Chiapas during the summers of 1988, 1989, and 1992 and went on to Guerrero to tape stories of survival in the languages of their narrators. In 1993, he accompanied refugees in the first mass return from Chiapas to Guatemala. *Brevísima Relación Testimonial de la Continua Destrucción del Mayab' (Guatemala)* (Montejo and Akab' 1992) is the fruit of Montejo's collaboration with other Mayas to produce evidence of government repression against isolated highland communities near the frontier with Mexico. For Montejo, his co-compiler's name evokes the collective collaboration inherent in the work and the inspiration he receives from Maya culture in his writings. Q'anil Akab' is both many voices and the transcendent unified diversity that Montejo advocates for Maya culture in Guatemala.

Safety was an issue for the refugees who offered their personal stories of military abuse for publication: in the book, each is protected by the use of a Maya pseudonym. There is, however, a complicated hopefulness in this naming. Through assumed names, the witnesses to violence are identified with their culture and the renewed practice of using indigenous names in Maya revitalization, all while they are able to maintain anonymity so they might return someday to Guatemala without fear of personal persecution for breaking the forced silence about violence.

Montejo structures his collection of testimonies of genocidal war to mirror Bartolomé de las Casas's famous description of the atrocities committed by the Spanish invaders against indigenous populations, as chronicled in the 1542 *Brevísima Relación de la Destrucción de las Indias* (Zimmerman 1995b, 114–15). Readers are reminded of the continuities of violence from the conquest to the present by Montejo's intercutting of fragments from the sixteenth-century las Casas account with each of the testimonies. The difference, Montejo reminds us, is that this *Brevísima Relación Testimonial*, unlike the original, contains the voices of Maya observers.

The modern chronicler celebrated the 1992 quincentenary of Spain's conquest of the New World with an open letter to the King of Spain, Juan Carlos I, whose sixteenth-century counterpart, Prince Felipe II, in his role as the chief negotiator with the Indies, served as the audience for the original las Casas account. As in past centuries, the correspondence urged the crown to direct its powers against colonial violence: "Here we present to your Highness a collection of testimonies, voices of the survivors of genocide, which the Guatemalan government has wanted to hide from the world's eyes" (Montejo and Akab' 1992, 9). Although Juan Carlos I did not reply when Montejo sent him the book, the antiquincentenary campaign was highly successful in bringing together circles of indigenous leaders throughout the Americas to share ideas for cultural demands in the face of continuing neocolonial violence.

Montejo signals other framings for this collection—both modern and ancient—by including the adjective *testimonial* in his title. This work is designed not as a synthesis of one narrator's survival but rather as a multivoiced contribution to the Latin American *testimonio* genre. Yet to mark this as an indigenous work, with its own cultural history that could not be assimilated into Cold War politics, the compiler offers an alternative subversive framing: the ancient prophesies by Maya priest-diviners of a foreign invasion described in the Maya *Chilam Balam* and in the Aztec chronicles of the conquest.[18] The editor imagined himself among the *aj-tziib'*, as an ancient scribe and poet in the present. Thus, Akab' links past and present as the prologue ends with these prophesies:

> 1980: Signs and Dreams. In dreams we saw great golden signs that appeared in the skies. Others saw sharp-edged machetes that fell from the heavens. Many machetes, a rain of machetes fell from the sky to the earth. But the most common dreams were of fires that razed the crops, along with animals and villages. Weeping, much weeping among the women and sighs among the elders. (Montejo and Akab' 1992, 12)

Drawn from Kuchumatan communities, Montejo's and Kaxh Pasil's testimony describes troubling signs of rare wild animals, grieving dogs, and the devil, which quickly gave way to visions of naked tortured bodies that gestured from perches in the trees at the banks of the river—long before the violence swept into the region. Most disconcerting were the elders' dreams in which the ancestors and patron saints abandoned their towns. Then angry waves of violence came in 1980, 1981, and 1982. Montejo historicizes the omens and eyewitness accounts with a chronology of the militarization and massacres in the Kuchumatans. In these years, thousands of refugees poured out of the mountains toward the frontier. At first, the Mexican authorities forced the refugees back into Guatemala. Then, as the scope of the violence became clear, refugee camps were set up in Chiapas[19]

The body of the work is composed of personal stories, called laments, which describe the physical intensity of military violence, the arbitrariness of torture and murder, and the double binds state violence created for civilians. Montejo's selection of these particular testimonies, among all the other possibilities, and his editing of the taped interviews would seem to reflect two interlocking and urgent issues: the public secret of "disappearances," which were in fact widespread brutal killings in isolated highland villages, and the involvement of Mayas in this violence.

The speakers graphically describe the horror of watching individuals—

young, old, men, and women—being hacked to death in front of unwilling witnesses because they were out of place or did not have the proper identity cards. They tell of others, who, after presenting their identity cards and being found on ever-growing lists of accused subversives, were unspeakably tortured in secret at military bases, their bodies burned or thrown from bridges to be carried away by the currents.[20] The testimonies dwell on deaths for no meaningful reason, on people with no chance to defend themselves from the military's lawlessness. As Hulum B'aq, a civil patroller, observed: "Not one soldier or military official was prosecuted for these crimes against the lives of thousands of peasants. Well they were the authorities, but criminal authorities" (Montejo and Akab' 1992: 78).

To make sense of this apparent senselessness, Montejo selects very specific voices for the book: a former soldier and member of the intelligence section, civil patrollers, and civilians who escaped from torture centers at military bases. In what I would argue is an autoethnography of a contact zone, the speakers can be seen as contributing important fragments from their own observational expertise, which when pulled together reveal the inner workings of the terrorist state: its tactics for civilian control and indoctrination, the treatment of prisoners and modes of torture at army bases, the structure of military-civilian authority, the connection of the armed forces with the death squads, and the ways a few lucky prisoners escaped from the bases.

Montejo is also interested in modes of justification for state violence as it escalated from surveillance to counterinsurgency sweeps and the extermination of civilian communities.[21] In the process, he traces the ways military rhetoric "shifted from Indians as savages to Indians as communists who threatened to seize private property and introduce a totalitarian system. . . . Indians were equated with guerrillas, subversives, and instruments of communism" (Montejo 1993a, 57–58).

Striking patterns emerge across from the disparate observations of these eyewitnesses. Rural Guatemala becomes a bloody and chaotic contact zone, where the terrorist state coerced complicity, transformed the subjectivities of its forced laborers, and created a climate where torture and massacres were inevitable. Since, for Montejo, ruthlessness is neither an inherent predisposition nor a characteristic flowing from a person's social position, the line between "good" and "bad" is continually blurred in this post-orientalist collection of narratives. Individuals who become complicit in the violence find themselves learning to be murderous through their "own" experiences and are purposefully taught by others to think in certain ways as a result of punishing, fragmenting, and isolating indoctrination, built on a foundational hierarchy of "good people" versus "savages who deserve extermination."

By resisting the ethnographic tendency to sum up the moral of the story, Montejo offers *Brevísima Relación Testimonial* as a polyphonic, interactive work, which calls on readers to discern patterns for themselves.[22] In the testimonies, some indigenous individuals resist complicity in small ways, others are sympathetic to the army. The patrollers condemn the brutality of soldiers who gang raped three young female Q'anjob'al Maya guerrillas before killing them. They show how some soldiers in the detachment drifted slowly to join the patrollers who had physically distanced themselves from the unbearable spectacle of the public torture of an old man and woman. Yet patrollers and soldiers alike rob "abandoned" homes and refugee camps of their residents' meager possessions and farm animals. At the military base, some guards encourage prisoners out of real empathy, others only in a cruel joke of betrayal to set them up for a terrifying end instead of their anticipated release.

Maya complicity in the atrocities is dealt with directly in the conflicted testimonies of Chilin Hultaxh, an ex-soldier and collaborator with the intelligence section, and Hulum B'aq, a former civil patroller—though, most significantly, no one in this collection actually speaks of his own personal violence toward others. What is revealed is the widespread routinization of violence in the everyday practices of the counterinsurgency forces, the torture centers at army bases, and local civil patrols.

So, too, the testimonies illustrate small acts of resistance on the part of soldiers and civil patrollers, who with more open opposition would have lost their lives. At one point, Hulum B'aq and his companions angrily confront a fellow patroller who, out of his own distress, attempted to curry favor with the military by loaning soldiers his machete, even as the other civilians found successful excuses for why they could not:

> We knew that the unfortunate indigenous women whom the soldiers had just killed were poor peasant women, not guerrillas, as the army is accustomed to accusing the thousands and thousands they have killed in the same way.
>
> "Why did you hand over your machete to them? Weren't you aware that they had their own arms with which to commit their crimes without our participation?" The man began crying with great sadness for having given them the machete, and in desperation threw the machete in the river. A machete that has been used to commit this kind of crime can't belong to us peasants. (Montejo and Akab' 1992, 75).

Here the narrative shows Mayas insisting on the nonviolent domestic utility of their most basic tool, the machete, in feeding people rather than killing them.

In these testimonies, a driving impulse of those whose lives were swallowed by the violence is to identify *other* individuals who were harmed: Ignacia, a pregnant women; Gilbertino a forty-year-old with six children; Doña Tulis, an old woman who could not bear to shed her traditional clothing at the refugee camp; Akux Lenam, a civil patroller who fled his duties; Doña Cristabel, a woman who found the courage to go to the military to ask where her son was held (Montejo and Akab' 1992, 23, 27, 31, 35, 49). At the end of the collection, Montejo continues this naming "to demonstrate to the world not just the statistics and the drama of the injustice in which the Maya people of Guatemala live, but also the names of these [302] victims" in San Francisco Netón, who were massacred by the army on July 17, 1982 (1992: 121–21). The list is important "evidence" to a world that undervalues narrative genres for documenting violence.

Another impulse brands complicity at the highest level by Presidents Lucas García, Ríos Montt, and Mejía Víctores, whose regimes authorized violence and organized the command structure and death squads that carried it out (Montejo and Akab' 1992, 9, 28–31, 49, 63–68, 91–96). The remembering of victims and protagonists by name becomes a powerful reply to the hopelessness of torture victims who were routinely forced to name "accomplices."

Reading Autoethnography in Dialogue with Foreign Ethnography

How might one read the Maya testimonial genre in dialogue with foreign interpretive ethnography—in this case, with my descriptions from those who stayed in San Andrés, a community far to the west and south of the Kuchumatans? Thematically, the accounts have much in common, though the intensity of militarization contrasted in the two regions. Both deal with existential dilemmas, with the fragmentation of community life, loyalty, and trust, and with the agony of witnessing brutal physical violence when one cannot intercede. Yet in other ways there are important differences in experience and genre.

Montejo's testimonies come in the form of sustained first-person narratives of torture, survival, and escape. Their immediacy is maintained by the erasure of the interview process and the omission of any metanarrative, abstraction, or analysis that might have continued after his introductory remarks.[23] As I have already argued, that is not to say there is no overall argument, for clearly this work makes the strongest possible case for the need to dismantle the terrorist state by demilitarizing the countryside, disbanding the civil patrols, giving refugees the opportunity to return to their communities and fields.

Reflexively, however, the compiler is submerged in this variant of the testimonial genre as just another voice in a collage of different positions and experiences. As interviewer and editor, Montejo took great care to maintain the distinctive language practices of each speaker in the Spanish edition and to include enough information to clarify their backgrounds. By contrast,

Montejo's personal narrative of exile, *Testimony: Death of a Guatemalan Village*, includes an independent narrative voice that more actively intervenes to explain issues, such as indoctrination, to a readership that may lack direct knowledge of rural community life.

These testimonies address the issue of survivorship by the repeated twinning of the speaker's own surprising survival with their companions' terrible deaths in the same situation. Thus, readers watch the arbitrariness of violence and survival. Hulum B'aq saw his connection with torture victims as he was on patrol duty:

> One day, when it was my turn to take care of the La Laguna bridge with my group, the soldiers came down to the bridge from Netón bringing three peasants who were all tied up. These three indigenous peasants looked so poor, just like us, the patrollers. We already knew the soldiers went down to the bridge at night to kill people they brought from different places and then they threw the bodies in the river to make them disappear (Montejo and Akab' 1992, 73–74).

Kaxh Maal-Ya's testimony tells how he and his younger brother Kaxhin were taken prisoner by their civil patrol for being absent when a military patrol made a visit to their community. Feeling they were going to be killed at the regional base, the older brother convinced Kaxhin to join him in an escape attempt, only to lose his younger brother at the base's perimeter fence while they were being pursued by the guards. Tumaxh K'em tells of a group of families, fleeing to Mexico, who were intercepted by their civil patrol and returned to the army base. Circumstances allowed the narrator to escape, but his neighbor Jesús was too weak from his beatings to follow. Shortly thereafter, another man was killed in Tumaxh's place. In both escapes, the survivors felt a moral compulsion, before fleeing across the border, to get in touch with the families of their counterparts and to tell them the sorrowful news behind the disappearance of their loved ones.

Miraculously amidst all the violence, these survivors' immediate families are reconstituted on the other side of the border, creating the possibility for a constructive future in the midst of personal tragedy. The book's final section presents children's fragmentary accounts of almost identical transitions from terror to safety,[24] and begs the question of the impact of state terrorism on them. To fill some of the silences from their stories, Montejo includes children's drawings, which give stark visual form to memories of soldiers shooting civilians and burning their homes.

Despite the shocking details, there are striking silences and absences in these testimonies: memories of what it meant to torture others not just to be a victim, children's enduring experiences of violence in other situations after their escape, refugee families both reunited and broken by the experience, and the dilemmas experienced by Mayas in exile that render their stories open ended and unfinished.[25] These silences no doubt reflect editorial choices but, as Montejo (1993a) explains, they also betray the great anxiety, vulnerability, and fear of strangers—especially of those who asked questions or probed memories of violence—that refugees, including these contributors, felt in the camps.

The collage of first-person accounts, rather than a voice-of-God expository style, leaves more of the work of analysis to the reader and makes the collection all the more powerful for those who have not directly experienced state terrorism and its fragmentation of everyday life. Yet, in remaining true to the genre, the lack of a narrator leaves the civil patrollers' and ex-soldier's silences about their own violence as unfinished business that can pass without being directly challenged and interrogated from an external, critical point of view. Nor do we hear from the ex-guerrillas who joined the flow of refugees to Mexico.

In contrast to Montejo's testimonies, the San Andrés accounts I collected during five months of field work in 1989 were much more fragmented and veiled in the naming of protagonists and victims. Most likely this is because people were still directly subject to terror tactics and systematic political monitoring when I returned to Guatemala to talk to the families I had been close to in the 1970s. It is also possible that people had not yet learned how to tell their stories as testimonies. They had less direct contact with human-rights groups than international refugees and had undoubtedly been exposed to the long-standing hostility on the part of the army and plantation owners, who held that human rights discourse was inherently "subversive."

In San Andrés, I was warned by friends that the local military commissioner would routinely monitor my behavior and that I should make no attempts to talk to youths or former soldiers. Initially I decided not to pursue the topic of violence out of concern for everyone's safety; in the end, I was compelled to deal with memories of the civil war because of the constant, if fragmentary, references to *la violencia* in public discourse. There were private stories of close escapes and of witnessing the disappearances of others—another version of twinning—, and many accounts of unidentified bodies on the highways. The denouement of exile was replaced in the narratives from San Andrés with a sense that "the violence, it always continues." There was no exit in sight at the end of the decade.

Like Montejo, I found the civil war bred terrible uncertainty, all sorts of survival tactics in the face of military and guerrilla intervention in community affairs, and the fear that violence would be internalized as individuals were tempted to take advantage of community divisions and antagonisms for personal profit or to settle old scores. For a number of reasons, San Andrés weathered four years of terror in the early 1980s with some killings, the short guerrilla occupation of the town, and the militarization of the region, but without major massacres. As the last chapter related, what weighed most heavily on townspeople was the public secret of a nearby clandestine cemetery where the army executed civilians. People were also aware of a smaller clandestine cemetery—this one the result of guerrilla killings—located outside a distant politicized hamlet.

Another tragic consequence of the violence was the constant fear on everyone's mind that neighbors or perhaps even relatives would denounce them to either the military or guerrillas. In effect, one had to rely on people one could not trust in order to survive the violence. Silence, strategic evasiveness, and ambiguity were used as verbal tactics for almost a decade by townspeople who felt that one could not know for certain the allegiances of those with whom they routinely dealt.

My published account, "Interpreting *la Violencia* in Guatemala: Shapes of Mayan Silence and Resistance" (1993) began in conventional academic expository style with the insurgency/counterinsurgency war as the context for understanding the impact of violence on civilians in San Andrés. Although my analysis masks the interactive interview process that accounted for my knowledge of the town, the challenge of representing the violence compelled me to shift to a more polyphonic text. From interviews, I quoted memories of daily life during the conflict to represent the immediacy and fragmenting experience of the violence for individuals and families. Given the political situation, however, the speakers remained unidentified in the text.

My analysis argued that townspeople survived the silence imposed by the corrosion of trust in others in part by revitalizing traditionalist magical realist narratives of transforming selves to address the haunting issue of interpersonal betrayal. Departing from social scientific conventions to make my case, I quoted a long, magical-realist narrative—which on the face of it had nothing to do with war but in practice had everything to do with the adversities it generated—and discussed Maya hermeneutics to show that realist fragments were only one of a variety of ways Mayas used to represent the effect of violence on their lives. The social relations that mediated the process of revitalization were striking, if ironic. Thus, like Montejo, I found that Maya culture—both in what we would consider its realist and magical realist ways of representing the world—was used by particular individuals to address the existential dilemmas and human costs of a world spinning out of control. One sees here a convergence between the ways testimonial and ethnographic accounts gain their authority and make their cases to readers.

In my ethnographic account, I had always wondered where to make space for my own presence and subjectivity as an outsider who had worked in Guatemala at various times for more than twenty years and returned there to continue research because it was "safer" than my other research site in the Peruvian Andes, which, at the time, was under siege by the Shining Path guerrilla movement.[26] Finally, with the urging of Begoña Aretxaga, I decided to add a self-reflexive epilogue through which I explored the role of anthropologists as witnesses to human-rights abuses, the issue of ethnography as a

dialogical project, and the fact that the U.S. political and military involvement in Guatemala was part of the problem. I considered the possibility that
the silences I found were produced in part by my presence not only the
trauma of the violence.[27] The epilogue also gave me the opportunity to note
that I too honored certain silences and ambiguities as someone who, like
others in the community in the late 1980s, had been caught in a nighttime
military sweep and knew more than she could reveal at the time in public
forums. My experience of state terror—though in no way comparable to
those who lived through the worst of the crisis or those who have had to
learn to survive prolonged periods of low-intensity warfare—had a fundamental impact on my own understandings and the themes I have elaborated
in writing about the impact of militarization on civilian lives.

I suspect that the silences imposed on San Andrés by the civil war left
community members hungry for precisely the kinds of accounts that Montejo and his collaborators produced to make sense of their own experiences.[28]
But, certainly through the early 1990s, the question was whether it was dangerous to be in possession of such books in a country where military sweeps
and political monitoring were still common. Thus, for some years these testimonies had a wide readership outside the country and little distribution
within.

In publishing first-person accounts of violent displacement, Montejo appropriated many of the conventions denounced by Pan-Maya critics of anthropology: the use of ethnographic interviews and autobiographical accounts that underscore individualism and divisions within the Maya
community. Yet his multiple framings, denunciations of racism, focus on
multiple subject positions, and inclusion of Maya narratives that transcend
the conventions of realist testimony may make the collection highly relevant
for the current process of healing and revitalization.

The framing of the collection to stress a subjectivity shaped by Maya
hermeneutics fits in with Montejo's other works, written throughout this period, which stress Maya cultural struggles and their distinctive moral discourse. Across these works, Montejo argues for the resilience of Maya culture in the face of fragmenting conflict and asserts that the experience of
violent displacement is yet another source of Pan-Mayanism. For their part,
Pan-Maya activists in Guatemala see this work as an important aspect of
their struggle for revindication.

Perhaps it is a hopeful sign of the times that the Spanish version of Montejo's *Testimony: Death of a Guatemalan Village* was published in Guatemala in 1993 with great acclaim and *Brevísima Relación Testimonial* will
be republished soon by the University of San Carlos Press in Guatemala.
Personal testimonies of the violence during the civil war in other parts of the
country can now be found at bookstores and open-air regional book fairs in
Guatemala, and Guatemalans are beginning to read Maya publications at

universities where the next generations of national leaders and professionals are being trained.

In recent years, Montejo has been able to return to Guatemala to speak at public forums organized by Mayanists, such as the 1994 *Primer Congreso de la Educación Maya* and the 1996 *Primer Congreso de Estudios Mayas.* Montejo's trips to his hometown, Jacaltenango, to work with others to build a library for adults and children represent still another encouraging sign. That he and others traveling through the highlands by bus and car have to fear for their lives because travelers are now being routinely threatened, robbed, kidnapped, and killed by unidentified gunmen only shows that violence has taken new twists and turns in the late 1990s.

Six

Interrogating Official History

As GUATEMALA MOVES from open warfare toward peace, one might ask if the Pan-Maya movement deploys cultural narratives not only to promote political change but also to heal and remake the world for the country's indigenous people. If so, it is important to ask why the movement has been as preoccupied with history critiquing as history making. Is this esoteric scholarship or something designed to contribute to more broadly based goals? Chapters six and seven introduce a variety of well-known Maya public intellectuals—Luis Enrique Sam Colop, Kab'lajuuj Tijax, and members of the linguistics group Oxlajuuj Keej Maya' Ajtz'iib', among them, B'alam and Waykan. Their activities illustrate Pan-Maya history writing and the practice of reading historical chronicles in study groups. Like multiculturalist movements elsewhere, Pan-Mayanists challenge national histories that exclude them and utilize history to build a collective sense of nation.

Elaine Scarry's (1985, 15) description of torture as an "unmaking of the world"—through fragmentation, the creation of divided selves, and physical destruction—strikes many observers as particularly insightful for situations of state terrorism. For her, a crucial act of resistance becomes the representation of pain—an elusive but vitally important experience to communicate. Echoing these concerns, the public intellectuals of the Pan-Maya movement are reweaving the story of "unmaking" into a narrative of cultural resurgence in writings on history, resistance, and rights.

It is not surprising that Mayanist commentators find a troubled past and room for a veiled presentism[1] in their revisionist histories. Maya historical sensibilities have been shaped not only by the experience of marginalization—that is, by "not being taken into account," as was the frustration in the early 1970s—but also by the war, which introduced the threat of being labeled a subversive or a collaborator and thus deserving torture and death. This stigmatizing language was used in public forums well into the 1990s to stifle social critique.

In 1993 President Serrano Elias, with support from elements of the army's high command, attempted an authoritarian takeover of his own government, instituted media censorship, and attempted to dissolve Congress, the Supreme Court, and the Constitution. This unsuccessful move toward formal authoritarianism once again reminded Guatemalans of the fragility of democracy, reestablished in a very tentative and contingent way in 1986 after thirty years of repressive military rule. A surprising alliance of business elites, union groups, students, and indigenous leaders convinced the army that such a regime would lack international and national legitimacy. The takeover's failure demonstrated the powerful fluidity of interests and factions in Guatemala and growing citizen involvement in national politics.

The subsequent selection of Ramiro de León Carpio, the national human-rights advocate, as president sparked hopefulness; but public confidence that he would confront the grave economic problems faced by the country was soon eroded. By 1994 he had become an apologist for counterinsurgency as a continuing national military policy, despite (or perhaps it is precisely because of) strong evidence that guerrillas had only a minor political presence in the countryside. The military appeared to be in control of national politics.

In this volatile political environment, it was extremely dangerous for Guatemalan commentators to write about contemporary political violence in any detail. Shortly before the takeover imposed media censorship, national newspapers printed reminders of intense political intolerance. They covered the trial and conviction of the soldiers (but not their commanding officers) who brutally killed Myrna Mack, a Ladina anthropologist on the Left, who was writing about internal refugees at the time of her death. Even as the newly democratized courts exposed past human-rights violations, the military used the national press to threaten its critics. They denounced Ricardo Falla, a Ladino priest from one of Guatemala's notable families, who as an anthropologist had written on indigenous resistance and most recently on human rights abuses in the highlands (1978a; 1994). After falsely accusing Falla of being a guerrilla leader, the military confiscated his field notes and marriage and baptism records. In addition, Rosalina Tuyúc, the outspoken Maya leader of CONAVIGUA, which had turned its efforts to exposing forced military recruitment, was branded a "guerrilla" by military officials. Although calling someone a communist had lost much of its sting in the rest of the world, this was not the case in Guatemala. The practice continued of public threats and violence to neutralize social criticism and punish activists. As one general put it, "as subversives [they] deserve whatever comes their way" (*Siglo Veintiuno*, March 1993).

This chapter outlines the dilemmas that Mayas living in Guatemala faced in remaking their world and asserting their presence in civil society during the early 1990s, when disappearances and repression continued yet mass killings had abated. For Pan-Mayanists, the issue was how to represent politics in an environment that sought to silence social commentary. This chapter offers a close reading of Luis Enrique Sam Colop's commentary on history, colonialism, and racism in Guatemala, which was written for release at the 1991 Segundo Encuentro Continental and distributed through a number of Pan-Maya organizations. The substance of his historical argument has been used in forums and adult education programs throughout the country.

Sam Colop is a prominent K'iche' Maya social commentator, linguist, lawyer, and writer in his forties. Originally from the activist agrarian hamlet Xecam outside the municipal center of Cantel, he joined other students who had exhausted local educational opportunities. They commuted on crowded public buses to Quetzaltenango, Guatemala's second largest city, which had a long history of indigenous commerce and politics. While finishing his law degree at the University of San Carlos in the early 1980s, Sam Colop (1983) wrote a thesis on national education policy and Maya nationhood. He was also recognized in his youth as a writer in Guatemala's largely Ladino literary circles. Sam Colop served as the director of the Maya archives at CEDIM in 1992–93, earned a Ph.D. in Maya linguistics at SUNY-Buffalo in 1994, and currently consults for the Academy of Maya Languages of Guatemala (ALMG), the Center for Regional Investigations of Mesoamerica (CIRMA), and a variety of legal reform projects, in addition to conducting his legal practice. Marking the postwar democratic opening, in 1996 he began to write a regular editorial column, *Ucha'xik*, in *Prensa Libre*, one of the country's leading dailies. The dangers of the early 1990s created another world.

Sam Colop's early essays were provocative in those years because they took Guatemalan racism head on, articulating Maya critiques of colonialism and signs of its persistence. He argued that racism and assimilationist policies are foundational forms of political violence, that cultural imperialism within was just as important to combat as imperialism without. His work reflected the Maya intellectual practice of trespassing disciplinary boundaries and divisions of knowledge in Western research. As the overview of recent politics suggests, Sam Colop was compelled by political circumstances to phrase his argument obliquely.

The Project of Recapturing the Racist Past

Public intellectuals active in promoting Maya resurgence were well aware of the ways the past was used to legitimize current social arrangements in Guatemala. "Official" national histories published by cultural elites, foreign scholars, and (interestingly enough) the Guatemalan military reappeared in school texts, newspaper articles, and advertisements. Maya teachers, parents, and community leaders on the periphery of the revitalization movement—not to speak of those directly involved—angrily complained about the national obsession with the indigenous defeat at the Spanish conquest and the virtual erasure of indigenous peoples as historical agents after their subjugation. Just mentioning Tecún Umán, the tragic hero in national mythology, made many Mayas livid.

Nationalist histories, such as the multivolume *Historia General de Guatemala*, were criticized for still being able to tell the story of the Guatemalan nation without systematically foregrounding Mayas as interpreters of the past. The issue was not a lack of Maya professional historians able to undertake detailed archival analysis since this has not been the primary focus of national history in Guatemala. Rather, academic history has formed an eclectic and fascinating genre that includes colonial chronicles, family genealogies, wide-ranging surveys of national political development, and polemical denunciations of capitalism. In many conventional histories, Mayas represented a past that could be covered quickly since it left few traces and had no historical future. Or Mayas were imagined as a class with a uniform history of exploitation.

Pan-Mayanists resented (and resent) their commodification and folklorization in national popular culture, the admiration of their civilization as Maya "ruins," and the transformation of their culture into a timeless tradition of brilliant hand-woven fabrics. Exalting Maya culture for the benefit of entrepreneurs and tourists was made all the more feasible by their constructed absence from the historical time of nation building and modernization.

Given this situation, it was not surprising that Mayas concerned with revitalization were beginning to formulate their own histories. One genre was contemporary essay, gaining its energy and authority not from focused archival work but rather from a juxtaposition of historical materials with contemporary scholarship, journalism, and national policy to produce a telling collage that exemplified the fragmenting persistence of corrosive racism in current events and commentators. One can see the Maya essayist taking the position of "piling wreckage upon wreckage" to condemn history's effect (Benjamin 1969, 257).

Enrique Sam Colop's programmatic essay "Jub'aqtun Omay Kuchum K'aslemal; Cinco Siglos de Encubrimiento" was published in monograph form for international and national distribution by the Maya publisher Cholsamaj.[2] Sam Colop sought to identify arguments that negate the humanity of specific segments of the country's population and legitimize violent political action against them. He made the case for Guatemalan racism as an accumulation of the historical discourses of "muting," "invasion," "the Indian," and "twentieth-century colonialism."[3]

Following the lead of Eduardo Galeano (1986, 115–16) and Beatriz Pastor (1988: 4–64), Sam Colop replaced the heroic language of the "discovery" of the New World with a discussion of the concealment or muting of indigenous culture by Spaniards who because of their own dominating worldviews were quick to condemn but unable to understand New World cultures in their own right. Muting captures the marginalization of indigenous communities but rejects arguments that European culture replaced local culture through forced assimilation. Rather, this language is used to suggest that those resisting domination employed strategic assimilation to buffer their cultural systems from the full weight of Spanish control. These writers argue that words such as *discovery* and *encounter* only obscure the effects of European expansionism. They criticize the language of "conquest" for its totalizing implication that denies indigenous culture and resistance. The term these Latin American scholars prefer is *invasion*, which conjures an image of territorial violation instead of the heroism of total conquest and gives the outcome critical indeterminacy.

Sam Colop wanted to create space for a public reassessment of racism as violence. He drew on the literary critics Tzventan Todorov (1984) and Beatriz Pastor (1988), who reveal the ideological nature of the sixteenth-century Spanish chronicles that recounted the initial European-indigenous contact in the New World. These critics are struck by the chronicles' disempowering double bind: *"If Columbus recognizes that the natives have language, then he refuses to accept it as different; if he recognizes that it is different, then he refuses to accept it as language"* (Sam Colop 1991, 12, emphasis mine). This paradigm justified violence to civilize the barbarous and to enforce Spanish terms of economic and moral exchange. Sam Colop explains the implications of this reasoning for New World populations:

> Columbus also perceives the natives with ambiguity: on one hand, he considers them equal and identical to himself and for this reason believes he understands their languages. In this respect, Columbus argues that the natives do not know how to speak their own languages well (Pastor 1988, 77–88). The perception of equals permits Columbus to propose a politics of assimilation that for him implies an "interchange" in which "the Spaniards give religion and take gold" (Todorov 1984, 45). The other perception considers them different and, in consequence, inferior. This permits him to propose his later objective. When Columbus becomes aware that gold is not abundant, he articulates a discourse that justifies slavery: dividing the natives into innocents and idolaters, into peaceful and warlike. The innocent and peaceful are subject to his power and the others to slavery. Columbus suggests that ships bringing livestock to America return to Spain full of slaves. (Sam Colop 1991, 11)

Sam Colop seeks to undermine the authoritativeness of accounts based on first-person observation. A key revelation is the constructed or fictional quality of Spanish chronicles of the invasion—a quality that has been accessible to all close readers of such colonial observers as Christopher Columbus, Hernán Cortés, Bernal Díaz, Francisco López de Gómara, Bartolomé de las Casas, and Pedro de Alvarado. He notes omissions, additions, and distortions, and shows how accounts created post hoc justifications of Spanish violence. His analysis dwells on the individualized self-interested subjectivity of the chroniclers. Citing the studies of Ramón Iglesia (1942), Lesley Byrd Simpson (1964), and Pastor (1988), Sam Colop illustrates the ways competitiveness, personal animosities, and individual biases colored accounts as writers attempted to enhance their own prestige and discredit other observers.

Sam Colop wonders not only about the motives behind the original authorship of the chronicles but also about the reasons for their use in more recent histories. What, he asks, would cause scholars in the present to continue to promote the dissemination of these chronicles as neutral windows for viewing the national past? In Guatemala, major twentieth-century Ladino research centers and historians—such as the Guatemalan Society for Geography and History (cf. Díaz del Castillo 1933), Luis Cardoza y Aragón (1965), and Francis Polo Sifontes (1986)—have treated these representations of the past as historical truth. They have republished colonial accounts with admiring introductions, excerpted them in their own writings, and justified colonial prejudices or left them unchallenged. As a result, sixteenth-century descriptions of indigenous people by López de Gómara as "stupid, savages, lacking feelings, vice ridden, sodomites, liars, ingrates, tale tellers, drunks"; Díaz's obsession with their "cannibalism"; Oviedo y Valdes's treatment of them as inanimate objects; and Ortiz's judgment that they were "stupid . . . ungrateful, unable to learn . . . without beards . . . and without art or industry" lived on (Sam Colop 1991, 14, 17, 23).[4] Outside Guatemala, such epithets are no longer taken at face value in the academic world. Rather, they are examined for the political logic of their constructions of "self" and "other" during periods of Western expansion and colonialism.

The theme central to twentieth-century versions of colonialist discourse is national unity to be achieved through Hispanization, *mestizaje* (biological blending), and homogenization. "*If Mayas are the 'other' then they are inferior; if they are not the 'other' then they can be assimilated*" (1991, 36, my emphasis) is the modern echo of Columbus. Sam Colop notes that today's journalists, historians, and politicians use this logic to argue that national history should tell the story of that fusion:

In 1990, *La Hora* newspaper (Aug. 11, 3, 29) argued against primary school instruction in Maya languages, based on what David Vela said: that these languages "are stuck in the middle of the sixteenth century and are *relatively poor* in expressing contexts and present values. There are many languages, and they are not mutually intelligible. . . ." Likewise, David Vela warned that one should "not carry enthusiasm for indigenous languages too far, even less be interested in studying them, because this is a *dangerous political game against national unity and is also bad for the destiny of our Indians*. . . ." The *La Hora* columnist continued from there: "The esteemed teacher sticks his finger in the wound. Unfortunately or fortunately, in reality *our Indians* were very backward when the Spaniards came. . . . [Many] wanted to cheat *our Indians* and take advantage of them, flattering them with the fiction they had superior culture. . . ." (1991, 35, emphasis Sam Colop).

Sam Colop's analysis of this column continues:

First, these statements show the continuing *encomienda*[5] spirit. They think of Mayas as property that must be protected. Second, the idea that instruction in Maya languages is "harmful" for the speakers is evidence of sixteenth-century thought that Indians only have those rights the colonizer deems convenient to give them. Third, the concept of "national unity" is what Carlos Fuentes calls the Legal *Patria* but not the Sovereign *Patria*. The Legal *Patria* denies Mayas their rights to language, culture, and self-determination—collective rights recognized by the Universal Declaration of Human Rights and international pacts through the United Nations (1991, 35–36).

This view ideologically opposes policies, such as bilingual education, that might slow assimilation on the grounds they undermine the nation-state. People, who despite the pressure to assimilate maintain their cultural distinctiveness, become folkloric exemplars of another time rather than modern citizens expected to exercise individual rights in contemporary civil society. Thus, nation building, the quintessence of modernity, refuses to recognize the contemporary relevance of cultural difference. This political logic produces a double bind that denies Mayas and their culture a *political* future (Sam Colop 1991, 29–35).

Sam Colop concludes his essay with a discussion of resistance, rights, and alternatives to colonialist ideology:

> For Native Nations of the Continent, 1992 signifies 500 Gregorian years of physical, cultural, and political resistance. Physical resistance is manifested in the survival of the Native Nations; resistance against cultural domination is manifested in the maintenance of Amerindian cultures and languages. Resistance against colonial domination is manifested by the struggle for the legitimate recovery of political, economic, cultural, and social rights (1991, 36–37).

In his view, the sixteenth-century Spanish priest Bartolomé de las Casas, who denounced colonial violence against indigenous people offered an interesting model: a plural society in which the only necessary relation between culturally distinctive groups would be the diplomatic-administrative machinery of the state.

> Historically, Bartolomé de las Casas is one of the great exceptions [to colonial intellectualism]. Although initially he was in agreement with the rest on the politics of assimilation, at the end of his life he insisted that only diplomatic-administrative relations existed between natives and Spaniards. Both peoples, Las Casas noted, are members of different states with different cultures (1991, 37).

With purposeful irony, Sam Colop chooses Spain as the modern exemplar:

> The Sovereign *Patria* can only be pluralist. Today Spain serves as an example of this process; it has not disappeared as a political entity with the recognition of its autonomous communities or its bilingual regions (1991, 36).

The Universal Declaration of Human Rights and United Nations proposals add a contemporary language of transcendent rights and self-determination for cultural minorities. Sam Colop observes that Germany, Russia, and the Vatican have admitted responsibility for past violence in other areas of the world, and in some instances even offered indemnization to survivors.[6] The *nunca más* for Guatemala would involve an international discussion of complicity—including Spaniards, North Americans, and others—and indemnization through Mayanist organizations working to actualize revitalization.

What is striking in Sam Colop's essay is his synthesis of colonial history with the languages of rights and pluralism from international sources and from his legal training in Guatemala. His goal is to reveal the power relations and paternalism ingrained in Guatemalan political practice: that rights are accorded to Mayas as Ladino society wishes rather than seen as inherently belonging to individuals and groups who will exercise them according to their own wishes. This is the explicit legacy of the past, the liberal moral of his analysis.

But additional dimensions of this analysis are muted if we only pay attention to the universalizing language of rights.

Relevance of Colonialist Structures of Representation for the Present

Sam Colop's project parallels recent multiculturalist challenges to U.S. educational and research establishments. In this sense, he is part of a transnational movement that has challenged established canons by questioning how the production of knowledge in education, government, and mass media politically marginalizes certain sectors of the population. Multicultural historical critiques fight a presentist battle.[7] They hope to lay the groundwork for transformations in the way nations represent and conceive of themselves. In education, for instance, reforms inspired by these critiques question the veiled prejudices children are taught as authoritative knowledge and the limits they are given for legitimate claims on national society. The substance of school curriculums and languages of public instruction are at issue.

It is important to see Sam Colop's analysis as firmly grounded in Guatemalan culture and politics. His view interrogates the invasion's savagery and discusses the genocidal decimation of an estimated 70 million of the 80 million inhabitants of the New World in the sixteenth century. One of Sam Colop's major sources, Todorov (1984, 133–45), excerpts jarring descriptions of Spanish cruelty from colonial chronicles—and judges the invaders responsible for the consequences of their actions—as they viciously murdered and enslaved indigenous people, exploited them through heartless labor conditions, demanded crushing amounts of tribute from struggling communities, and understood epidemics of European diseases as effective weapons against the infidels.

To drive his case home, Sam Colop draws on early indigenous accounts of the invasion. The Florentine Codex narrates Alvarado's slaughter of unsuspecting Aztec soldiers during a celebration at the Main Temple:

> [The Spaniards] ran in among the dancers, forcing their way to the place where the drums were played. They attacked the man who was drumming and cut off his arms. They cut off his head, and it rolled across the floor.
>
> They attacked all the celebrants, stabbing them, spearing them, striking them with their swords. They attacked some of them from behind, and these fell instantly to the ground with their entrails hanging out. Others they beheaded: they cut off their heads, or split their heads into pieces.
>
> They struck others in the shoulders, and their arms were torn from their bodies. They wounded some in the thigh and some in the calf. They slashed others in the abdomen, and their entrails all spilled to the ground. Some attempted to run away, but their intestines dragged as they ran; they seemed to tangle their feet in their own entrails. No matter how they tried to save themselves, they could find no escape (Léon-Portilla 1962, 74–76 as quoted in Sam Colop 1991, 25).

The "Black Legend" of Spanish cruelty, however, has been challenged by revisionists. Many scholars point to the importance of contextualizing Spanish actions in terms of sixteen-century European conventions for religious and political sanction, which were brutal and sadistic by today's standards. Critics further argue that to generalize early accounts of atrocities to other regions and centuries in Latin America misses important transformations in Spanish and indigenous societies that occurred with the emergence of a hybrid colonial society. Both groups had to adjust to the population collapse that followed the unwitting initial introduction of infectious diseases against which indigenous populations had no effective defense (cf. Klor de Alva n.d.).

Another revisionist voice, William Maltby (1968), argues that the Black Legend of Spanish cruelty, treacherousness, and greed was elaborated by the English for their own political ends. Sixteenth- and seventeenth-century English historians and pamphleteers eagerly cited examples of Spanish violence from chroniclers such as Las Casas, whose work was first translated into English in 1583.[8]

The English transformed these accounts into anti-Hispanic propaganda to arouse English Protestant hatred of Iberian Catholics; to express the resentment of Spanish interference in the political affairs of France, Italy, and Germany; and to personalize English-Spanish tensions during two hundred years of intermittent hostilities. Maltby argues it is vital to trace the politics that governed the repeated revival of the legend of national depravity, given that Spaniards were no more cruel than others involved in empire-building and did not pursue a premeditated policy of genocide. The English—clearly it would be important to specify who and when—wove this antagonistic imagery of national character into a discourse of contrast and opposition that became a central element in their consciousness of nation (1968, 18, 135).[9]

In retelling rather than debunking the Black Legend, Sam Colop would seem to be writing against the grain of current scholarship and in tension with Guatemalan historians such as Francis Polo Sifontes (1986, 57), who argues a historical relativist line. A closer look at Sam Colop's treatment, however, reveals a different goal for his historical project: the unmasking and critique of colonial structures of representation of "self" and "other." His commentary pursues a specific angle: Alvarado's violence toward indigenous populations when the Spanish invaded Guatemala in 1524 and the displacement of blame for their deaths onto the indigenous leaders themselves.

He quotes from Alvarado's letters, which recounted victories over the K'iche's and were used by Cortés in reports to the Spanish Crown:

> And seeing that by fire and sword I might bring these people to the service of His Majesty, *I determined to burn the chiefs*[10] *who, at the time that I wanted to burn them, told me, as it will appear in their confessions, that they were the ones who had ordered the war against me and were the ones also who made it*. They told me about the way they were to do so, to burn me in the city, and that with this thought (in their minds) they had brought me there, and that they had ordered their vassals not to come and give obedience to our Lord the Emperor, nor help us, nor do anything else that was right. And as I knew them to have such a bad disposition towards the service of His Majesty, and to insure the good and peace of this land, I burnt them, and sent to burn the town and to destroy it, for it is a very strong and dangerous place, that more resembles a robber's stronghold than a city (translation by Mackie 1924, 62–63, emphasis mine; cf. Sam Colop 1991: 19–20).[11]

Sam Colop singles out Alvarado as "the cruel and ruthless prototype of the 'conqueror'" for his actions in Mexico and Guatemala (1991, 19). According to sixteenth-century Spanish accounts, he massacred unarmed populations and torched towns; raped, kidnapped, and intimidated those from whom he demanded tribute; and executed other Maya leaders (*ajpopi'*)—including Kaji' Imox and the son of Oxib' Kej, Kiyawit Kawoq—by hanging. His policy was one of "*tierra arrasada con sangre y fuego*" (scorched earth by blood and fire) (1991, 19–21).

The fact of Alvarado's cruelty is not the only issue that stands out. Just as significant for Sam Colop is the driving logic of his brutality:

> There is an elaboration of certain materials in Alvarado's discourse. Note three key elements: (1) Alvarado's determination to burn the rulers alive, (2) the rulers' confessions under Alvarado's compulsion, and (3) the confessions as justification for the burning to death of the *ajpopi'*. Alvarado manipulates these elements so that

the K'iche' leaders are responsible for their own misfortune, for not wanting to submit themselves. In this way, Alvarado's responsibility is less important than the victims' guilt. This framing of the discourse goes beyond the facts. Alvarado, according to Recinos (1952, 77), has the common practice of "bringing up other people's *possible intentions* and imposing punishment before an offense takes material form." (Sam Colop 1991, 21)

The striking connection for me is with Elaine Scarry's (1985) theorization of the archetypal torturer who sets the stage so that the blame falls on the victim who therefore merits punishment, rather than on the instigator of violence. A variety of historical themes in Sam Colop's writings resonate with this preoccupation: the forced confessions of the Maya rulers that could not alter the inevitable, the power of language to stigmatize, the concern with collective dehumanization, and the legitimation of violence as redemptive. Scarry sees torture as a crisis of power, language, and communication:

> The physical pain [of torture] is so incontestably real that it seems to confer its quality of "uncontestable reality" on that power that has brought it into being. It is, of course, precisely because the reality of that power is so highly contestable, the regime so unstable, that torture is being used. (1985, 27)

Sam Colop cites Spanish and Maya chronicles of the invasion to document the new regime of power and its brutality/vulnerability.

The unmaking of the Maya world involved the tragedy of coerced (or imputed) confessions in which the victim—such as the Maya *ajpopi'*—"shifts into being the agent of his own annihilation" (1985, 47). Coerced confessions raised the specter of betrayal even though the stripping of "all control over, and therefore responsibility for his world, his words, and his body" effectively moots any such judgment (1985, 47). The Spanish torturer sought the displacement of blame in order to deny responsibility for physical violence. As Scarry observed:

> It is not merely that his power makes him blind, nor that his power is accompanied by blindness, nor even that his power required blindness; it is, instead, quite simply that his blindness, his willed amorality, *is* his power, or a large part of it (1985, 57).

Sam Colop's extensive quotes from Maya chronicles focus on Spanish brutality—on agency and damage—to represent the experience of pain.

From an anthropological point of view, Scarry offers many insights into colonial structures of representation even as her striking imagery reduces torture to a unitary discourse of power and pain, the product of the interpersonal relation of the torturer and tortured. One must step outside the torture chamber to see the wider cultural context of violence and to discover that the unmaking and making of the world is a continual issue for subordinates in repressive regimes. Sam Colop's style—his strategic pause after describing Spanish and Maya accounts of torture and executions—purposefully leaves to the reader the task of contemplating the pain of violent physical extinction for the Maya rulers. His analytical work shifts to another issue: the political psychology of domination and racism.

Concealed, yet waiting to be discovered in Sam Colop's essay, is an important lesson about the logic of terror that blamed its early victims in the sixteenth century. In Guatemala, as elsewhere, virulent hate speech—whether blatant or indirect—has often rendered violence logical, appropriate, and just. Sam Colop attunes the reader to reciprocity and morality, asserted *and* negated in accounts of Alvarado's execution/slaughter of Maya leaders. The focus on torture-confession-punishment signals reverberations between the sixteenth and twentieth centuries that Mayas found important as the war wound down. Torture and execution were common practices during Guatemala's civil war, when tens of thousands of civilians were killed. Those in structural positions of power—be they Spanish invaders or Guatemalan military officers—found ways of absolving themselves of responsibility for their violence against others.[12]

Maya historical commentaries constitute a presentism that challenges the civic nationalism and authoritativeness of official histories written by Ladinos. Enrique Sam Colop's work argues that racism operates through transforming analogies of sameness and difference. The creation of counter-histories involves a multiculturalist rereading of accounts of the past and an appraisal of the existential dilemmas that continue in the often turbulent present. As I have suggested, his work can be read on several levels for its analysis of domination and the scope of effective resistance.

Selective Appropriations of Latin American Social Criticism

There are diverse others in this history making. Sam Colop draws inspiration from European and Latin American literary critics and social commentators. But his appropriations are cautious given the nature of his project. Eduardo Galeano—an anti-imperialist social critic who has lived in Uruguay, Argentina, and Spain and is best known for *The Open Veins of Latin America* (1973)—is useful for his discussion of the conquest as concealment. In *El Descubrimiento de América que Todavía No Fue y Otros Escritos* (1986), he writes with special intensity about indigenous struggles, human-rights abuses, and government censorship of free expression and Latin American writers. Interestingly, he concludes the book with a ray of hope: with Spain, after confronting the cultural violence of its authoritarian past, rediscovering its own internal cultural and linguistic pluralism as it struggles for democracy in the present. Suddenly, instead of "the Spaniards," we see Castilians, Basques, Catalans, Andalusians, and Galicians. Galeano's lesson from his years of exile in Spain was a more nuanced colonial critique that acknowledges the dialectics of identity construction for both indigenous peoples and Europeans.

Sam Colop made a place for this complicating irony when he dealt with twentieth-century Spain as a multicultural society in his earlier writings (1983). For Pan-Mayanists, the colonizing other does not have to be frozen in history to play the role of the European dominator and the progenitor of the Ladino. His observation parallels the current wave of revaluing European cultural and linguistic pluralism that has accompanied the creation of the European Community in the 1990s (Rajasingham 1993; *New York Times*, May 3, 1993). Pan-Mayanist intellectuals, like Sam Colop, have found two lines of multicultural identification: ties with the originating peoples of the New World and with linguistic minorities such as the Basques in Europe.

Sam Colop also draws on the Latin American literary critic Beatriz Pastor, who provides a detailed analysis of the "mythification" of New World cultures by the Spanish explorers. In *Discurso Narrativo de la Conquista de América* (1988), however, she goes on to discuss the failure of heroic domination evident in the wider corpus of colonial chronicles. Many accounts describe Spanish vulnerability and failure in the face of the untamed natural world that threatened the invaders with disease, starvation, and economic ruin. They also depict Spanish rebellions against Crown representatives who were denounced as deceitful, corrupt, and dishonorable when expeditions suffered heavy losses and failed to find promised wealth. In Pastor's view, the process eroded and blurred the hierarchies Spaniard/native, and civilized/barbarous.

Pastor's narrative culminates in the genesis of a unique New World culture, a Hispanic-American consciousness that celebrates marginality, the paradoxes of its dual origin, and a critical view of its own past (1988, 439). By focusing on the ethnogenesis of the *mestizo* through the fusion of Spaniards, their New World descendants, and diverse indigenous peoples, Pastor reaffirms a modernist trajectory for Mexican history and naturalizes the dominance of the *mestizo* mainstream. Physical and cultural amalgamation— a *mestizo* melting pot—displaces (through idealization or erasure) the historical progenitors, indigenous and European alike.

As one would expect, Sam Colop becomes very selective in his appropriation of Pastor. He rejects any solution to the riddle of domination-and-resistance that implies the cultural and physical merging of the colonized "self" and "other" through *mestizaje*. Maya fusion into a *kaxlan* mainstream is unacceptable. Interestingly enough, Pastor apologizes for ignoring indigenous chronicles and peoples in her analysis. But that is the point: the New World becomes a sui generis creation in her view. The obvious problem in her narrative is the bracketing and marginalization of substantial New World populations who have continued to count themselves as indigenous.

Finally, Sam Colop uses Tzvetan Todorov's analysis of the power relations and double binds built into Spanish colonial assessments of the sameness/difference of New World populations and their civilized conquerors. He selects aspects of Todorov useful for his argument about continuities in the political psychology of violence and racism. The rest of Todorov's argument—especially the problematic thesis of Aztec vulnerability to the superior Spanish capacity to improvise contingent political moves and his argument about the suppressed individuality in Aztec society[13]—is ignored.

Interactive Remembering

Enrique Sam Colop recommends the critical study of history to unlock the terms and tenacity of prejudice in the present and to clarify current existential dilemmas by projecting them on the past. The cumulative wreckage of racism—which subverts narratives of national progress and modernization—is the overt message of his essay. The reverberation of terror across centuries—his Benjaminian moment of danger[14]—is a connection left to individuals to make, perhaps half-consciously as they read the essay. The connection is made overt when Sam Colop uses the language *tierra arrasada con sangre y fuego* (scorched earth by blood and fire) to sum up the horror of the sixteenth-century invasion. No one has to point out to Guatemalan audiences that this was the language of government counterinsurgency policies.

Connective flashes are not one-way temporal insights, the intrusion of the past into the present. Rather, given the Maya use of history to understand the political-psychology of violence and domination, these flashes represent the play of the present in a past of which it is a part.[15] Thus, the Maya historical project is strikingly different from Ladino nationalist histories, from new university projects in municipal archives, from quincentenary revisionism that sought to be fair to the Spaniards, and from historically compartmentalized studies of resistance. The Maya echo of a cycle in the present's relation to the past is not, I suspect, accidental. It seems to echo the historicizing cyclicity of Maya constructions of time, so often misunderstood by those structuralists who see Mayas as deterministically driven by their elaborate calendrics.[16]

Sam Colop's work challenges nationalist histories that focus on the development of the modern state and materialist histories that see foreign imperialism and class conflict as the only driving issues. Sam Colop sees reality as a consequence of power relations wherever they are manifested. To this end, his analysis draws the reader into the realm of political psychology, colonialism, and racism, which are related but not reducible to class exploitation. Like Cojtí, Sam Colop's strategic essentialism is creative, unstable, and self-contradictory, at once essentializing the other as the racist *kaxlan*, selectively appropriating foreign research, and from time to time collaborating with North Americans.[17] The overriding rationale for his essentialism is an ideological one: the forging of a unified Maya consciousness.

Sam Colop radically questions why established works are treated as authoritative in Guatemalan schools, universities, and public culture. His analysis arms Maya readers with important critical tools by demonstrating that first-person accounts—whether written by the observer or recycled in others' works—should never be taken at face value but rather seen as motivated and shaped by a flux of intentions suppressed by their creators and appropriators.[18] He demonstrates that not all *kaxlan* are the same or need to be appropriated wholesale. His major insight is to question the political and personal stakes involved in portraying the past.

Is there an inevitable divergence between postoriental academic history and activists' efforts to promote the revitalization of Maya culture, challenge racism, and combat internalized prejudice? For the postcolonial world, Prakash argues that nationalists' attempts to create a dismissive condemnation of Western society as repressive and a romanticized cultural essence for themselves run the risk of marginalizing other conflicts and heterogeneities within subaltern and metropole realities. At worst they bolster the West–Third World contrast that underpins the very power relations anticolonial studies seek to destabilize. Prakash warns, "Essentialism carries an enormous risk, even when it takes the self-canceling form," as in subaltern studies (1992a, 373). For the Pan-Maya movement, gender politics, specifically women's concern for a voice in movement decisions and agendas, has often been dismissed and suppressed as a legitimate heterogeneity that would diversify indigenous political interests.[19]

Darini Rajasingham suggested to me that essentialism and reverse orientalism[20] may characterize the first wave of anti-colonial subaltern indigenous authors. Following Prakash (1992a), a subsequent post-orientalist wave would acknowledge its historical debt but find reasons to move beyond the subaltern critique by dealing with the dialectics of identity construction on all sides: not only with the colonizer and colonized in all their heterogeneity but also with the transcultural flow of individuals, institutions, and signs that elude or subvert national boundaries.[21] The appropriation of ideas for rethinking politics and culture is a global phenomenon.

It is important, however, to remain wary of any universalizing framework, certainly of one that suggests global stages in political consciousness.[22] As in the past, Mayas now transform what they borrow—indigenous rights discourses, African-American multiculturalism in the schools, European literary criticism, *testimonio* genres, and Latin American anti-imperialism—and make it their own in a way that reflects and reshapes their particular concerns and circumstances. In the process, multiculturalist strategies become Mayanist strategies for social critique. An interweaving of political voices, rather than discrete stages leading to a transcendent post-orientalism, best captures the Pan-Maya movement. Current dilemmas for return refugees, land conflicts, and simmering controversies over women's voices in Pan-Maya politics remind activists of issues that need to be addressed *among* Maya communities, among the fragments they see as building blocks for a wider movement.[23]

Finally, it is important to follow the dynamics and scope of Maya Studies as it defines its mission in practice—to turn to the local grounding of Maya programs for cultural resurgence—rather than to freeze the emerging field in any characteristic mode of analysis. At present, the field both condemns the "other" as racist by definition and finds continual exceptions to this rule, as in the cases of Las Casas, modern Spanish policies toward the nation's own pluralism, and foreign intellectual collaborators.[24]

In bringing these chapters to a close, it is vital to confront the limits of the interpretive schemes I have used, even as one can hope they have generated some measure of insight. Rich texts, such as these, deserve close readings rather than the quick characterizations they often receive. This literary analysis has attempted to evoke Montejo's play of eyewitness narrative and subtle framing in his testimonial collections and Sam Colop's abstract distancing language in his collage of the past and present. As we have seen, a fuller sense of what Pan-Mayanists define as political results from an examination of the genres, imagery, ideas, and ironies these authors generate and borrow to express themselves. Like these writers, I have appropriated a variety of thinkers and ideas so that my thick description of their works might become an effective mode of interpretation and analysis. Yet, as I have suggested, a wider understanding of the Pan-Maya movement must continue beyond the genealogy of knowledge for the emergence of Maya Studies.

The way out of this dilemma is to continue the process of locating the sources of inspiration for Mayanist discourse outside the realm of published texts and to trace the effects of this emerging discourse in practical affairs. This is where anthropology, literary criticism, subaltern studies, and history often part ways. Rather than accepting the silences publicly imposed on published social commentary as the end of the story, it is critical to deal with Maya experiences of contemporary democracy and the practical sites where history and culture are studied and taught by Maya activists as part of their decentralized efforts to forge a national movement. Mayas writing from exile, such as Victor Montejo and his collaborators, have been able to personalize the violence, while, as will be evident in the next chapter, Pan-Mayanists in Guatemala are now working on ways to displace violence with revitalization.

Seven

Finding Oneself in a Sixteenth-century Chronicle of Conquest

IN RESEARCH on the Spanish conquest of the New World and on the European voyages of discovery, scholars such as Tzvetan Todorov (1984), Marshall Sahlins (1981; 1985; 1995), and Gananath Obeyesekere (1992) debated the indigenous interpretation of Europeans at first contact. None of these authors, however, asks about the stakes twentieth-century indigenous activists might find in these arguments, or the very different interests indigenous readers currently bring to the colonial frontier.[1] This essay deals with Maya intellectuals, with their practice of reading history, the political issues they find riveting in ancient texts, and the significance of history for current struggles. Michael Taussig's (1993) tactic of tacking back and forth between historicist and presentist perspectives inspires this inquiry. There are echoes as well of Dennis Tedlock's (1983) ethnopaleography. Yet my approach is more ethnographic than that of either Taussig or Tedlock, in the sense of an overarching concern with community building and cultural context, with mimetic moments Mayas find important at this political juncture. The project takes on special importance in Guatemala, where Maya intellectuals have become the architects of a national movement for ethnic revindication.

Each year, Pan-Mayanists host hundreds of informal meetings, lectures, workshops, conferences, and short courses for activists and community members. Whatever their format, these events are opportunities to contest the representation of Mayas in national culture, to imagine a Maya-centric history, and to reveal the paradoxes of the movement. Maya intellectuals active in culturalist networks now meet in large and small study groups, where they read Maya chronicles dating from the sixteenth to nineteenth centuries and discuss advances in the decipherment of ancient glyphs. Chronicles and legal documents (*títulos*) were written in Latin script in indigenous languages such as K'ichee' or Kaqchikel with sixteenth-century innovations to represent sounds foreign to Spanish. These documents are now considered sacred, in some cases biblical, texts.

This analysis traces the work of a group of prominent linguists from Oxlajuuj Keej Maya' Ajtz'iib' (OKMA) and the Rafael Landívar Linguistics Institute as they spent a week studying the celebrated *Annals of the Kaqchikels*, which were written at the time of the first contact between Mayas and Spaniards in 1524.[2] These linguists are involved in a wide variety of community-education projects as teachers and producers of nationally distributed educational materials. Our focus will be on issues they found compelling in this eyewitness portrayal of Maya life before and after the Spanish invasion. Pan-Mayanists see these chronicles as vital windows on the past and as useful guides for a variety of difficult projects in the present.[3] The group's engagement—what I would describe as having a Talmudic sense of the text's complexity—is central to this analysis. Following the Maya stress on the multiple layering of meaning, this analysis finds the history work group revealing in its explicit agenda for the meeting and its hidden transcript of cultural preoccupations.[4]

To read a Maya chronicle is to confront its plurality. Chronicles often include transliterations of pre-Columbian glyphic and pictorial texts, oral histories, and eyewitness observations. Documents were copied and recopied at various times, and "originals" were lost, hidden, sometimes destroyed. Subsequent generations inserted marginal annotations, addenda, updated histories, and new introductions or dropped sections they found uninteresting (or sometimes too interesting). In Guatemala, most are known only through early Spanish translations, which are often wildly inaccurate. In many cases the originals are not accessible to native speakers because of differences between ancient and modern forms of the languages and because so few people are literate in Maya languages.

Why is this project important to the very busy public intellectuals of the Maya movement? Pakal B'alam—an intense, fast-speaking *ch'ip* (youngest son) from one of the most prominent Pan-Mayanist families with roots in Tecpán—observed that origins are important because "true 'history' or not, they show the Kaqchikels have their own origin."[5] The *Annals* are consulted to answer the question: "From what point [in history] did we exist as Kaqchikels, who said we were Kaqchikels?" The chronicle is also seen as having wider lessons about the depth and genesis of Maya culture, which few Guatemalans know in any detail. As a non-Kaqchikel participant from Palin, Waykan added:

> We are studying the chronicles, the *Popol Wuj*, *Annals of the Kaqchikels*, and *Rabinal Achi*. They will teach us a great deal, more still since we are so locally oriented and study localized languages. It will teach us not only other means of expression but how to relate to others in general, how people related before and how they relate now. This can help us a lot.

Given the number of Maya languages in Guatemala, the long-range goal is to produce modernized versions of the chronicles in their original language and to disseminate Spanish translations that will reach wider audiences. The linguists see the project as one of creating larger identifications and counterhistories, which, as Pakal B'alam put it, "do not argue the opposite of official histories for their own sake but rather seek truths that have not been fully aired."

In the spring of 1992, an informal group of Maya linguists met for day-long sessions to study the sixteenth-century version of the *Annals* and its nineteenth- and twentieth-century Spanish translations. Kab'lajuj Tijax—a highly respected professional and Kaqchikel elder in Maya linguistics, originally from Comalapa—talked about the substance of the text with great reverence. This masterwork depicts "official Maya history," a view from the past of the origins of a major indigenous people, their common cosmology, experiences of armed European invasion, and, critically, their genealogical continuity and survival over the centuries. These are the truths that he believes need airing. Official state histories in the schools and beyond allude to this chronicle but most often to tell of the defeat of the Mayas at the conquest. Tellingly, none of its official translators has been a native speaker of Kaqchikel.

The *Annals* manuscript represents a distillation of ancient cosmogonic knowledge and of first-person accounts that span the years of 1510 to 1604. Compiled first by Francisco Hernández Arana, who witnessed the Spanish invasion in 1524, and after 1583 by Francisco Díaz, who added a running account of important events in Sololá,[6] the manuscript was recopied in the mid seventeenth century by a professional scribe.

The original historians were members of the Xajila family, direct descendants of early Kaqchikel rulers, and at different times mayors of Sololá during the early colonial period (Recinos and Goetz 1953, 13–14). At the end of the manuscript, five additional short narratives appear, composed between 1550 and 1590 by Diego López. The additions describe the genealogy of the Pakal lineage, its connection to the governing Xajil political-descent group, as well as specifics on land rights, political offices, and rights to succession.

The study group highlighted worldview, or *cosmovisión*, as a fundamental philosophical and aesthetic element of the chronicles. As Pakal B'alam observed: "Myths don't just relate the history of a people but their way of thinking." The group decided to focus on specific topics since it was not feasible to do a careful reading of the entire chronicle in the time available. In a quick consensus, the group agreed on the mythic origins of the Kaqchikels, the indigenous rebellion at the pre-Hispanic capital Iximche', the Spanish invasion, and the Pakal B'alam genealogy.[7] These eclectic choices reveal important subthemes in Maya revitalization.

Origins and the Tulan Diaspora

The work group began with the Maya genesis, with the chronicle's portrayal of the origins of divine ancestors, the physical world, and humanity. Creation does not begin from nothingness in Maya cosmogonies. Inevitably, there are plural formative beings before pivotal moments of origin and an interplay of creations—some successful, others failed.[8] In the *Annals*, the narrator addresses his readers, the children of Tulan and members of the Xajila lineage, telling them of their mythistory in distant times, places, and generations:[9]

[1] Behold, I will write part of the history of our first fathers, our grandfathers,
    those who engendered people in the past
    when the hills and valleys had not yet been created,
    when there was only the rabbit, the bird,
    they say.
    Then the hills and valleys were in fact created;
    they are our fathers, our grandfathers,
    my children of Tulan.[10]

The history then becomes genealogical, tracing the ancestors Q'aq'awitz and Saqtekaw and their relation to the founders of the four Kaqchikel lineages from the distant Tulan.

After the genealogies, the *Annals* speak in a series of spatial metaphors about Kaqchikel ethnogenesis. The chronicle narrates the foundational migration from Tulan and describes interdependent cycles of creation for humans and corn. The failed creations on the way to a new ordering are another signature of Maya cosmogony.

[4] These are the words of Q'aq'awitz and Saqtekaw.
    This is the true origin of the words that Q'aqawitz and Saqtekaw tell.
    From the four directions came the people of Tulan.
    There is a Tulan in the east,
    another in the south,
    one out in the west from whence we came,
    another in the north.
    These are four Tulans,
    you, our children,
    they say.
    From the west we came from Tulan to the other side of the sea. . . .
[5] Soon came Chay Ab'aj[11] created
    by Raxaxib'alb'ay, Q'anaxib'alb'ay.
    Soon man was created by Tz'aqol B'itol[12];
    he who feeds the obsidian stone.
    It was hard to create mankind,
    to finish mankind.
    He was made of wood,
    he was made only of earth.
    He did not speak,
    he did not walk.
    What was made had neither blood nor flesh

they say, our first fathers, grandfathers,
you, our children.
They did not find the right element for his creation,
finally they found the element:
Only two animals knew where it was
in the mountain called Paxil.
These animals were the coyote and the raven.
It was found in the intestines
of the coyote when it was killed,
was cut open.
Corn sprang from his insides. . . .

The entrance to Tulan was closed.
The place from whence we came was in the form of a bat
which enclosed the entrance to Tulan
the place where we were born
and were engendered;
there we were given our responsibility
in the darkness, in the night,
you, our children.
That which Q'aqa'witz, Saqtekaw said,
you our children,
has not been forgotten.
There have been many generations
which nourished themselves with these words in the past.

The passages evoked strong visual images for the linguists. They circulated a drawing of the walled city of their origin with its totemic main gate, which had been done by a student of Linda Schele. There the bat (*sotz'*) portal was pictured with massive doors and an indecipherable greeting traced in glyphs. The linguists discussed the autochthonous writing system, created by their ancestors and never understood by the colonizers. "They nourished themselves with their words" takes on another layer of meaning in the drawing. I can only add that this is doubly interesting given the possible existence of the *Annals* mythistory in codex form, as Carmack (1973) speculates.

The linguists also drew a geometric illustration to represent the abstract spatial imagery underlying the origins narrative. Their four-cornered universe highlighted the underworld (not hell), overworld, cardinal directions, and central axis. Creation unfolded on a cosmic stage, marked in numerous subtle ways—such as the mention of Raxaxib'albay (*rax* = green) and Q'anaxib'albay (*q'an* = yellow)—yet elusive to many students of the text. Translators frequently passed by oblique references to this spatial imagery, apparently because they were unimpressed with the nuances of origins symbolism. The veiled language reminded earlier audiences of the cosmic stage on which human history unfolded in cyclic time.

When Maya cosmology was translated into Spanish and given greater scholarly attention in the nineteen and twentieth centuries, it was incorporated into Christian categories. Intensifying the tendencies of colonial transcribers who had been trained by Catholic priests, later translators equated the Maya underworld (*xib'alb'ay*) with hell, Maya divinities with the devil, Spaniards with gods, and Mayas with pagans. It has always been a temptation to translate Maya worldview, with its abundant twins and dualisms, into the mutually exclusive good/evil dichotomies in Christianity. This is a chronic problem, something that Pan-Mayanists fight in their own discussions as they attempt to purge Maya worldview from its encounter with various historical waves of European religion.

Rebellion at Iximche' the Ancient Capital

The group turned next to the ancient political intrigues through which the Kaqchikels emerged as an autonomous indigenous state capable of jockeying with other Maya states for territory and dominance. The rebellion occurred after the Kaqchikel separation from its political progenitor, the ever-dominant K'ichee' state. A pivotal event in early Kaqchikel history was the struggle between rival ruling lineages, which culminated with a rebellion of the Tuquche' political-descent group at the Kaqchikel capital Iximche'. As leaders strategized to amass power, the envious Tuquche' leader Kai' Junapu confronted the leaders Oxlajuuj Tz'ii' and Kab'lajuj Tijax, "who did not want war/their daughters and sons suffered" (passage 100). The battle began in classical form with the amassing of Tuquche' forces. Among other combatants, four women fought with lances and bows and arrows:

> [102] . . . Four women were prepared
> They carried double-bladed lances,
> their bows and arrows.
> They found themselves in battle,
> always the four daughters. . . .
> Their arrows reached the shield of Chukuyb'atz'in.[13]
> For this reason the men were frightened
> because of the great battle the old leaders gave them.
> Once again the war leaders showed the bodies of the
> women. . . .
> Our grandparents Oxlajuj Tz'ii' and Kab'lajuj Tijax
> dispersed the Tuquche'.

The political history at the Kaqchikel capital was absorbing. As the group reviewed this passage, linguist Kab'lajuj Tijax followed the victory of his namesake, who as it turned out was one of the last rulers independently chosen by the Kaqchikels. The victory over the Tuquche' marked the emergence of the Kaqchikels as an expansive state force.

There was one puzzle in the study group's work on early political history. Why, in the midst of studying Kaqchikel political emergence, was the group interested in a passage describing women warriors? No one in the group seemed particularly concerned with women's issues as defined by current social movements. Later, I had a chance to pursue the topic. As is common knowledge, gender has become increasingly politicized by feminist groups in Latin America and the United States. It is now an important consideration in development programming by agencies such as U.S.-AID and European foundations and is routinely raised by activists as an issue at international rights conferences. Maya women, especially professionals, feel they are under pressure to see women as exploited by men; the male leadership worries about being portrayed as sexist in what remains a decidedly androcentric cultural system.

Members of the group explained that the idea of women warriors, even if mentioned only in passing, is appealing because it demonstrates that women were held in respect and occupied positions of prestige in the original cultural system. Thus, Maya women would be right in opting to join with men, as they did at Iximche', stressing joint ethnic goals over their personal struggles. For today's readers, this image is not one of Amazon independence, as the well-known translator Recinos had speculated (1950, 112 fn. 205), but rather a hopeful rationale for common purpose across social cleavages. It is interesting how often the gender issue bubbles up in Pan-Mayanist meetings. This momentary taming of the suppressed was more easily accomplished than at other conferences, where flashes of female anger have jolted audiences, only to be swallowed up by the dynamics of Mayanist consensus making.[14]

The Spanish Conquest and Maya Betrayal

The Spanish invasion was destined to become a major pursuit of the study group since it defined colonial power structures and provoked resistance that has continued over the last five hundred years. The group disputed the classic Western portrayal of awed reactions at the first Maya encounter with the Spaniards (as described in passage 148). The Brinton translation reads "but it was a fearful thing when they entered; their faces were strange, and the chiefs *took them for gods.*" Recinos and Goetz[15] offer a similar version: "In truth they inspired fear when they arrived. Their faces were strange. The Lords *took them for gods*" (1953, 121). Instead, the study group argued that the sixteenth-century Kaqchikel chronicles described Europeans as unnatural and menacing: "*It was really terrifying* when they came, they were not known, the leaders assumed *they were unnatural beings.*"[16] Thus in Maya revisionist translations, terror not awe foreshadows armed clashes and the Spanish military victory over the indigenous states.[17]

Stories of Pedro de Alvarado's defeat of the Maya leader Tecún Umán have been given legendary status in national schools and state-sponsored histories.[18] According to official accounts, Tecún Umán's heroic though tragic death is the culmination of the conquest. Finding himself in hand-to-hand combat with the Spanish leader, Tecún Umán is said to have taken the unfamiliar horse and conqueror as one. Unknowingly, he plunged his weapon into the horse, leaving the final counter blow to the foreign conqueror. Mayanists simply do not believe this story, which they feel has been created to assert Maya stupidity and ignorance: Their ancient leaders were unable to distinguish man and beast! Such stories—like the long reputed association of the Spaniards with gods—are seen as legitimizing the inevitable domination of Mayas by the European other. Mayanists see little to admire in this tale of so-called heroic death. From small town schools to national meetings, this story instantly triggers Mayanist resentment.

Recently, Mayanists in Guatemala have begun to search for alternative images of Maya heroism. One Kaqchikel option appears in the *Annals*. The leader Kaji' Imox survived the initial invasion and is now seen as having engaged in a campaign of nonconventional warfare against Spaniards for years afterwards. Eventually he was killed. But his flexibility in adjusting to Spanish preeminence in the open field of battle, when Maya war maneuvers proved unsuccessful against a technologically superior force, is felt to be emblematic of the tactical ingenuity necessary to resist colonial domination (see, for example, passages 154 and 156). Given the failure of Guatemala's armed insurgency, however, it would be a mistake to read this fascination narrowly. Rather, one can see this tactical ingenuity reflected in the development of hundreds of loosely connected research centers, language committees, and nonformal education projects throughout the highlands.

The image of Kaji' Imox is compelling to Kaqchikels, who look for exemplars of resistance to counterbalance another painful theme in their history, betrayal. At issue is their state's early alliance with the Spaniards against their historical rivals, the K'ichee's. Kaqchikels carry the stigma of being "traitors" at the invasion, and epithets still fly in moments of interpersonal hostility. Waykan explained:

> I've heard people say, "Well, if the K'ichee's and the Kaqchikels were enemies, and the Kaqchikels betrayed the K'ichee's. . . ." They try to use this as a weapon against others to assert "You are not our equals." It's now sometimes used to reject a Kaqchikel or K'ichee' proposal.

This is not a minor issue, given the size and importance of these groups. K'ichee's, the largest subgroup in Guatemala, number more than 1 million. Kaqchikels, the third largest and most active in Pan-Mayanist leadership, number slightly more than four hundred thousand (Oxlajuuj Keej 1993, 13, 16).

The study group, however, did not want to rewrite history to cover up this enmity if in fact that was the substance of the chronicle. Rather, as Waykan observed, they sought a wider context:

> We need a deeper understanding of what happened. It's not enough to say, "*You are fighting* each other; *you were* enemies." In so doing we only feed this enmity.

How did the early Kaqchikels see their alliance with the Spaniards? Does an understanding of historical patterns of intergroup warfare make their momentary alliance with the Spaniards more intelligible? In fact, the work group discovered more resistance and more Spanish manipulation of the Mayas than has been apparent in the standard Spanish translations.

In the study group, as the linguists came to the narration of the conquest, they paused and for a moment imagined an alternative story in which the Spanish invaders had not enlisted eager Kaqchikels in the attack of their regional rivals. But among all the other errors and ambiguities, the text would not yield this wished-for interpretation (see passages 148–49). After using Kaqchikel forces to vanquish the K'ichee' armies, the Spaniards turned their attention to looting their recent allies. The painfulness of Kaqchikel complicity and betrayal—though clearly manipulated in the sense that the Spaniards took advantage of existing divisions to dominate all Maya groups in the end (see, for example, passages 152, 154, and 156)—stands as a reminder that Maya unity is something new and vulnerable.

Genealogical Echoes in the Present

Finally, the Maya linguists turned with great interest to the later genealogical section of the *Annals*, the section most translators have not even bothered to transcribe or translate. For the study group, the Pakal B'alam genealogy demonstrated crucial physical and cultural continuity from the mythic origins of the Kaqchikel Maya to the historical moment in the sixteenth century when the oral version of the *Annals* was written down. The continuity of generation begetting generation is double voiced in a particularly revealing way. The first male ancestor, Pakal B'alam, gives rise to a generation of sons: Pakal Tojin, Pakal Ajmaq, and Pakal Kej. In turn they beget another male generation: Pakal Jun Ajpu, Pakal Ajin, and Pakal Kej. Finally, in the narrator's generation, when the *Annals* were set down in Latin script, Maya names suddenly take a Hispanicized form: Francisco Kechelaj, Diego Méndez, and finally the historian himself, Diego López (see passage "o" in Villacorta C. 1934).

In essence, the text depicts the mirror image of what the linguists are currently doing in their lives. As is the convention for Pan-Mayanists, each has readopted a Maya name—drawn from sacred texts or from day names in the Maya calendar—to displace at least situationally their given names in Spanish. So during the workshop, Pakal B'alam appeared twice: as a famous ancestor and progenitor in the text and as a twentieth-century linguist checking the Kaqchikel transcription of the *Annals* on his laptop computer. Following Benjamin, this flash of recognition is fundamental to historical consciousness, urging the oppressed not to "forget both its hatred and its spirit of sacrifice, for both are nourished by the image of enslaved ancestors rather than liberated grandchildren" (1969, 260). Kaqchikel intellectuals would agree with Benjamin and add that the intimacy of remembering in these small face-to-face groups builds personal commitment to cultural resurgence. Finding oneself in the Kab'lajuj Tijax history or the Pakal B'alam genealogy reaffirms the significance of renaming for revitalization and nationalist identity.[19]

It is now clear, however, that if Mayanists do not publish research on the chronicles, others will. The translation of indigenous culture is big business along several fronts: schools are under pressure to include more materials on Maya culture; the tourist market includes many who have passionate interests in Indian culture; and human-rights struggles, Rigoberta Menchú, and United Nations conferences have spurred international concern. Not to speak of foreign anthropologists and their students in university courses.

In fact, Oxlajuuj Keej Maya' Ajtz'iib' (OKMA)—the linguistic research center whose members were active in the history reading group—decided to include a short excerpt from the *Annals* in their new book on Maya linguistics, *Maya' Chii': Los Idiomas Mayas de Guatemala* (1993). The book was written to be used by activists, by students taking adult education courses, and by teachers in Maya schools. Interestingly, they did not use any of the passages from the informal meetings; rather, they chose a passage about diaspora for its transcendent message. Their brief introduction frames the selection for Maya readers in the following terms:

> This fragment of the *Annals* is a prophesy directed to the groups of pilgrims on their march in search of their own land. This exhortation speaks of the difficulties there will be on the journey, and of their possible future glory. It is transmitted from generation to generation and is one of the literary legacies of the Maya culture.

> At once they took their bows, shields,
> lances, plumes, paintings,
> with bumblebees and wasps,

the mud, the flood, the swamp, the fog.
When we were given advice:
"Great will be your burden,
you will not sleep,
you will not be defeated,
you will not be trampled.
Oh my children!
You will be strong,
you will be powerful,
you will have strength.
Take your bows, arrows, and shields.
If you pay tribute
jade, metal, plumes, songs,
for this you will also
possess them and have them
the jade, the metal, and the plumes
painted and engraved objects.
All the seven communities have given tribute
even up to the distant hills
You will have and you will demolish everything.
Lay out your bows and shields,
one will be the first, the other the last
you thirteen warriors,
you thirteen princes,
you thirteen elders,
assemble your bows and shields
that I gave you.
Then go to lay out
the tribute, your bows and shields.
There is a war there
in the west,
in a place named Suywa,
there you will go to test
the bows and shields I gave you,
Go my children!"
It was said to us
when we came from Tulan,
when the warriors came from the seven communities.
When we came from Tulan
in reality it was terrible
when we encountered the bumblebees,
the wasps, the swamps, the fog, the mud, the flood.

(OKMA 1993: 105–7).

Pan-Mayanists are reviving the heroic imagery of Maya warriors in an attempt to deal with the passivity they see as one of the scars of Ladino racism and its language of inferiority for indigenous populations. Images of self-determination and adversity are weapons for a population that has been defined by conquest rather than by their own historical agency. Most important, this narrative resonates with experience of displacement suffered by many Maya refugees during the violence and with the struggles youths face with extreme pressures to assimilate. Today's quest echoes the first Tulan migrations and the continuing process of creation in Maya cosmology. The *Anales* are being mined for both personalized and more global imageries, depending on the context and audience.

The *Annals of the Kaqchikels* amply document, in an elite-centered way, the complex political history of preconquest states, the violence of first contact with the Spaniards, and the aftermath of colonialism. Carmack argues that these writings illustrate the colonial persistence of ancient Maya strategies to legitimize elite control of state policy and sacred knowledge. In fact, chronicles and genealogies were often presented in Spanish colonial courts in support of the rights of Maya elites to political office, tribute, rents, natural resources, and arms (1973, 18–21).

Interestingly enough, the power of hereditary elites was not controversial for the Maya activists in the 1992 history work group. Like most of the national leadership, they are from modest rural backgrounds but have found the path to geographical and economic mobility, at least for the moment, through education and their work in linguistics. Moments of identification across centuries, descent groups, and political divisions are not being used by this branch of the movement to consolidate elite status in the ancient style of monopolies over literacy and knowledge.[20] In support of their views, movement intellectuals, such as historian Víctor Racancoj (1994), have argued for an egalitarian and communal view of ancient Maya civilization as a cultural form that emerged independently of the Western tradition and without entrenched class differences. In practice, these intellectuals are trying to democratize access to knowledge through an activist ethic of community service. Their goal is to promote universal literacy, in contrast to the ancient practices of the culture they celebrate. They also want to see resistance and cultural continuity displace the tragic death of Maya culture in the person of Tecún Umán.

In contrast to earlier non-Maya scholars who felt the Xajila genealogies were not important enough to translate, family affairs are once again affairs of a nation. Maya identity politics seeks to tie the intimate and familiar to nationhood in ways that earlier historians and translators would not have imagined. Continuity in descent, culture, and language is being constructed as a challenge to histories of conquest and assimilation.

There were ironies and striking instances of unfinished business in the group's reading of the *Annals*. Sixteenth-century chroniclers were regarded as primary sources on autochthonous culture yet used Hispanicized names for themselves. Genealogies fell silent on the place of women in andro-centric accountings of state building and continuity. Class issues remained unexplored at that juncture. Yet the history group challenged linear render-ings of change. They made a place for a return of the suppressed, exem-plified in this instance by linguists who used their Maya names for the occa-sion, four women warriors on the field of battle, and new elites who seek in their daily lives to share their knowledge and the tools of literacy with im-poverished Mayas in the countryside.

Self-Determination and Polyculturalism

If self-determination represents a distinctive collectively and historically constituted form of agency, then an integral aspect of self-determination is the particular transcultural, dialogical processes through which Mayas assert its meaning. Chapters six and seven have shown how Pan-Mayanists have been pulled in several directions as they define cultural resurgence. In reply to widespread racism, they have chosen to elaborate a nonracial model of identification. Indigenous language has been embraced to emphasize cultural uniqueness, pre-Hispanic origins, and the diversity/unity duality critical to revitalization efforts. History is being experienced and told in a way that adds substance to these claims. The contested nature of who authors and translates difference (that is, the power structures of naming) has become a central issue—although more so for national histories and translations than for chronicles in indigenous languages. By renaming themselves and the world in Maya languages, Pan-Mayanists reassert a continuity of difference that defeats European colonialism. At war with this process is the Gua-temalan racist who continues to assert differences designed to render Mayas less than human.[21] This clash of agencies is central to Maya unification and self-determination.

The diversity/unity dualism of Maya languages is mirrored in the histori-cal structure of the Pan-Maya movement: a network of decentralized re-search, cultural, and educational centers. Decentralization as a movement strategy is further reinforced by Maya cultural practices, national political realities, and foreign funders. Maya communities generate a great deal of local leadership and marked tolerance for individual variation within wider collective efforts. (See the next chapter for details.) Research centers—even as they foster novel cultural hybrids after bringing together Pan-Mayanists from different language groups—value investing in local communities and their notions of cultural authority. National political uncertainties also favor decentralized strategies, which can quickly respond to changing political circumstances. Finally NGO[22] funders long favored small projects in their particular areas of interest. Pan-Maya research centers and their activities are supported by an array of Maya entrepreneurs, Maya professionals, the Guatemalan government, European and American foundations, and transnational academic networks.[23]

From works like Sam Colop's (1991) quincentenary essay, the *Anales* study group, and Racancoj's history of Maya civilization (1994) counter-histories are emerging. Mayas reveal the persistence of racial prejudice—echoes of invidious stereotyping with the unquestioning use of demeaning colonial accounts by contemporary historians. Moreover, they see flashes of the present, with its painful existential dilemmas, reflected in the past. By renaming themselves and studying Maya historical chronicles that survived the burning of many indigenous manuscripts by the Spanish, Mayas are challenging radical discontinuities in culture and identity and reasserting the viability of cultural difference. There is much material in the chronicles for Maya-centric historical scholarship to challenge national histories that debase or distantly idealize the Maya past. There is also much to shed light on the dilemmas of identity politics for Pan-Mayanists in a world of crosscutting loyalties and alliances and in a world of old and new hierarchies of knowledge and power.

Interestingly enough, U.S. culture has played at least a small part in the development of Maya Studies. After earning a law degree in Guatemala, Sam Colop pursued graduate work in linguistics at the University of Iowa, SUNY-Albany, and SUNY-Buffalo, working with Nora England and Dennis Tedlock. He is widely read in critical anthropology and anticolonial studies, has cochaired joint Maya–North American panels at academic conferences, and lectures widely at American universities. Members of the *Annals* study group, whose informal group met this time at the University of Texas at Austin under the auspices of art historian Linda Schele's workshops on Maya glyphs, were from two of the major Maya research networks in Guatemala. Kab'lajuj Tijax had been to the United States before; for the others this was a new experience. All had worked with North American linguists for sustained periods of time in Guatemala.

Despite the complex enjoyment of international travel and the admiring recognition from U.S. audiences, personal familiarity with the United States has not deflected Maya critiques of foreign scholarship as a neocolonial enterprise. Exposure to the anticolonialism of the *popular* Left—reinforced in meetings with North American Indians at the 1991 Second Continental Meeting of Indigenous, Black, and Popular Resistance—has led to denunciations of the built-in asymmetries in the research process, doubts about foreign anthropologists' motives for research, and concerns that foreign research will continue to reinforce divide-and-conquer politics in Guatemala.

In this moment of revitalization through Maya Studies, the issue for

Mayas is self-determination in a world in which polyculturalism is a common experience. These intellectuals want recognition as individuals who bring insights from their own studies and experiences to wider forums for social criticism and cultural revitalization. In forging a novel cultural nationalism, these scholars locate themselves at the nexus of local and international identity streams. Most strikingly, they bring together a combination of talents, training, and international experience—the ancient and the new, the local and the international—that defies the conventional grammar of Guatemalan ethnic divisions of labor. Their hosting of major international congresses of Maya Studies in 1996 and 1997 at the Rafael Landívar University in Guatemala City—complete with a wide variety of panels, plenaries, and book displays—marked the development critical mass of Maya scholars and public intellectuals who were happy to engage North American, Latin American, and Guatemalan Ladino scholars on their own terms (see Universidad Rafael Landívar 1997).

Ladinos by definition are supposed to have privileged access to the wider modern world; Maya culture is supposed to isolate, buffer, and localize one's view of the world. Clearly, Maya Studies subverts this view in its transcultural practice. The personal satisfaction of being active in these foreign worlds stems from the fact that the foreign "other" outside Guatemala appears to value Maya culture more than Ladinos and that these travels make Mayas authoritative insiders when speaking of high status "American" culture. Knowledge and power are important elements of this process, which subverts the national hierarchy only, it would seem, to leave intact an international one.[24]

Eight

"Each Mind Is a World": Person, Authority, and Community

MAYA VIEWS of the social world hold that the reasoning of others is not fully accessible, that actions may mask secret intentions at odds with self-presentation, and that estrangement and envy are ever-present dangers. In turning to local agendas for the revitalization of indigenous culture, it is essential to explore the distinctive signature that Kaqchikel Maya culture gives to social tensions and the ways leadership styles have been adapted to the uncertainties raised by recent decades of striking interpersonal change. As we have already seen, deeply felt anxieties are the subject of traditionalist narratives of transforming selves and newly articulated *testimonios* of human rights abuses—both used to make sense of contemporary political crises. In the past, interpersonal uncertainty was also a major theme of ritual prayers offered during the celebrations of the civil-religious hierarchy, the vital traditionalist institution that structured public life in many rural communities from the colonial period through the 1970s. This chapter discusses the cultural meanings—born of pre-Columbian, colonial, nineteenth-, and twentieth-century waves of transculturalism—that give interpersonal relations and leadership their Kaqchikel Maya character. The next chapter personalizes these issues by presenting the family biography of three generations of antiracism activists in San Andrés, some of whom are sympathetic and others skeptical of Pan-Mayanism.

"Each mind is a world" is a phrase I heard in the early 1970s as well as the late 1980s. The reminder is spoken by Mayas in combinations of Spanish and Kaqchikel. *Jun jolomaj jun ruch'ulew* in San Andrés Kaqchikel or *cada cabeza es un mundo* in Spanish was also said as *cada jolomaj jun mundo*, an interweaving of both languages. Regardless of the phrasing, the point is clear: it is expected that each person thinks in a different way from any other; each will assess his or her life chances and reasons for social participation from a distinctive vantage point. "Each mind is a world" was evoked to explain that one could not know with any great certainty the specific motivations, the internal thoughts, of another. The comment was often accompanied with a body language of resignation, a shrug designed to cut off further speculation. I would argue that this phrase reflects for its users both a cultural style and strategic evasiveness. The fact that there never was a transparent connection between act and intent for this community has only been heightened by chronic political insecurities.

I first heard the "each mind is a world" philosophy when talking to the leaders of the civil-religious hierarchy, the key traditionalist institution and an important source of public ritual until the mid 1970s.[1] Each saint society was named after a central figure: the Virgen de María, Virgen de Dolores, Jesús, San Andrés, and San Nicolás. Saint societies were composed of hierarchies of officers from the head or *kofradio* (from *cofrade* in Spanish) to the lowest *mortomo* (from *mayordomo* in Spanish). The hierarchy also ranked Maya civil authorities from the Maya mayor through grades of councillors (*regidores*) to the lowest messengers (*alguaciles*). Finally, the church had a ranking of officials from the head *pixcal* (*fiscal*) to *sacristanes* and their assistants called *chajales*.

Expectations were high that all men who were physically and financially able would participate in the hierarchy, moving up and among the branches during their lifetimes of community service. Service was costly in time and donations for not only the officials but also their wives and families. After a career of significant posts and responsibilities, an activist would become a principal elder, or *krunsipal* (from the Spanish *principal*, a term that is also used). These honored elders monitored the Maya mayor's activities and served as advisers when decisions were made within the Maya community. They discussed who should serve when annual selections of officeholders were made, volunteered their sons for lower posts, and became *kofradios* themselves when needed. It is clear the most respected *principales* in San Andrés, such as Don Emiliano Matzar, cared deeply about the civil-religious hierarchy, especially the *cofradías*, and tried over the course of time and against great odds to keep their positions alive. They took more than their share of the demanding *kofradio* positions. Several other elders chose to specialize in the recitation of ritual discourses at important celebrations, acting as speakers and guides (*k'amöl b'ey*) for municipal authorities and saint societies.

The *k'amöl b'ey* were leaders in a special sense. As *principales*, they were vested with the moral authority to demand service. As *k'amöl b'ey* in the civil-religious hierarchy, they stood for the "goodwill" (*voluntad* or *rachuxlal*) of individuals who participated in and thus perpetuated *costumbre*, the rituals and town-focused practices of the ancestors. They also served as marriage negotiators between families, an elaborate and formalized process. In the civil-religious hierarchy, "each mind is a world" meant that people were assumed to have very different reasons for serving, all of which were valid as long as one participated. As one elder put it: "Your mind is of one thought, another's is of another thought, and so it goes." Some participants were devoted to a particular saint, others had made a pledge to a saint and were obligated to pay it back in service. Still others sought access to communal lands available to those who held posts in the community hierarchy. Imputing motives was not important, only the outcome. What mattered was that different wills managed to converge to celebrate the commonality of place that defined their community.[2] Outcomes had their own drama as individuals failed to show up or showed up very late for a particular preparation or event. There was always the chance in the early 1970s that individual wills would not come together, that the system would falter in the face of aggressive evangelization by Catholic and Protestant groups. For traditionalists, action and joint participation were more important than state of mind.

In the face of this individuality, rituals—where members looked to altar tables crowded with saints and candles from narrow benches that ringed the dark room with its carpet of pungent pine-needles—called for elaborate etiquette. Social status was observed in the procession, seating, and service of ritual foods and drinks by rank in the civil-religious hierarchy.[3] Rituals reaffirmed the interconnectedness of all individuals in a ranking where each person had a clearly defined place and duty and through which the life cycle was defined by evolving social responsibilities and authority. Just as the etiquette of rituals and processions was felt to express the central value of "respect," so, too, the ways in which these rituals were articulated was integral to the sense of order by which the community was fundamentally organized.

Recited in rapid-fire old Kaqchikel, ritual prayers were given at all major celebrations as dialogues between the guide of the municipal authorities and the guide of the host saint society. The wording was strikingly similar from event to event. Although many participants did not understand all the old Kaqchikel, most were well aware of the dominant themes and images. What did the *k'amöl b'ey*, literally "the taker of the path," say to the assembly of municipal authorities and religious officials who waited for his greetings at the shrine? His message spelled out Kaqchikel hopes and fears in a world of emotional estrangement. The fear was that people would commit the sin of disrespect.

The *k'amöl b'ey* began with a description of the special powers of divinities who are able to see inside individuals as people could not. The angel San Bernadino is the sun, who warms the land and the crops. Rising and setting, he guides and illuminates the world. San Bernadino sees peoples' inner feelings, becomes aware of those who do and do not merit punishment, and pardons bad actions even as the discourses are recited:[4]

The angel San Bernadino,
saw this day,
this hour.
It was he who saw,
who gave the gift,

where there is sadness,
where there is lamenting,
where there is happiness here on earth.
They were present to witness
below the sky,
below the earth,
God the Father.[5]

One person explained that the sun's "gift" was seeing those who were not guilty and thus did not deserve God's punishment.

The guide went on to talk about estrangement, that people in a community where "we share ancestors and *costumbre*," where "we should be united," might not care. Here the prayers described church bells being rung in "doubles" announcing someone's death:

Where does he raise his hand,
his foot,
that relative,
that mother?
The holy bells ring out
over our ravine,
over our town.[6]

Thus, thus our spirit goes with God.
"Oh God, who is coming?
Who is this father,
who is this brother
who goes away,
who returns,
at the hands,
at the feet of God?"[7]

"It will be God who will take you,
it will be God who will take care of you,
it will be God who will pardon you."[8]

We are born for tomorrow,
we are born for the future.
Only one our God is given us,
we give ———,[9]
Our brother is a very good Christian.

Perhaps we have only one more day,
now we have only one more deed.
Perhaps we are happy for it,
Perhaps we express a bad word,

an evil thought,
About the departure,
about the return.[10]

But this is not what God commands,
Only a few holy words,
only ————,
Let us say.
But we cannot recover these expressions.
Perhaps we have just one more day.
Perhaps we have just one more deed.

————

our mothers came,
our grandmothers,
our grandfathers,
in ancient times,
with ancient history.
They had good words.
Good words were in their thoughts.
They knelt before the Earth.[11]

This was a plea for townspeople to see others as members of the same family, to care about their deaths, and to express concern by wishing people well in God's protection. The legitimacy of the plea was rooted in the past, in ancestors' thoughts and actions. It was the present that was in doubt.

The prayers continued with another image of alienation, that younger generations might not respect their elders:

Here, then, they were given their days,
they were given their time.
Perhaps they did their work,
once, twice,
in the sacred house of the government.
Perhaps they did their service,
once, twice,
in the holy church.
Perhaps they did their work, their service
once, twice,
in the great house of the saint society.[12]

There then, they were given their days,
they were given their time.
Perhaps their hair became white,
their heads became white.

Perhaps they returned there,
Perhaps they obeyed,
Perhaps they grew old in their service.[13]

We then are their daughters,
their sons,
their buds,
their shoots.
But perhaps this is not what we say to
our mother, our father,
one with white hair, white-headed.[14]

They will not do anything,
our mother, our father,
if our souls are incomplete,
are still lacking.
On their path, their life of their service.
Perhaps in place of obeying them,
we push them down.[15]

"This is what makes me suffer,"
our mother, our father,
one with white hair, white-headed.

"Oh God, you are my daughter, you are my child,
you are my bud, you are my shoot.
This is what you do to me.
Because you are so vigorous,
because of your strength, your knowledge,[16]
you want to push me from the path,
perhaps with your mouth, perhaps with your eyes."[17]

The days will go, the time will go.
Perhaps he will call for your return,
perhaps he will kneel,
perhaps he will prostrate himself,
at the rising,[18] at the setting of San Bernardino.[19]

There our destiny will be made clear,
If the day arrives or does not arrive,
If the hour arrives or does not arrive,
of our departure, our return,
at the hands, at the feet of God.[20]
Only our voice, only our intelligence
our obeying, our pushing.

Perhaps the word will continue,
perhaps the voice will continue.
But now we cannot express ourselves well
in the presence of the Earth/the World.[21]

Here the fear was the loss of interdependence between generations, that youths might reject their elders even though they would not exist without them. What is interesting in this prayer is the threat of punishment when the elder is pushed off the path of life and ignored as a point of reference by younger generations, who have their own ideas. The elder weighs the alternative of praying to God to punish those who show disrespect. When discussing these rituals, however, people noted that the real punishment for the youth would be that later in his life, when he is old and infirm, he would be subject to the same mistreatment and suffering that he gave his grandfather, his ancestor.

Maya Costumbre as Memory

Both memory and its various embodiments—recalling, forgetting, denying, repressing, erasing, revitalizing, replacing, veiling, rejecting, reenacting—are preoccupations in Maya communities. Classical North American studies of Maya worldview tended to essentialize and conflate memory-continuity as "Maya culture" and bemoan its contrast as "culture loss." These ethnographic descriptions noted that *costumbre*, reenacted continuities in religion and social organization, was central to traditionalist Maya culture. "Why do you do this?" asked the ethnographer. "Because of *costumbre*," was the inevitable reply, which was taken as self-evident consensus and continuity. *Costumbre* was mandated by high-status elders and associated with the activities of the civil-religious hierarchy, which defined the moral authority, community membership, and the nature of collective identification.

In describing *costumbre* before its erosion, North American anthropologists often adopted a language of Durkheimian metaphors: continuity, cohesiveness, solidarity, consensus, integration. This cultural system condensed ethnicity onto each community, which had its own ancestors, lands, saints, saint societies, and dialect of a Maya language.

But two issues complicated this analysis of memory-continuity. In towns like San Andrés the elders spoke of the saint societies as alternatively "invented" by the Spanish conquerors and by the Maya ancestors. Some noted with pride particular additions their families had contributed to *costumbre* in specific years. Moreover, the prayers offered at rituals spoke of the tenuousness of *costumbre*, as something that was only partially remembered, an echo of a different but not completely knowable past. Ruptures, rather than a simple continuity of memory, were commemorated at these rituals. In the rush to document continuities—an ironic process since ethnographers and Mayas alike were well aware of the Spanish colonialism—most anthropologists overlooked the anxieties expressed in the prayers of the exemplar of continuity, the ritual guide of the civil-religious hierarchy. The *k'amöl b'ey's* prayers described rituals as an imperfect mimesis because the ancestors had "better words, better expressions," which they used before Maya authorities and before God. "Ours is another generation," they concluded. These prayers spoke of other ruptures: the alienation of youths from the elders they were supposed to respect and the lack of empathy in the community for others in pain.

Remembering was a specialized activity in a system in which public religious participation in processions and service in the hierarchy was all that was important for most participants. A few of the most active elders were known as specialists, as archives of the important prayers, narratives, and explanatory details representing the past. In San Andrés, ritual knowledge and generosity in time and devotion translated into great personal respect and authority for specialists in religious matters but not into specific powers. Financial incentives, particularly access to communal lands and their harvests, were available to participants in general and allocated by the civil wing of the hierarchy. For Kaqchikels, "we do this out of *costumbre*" was not really an affirmation of unproblematic continuities, consensus, common knowledge, integration, or the coercive powers of a closed corporate community.

In the mid 1970s, after a decade of difficulties, the civil-religious hierarchy, which dated from the Spanish colonial period and had roots in pre-Columbian structures of moral authority, collapsed.[22] When asked why this occurred, everyone agreed that community service became too expensive, that with the skyrocketing cost of staples and essentials and depressed earnings people could not afford the time or money to participate. The mid-1970s were certainly a period of hardship as the buying power of the national currency, the *quetzal*, declined 40 percent in a three-year period. But the explanation of common suffering hides other factors that were undoubtedly just as important.

On the one hand, a politicized younger generation successfully challenged the legality of obligatory unpaid community service and the right of saint societies to hold communal lands for their own benefit. These actions echoed fears expressed by the *k'amöl b'ey*, that youths would refuse to follow traditionalist constructions of authority. On the other hand, local evangelizing groups, including Catholic Action and several Protestant denominations, had eroded the monopoly of the *cofradías* by converting traditionalists, who were no longer permitted by their new congregations to participate in the activities of *costumbre*. Why did people convert? Economics is the reason most often cited, though there are myriad others. Ultimately, "each mind is a world" is used by traditionalists to explain individual decisions that led to Catholic Action's early success and by traditionalists and new Catholics to generalize about conversions resulting in the slower but striking growth of the Evangelicals. This construction of the person holds that a diversity of thought is the natural state of affairs and there are distinct limits to powers of persuasion if an individual dissents.

The Problem of Unstable Selves

While those in the contemporary "West" struggle through all kinds of therapy and self-discovery to find and display their real selves, Kaqchikel Mayas are not fully convinced that this is possible. Central to their constructions of the person are beliefs that individual minds are different worlds and that some individuals have the capacity to transform themselves, sometimes benignly but most often disruptively, into other beings. In Kaqchikel the word *nuk'exri'* means to transform or change oneself. It is also used in the sense of exchanging one thing or form for another.[23] These preoccupations are captured by a range of mythistories that were part of a vibrant oral tradition in San Andrés. Narratives concerning the masters of the night, the master of sickness, *la llorona*, and the guardian of the wilds gave form to the lack of constancy of certain selves.

Certain kinds of people and animals are unstable and worrisome transformations of something else (see chapter three). In some cases humans, who appear normal, regularly assume animal form. They are *sub'unel*: "deceivers" and "confounders." They are often described as driven to certain actions, just as animals are driven by an inner compulsion to do what they must.[24] The master of the night is a being who is human during the day but becomes an animal, often a goat, sheep, or dog, at night, when it is compelled to wander and disturb people. Those who are born with this capacity display it later in life, long after they are accepted members of the community. Their own families do not suspect their true nature, that they are not in fact human.[25]

Every town has other beings who appear as normal people in every respect during the day, but at night transform themselves into supernatural animals who bring disease. Most often the "master of sickness" (*rajaw yab'il*) is pictured as acting alone, bringing deadly epidemics of flu and fevers to neighboring towns. But on at least one occasion, the masters of sickness of San Andrés were mustered as allies when their counterparts in a rival town, Concepción, attacked the community. As the narrative goes, people from Concepción sought to destroy San Andrés some years ago because townspeople were envious of the better treatment Trixanos got on the coastal plantation where they both worked. Angry at what they felt was an injustice, the people of Concepción asked their shaman-priest to send an epidemic. As people began to die, as those who had just buried the dead began to die themselves, the terrified populace called on their own master of sickness for a counterattack. To stop the escalating violence, Maya priests and the guardian divinity (the *rajaw juyu* or "master of the mountain") of each town finally met to negotiate a truce.

The human identities of the masters of sickness are said not to be known, except among themselves. When worries about strange animals are aroused, people pursue and attack the suspected master of sickness to drive it back to its own community. It must be completely destroyed because, even if only a few hairs are left, these beings are able to reconstitute themselves. Because of the nature of their work, the masters of sickness must suffer forever after death, when, along with other beings associated with witchcraft, they are transformed into cooking stones at the guardian divinity's magical plantation inside the mountain.

Other beings capable of transformation exist to punish people for misdeeds. In narratives, *la llorona* appears as a howling spirit who pursues nervous municipal patrols as they check the town late at night. She takes the form of the lover of one of the married men on the patrol. Specific men are always named in these accounts. Men are portrayed as inevitably fooled by the ruse, even though everyone knows of the existence of *la llorona*. Drawn to *la llorona* for the pleasures of a late night encounter, the adulterer must lie to his companions in order to leave them behind. Upon embracing his counterfeit lover, the man is horrified by her abrupt shape change into a monster with hooves, fangs, and a terrible face. Shouting in pain and confusion, the adulterer, in turn, reveals himself to his companions, who, against his protests, carry him home to his family. His wife's reaction is anger because she knows full well what this means, and the family finally seeks help from Maya shaman-priests to confirm the cause of the husband's illness and see if he can be restored to health. In the end, they administer whatever punishment the Maya priest prescribes.

Another, supernatural figure, the master of the wilds (*rajaw juyu*), takes people from society to a parallel world inside his sacred mountain. He is a powerful, enigmatic figure in Kaqchikel religion, because each sacred mountain has its own guardian, who may protect his people but may also lure them away from the town's patron saint. The guardian is a tall, powerful, extraordinarily rich Ladino divinity with dominion over the wilds and an enchanted plantation inside his mountain. Some Mayas petition him for fertility and good crops with the help of a diviner. To others he makes sudden, unsolicited offers of wealth. Those who receive anything from the guardian, however, soon realize that they are in debt, that they must pay back what they have received with hard labor inside the mountain. Those who are returned "to pay back their word" are changed into animals who must suffer on the plantation, their transformation from human to animal to human being accomplished by lashes from the guardian's assistants. Others are brought back to work as supernatural animals inside the mountain as a punishment for incest or having sexual relations across ethnic lines. Human-burros are fated to be burned as they stoke the fires of the volcano with stacks of bones carried on their backs. Human-pigs are raised to be slaughtered, only to be reborn and fattened once again.

When I was in San Andrés in the 1970s, elders told me that young people who had the nonvolitional "luck–destiny" to pursue careers that violated the ethnic division of labor would also be brought to the guardian's plantation. At that point, elders felt that Ladino occupations, such as white-collar work involving literacy in Spanish or truck driving instead of agricultural work in the fields, involved the risk that youths would become Ladino-like with the capacity to dominate and exploit other Mayas. While elders dreaded this eventuality, such change was associated with an individual's immutable destiny and, therefore, considered outside the powers of the community and the individual to control.

Just as these narratives in all their variety are believed to document examples of the capacity of transformation, they also describe the process of the successful *unmasking* of someone or something that appears to be something else. In the case of the master of the night, the husband sensed that he had been deceived by his wife, overcame obstacles to find out what she became when she sneaked out at night, and neutralized her ability to reassume human form by salting the pile of flesh she had left behind. In the case of the *rajaw yab'il*, when an epidemic threatened San Andrés, Maya priests were consulted to determine the cause and negotiate a truce between the guardians of the neighboring towns. When *la llorona* revealed herself to be a monster, not an impassioned lover, the adulterer was unmasked for all to see. Though protesting innocence, the man's guilt was quickly established by the Maya priests.

In an unstable world, people are transformed into supernatural animals while trying to conceal their natures and spirits transform themselves into animal and human forms. Humans can struggle to reveal the awful truth and at least neutralize it with the help of diviners. As a corpus, the narratives deal with intention by elaborating the theme of unmasking deceit. Yet, at least some of the deceit is involuntary. Masters of the night and masters of sickness are most often, but not always, compelled to act as animals, "without shame." One Catholic Action catechist concluded that their souls, their consciences have "no feeling, no response." In contrast, the adulterers in the stories of *la llorona* or the women in the accounts of those who must work inside the mountain as a punishment for sleeping with Ladinos are unmasked as people who had a choice.

These narratives live on past the traditionalist civil-religious hierarchy. For instance, some evangelical converts have rewoven these themes into personal conversion stories, which they tell in evangelizing conversations with others. In witnessing how they found Christ, individuals routinely denigrate their past in order to demonstrate the magnitude of their personal transformation in the present.[26] At first hearing, these autobiographical narratives might appear alien to traditionalist religious practices, which call on diviners to interpret the past's relevance for the present and offer stories of moral unmasking with appropriate biographical allusions. Yet, traditionalists, Catholic Action members, and Evangelicals do not necessarily honor the religious cleavages that analysts describe as absolute. Evangelical conversion stories, for example, often evoke Kaqchikel constructions of the person. In San Andrés, one well known convert and leader of his congregation appropriated the traditionalist *la llorona* narrative. In evoking this story, the new Evangelical transformed himself—that is, he converted—to escape the consequences of the unmasking of his adultery. His strategic use of the *la llorona* narrative to tell his now valuable story of conversion was thought to be particularly entertaining and clever by others, including Catholics.

The issues of transformation and unmasking appear not only in stories that are told at home to instruct children or at wakes for entertainment; they are also manifested in everyday social relations and the politics of the community. The problem of people who may not be what they appear is an ever-present subtext to political life. As one Maya leader put it:

> Yes there are people who have this capacity [to transform themselves], perhaps they're good, perhaps they're bad. Yes, this definitely exists in all areas of life. For this reason I do my investigating and make my own conclusions: Who are we in the town? For this reason people made me a leader. I have this obligation to find out who we are. Are we all united, are we loyal? Are we all the same, do we have the same thoughts? Why do I need to know this? To know who I am talking to. To know what assistance, what advice to give this person. To know what to avoid, because with some you can't. These people might be that. These people are this and are capable of that. But I keep it to myself.

Unmasking is as important as it is difficult. After the 1976 earthquake, which killed twenty thousand people in Guatemala and in which virtually everyone in the town lost their homes and businesses, the critical issue in San Andrés was who was taking advantage of volunteer positions on earthquake relief committees to divert supplies from those in great need. Similarly, during the civil war the issue was everyone's hidden politics and potential secret alliances with the military or the guerrillas. One needed to know, but one could not trust, others' self-presentations since deception was felt to be ubiquitous. As one leader concluded in discussing local political uncertainty during the violence: "There is a saying: you can't even trust your own body."[27] In this context, not trusting your own body meant doubting neighbors, coreligionists, friends, and ultimately your own family. Violence intensified distrust both outside and inside the town. In this situation, people were skeptical, not only of the body politic but also of their families, their community.

George Foster's characterization of certain Latin American communities as driven by an image of "limited good" (1967)—a world in which the moral universe is likened to a zero-sum game—may have fallen out of favor with North American anthropologists, but Mayas find this conception accurate to their situation. It resonates with people's sense of the competitiveness and danger of interpersonal relations. The social world is saturated with the strong emotion of *envidia* ("envy"), a visceral judgment that someone has more only at one's own expense. As one person explained: "People will envy the person who has a little more in life, who has more corn or another product. So someone begins to do witchcraft (*brujería*) against the person. I know people who are envious. In the past, if one had a cow, people who were poor didn't like that, they envied the person with the cow."

Those who felt they had been wronged could go to a *zajorín*, a diviner, particularly to the *ajitz* (the shaman who specialized in bringing harm to others, from *itzel*, "evil," in Kaqchikel). Illness, dreams, and lurking animal spirits had to be interpreted to see if they were the consequences of an enemy's revenge or a saint's punishment. In ambiguous situations, an individual went to a Maya priest, the *ajq'ij* (from *q'ij*, "day," in Kaqchikel), to have the situation diagnosed and rituals of healing or defense performed. Alternatively a person could visit images of the saints, asking for protection and the punishment of enemies, offering candles on a Monday, the most powerful day for diviners. Diviners clarified problems by casting and arranging red divining seeds on a table seven times to see if they fell in pairs, asking the family questions during the process.[28] They prayed with the petitioner or his family at mountain shrines, offering candles and chickens. While most anthropologists associate divining with Maya calendrics and healing, in San Andrés narratives about divining are often about unmasking dangerous emotions of those around oneself.

How to Lead in an Ambiguous World of Conflicting Interests

In Kaqchikel Maya communities like San Andrés, inner states present ambiguities that call for interpretation, even if there are limits to their interpretability. A person's inner thoughts have their own powers because they are stubbornly individualized, underscore the fragility of authority, and may be aimed at misrepresentation or the harm of another. Thus it should not be surprising that Maya culture generates leaders who are intermediaries, "third persons" as they are called. These intermediaries—be they guides of the civil-religious hierarchy, Maya priests, or, given the decline of the traditionalist system, contemporary religious and political leaders—take on the never completed work of making sense of other minds and intentions. In the past, the ritual guides of the civil-religious hierarchy celebrated moments of commonality and connection for diverse minds and focused the problem of authority and disrespect on the inner states of younger generations. Maya priests interpreted illness, accidents, misfortunes, and family deaths as the consequences of an individual's own moral failings or as the result of another's envy and anger. Contemporary leaders continue these practices, focusing their energies on the capacities of people to transform themselves and the deceits this may involve. In fact they are very proud of working well with people whom they feel they cannot really trust.

These days, however, the problem of transformation takes on a contemporary twist. Kaqchikel leaders now fear that the younger generation is involved in another kind of self-transformation, a freely chosen denial of their Maya identity. Youths can become the cultural other—they can actually pass as educated, Ladino professionals—because this generation has options that were unimaginable twenty years ago. Mayas in their twenties now have teaching degrees and are going on for university educations, radically violating the ethnic division of labor that in past generations relegated Mayas to heavy manual work and channeled Ladinos to higher status, nonmanual jobs involving literacy in Spanish and national patronage networks. Unconventional aspirations of young Mayas are no longer regarded as oddities or manifestations of a compelled luck-destiny to be punished in the plantation counterworld by the master of the mountain.

This situation has given birth to a new narrative. The San Andrés version echoes similar stories throughout the highlands. The story describes an educated youth away at high school, visited by his father, who wears the traditional white pants and the black-and-white plaid wool apron of his indigenous community. Seeing his father at the edge of the schoolyard, the youth tells his friends he will be right back. He greets his father with news that all is well at school, makes plans for a visit home during the next vacation, and receives his favorite food and praise from home. Returning to his friends, the youth explains the encounter to them: how thoughtful it was that an old family *servant* came to bring presents and good wishes from his family. How loyal the man has been to them.

The story, of course, is one of betrayal and denial. Maya youths can avoid painful confrontations with their peers' racism by presenting themselves as Ladinos in urban high schools and universities but only if they deny their own families and communities. Community leaders have responded to this dilemma by attempting to "modernize" Kaqchikel culture. Their goal has been to make it attractive and relevant to Kaqchikel youth so the cruelest deception, that of denying one's parents at the moment of one's greatest success, will not be the history of this generation.

Nine

Indigenous Activism across Generations

How is political struggle reproduced over time in Maya communities? How do succeeding generations of activists see the process? This chapter seeks to examine these issues ethnographically by retracing lifetimes of antiracism activism. Our focus will be on the social history of a Kaqchikel family and the complex interplay of these individuals as protagonists in the structured social worlds they inhabit. I am interested, on the one hand, in continuities of tacit knowledge that inform Kaqchikel family life and, on the other, in self-conscious disjunctures in cultural transmission. To paraphrase Holland and Lave (1998), this analysis will pursue contestations and oppositions that arise historically, yet—as they are reproduced across generations—become conventions that inform a variety of spheres of life. Identity, in this account, becomes a shifting composite, complexly influenced by individual protagonists, the transnational discourses they appropriate, and the shifting arenas of their activism.

The irony of an "across-generations" framing of activism and cultural transmission is that it forces anthropologists to double back on the discipline's conventional method for ethnographic production. Anthropological writing seeks to bring social institutions and events into focus, yet much of the raw data for our general images of social life comes through personal and autobiographical encounters with specific individuals who narrativize their reality in ways that catch our attention. Writing becomes the process of effacing the personal encounter of fieldwork to achieve the appearance of a higher level of abstraction. Recent ethnographic experiments have attempted to remind us of the intimacy of cultural production for those we study and the dialogical method of knowing central to anthropological research.[1] What I attempt to retain in this chapter is the initial autobiographical dimension from the accounts of Maya activists and institution builders.

An across-generations inquiry also raises the issue of how anthropologists conceptualize generations and how Mayas inevitably confound analysts' reified expectations with social practices that draw in issues far beyond Western conceptions of generation.[2] Central to this formulation is the issue of Maya family dynamics and the ways social relations and patrilocal kinship ideologies constitute individual experiences and are transformed in the unfolding of actual lives. That *intra*generational relations turn out to be as important as relations across generations should not surprise us; the question is how individuals instantiate particular social forms, with their inevitable tensions, and how social forms in all their variety shape the process. Further implicated in the consideration of kinship relations is the issue of *historical generation* in the sense of the formative political and economic conditions that create different experiential environments and existential dilemmas for individuals in the same cohort. As this analysis will show, Maya social ideologies, their structuring of kinship relations, and the political experiences of historical generations are central to the understanding of individual agency and the persistence of oppositions beyond their formative origins. Moreover, one cannot really talk about the practice of kinship, community authority, or historical generations without dealing with Maya constructions of the person and the complications this cultural formation creates for all sorts of social relations.

The ethnographic element of this analysis illustrates the ways Mayas have employed and transformed their culture to challenge social arrangements that have historically subordinated and marginalized them. Throughout the chapter, I juxtapose Maya imaginaries of the relations between generations—drawn from rituals, fantasy, and social critiques—with the political biography of a prominent Kaqchikel Maya activist family in San Andrés, whom I will call the Ixims. The constant in this family has been social activism, first local and regional and most recently national. But their tactics, sense of indigenous identity, and ways of moralizing continuity versus discontinuity have often put members of this extended family at odds with each other. It is in this intimate family context that the analysis examines cultural transmission and political action.

Before engaging these issues ethnographically, however, I want to revisit current anthropological framings of indigenous identity in Guatemala. My goal is to introduce a reflexive element to this analysis. That is, we need to identify another anthropological level on which oppositions arise historically, become conventionalized, and are reproduced through the interventions of particular individuals.

Narrating Identity Politics: A Clash of Anthropologies

Anthropologists have found many ways of narrating Guatemalan history and identity politics. *Anti-racism narratives* speak of agrarian communities as centers of cultural resistance to colonial rule.[3] According to this perspective, Maya culture has gained its colonial and postcolonial forms as an oppositional discourse to Guatemalan racism, which has changed in character in response to economic transformations without losing its ethnic hierarchy or invidiousness over the last five hundred years. Mayas have replied to domination and exploitation with a striking blend of Maya and Catholic religions, strategies of separatism, and regional economic practices that have allowed some Mayas greater commercial autonomy.[4] This line of analysis conventionally begins with the colonially imposed ethnic division of labor that forced Mayas into the role of impoverished agricultural laborers who, in order to make a living, worked on Spanish and Ladino plantations and more recently on commercial farms for export.

By contrast, *continuity narratives* focus on the persistence across centuries of pre-Columbian beliefs and practices that demonstrate the success Mayas have had in constituting a cultural world that is more than a reflection of colonial society.[5] Maya languages, cosmology, beliefs in transforming selves, distinctive notions of "soul," shamanism, base-twenty mathematics, and distinctive calendrics would be examples of generalized continuities over great periods of time despite tremendous changes in other aspects of culture. Rather than existing outside history, Mayas inhabit a distinctive stream of history, perpetuated through languages and beliefs that antedate the conquest. This narration argues against Maya culture as a reaction to ethnic oppression.

Challenging both views, *mestizaje narratives* deny that there is a specifically "indigenous" story to tell by pointing out the blend of cultures and of family lines that occurred during the colonial period. From this perspective, waves of indigenous acculturation and physical *mestizaje* undermined Ladino and *indígena* as mutually exclusive entities and erased the salience of claims of ethnic distinctiveness. To talk in terms of ethnic categories is to hide the real issue of the cross-ethnic character of class oppression for the rural poor and to ignore the fact that Ladinos do not collectively oppress Mayas. Ethnic arguments are examples of the lingering of conventional distinctions—indigenous and Ladino—past their time of social relevance.

Anthropologists, including the present author, have tended to see these alternative formulations as being at war with each other. We have tended to teach each others' analyses not for their heterodox moments, but for the ways in which they represent opposing schools of thought. This chapter explores the possibility of an excluded middle for the analysis of identity politics—the coexistence of multiple politics and histories that are hidden by the antagonism of these anthropological constructions. Both continuity and resistance narratives are salient to anthropological understandings of the impetus and dilemmas of activism. Being Maya is not a singular identity for these activists, ethnicity is not a separate domain but rather a product of all sorts of transnational culture flows, and the struggle for justice involves the creation of very different activist communities. Furthermore, the ambiguous nature of social relations—their zero-sum character in a world where other selves are not fully knowable or constant—continues to serve as a formative medium for community affairs. Activism, leadership styles, and Maya cultural resurgence have been influenced by local culture in all its diversity and by the need to reply to the character of ethnic domination—with its own continuities and ruptures—current in the country at any one historical moment.[6]

The Older Generations: Traditionalism and Religious Rebellion

In 1993, from the living room of his house just outside San Andrés, Don Gustavo's harangue to me about his nephews, Alfonso and No'j, was spontaneous and intense:

> I've talked to those who head this movement. To really recover Maya culture, we would have to return to the ways of our ancestors. To recover everything we would have to speak our indigenous language. Yet we are the guilty ones with our children. None of our children speaks our language. I'm not going to correct these people; they are very educated. But my view is: how are we going to recover our culture, how are our children to recover it if we are the ones who teach our children modern things, new things? To recover this, we would have to go back to the kitchen and cook on the floor over the three stones, the *tenemastes*. But these intellectuals don't have hearth stones, they probably have something even better than my wood stove.
>
> At the great university and grand meetings of our indigenous people, the indigenous intellectual gives his talk on indigenous culture. But when he goes to give the talk, he should be wearing indigenous dress. But no. Why? To recover our culture, he should wear indigenous dress. I tell you with pride this is what I wear. Some may say we look like clowns. But they should put on indigenous dress.
>
> Once, two of these great intellectuals argued. One said to the other, "If you are going to give these talks, you have to wear indigenous dress. No one will believe you, dressed as you are now."

Don Gustavo Ixim, the focus of this family biography, has struggled for five decades to organize the community of San Andrés within the scope of regional networks of Catholic Action groups. Now eighty years old, he narrates his life as one of tireless leadership, community building, and political savvy in religious and civic affairs. His personal identification with and submission to the authority of the Catholic Church and its teachings are fundamental to his life, as it has been to his brothers, who are also catechists. There have been times of deep disillusionment in his life. As a youth he struggled personally over his wife's inability to have more children after dangerous pregnancies and the birth of their only daughter early in the marriage. Then, and later in his life when he was caught up in the hard-drinking political culture of public office, Don Gustavo faced self-destructive bouts of alcoholism. With his health and credibility seriously threatened by drunkenness—he was killing himself, as everyone could see—he struggled back by quietly joining AA in a neighboring community. He presents his life story as a witness to the struggle against alcohol abuse and the constancy of religious faith that informs his ceaseless drive for institution building in the community.

In his youth, Don Gustavo's father migrated from the K'ichee' town of Totonicapán to San Andrés and sought, with only partial success, to shed his image as an outsider in the endogamous community. To gain membership, he offered service in the Maya-run saint societies, participated in other traditionalist activities, and "invented" the practice of bringing well-known marimbas to the town for the liminal dances at major festivals. His four sons assisted their father, learned traditionalist beliefs, and took advantage of the education available to peasant families—three years of local elementary school, during which they learned Spanish. They married women from quite humble families in the *municipio*. The youths, however, decided on a nonconventional path when they opted to join a new religious group organizing in the community. Catholic Action, part of a national movement to bring indigenous people into the fold of sacramental Catholicism, categorically opposed the gerontocracy of the traditionalist civil-religious hierarchy, welcomed all Catholics as equals before God, and encouraged youthful leadership. Don Gustavo's conversion was a stunning move because it meant not just turning his back on his father's tactic for community membership but challenging the delicate balance of ethnic relations in the town.

Community-focused traditionalism can be seen as an attempt to maintain moral space in a world dominated by the ethnic other, the Ladino landholder. Ladinos understood the politics of traditionalism as a nonthreatening form of separatism. In their minds, it encouraged submission to a division of labor that compelled Mayas to work as laborers for non-Mayas. The "hidden transcript" of traditionalism—liminal moments when social dramas[7] and communal dances ridiculed and inverted local power structures, including plantation life, the authority of Maya elders, and parental authority over their offspring—was either accepted as entertainment at major religious festivals or never understood by the dominant ethnic group for what it was. Significantly, when Catholic Action began to organize, local Ladinos threw their support to the traditionalists.[8]

In the narrow construction, Catholic Action was an attempt to counteract the religious authority of traditionalist Catholicism and shamanism and to reintegrate local congregations into the formal hierarchy of the Catholic church. Catechists—who were literate, bilingual, and specially trained lay leaders of the congregation—worked to convert townspeople away from the heterodox practices of the saint societies. Politically, Catholic Action was part of Archbishop Rossell y Arellana's program in the 1940s and 1950s to depoliticize impoverished indigenous populations, whom national elites feared might find communism more attractive than grueling, poorly paid plantation labor.

During the revolutionary presidency of Jacobo Arbenz (1951–54), Don Gustavo awakened politically when, as a young adult who had worked on local plantations, he was invited to join one of the newly constituted agrarian reform committees. The committee's mandate was to identify, for possible redistribution, plantations in the region that were not cultivating all their land. The group had barely begun when a U.S.-bolstered counterrevolutionary force, led by Carlos Castillo Armas, successfully invaded Guatemala and took over the government in 1954. Although the redistributive policies that involved peasants in mainstream politics were quickly dismantled, a younger indigenous generation had experienced something novel—politics outside the scope and age structure of their communities. This early exposure appears to have had a catalytic impact on Don Gustavo's life, even as he turned to Catholic Action, the organization that conservative elites had chartered for young activists, and internalized the archbishop's hatred of the revolutionary period for its radical politics and anticlericalism.

In practice, local catechists such as Don Gustavo repoliticized the Catholic movement, using its universalist language to legitimize the struggle against ethnic discrimination, hateful stereotypes, and social hierarchies that marginalized indigenous people in community affairs. Catechists urged this worldly action to mirror their newly found religious universalism, and organized community groups to promote agrarian cooperative membership and school attendance. In so doing, they were responding to the agrarian poverty of their congregations. U.S. development agencies encouraged these efforts and financially supported the cooperative movement as an antidote to leftist politics. Thus, with external support from various sources, the catechists began the long process of undermining traditionalism and challenging the ethnic division of labor and politics.

To differentiate their Christ-centric sense of Christianity from the worship of the saint societies, the catechists dispensed with the practice of elaborate processions of the saints and focused on study sessions and rosaries during the week and on mass on Sundays. They rejected the social relations that structured the saint societies: the elaborate ascending scale of offices, through which adult men moved during the course of their lives to gain moral authority and finally become community elders. Rather, Catholic Action offered leadership positions and continuing education on a wide variety of topics and created a generation of locally based cultural brokers in wider social and political affairs. Young men, and in some cases young women, could now speak out on morality, though their authority and frame of reference were rooted in contemporary institutionalized Catholicism rather than in the local community.

In an interesting way, however, Catholic Action came to reenact the older principle of gerontocracy: as the first catechists matured, they became elders and overseers of the movement, and youths were channeled to specialized groups and choirs. The life cycle of the founding catechists created a new social hierarchy, a large and very active congregation, and qualms among secular youths about this religious reply to traditionalism.

There have been other limits to Catholic Action's universalism. On the whole, wives play private supportive roles to their husbands' leadership. Don Gustavo's wife, Elena, who remains illiterate despite the group's stress on continuing education, keeps their busy homestead running. Few girls of her generation had access to much schooling, and those who came from outlying hamlets, as she did, often worked at home and failed to attend school. There was never an opportunity to catch up. Don Gustavo's sister-in-law, María, has always been an entrepreneur, adding important income to the family economy through her regional weaving business. Neither woman has the time or inclination to serve actively in the organization founded by their husbands.

Younger members of the Ixim family, including Alfonso—Gustavo's older brother's eldest son—chafed at the personal discipline required of leaders in Catholic Action. Rather, these youths decided to use their education, the right to which had been won by activist parents, to dispute the conventional ethnic division of labor. They were looking for something other than hard manual labor and subsistence farming to support their families. These youths finished the project of tearing down traditionalism through a legal challenge of the unpaid service demanded by traditionalists for their organizations. Some became development workers and teachers, others migrated to the capital and the coast for work. Activists who stayed in their home communities found pathways to local influence through community youth work and neighborhood improvement projects.

The catechist parents of these educated youths grew worried about the younger generation, about their capacity for betrayal. Some parents fantasized that their children would learn martial arts and beat them up. Others worried their children would pass as Ladinos outside San Andrés to get ahead on their own.

Back to the Future: An Experiment in Revitalization

In San Andrés, the catechists felt that one way out of this double bind was to involve their children in efforts to reinvigorate Kaqchikel culture. After Catholic Action's earlier hostility toward *costumbre*, I was surprised to see Don Gustavo spearheading an effort to revive traditionalism in 1989. In the 1970s, Catholic Action had undercut traditionalism through direct competition, a tactic it used after its initial attempts at accommodation foundered. It deprived the saints societies of willing participants by demanding that converts stay away from processions, rituals, and community festivals. They denounced the heterodoxy and "impurity" of the civil-religious hierarchy whose celebrations involved liminal drunkenness and sexual license at major celebrations such as Holy Week and the feast of the community's patron saint.

Catholic Action, with help from growing evangelical congregations, emerged triumphant. By the mid 1970s, the statues of the saints were cared for in private homes rather than in the brotherhood shrines, which had fallen into disuse. Respected *principales* no longer called everyone to serve the community for a year at a time in the saint societies, the community church, or the municipal offices. Ritual guides no longer choreographed the meetings and processions of the civil-religious hierarchy so that each wing of the organization was well represented and people found their rightful place in the elaborate social rankings. The poetic dialogues of prayer were no longer recited before ritual meals. Occasionally, a particularly devoted person would refurbish a shrine and take on public duties; at one point Ladinos assumed the task, then a highly religious Maya woman. But the communal dimensions of the celebration withered.

What astounded me most in 1989 was the surprising resurrection of saint society rituals long after their apparent demise. Catholic Action decided to dramatize them as *actos culturales* to audiences of hundreds of Mayas, who found themselves absolutely entranced by the productions, held to inaugurate the new social salon at the church. Moreover, Don Gustavo, who had done everything he could to undermine the legitimacy of the traditionalists, enthusiastically described his duties as the work of a *k'amöl b'ey*, a ritual guide.

In this experiment, Don Gustavo saw his role as rekindling memories to teach young people about their cultural identity. For the catechists, the rituals were no longer sacred ceremonies; rather, they were plays in which young people—always in male-female pairs dressed in newly acquired traditionalist outfits instead of their everyday Western clothing—played the parts of the ritual guide, the saint society head, his assistants, and their respective wives. As the catechists emphasized, the plays were not held in sacred space, not in the Church's sanctuary, but rather in the new hall, which they anticipated would be the center of active youth programming for the congregation. The vignettes were perhaps an hour long, in contrast to the three to five days of rituals and processions at the key junctures of the sacred calendar in the past.

With the blessing of several Catholic priests who watched the event, Don Gustavo and the other catechists organized a selective remembering of saint society rituals with the explicit goal of affirming what had now become problematic: the continuity of Maya culture. This was "imperialist nostalgia" (Rosaldo 1990) from indigenous insiders, for clearly, in challenging *costumbre* and promoting nontraditional education, the activities of Catholic Action had eroded local commitments to these forms of identity and cultural distinctiveness. Nevertheless, for Catholic Action the authenticity of the skits rested in the immediacy of their connection to traditionalist rituals in San Andrés. Knowledgeable grandparents had been consulted along with a retired ritual guide so that the rituals would be just right. As one leader put it, "We are doing our own ethnography for these rituals."

The festival showcased young couples who marched in procession to the stage, reenacted the saint society's preparations for the titular feast of the town, and celebrated the harvest ceremonies including the storage of the crops and the hand-grinding of corn for tortilla dough, a process long ago replaced by machines. Notably missing were the high points of traditionalist practices: the fraternal ritual meals during which the guides offered their dialogues, the worship at altars overflowing with saints who were periodically taken through the town in procession, the drunken nights of marimba music and dancing at the end of major celebrations, and the shamanic rituals. The selectivity of religious memory appeared to be driven by the compatibility of certain traditionalist activities with Catholic orthodoxy and the continuing unacceptability of other activities, officials, and icons.

What became compatible or incompatible for Catholic Action was the historical product of the interplay of the two religious organizations.[9] Thus, echoes of the older tensions between Catholic Action and the traditionalist saint societies resurfaced in the commemoration even as the event was explicitly about recapturing the ever-problematic youth.

The focus on the next generation was strategic, given the prevailing fear that youths who associated Maya culture with agrarian poverty and marginalization would abandon their community. In response, catechists deliberately tried to update Maya culture so it would be more attractive to current social needs. This meant acknowledging that young adults, especially those with high-school educations and nonagricultural aspirations as teachers and office workers, needed social recognition and a respected place in the community. They, not the elders, were the new commentators and organizers of skits during the festival. Another anxiety very close to the surface was that the Catholic Church would lose the next generation to the Evangelicals. The festival was designed to counterbalance the Evangelicals' alleged lack of interest in maintaining Kaqchikel culture.

These concerns may well explain the focus on couples and the interest among catechists in reviving traditionalist marriage negotiation rituals. Historically, the *pedida*—which involved ritual guides as go-betweens for the families of the groom and bride in an endogamous community—called for a prolonged and stylized set of rituals to express heightened respect for parental authority. Narrative tension, one of the most enjoyable parts of the ritual in people's personal and historical accounts, was interjected as the bride's family feigned lack of interest or coolly asked for more time to deliberate. The *pedida* was another focal point of Maya traditionalism, although I did not understand its importance in my first fieldwork in 1970 because of my own bias—an uncritical reflection of the sentiments of my department and the discipline at the time—against doing research on devalued "private" family issues or on women.[10]

Traditionalist marriage negotiations were part of a discovery procedure, another variant of unmasking, to see if the girl's parents opposed the union. Initial refusals on the part of her parents were expected; in the event of serious impediments, it is said that the family would throw chiles on their cooking fire or bring hot water to the door to signal an unacceptable match. Rituals called for gift giving and a marriage ceremony, after which the couple lived together, often with the parents of the girl, until the groom paid off his obligation, at which time his family was expected to offer a house site near those of his father and brothers, where the family home would be constructed.

The emphasis in 1989 was on the use of the ritual to promote the continuity of congregations and Maya identity, insuring that young people could marry within the town into families that shared religious commitments. Another veiled concern might well have been the growing numbers of single mothers, something that is said not to have been a problem in the old days as marriages were arranged as soon as adolescents showed any sexual interest. As memories of the past were filtered through the needs of the present, it was not surprising that the catechists saw themselves as *k'amöl b'ey*. During the public events, they yielded the contemporary role of the microphoned hosts to activist youths, who with great élan narrated events and played tapes of traditionalist marimba music on their prominently displayed boom boxes. The catechists, however, safeguarded the role of neo-traditionalist marriage negotiators for themselves. The line between orthodoxy and heterodoxy was remembered in novel ways.

As much as everyone enjoyed the excitement of two days of reenactments and nightlife in a normally quiet, dusty town, the festive celebrations soon lost momentum and were abandoned by Catholic Action. Don Gustavo explained that the church hierarchy, despite its great consternation about evangelical conversions of young people, had decided not to sanction these practices. Another aspect of this decision was most likely the fact that Trixano youths active in the Pan-Maya movement, which was just picking up steam at that point, had a convergent project of revitalization, but one with very different religious goals, including the revitalization of the authority of traditionalist shaman-priests (*ajq'ij*).

The Restlessness of the Next Generation

Alfonso, now fifty years old, experimented with ethnic passing when he worked in Guatemala City as a mechanic in the late 1960s. With six years of education, including studies outside the town in Quetzaltenango, he might easily have disappeared into urban life; he was literate, fluent in Spanish, and restless. When home in San Andrés, he refused to carry firewood with a tumpline across his forehead because, for him, it marked the submission of Mayas to degrading poverty. Alfonso had inherited his family's disdain for traditionalism and thirst for authority, but there was no employment outlet in the town for his energy. At home for a quick visit in 1970, Alfonso met a young anthropologist and worked for her as a field assistant for six months. To his parents' delight, the work reconnected him with San Andrés and his family after an absence of three years. The anthropologist's fascination with Maya culture had little impact on Alfonso, who demeaned traditionalism as archaic and shamanism as witchcraft. As he explains it, anthropological research helped him refine skills that he later used as an office worker and cooperative organizer for the national federation of agricultural cooperatives.

Alfonso narrates his life as an individual who successfully organized Maya peasants into agrarian and housing cooperatives and gained a regional following through his knowledge of bureaucratic procedures, national law, Maya culture, and the Kaqchikel and Spanish languages. His antiracism work was decidedly secular. During the day, he visited the agrarian communities in the region to establish new cooperatives. At night, his house always had visitors: illiterate farmers with a bureaucratic worry they could only express in Kaqchikel, someone who needed legal help in a dispute, school children with assignments on the history of the town.

As the only Maya operating out of the district office, Alfonso enjoyed regional influence; he became an avid participant in national cooperative organizations, advanced technical courses, and political meetings, where local leaders were courted by national political figures who sought rural votes. His political base grew as did his ties with politicians and party organizations; he yearned for political office. Alfonso had found his way in a system that cynically patronized Mayas; he was locally based but transregionally concerned. In the late 1970s he ran for a congressional seat and apparently won the election only to find that, in the turmoil of the counterinsurgency war, the election results had been nullified.

Alfonso's work in the cooperative movement reemerged in the mid 1980s, when it was again safe to be involved in development organizations and institution building. His many scrapbooks document his activism, marriage to a Maya schoolteacher from a prominent family in the region, and the achievements of their children in school. Their house was a center of activity for the extended family and his public responsibilities. The rooms were comfortable and brimming with technology: a typewriter for late-night work in his office, a refrigerator in the storeroom, a propane stove in the kitchen (which had yet to displace the raised wood fire for cooking because of the fear of explosions), and, in the family room/bedroom, a stereo for daytime music and a television for evening favorites like *MacGyver*, *Sábado Gigante*, Mexican cowboy movies, and the national news.

Different Paths to Pan-Maya Activism

Both Gustavo and Alfonso were lucky to have survived the violence. They ceased virtually all public activities, avoided unnecessary travel, and kept to themselves politically. Alfonso's youngest brother, No'j, now thirty years old, lived through the violence as a young teenager. Later he was offered a scholarship by a linguistics project and, with years of advanced training, grew active in the Maya movement's efforts in language revitalization. With support from North American linguists and European funders, his group has published sophisticated linguistics research on major indigenous languages and general education materials on Maya language and culture. Their antiracism work has taken the shape of promoting cultural resurgence and autonomy in a project that seeks rededication to the *cultural* needs of rural communities. The group has the urgency of working against the flow of history and the *mestizaje* narrative (which they call *ladinización*) in an attempt to halt the process of assimilation and the loss of native speakers of Guatemala's twenty-one Maya languages.

No'j's historical generation is the first in town to aspire to university education. In Quetzaltenango, special part-time programs were established for Maya commuters, many of whom already have jobs and families to support. In the capital, Maya linguistics programs at two universities have attracted activists, who study in addition to their regular jobs and volunteer teaching. Like many other Mayanists, No'j maintains strong ties with his home community. His young wife and their children live back in San Andrés, where the younger brothers of the family have constructed homes. Despite urban work and ongoing college studies elsewhere, No'j's generation is striving to follow the Maya preference for brothers to co-reside with their parents in a patrilocal configuration. As families grow past the size of the parental compound, older brothers move to nearby parcels if they can, and maintain the extended family through frequent visits, joint meals, and day-care arrangements.

As a youngest son, No'j will inherit his parents' household and the responsibility for their care late in life. This practice has given No'j other ways in which to be Maya. Like many Pan-Mayanists, however, he has broken with the endogamy of the community and married a fellow activist from another region of the country, whom he met at work. In his practice of cultural resurgence, No'j has the passion of a convert. He speaks only Kaqchikel in the family compound so his children might begin their lives as monolingual Maya speakers. This self-conscious practice seeks to counter the shift to Spanish that has occurred in many Kaqchikel-Maya homes since the 1970s. Moreover, No'j insists on speaking the Pan-Mayanist version of Kaqchikel, which strives toward regional standardization and avoids common Spanish loan words in order to signify the modern capacity and autonomy of the language. Strikingly, No'j's revitalization inverts the conventional generational authority of cultural transmission and substitutes standardized Maya culture disseminated by Pan-Maya research centers, such as his own, for local practices.

On the home front, No'j has only been partially successful. In a quiet way, his parents have proven to be unwilling to submit themselves to the discipline of revitalization, primarily because their family strategy has always been a bicultural one, in which it is important for children to master Spanish and Ladino practices in order to make their way in the world. During the week, while No'j works in the city, his mother and father subversively switch to Spanish in dealing with their grandchildren and daughter-in-law, who in any event speaks a different Maya language and still finds Kaqchikel a challenge.

The hardest part of revitalization for the older generation has been the renunciation of Christianity by many Pan-Mayanists. No'j and his older brother, Alfonso, now see Christianity, in all its incarnations,[11] as colonialism. No'j remains decidedly secular at this point in his life and rejects all religious authority, much as his older brother once did. Alfonso feels that Christianity would be better replaced by shamanism for family rituals and communal celebrations of the Maya New Year. In a surprising move, he has become a shaman-priest, training with other regional Maya priests in rituals and calendrics and now using the name Nimajay. For a while he left office work—which had soured with dangerous interpersonal tensions—and dedicated himself to the revitalization of traditionalist councils of elders through COCADI, a national organization. His wife, a professional in her own right as one of the first generation of Maya teachers in the San Andrés schools, has family and revitalization contacts in Chimaltenango, which has facilitated a new geographic connection. But Alfonso worried about giving up his local authority, feeling that in middle age a definitive move to build a new career from scratch would be very difficult. Moreover, forgoing the entitlements of patrilocality would deprive him of his familial power base in San Andrés. No doubt there is a gender politics to these ongoing calculations.

Alfonso has found deep personal satisfaction in performing family rituals for blessings and healing, in nationally promoting traditionalist authority in communal affairs, and in public conferences where shaman-priests add seriousness of purpose and authenticity to the proceedings. Many of his old organizational talents have been transferred to this new interest. He is now an insider in a wing of the movement where practical experience in community organizing, not university education, is important.

At times, tensions have emerged between the academic and shamanistic wings of the movement, though they are engaged in overlapping forms of transculturalism to promote Maya culture. Both groups invited the art historian, Linda Schele, to conduct workshops on Maya glyphs and their translation. In 1993, she gave a workshop in San Andrés, which brought catechists, teachers, shaman-priests, and other community leaders together. Many minicourses for Maya leaders have been held in Antigua and Chimaltenango.

The scholarly wing prizes the esoteric, practical knowledge that shamans have of ancient culture, religion, and calendrics. Many seek shamanic assistance and have the interlocking cycles of the Maya calendar programmed on their laptops. Yet the young professionals, now caught in a culture of bureaucratic credentialing as they seek funding for their projects, also wonder how one knows whether a shaman-priest is deserving of his or her authority, given that they know of no formal body that regulates this status. (In fact, shamans now have their own federation, training programs, and investitures, though their activities are often not public.) At Pan-Maya meetings of the scholarly wing, such as the 1994 national conference on Maya educational policy, shaman-priests found themselves invited to officiate at rituals but having to protest to gain voice as educators with their own concerns for revitalization.

The older generation of the Ixim family is confounded by their children's participation in Pan-Mayanism. They see great irony in a movement that idealizes respect for elders yet in practice takes away their authority and moral voice. In his 1993 harangue, Uncle Gustavo bitterly outlined the contradictions he sees in the movement: its selective language of cultural recovery, embrace of modern technology, use of Spanish, and men's avoidance of indigenous dress that would mark them as ethnically distinctive and tied to rural communities. He used subversively ironic language—"the great university," "the grand meetings," "the indigenous intellectual"—to widen the distance between university and community affairs. In practice, the children of his family have eroded these separations. For his part, Don Gustavo is a respected local and regional intellectual who has organized hundreds of meetings, great and small, and has made a very successful living with his hands. Most recently, he has explored the feasibility of growing indigenous medicinal plants for a company that offers organic products to customers through catalogue sales. One wonders if Don Gustavo uses this ironic language to express his resentment of emerging class tensions and a youthful generation that has done little if any direct agricultural work but rather celebrates its achievements in other technologies. So he has invented new narratives of betrayal—animated with stoves that everyone fears will blow up.

By contrast, his older brother, Don Luis, speaks with equanimity of the cosmic Maya life cycle in which an older generation dies so new generations might be born. He sees the inevitable end of what his generation has been able to achieve through their efforts in the church, schools, commercial crop production, and local government. Given the historical circumstances, they have advanced the cause, especially from the days when indigenous people were expected to step off the sidewalk with hats in hand so Ladinos could pass unimpeded. Now the next generation will assume the struggle with different tactics, only to be replaced by still other generations.[12] Both elders deeply value the dedication of their entire adult lives to faith in Christ and religious activism. No doubt they are pleased that one of the family's sons has combined leadership in neighborhood improvement projects with religious devotion as a catechist offering religious instruction at a nearby Catholic girls school. The idea that the God of their people and their children might be another divinity—the builder-modeler Tz'aqol B'itol of ancient Maya mythistory—is far beyond these elders' capacity for personal transformation.

Generational Change and Ideological Diversity in Pan-Mayanism

What is striking in this family biography of Maya activists is the interweaving of generation, life-cycle dynamics, organizational genesis, and national politics. There has been an interplay of discontinuity and rejection of Maya practices with continuity and revitalization. Each generation and subgeneration has found its own language for critiquing racism and discrimination and has often been judged in some way as complicit by the next generation. Tensions generated by changing political and economic circumstances have been expressed and experienced in the language of generational change. Sherry Ortner's (1995) call for thick ethnographic description to examine subgroup politics as something beyond an overdetermined reflection of wider social hierarchies and her challenge to anthropologists to pursue the interplay of resistance and complicity in intergroup relations finds strong resonance in this analysis.

As we have found, there are important, specifically *intra*generational dynamics in this family grammar of identity and activism. In Maya families, the eldest and youngest sons are important markers of generation. The eldest has important authority and becomes almost a father figure to the family. Even today, the eldest son (*nimalaxel*) is routinely consulted for personal advice by younger brothers and sisters. Alfonso's easy authority, articulateness, and activism was reinforced by his position as an eldest and by his experiences of organizational authority. The youngest (*ch'ip*), who is expected to be indulged by his parents, inherits the family homestead and the responsibility for caring for his parents at the end of their lives. Thus,

No'j—who might have drifted off to Guatemala City like his brother or to the United States as other Mayas of his generation did—was called back to San Andrés by kinship obligations and by an ideology that stresses the importance of Maya language and family ties to community. Kinship served as a crosscurrent to the urbanization of the Pan-Maya movement.

It would be a mistake, however, to talk about Guatemalan politics as if they were external to and separate from family dynamics—a reinvention of the domestic/public split that feminist anthropology has critiqued so successfully. Clearly, in the Maya case, generational politics has a synergistic relation with community and national politics. This analysis suggests that the ideological diversity of the Pan-Maya movement is not just produced by differences in regional language groups or by decentralized community loyalties. In addition, Maya constructions of kinship and the person contribute to this diversity. It also suggests that the structural tensions of Maya kinship are being enacted at least in some families through the *intra*-movement dynamics of Pan-Mayanism. Much anthropological ink has been spilled on the Ladino/Maya opposition in Guatemala. Yet, this analysis reveals additional sets of contestations and oppositions that shape and are shaped by participants' identities within the dynamics of Maya identity: revitalization ideologies, kinship, religion, and gender.

Clearly, elements of the antiracism, cultural continuity, and *mestizaje* narratives are at work in this phenomenology. The present analysis suggests that antiracism narratives are incomplete to the extent that they focus on "the other"—the racist—without a full consideration of the dynamics and diversity of indigenous identity. As we have seen, the continuity narrative is not as linear as its language suggests. Rather there is an interweaving of historically deep and tacit elements of Maya culture with the current debates about community and identity. This analysis also suggests a wider construction of *mestizaje*, one that considers the Pan-Maya distrust of this language and, rather than biologizing the process or treating it as a fait accompli, traces the transnational cultural flows that at different moments have intensified Maya identity—religious and cultural.

In the past, tension among the generations was expressed in ritual dialogues and mythistories and enacted in liminal rituals. For traditionalists, the rejection of respect for elders could bring moral wrath and punishment from God at their calling. For Catholic Action, there were fantasies that the youth would rebel and betray their elders. Now, at the turn of generations, when a younger set of elders is about to replace another, there is a combination of anger at a new betrayal and peaceful resignation in the face of cosmic cycles of rebirth through destruction.

This analysis has implications for the way we conceptualize politics, the interplay (rather than any mutually exclusive nature) of continuity and discontinuity, and the relation of individuals to social criticism. It may also shed light on Maya creativity and their proclivity to generate a tremendous number of leaders only to find that others resist their constituted authority. Many have commented on the proliferation of Maya organizations in the Pan-Maya movement—at each conference, new organizations and networks are launched to transcend the divisions of existing groups. Some anthropologists have pointed out that Mayas have not had the political or economic resources to build large formal organizations. This situation, however, appears to be changing with the involvement of European funders who have opened up new possibilities and generated demands for centralized indigenous organizations through their peace accord projects. Other observers have argued that the proliferation of grassroots organizations is a cultural tactic, born of the uncertainties of Guatemalan politics that brutally punished overt opposition during the recent civil war. This analysis suggests an additional factor: the social relations of generational change as a mediator of political struggle.

Conclusions _____

Tracing the "Invisible Thread
of Ethnicity"

> There are Mayas who argue these studies do more
> harm than good for the movement.
>   *Demetrio Cojtí Cuxil (1997, 133)*

DESPITE THE hegemonic image Ladino culture enjoys in national affairs, alternative realities erupt from time to time to defy its terms, even on the highest level. While addressing the Guatemalan National Congress in 1975 about Ladino land seizures that had victimized Maya peasants, Representative Fernando Tesagüic Tohom (one of only two Maya representatives in Congress at that point) was said to have suddenly lapsed into his Maya language. He was immediately called to order for not speaking in the official national language, Spanish. The incident was reported in the national press and is still referred to years later. Pan-Maya activist Enrique Sam Colop interprets this as a moment when the representative, speaking about an issue that affected him deeply, switched unconsciously to his maternal language in order to express himself freely. This was not simply a tactical move or protest. For Mayanists, the unintentional "failure to observe order" (*falta al orden*) and the anger it evoked in Congress reveal the arbitrary and imposed nature of the official system (1983, 66).

In their writings, Mayanists suggest that the national order is fated to crack and fissure only to expose other underlying realities: how little is actually shared, how much is unintelligible to those in power, how fragile the claim is to a singular nationality, and how social critiques claim audiences in other than the official language. Thus, the belligerent call to order—a dramatic show of control—only revealed a much more fundamental lack of control. As Alberto Melucci (1989) would suggest, remembering the event in this vein pushes the discourse of power to its limits and demonstrates the self-contradictory character of state rationality. Once the instability and arbitrariness of existing arrangements is unmasked, Mayanists argue it is imperative that the government and wider public recognize the national stature of the country's cultural pluralism. Given that Mayas make up a substantial percentage of the national population and that indigenous rights were propelled to center stage in the 1996 peace accords, these issues are likely to gain greater attention in the next decade. As Cojtí Cuxil has announced: "Guatemala is a multinational society. . . . That is to say 'Guatemalan culture' cannot be other than a confederation of cultures and languages in which each preserves its originality" (1991a, 6, 84).

History, of course, provides complex protagonists, and so it turns out that Tezahuic Tohón is most often remembered in silence as a warning rather than a hero. In 1976 he attempted to create the Indigenous Party of Guatemala and become "the maximal leader of the indigenous people," only to be forced—after hostile accusations in the press and congress that he was promoting racism and class conflict—to repackage the political party as nondiscriminatory and nationalist. The renamed Front for National Integration was compelled to retool its nascent indigenous agenda and forge alliances with existing parties as Tezahuic Tohón sought votes to extend its base past the core of several hundred activists. In what are portrayed as desperate attempts to consolidate power within the raw hegemony of insider party politics, Tezahuic Tohón courted parties across the spectrum only to end up joining the right-wing alliance supporting General Lucas García for president. This futile alliance generated few votes and no momentum or enduring party structure. In hindsight, it was also a terrible political misstep, as Lucas García soon became one of the chief architects of state terrorism directed toward the Maya highlands in the early 1980s.[1]

This whispered story of the dangers of Guatemalan democracy and the complex vulnerability of those who seek political power haunts Mayanists who acknowledge the formidable obstacles to entering party politics on the national level despite the Maya numerical majority in many highland communities. It illustrates why a movement that holds presidential candidate forums and is proud of the election of Maya mayors and congressional representatives and the formation of civic committees to promote local candidates has nevertheless been extremely cautious about organizing politically as long as other paths to influence prove effective and parties resist change.

At the heart of Pan-Maya activism is the project of rendering "national culture" explicitly problematic. Most officials in the country's legal and educational systems have not shared this concern; for them, national culture remains obviously synonymous with urban Ladino culture. According to Sam Colop (1983, 61), however, this self-satisfaction only masks a submerged identity crisis:

"National culture" is the set of habits that Ladinos practice, a sum of North American–Hispanic elements that do not diminish it yet render it dependent. Jean-Loup Herbert says of this culture: They look endlessly for a definition of national culture: *mestizo*, Hispanic-American, Iberian-American, Latin American, or modern— empty terms that reflect the alienated search of a minority. Paradoxically they hope for and predict the disappearance of indigenous culture into this historic nothingness: [According to Joaquin Noval,] "integration does not require that all indigenous people are transformed into Ladinos, but this will probably be their destiny."

Sam Colop's quotations of Ladino skepticism deconstruct the rightful authority and authoritativeness of existing constructions of "national culture" to represent the country.[2] It is clear to Mayanists how Ladinos have been able to reproduce the illusion of a hegemonic national culture—through their monopoly of the schools, church, mass media, and political structures.

History continues to be on the mind of these activists. Movement intellectuals and students have studied the sixteenth-century chronicles—Spanish and Maya—of the foreign invasion of what later came to be Guatemala. They have been quick to demonstrate the tactical and debilitating use of these documentary sources in official histories that portray Maya culture as timeless and marginalize indigenous Guatemalans from the development of the modern state. Pan-Mayanists have also produced powerful testimonial histories of the recent civil war. A preoccupation with genesis crosscuts these projects: a concern with the pre-Columbian sources of Maya culture and the colonial and contemporary sources of Guatemala's ethnic formation through which indigenous populations have been designated as the devalued other.

Another issue for Pan-Mayanism has been the exploration of the powerful fiction of the unitary, all-powerful state—or, in Michael Taussig's (1993) terminology, state fetishism—in a situation of tremendous state violence. Sam Colop's analysis of Spanish chronicles and their use in official history shows how Guatemalan nationalism is strategically constituted as standing above ethnicity; Montejo's testimonial ethnography demythologizes the state as a singular protagonist.

With a focus on the logics of racism, this activist research continually runs the risk of elevating the indigenous "self" by categorically denouncing the Spanish/Ladino "other" as a racist, thus creating a variant of reverse orientalism. Yet, in a different move, Maya intellectuals have also read indigenous narratives of struggle and resistance across the grain to examine the underside of state fetishism—the painful complicity of some Mayas, as soldiers and civil patrollers, with military forces that brutally oppressed other Mayas. These observers ask in realist ethnographic terms: How precisely does a terrorist state exert its coercive powers over individuals, some who internalize violence and come to enjoy it and others who in the worst of circumstances find an exit or discover small ways to draw a line even when overt resistance is impossible? This book has argued that Mayas both inside and outside the Maya movement have felt compelled to produce culture that expresses the existential dilemmas they faced during the heightened uncertainties and ambiguities of the counterinsurgency war.

These issues will not disappear with the peace accords. From all reports, the military, even as it downsizes and disbands civil patrols, is currently organizing new structures of surveillance. Many Guatemalans feared that demobilized soldiers, police, and guerrillas would only find violent lines of work that exploit their combat training. They were right. Unless employment and land issues are effectively addressed in the peace implementation process, robberies, kidnappings, murders, and extortion are likely to escalate still further. In the past, rising anxiety has sometimes led people in unexpected quarters to call for authoritarian regimes to reestablish order in civil society or for renewed militarization (which may involve U.S. intervention) to deal with increased drug-related violence and corruption.

Current analyses of language and politics have important implications for models of national political organization. Mayanists and others are proposing models for democratic organization that range from territorial autonomy to administrative regionalization to class-based and transethnic political blocs acting within existing forms of participatory democracy. For Mayanists, the emerging metaphor is "nation" as contrasted with "state." Sam Colop (1983, 35) defines nation in the following terms:

> Nation is a state of social consciousness, a psychological phenomenon. It is collective loyalty that unites a society with its collective past and involves it in common aspirations. It is cultural identification, sentiment, and a common means of communication: language. We do not include the term race[3] because this biological terminology has been surpassed. This means that a legislated or objective standard does not make a nation. Rather, we insist that it is the psychological or intellectual self-conception of the human group to which we are referring.

A nation, in this view, becomes synonymous with a people or community, which echoes UN rights discourse and the Spanish word *pueblo*.

On the one hand, Mayanists differentiate between "state," a sovereign instrument of administration and control over a territory, and "nation," which does not always have juridic or political power or even territorial expression (Cojtí Cuxil 1991a, 4; Sam Colop 1983, 36). Jews were recognized as a nation before the state of Israel, Enrique Sam Colop reminds us. This, of course, is a telling example of dispersion and reunification. Elements of nation emerge from the "*hilo invisible de la etnia*" (the invisible thread of ethnicity), which involves identification with a group having a common history, its own culture, a collective memory, religion, ways of dress, and future aspirations—in short, a deeply felt essence no one else shares. In a Barthian way (1969), one can change in innumerable ways—shifting dress, religion, language, work, and the region where one lives—without losing the essence, the thread of common consciousness. Mayanists argue that constitutions and statutes do not really have the capacity to argue against this essence, for theirs is another nature: as political texts they are vulnerable and ephemeral, as Guatemalan history certainly shows. A common judicial system does not unify distinct nations into a singularity because this imposed abstract uniformity fails to relate to the cultural reality of the indigenous majority (Sam Colop 1983, 37–39; Cojtí Cuxil 1991a, 11, 20, 36–39).

In imagining a multinational state, Cojtí Cuxil (1991a, 68–71) suggests a new role for Maya languages, as indicators of regionalized cultural identities, or nationalities, which would serve as the basis for territorial subdivisions and self-government. As such they would become the basis of political mobilization to break with existing models of internal colonialism, which subdivide the country into departments without attention to the ways language and history have shaped the landscape.[4]

This federalist vision is where Mayanists differed from the *popular* Left in the early 1990s. At the Second Continental Meeting for Indigenous, Black, and Popular Resistance, the national goal was to bring Guatemalans together on the basis of class and work affiliations for a transethnic movement of Ladinos and Mayas. Through working papers distributed at the conference and ongoing work groups on "indigenous and mass unity," the Left stressed a language of cultural respect and autonomy for indigenous peoples of the Americas. Yet, the idea that autonomy might be expressed in administrative regionalization in Guatemala was troubling to the *popular* leadership. On the whole, Mayanists judged the *popular* model as calling for their assimilation into national society, much as the Guatemalan state has acted in educational policy. *Popular* organizers were seen as externalizing injustice by focusing their critiques on U.S. imperialism and colonialism—and more recently on global "neoliberalism"—rather than giving high priority to patterns of Guatemalan racism, internal colonialism, and cultural distinctiveness.

As this analysis has argued, Mayanists and Maya activists from the Left were brought together more successfully during the peace process through the Assembly of Civil Society and the COPMAGUA forums. The result was a striking coalitional consensus on the importance of "identity and rights of indigenous peoples," which became a separate section of the accords, signed by government and guerrilla representatives. As offshoots of the COPMAGUA process continue to meet to plan agendas for the implementation of the accords, it will be interesting to follow the next stage of consensus building and strategies to influence the national congress.

The process will be highly charged on all sides. After emerging from a 1996 meeting, one Mayanist complained that coalitions dominated by URNG guerilla allies were still creating documents peppered with "*lucha, lucha, lucha*" ([class] struggle, struggle, struggle) and that he felt ostracized for raising the issue of new political languages—including cross-class alliances—to replace old paradigms. Strong Ladino backlash in the face of indigenous organizing has caused public intellectuals such as Marta Elena Casaus Arzú to call for a rethinking of the Ladino stakes in prevailing definitions of nation and state, which marginalize indigenous citizens. Rightist parties, especially Rios Montt's allies in the Guatemalan Republican Front (FRG), will continue to block reforms using strategies developed during their furious, though ultimately unsuccessful, opposition to Guatemala's endorsement of the ILO 169 accords on indigenous rights, which they sidelined for years in the legislature and the courts.

Cojtí Cuxil (1991a, 12–13, 70–76) and other leaders will continue to work toward an image of Guatemala as a federation of nations, each with its own government, territory, laws, and means for cultural development. Public administration would, in this vision, speak the language of those governed, not the other way around; state government would routinely translate documents into regional languages. Representatives from national subunits—Maya and Ladino—would make up the overarching government of the state.

While the 1996 Peace Accords brought recognition of Maya culture, so far the issue of alternative state structures has fallen outside the scope of actual reforms. Thus, Cojtí Cuxil's early condemnation of national politics still holds:

> We have to admit that until now the problem of nationalities has not been resolved by any revolution or counterrevolution, by any reform or counterreform, by any independence or annexation, by a coup or countercoup. (1991a, 13)[5]

The problem remains more than recognizing different nationalities or assuming that an abstract language of rights will easily transcend diversity. Rather it involves conceiving a formula "to federate diverse nationalities [and] articulate diverse national identities democratically" (Cojtí Cuxil 1991a, 13). In his view, to govern without wider legitimacy is to risk cycles of violence, as those who govern seek to impose their system and those who want to evade domination push for a more radical decentralization. In early writings, Mayanists cited Lebanon during its civil war,[6] although the world abounds with more timely examples that argue their point. Without a concern for the multinational character of the country, Mayanists hold that neoliberal regional development plans that seek only decentralization are bound to be insufficient (Cojtí Cuxil 1991a, 13, 15).

Mayanists have used comparative examples to make their case for the viability and necessity of national reform. First, they show the range of European societies—all high status and democratic, such as Belgium and Spain—that have achieved what some would dismiss as an apocalyptic goal for Guatemala. Latin American examples, such as Peru during its reformist period, are included to establish that multicultural reforms have been attempted in New World countries with substantial indigenous populations. Second, they point out that peoples caught in much more dramatic diasporas have reunified through the thread of a common consciousness to create viable nation-states. Finally, they argue that suppressed ethnicities do not disappear when the larger system mutes them. The failure to negotiate *plu-*

ricultural alternatives has torn other states apart. Pan-Maya comparative politics shows another dimension of nations as "imagined communities"[7]: other systems, perceived as counterparts, can be evoked as political leverage to demonstrate the feasibility of imagined alternatives and the dangers of failing to address the existing social order. The threat is as real as it is oblique.

How does one measure the success or influence of Pan-Mayanism in Guatemala? Mayanists have not organized their own political party. They have avoided the term "activist" for their participants and "political" for their organizations. Rather than seeking to demonstrate their strength through mass demonstrations, they have organized all sorts of conferences, meetings, workshops, educational programs, and editorial campaigns. The goal of these efforts has been to incorporate new generations of Maya professionals, elementary school teachers, councils of elders, and working adults into their discursive community. The decision to stress "cultural" issues—language, education, religion, community leadership, and ecologically sensitive "development" strategies—reflects the Pan-Maya analysis of cultural difference, Guatemalan racism, and state violence. The ruthlessness of the counterinsurgency war during the late 1970s and 1980s, which severely punished any activism deemed political, shaped Pan-Mayanism in important ways.

Institutionally, Mayanists have founded a vast array of research and educational organizations, linked by national networks, such as COMG and its successors, which keep groups in touch with each other. Many of these organizations have local representatives and agents, some have community committees throughout the highlands. Perhaps the most visibly successful program has been the network of private Maya schools. In the 1980s, Maya leaders began to critique the national school system as marginalizing impoverished agriculturalists, some of whom are monolingual in indigenous languages and many of whom are illiterate in Spanish, which serves as the medium of instruction for their children in school. In the subsequent decade, Mayanists have been acting on their critiques by creating alternative schools, textbooks, national educational alliances, and images of nation with more than one official language. There are now several hundred private Maya elementary schools and adult education programs, supported by a variety of foreign funders.

Beyond their successes with Maya schools and centers for research and cultural programming, Pan-Mayanism has had a wider, though much more difficult to measure, effect on Guatemalan society. Like the powerful continuing effects of feminism in the "post-feminist" United States, Pan-Mayanism has promulgated new languages to personalize identity politics, understand inequality, and organize across communities. Cultural innovations—such as the linking of human, civil, and cultural rights—have had a diffuse yet striking effect on the terms of debate in national and local politics. Just as Mayanists adopted and expanded the rights language used by the *popular* movement to include cultural rights, so groups with very distinctive politics have over time found themselves adopting aspects of the Pan-Maya analysis of cultural diversity, although they are highly ambivalent about ethnic organizing per se. The clashing interplay of movements and critics is evident in such shifts in political language.

In debates over the legitimacy and the social vision of Pan-Mayanism, Maya public intellectuals have selectively marshalled essentialist arguments about the deep stability of Maya culture under siege and the foundational wound of racism in marginalizing indigenous peoples. Their critics have countered with tactical post-modernist deconstructions to denaturalize Maya culture, reveal the hybridity of current cultural practices, and highlight moments when Maya class mobility has trumped racism. The dynamic tension between modes of argument—in practice, all sides use foundational and deconstructionist rhetorics—has proved difficult to control. For instance, critic Mario Roberto Morales's spoof of "Ladino identity," originally designed as a foil to ridicule Maya identity politics, helped fuel serious self-questioning among progressive Ladinos about their sense of identity and taken-for-granted entitlement to national culture. For Mayanists, their vital sense of cultural difference has never been able to displace the urgency of widespread poverty that cross-cuts yet is reinforced by fierce ethnic discrimination.

These cultural transformations have been accompanied by the emergence of a new class of indigenous professionals, who, given Guatemala's ethnic formation, might have passed as Ladinos in past decades or disappeared from the national scene in diasporas of Guatemalan refugees, yet now assert their Mayaness. I have argued that while anthropology has important conceptual and ethnographic contributions to make to the study of hybrid class formation, the field seems hobbled by the way class issues have been framed in the past, especially in works on rural Latin America. In many ways there has been an unexamined ambivalence about class mobility for the rural poor. Perhaps this is a consequence of classical historical materialist frameworks, which, given Latin America's rural poverty, justifiably focused on exposing structural exploitation, yet, in the process, produced reductive views of class identity. Yet, dismissive or cynical judgments of mobility reappear in more recent non-Marxist works. The irony, as Mayanists have pointed out, is that most U.S. analysts are middle-class intellectuals with urban and rural working-class roots in their parents' or grandparents' generations.

As this book has argued, many Mayanists are members of new parallel middle classes in rural and urban spheres, which have complex relations with their Ladino counterparts. Thus, one extraordinarily important effect of the movement has been its service as a conduit for novel class-ethnic blends in a society slow to open doors to indigenous employees. Given Pan-Mayanism's leadership, composed in some cases of professionals who pulled themselves back from the brink of passing—by becoming active in Maya organizations and gaining fluency in their hometown's Maya language, sometimes as adults—it is interesting that the movement has not chosen to work with migrants who have passed into Ladino society over the last generation or two. Rather, in a move that reveals another important source of contemporary Maya culture, Pan-Mayanism has focused on forging cross-class alliances with rural middle and agricultural classes in the highland communities where Maya languages are commonly spoken. Here the political contours of Pan-Mayanism's selective definition of communities of shared discourse become evident.

As this analysis has argued, the rural interplay of class, ethnicity, and Pan-Mayanism needs to be examined from multiple points of view. While anthropologists such as Carol Smith (1992a) argue that Maya university students forged the movement through debates with their neo-Marxist peers, this analysis has found a wider array of rural as well as urban sources for Pan-Maya activism. It is important to recognize the longer tradition of indigenous intellectuals in rural communities—from the *k'amöl b'ey* archives of traditional knowledge and the *ajq'ij* shaman-priests to catechists and development experts—whose leadership is informed by Maya leadership norms, historical generations, and waves of community organizing by international groups. In San Andrés, local intellectuals have long seen their work in traditionalist saint societies and in sacramental Catholic groups as involving social criticism and activism for the indigenous community. Arjun Appadurai's (1996, 18) insight applies here. Rather than being primordial, the localism of Maya communities is itself a historical product that reflects and inflects the dynamics of the global.

Today, the relation of Mayanists to local intellectuals is played out in the sometimes clashing, sometimes coalitional involvements of generations of activists in local affairs. Pan-Mayanism continues to generate some leaders—such as Alfonso Ixim—who, though active in national organizations, most value the perspective of localized communities, and others—such as No'j Ixim—who advocate pan-community standardization yet maintain close ties to their hometowns. To the extent that decentralized rural schools actually incorporate traditionalist or neotraditionalist elders with localized cultural commitments, these creative and sometimes highly politicized tensions will continue. More likely, the standardized Maya culture and linguistics taught on the high-school level will impress families when it reaffirms generalized translocal values and will be treated as just another form of esoteric knowledge—another academic discipline, like calculus or chemistry—when it strays from recognized norms.

The capacity of the local community of San Andrés to withstand the intrusion of powerful organizations, even when they appear poised to overrun the municipal center, is legendary and subject to a good measure of local pride. In some instances, as with the 1950s establishment of Catholic Action, young adults in the community used the new organization to address the tensions between generations, yet they also reworked the national organization's anticommunist ideology to reflect local concerns about poverty and ethnic tensions. Responding to the establishment of a conservative, extremely hierarchical Opus Dei seminary in the early 1990s, the Catholic community easily buffered itself from external control by selectively channeling outsider participation in local affairs. Soon enough the seminarians relocated to another venue, and the residential complex became the regional Catholic girls school.

That Maya schools are meeting important educational needs and that teachers are engaging in very creative teaching of young children is clear from my classroom observations in San Andrés. The school, which offers subsidized meals, reaches the children of poor families as well as working adults who can afford small tuition payments to study at night. Teaching in Maya languages at the post-elementary level, however, is a greater challenge, given that the civil war and the availability of work have pulled many adults (teachers and students) away from their home regions. Maya secondary schools will be under much greater competitive pressure to respond to parents' assessments of skills that will give their children highly valued advantages in the wider job market. I suspect that the schools will receive the same treatment as other imports in this tactically syncretic and resilient rural culture.

For both national and local intellectuals, John Watanabe's (forthcoming, 4) insight holds:

> Rather than objectifying culture as essential traits that endure or erode, anthropologists have come to treat Maya cultures in Guatemala as strategic self-expressions of Maya identity, motivated—and thus presumably more appropriately authenticated—by Maya propensities and possibilities in the present rather than by pre-Hispanic primordialisms.

There are ongoing tensions and debates in the political process of authenticating Maya culture rather than an easy emergence of standardized forms through the movement. Mayanists stand on both sides of these divides with locally anchored intellectuals not infrequently at odds with transcommunity activists on issues of language and dialect loyalty, though both groups agree on other issues. Norms of community consultation and consensus decision-making have brought the two halves of the movement together at critical junctures, such as in commission meetings designed to make policy recommendations about accord implementation.

Foreign funding of peace accord initiatives will have a great impact on the movement over the next five years. Mayanists are directing attention to the transnational patterns of World Bank and Inter-American Development Bank support for the reconstruction of civil society. At meetings on democracy and development in March 1998, Cojtí Cuxil questioned whether international donors plan to respect and support Maya culture. Or will funding serve to recreate ethnic hierarchies in which Creoles become the project directors and Mayas the beneficiaries of democratization funding? The paradigm shift he hopes for would be a decolonizing one in which protagonists are routinely Mayas, projects make active use of indigenous culture, Mayas would have decision-making power and encourage direct consultation on local preferences, and the aid process could be used to realize the autonomous potential of indigenous culture.

In practice, projects arising from the indigenous accords have favored standardized strategies to train experts in a range of innovative fields and provided temporary employment opportunities for bilingual professionals in the urban and rural middle classes. Standardized elementary-school materials are published by Maya presses in a range of indigenous languages. International funding has raised and transformed the stakes for the credentialing of intellectuals at the same time that access to high school and college has been expanded. But the wider accords have also favored decentralized strategies to cultivate democratic participation and deal with socioeconomic needs.

In this situation, Pan-Mayanism will experience conflicting tensions and continuing challenges to its development as a movement. To continue its success, Mayanists will have to generate effective cross-class and cross-generation connections at the very moment when stratification within Maya communities is growing and marked in novel ways. The movement will have to continue its national networking across organizations yet articulate with the country's very different regional economies. Most importantly, Pan-Mayanism will have to find ways of appealing to geographically mobile Mayas, including restless youths, refugees, former soldiers, and urban migrants. If Michael Kearney (1996) is right, the ethnic appeal has great potential for these groups. In the event that Pan-Mayanism does not expand its outreach, other groups will make their appeals in the name of Maya culture.

The accord process has made it very clear that funding models are not designed by Mayanists but rather by the international community and increasingly by groups like the World Bank, which has less experience with indigenous issues. In 1997, $1.9 billion was pledged to Guatemala in reconstruction assistance through the Inter-American Development Bank and the World Bank (Ruthrauff 1997; Ruthrauff and Carlson 1997). While the movement has benefited greatly from foreign support in the past, it will not be given high priority in programs that focus on other aspects of the accords. At issue in the future will be income-generating activities from well-established organizations such as the Maya publisher Cholsamaj and new initiatives such as the founding of a Maya university.

There are various possible futures for the Maya movement. Pan-Mayanism may find a way to ride the global wave of decentralized government services and successfully promote regional cultural autonomy in education and self-administration. In the process, the movement may widen its base by recruiting educated youths active in local bread-and-butter issues and rural politics. A federalist solution to multiculturalism and self-determination would reconfigure the Guatemalan state and generate novel institutions to represent linguistic regions in local and national affairs in which Mayanists would play a central role. Mayanists would become institution builders and take an active role in designing a Maya university, public school system, consensus decision-making bodies to represent local communities in wider affairs, an intercultural court system, and regionalized development projects.

Alternatively, the movement will continue to produce urban-trained and rurally affiliated professionals for existing organizations that deal with indigenous issues. This specialization would fuel the three-decade expansion of the bicultural Maya-identified middle class, consolidate routes for mobility across generations in rural families, and give Maya elites a greater voice in national affairs. As we know from the work of Florencia Mallon (1995), James Ferguson (1994), Claudio Lomnitz-Adler (1992), and Steven Feierman (1990), however, there are great risks in bureaucratic reforms driven from the center. In the worst case scenario, the creation of centralized bureaucratic power structures in the name of reform and decentralization will foster tactical political alliances to constrain alternatives, remove important social issues from the realm of political debate, and generate images of rural life that further naturalize inequalities. More optimistically, after a peace process in which social issues were repoliticized, Maya public intellectuals will continue to cultivate media access in order to publicize their running critiques of national policy and confront the moral consequences of the growing disparity between the life chances of middle income and impoverished Mayas. Similar preoccupations have been powerfully expressed in the writings of Henry Louis Gates and Cornel West (1996) for the urban African-American professional class in United States.

Still another possible future for the movement is the generative, cultural one of authoring novel discourses of identity and citizenship for the country as a whole. Even in the event that Pan-Mayanism does not expand far beyond its current national network of highly committed advocates, the movement's centers and coalitions will continue to circulate innovative ideas— such as the multiculturalism of Guatemalan society, the revitalization of Maya language and culture, the interlocking agenda of cultural rights, and the rethinking of national education—that other political actors will absorb and appropriate. There is little doubt that the movement has already contributed to a paradigm shift in the way the international community and many indigenous and Ladino Guatemalans think about the country. Political groups on the Right and the Left are now forced to articulate their stands on a range of Maya initiatives that were unheard of or ridiculed in the early 1970s.

In their own ways, each of these imagined outcomes underscores the power of indigenous rights—as a social movement and a critical discourse—to raise important issues for emerging democracies at this historical moment. As Deborah Yashar (1996) argues, this complex power comes from the fundamental tensions in post–Cold War democracy, neoliberal economic policy, and groups marginalized by the hypocritical winds of change. In the next decade, after the efflorescence and likely decline of international funding, Pan-Maya research centers may find ways to become self-sustaining and independent through entrepreneurial activities that marshall Maya cultural capital (in multilingual publications, training centers, continuing education activities, holistic health and development programs, and consulting for the organizational legacies of the peace accords), through specialized international support, and through joint economic endeavors with other indigenous groups in the Americas. Or the movement may be supplanted by new organizations with related agendas, wider membership, different coalitional possibilities, and more direct influence in the congress and political parties. As individuals decide where to put their energies in the future, the compelling issues for these activists will include the consequences of maintaining or losing control over their central philosophy and political vision, the profound heterogeneity of the Maya *pueblo*, the ways different political interests recast Maya culture for their own political aspirations, and the necessity of finding new ways to work with Ladinos.

As of 1998, members of prominent Pan-Maya organizations eagerly anticipate the formation of exclusively Maya-speaking workplaces within their urban organizations—with Kaqchikel or K'ichee' as their lingua franca—while they have begun to employ sympathetic Ladinos for the first time. One can see these moves as paradoxical responses to political pressures and hostile critics or as inventive next steps in coalition building to mainstream the movement. The internal politics of these moves are just as complex as their intercultural politics. Clearly Pan-Mayanism's ongoing history is much more absorbing to follow than to predict.

Anthropologically Contextualizing the Movement

In closing, I want to turn to the choices and political dilemmas we face in representing Pan-Mayanism and contextualizing it in current social scientific literatures. Neil Larsen (1995) argues that the maneuver of "reading North by South" underscores the relational character of understanding other situations and subjectivities. For all parties, it is a power-inflected act that raises important questions for Northern writers about sympathetic observers and their internalized political legacies, the romance of attributing radical cultural difference to some but not all others, and the politics of the choices of engagement by professional observers.

The scope of issues that "indigenous intellectuals in non-western societies" raise for the anthropology and development establishments is a fascinating one. In the late 1970s, Hussein Fahim (1982) convened an international seminar to ask if indigenous anthropology should be recognized and supported as an ally in national development efforts. The question was hotly contested at that time. Some participants worried that the formation of multiple anthropologies would dangerously undercut the legitimacy of Western anthropology as a science that generates objective knowledge for its own sake and for practical development needs. Others talked about their desire to move past the colonialism of the past and create a world anthropology based on a common conceptual language. Universalism was advocated as the way to break the Western monopoly of the social sciences and challenge Western bias and ethnocentrism. Some saw applied anthropology's rightful role as helping states to more effectively implement development policies by measuring the costs and benefits of change. Others talked about the anti-state bias of anthropologists who identified with local communities and saw state planning as limiting individual freedom. Discussants viewed indigenous anthropologists as advantaged by their specialized knowledge of local situations yet adversely influenced by nationalist pressures and politics that compromise their scientific findings.

From the vantage point of the present, these discussions prove both patronizing and insightful. It is clear that the status of anthropology as a science with a unitary sense of method and objectivity has become a central debate in anthropology. The field has taken the older ambivalence about its relation to the state and become actively engaged in conceptualizing state power. A concern with the sources of politics and bias for all researchers has replaced the sense that Western ethnocentrism can be easily mastered and that the real difficulty lies with indigenous anthropologists' struggle with the biases brought by local involvements, national political pressures, and fears that unpopular research will cause ostracism and estrangement. Most arresting is the seminar participants' sense that they were the rightful judges of whether others should do anthropology and what the field's disciplinary mandate should be. The present reality of indigenous intellectuals with their own movement agendas and transnational involvements, judgments of the role of science and foreign research, and plans to reconfigure the state and nation was not really anticipated by the seminar. But the seminar's central preoccupation appears to foreshadow the unfolding of diverse anthropologies and raises the issue of the meaning of recognition in a world that has politicized reading North by South in new ways. How do current anthropological frameworks resonate with Pan-Mayanism?

First, we can see Pan-Mayanism as an instance of revitalization, a metaphor I use along with resurgence in this book. Following Anthony F. C. Wallace's classic ethnography (1972), revitalization is not simply a process of reasserting the viability of earlier cultural forms. Rather, it is a self-conscious cultural resynthesis in the face of extraordinary pressure and conflict, when older models no longer orient people in increasingly unstable social environments. For Wallace, the issue was the politics of a resynthesis, the authors of which have been compelled to reach across cultural divides to imagine a radical transformation of indigenous culture. Competing formulations, visionary inspiration, charismatic leaders, and cultural hybrids are part of the process of revitalization before the politics of institutionalization takes over and routinizes or standardizes the outcome.

A second framing would point to the "invented traditions" of Pan-Maya revitalization. In Eric Hobsbawm and Terence Ranger's (1983) formulation, culturally distinctive traditions of a timeless past are often, in fact, recent innovations that involve the mimetic appropriation of colonial culture by indigenous elites to consolidate political authority or involve tactical market segmentation for a lucrative commerce to clothe distinctive identities.

A third literature for understanding Pan-Mayanism would include current formulations of ethnic nationalism, imagined communities, and oppositional politics. Following Ronald Horowitz (1985), this literature is highly ambivalent about the project of ethnic intensification. Ethnic nationalism is often condemned for destructive essentialism, polarized politics, and state disintegration. In political science and anthropology, there is cynicism about movement leaders, a sense that powerful individuals will take advantage of the moment for their own personal gain, even if it comes to promoting widespread violence. Little room is left for Maya multiculturalism in the last two models.

A fourth literature would examine Pan-Mayanism in the context of new social movements, à la Arturo Escobar and Sonia Alvarez (1992) and Sonia Alvarez, Evelina Dagnino, and Arturo Escobar (1998). In the Latin American case, this research has focused on the recent surge of grassroots activism working, often militantly, within democratic systems for change through the women's, ecology, labor, Afro-Latin American, human rights, gay rights, and indigenous movements.[8] These movements have global ties and transnational languages, yet quite localized and culturally specific goals. Here the Maya movement would be considered a rights-based movement and would be further contextualized in terms of a transnational indigenous agenda that has grown in importance throughout Latin America. As in James Clifford's analysis (1988), the issue is how a culture transforms itself to articulate with powerful institutional structures offering access to wider resources.

That Pan-Mayanism fails to rest comfortably in any one of these social scientific literatures helps us characterize the limitations of each. The "revitalization model" fascinates with its combination of psychology and politics, yet Wallace's formulation (1956) always had an odd functionalism. One shortcoming involves the assumption that cultures find a steady state between times of crisis, rather than the more dynamic, heterogeneous views of culture now advocated by many anthropologists. Wallace's ethnography was much richer historically than his abstract model. Yet even in his ethnography, his psychoanalytic argument stood in the way of a fuller exploration of historicized self-consciousness and agency.

The "invented cultures" model questions who initially authored the aspects of culture now seen as "traditional" or definitive, with what political or economic goals. A great deal of cultural difference is, in effect, recycled colonial culture.[9] Of course, by definition all culture has a history, often transcultural, of construction. Hobsbawm and Ranger's concern with who benefits when invented culture becomes standard practice is important for all social analysis. Yet there is another political issue here, as anthropologists[10] have recently pointed out: What politics drives this selective labeling of invented culture—as in the case of the editorial polemics analyzed in the first chapter—so that it discredits indigenous voices when the stakes are high and authenticity is more than an academic issue?

The "ethnic nationalist" model also turns out to be rocky terrain for anthropology because in practice this label quickly reduces multifaceted movements to territorial nationalism, state-endangering opposition, and the corrupt politics of a newly consolidating elite. Crawford Young (1976; 1993) initially felt that nationalist movements would not be an issue for Latin American indigenous populations who found themselves fragmented, assimilated into the peasantry, and "deprived of the cultural resources for a collective response to their subordinate status" (1976, 457; 1993). How wrong Young now admits he was. Yet Guatemala is not the former Yugoslavia or Rwanda. Maya intellectuals see *nationalist* as a threatening label for their situation because it allows governments to point to international examples of state fragmentation to justify repression in the name of national security at home.

Nor do Maya culturalists find that "ethnic" or "minority" appropriately describes their struggle. In their view, the discourse of "minority rights" emanates from the United States, where it disempowers social movements, promotes assimilation into the mainstream, and limits activists' ability to reconfigure national culture. They reject this language as marginalizing. Moreover, they are aware that this language has been used in Guatemala and the United States to argue that Maya cultural elites who work in non-agricultural occupations outside their home communities are no longer really Mayas but rather a "third ethnicity" between indigenous and Ladino. Thus, they become unauthentic representatives of their own people.

Finally, anthropology seems both intrigued and worried by the new-social-movements literature. Anthropologists are excited about pursuing this local yet transcultural formulation of change. Yet, there is a legitimate fear that key issues of cultural meaning and distinctiveness will disappear in the transcultural (but strikingly Western sounding) grammar of movements. It is not uncommon for scholars of new social movements to treat their goals and organizations as self-evident and, thus, to focus on the formal ideologies and established collectivities that people embrace. Much less attention is directed to the internal dynamics of these movements: to the particular ways participants contest, create, and consume culture through their activism; to the ways social relations (not just individual choice) mediate involvements; or to the ironies of identity politics in movements that foreground one of many identities relevant to activists.

Perhaps, in its own particular hybrid form, the Pan-Maya movement in Guatemala will offer lessons about nonviolent options for rethinking political marginalization in multi-ethnic states that seek democratic futures. The Pan-Mayanist turn to educational reform for the rural poor has attracted widespread attention in local, national, and international arenas. It has also generated competitors, such as the Ministry of Education's PRONADE program, which began with a mission of extending school coverage to communities without elementary schools and now speaks of improving multicultural curricular content. The movement's concern with bilingual teachers and with court interpreters has provoked U.S.-AID, a former antagonist, once again to expand its college scholarship program in these fields. Pan-Mayanism's impact appears evident even in its competitors' efforts.[11] There is, of course, a great deal of unfinished business in the movement, including gender issues, religious diversity, and appeal to impoverished urban migrants from the highlands.

The national leadership is well aware that Guatemala's transition is also a crucial moment for Pan-Mayanism. How will Pan-Mayanists negotiate with others—including their *popular* Maya allies, Ladinos with intercultural concerns, and international NGO sympathizers—to pressure for the implementation of peace-accord reforms, despite a recalcitrant Congress? How will the movement respond to the World Bank's now-prominent role in distributing funds for grassroots democratization projects, its preference for centralized initiatives and community-based projects at the expense of federalist institution-building support, and its misreading of Maya norms for consensus decision-making as inefficiency in umbrella groups such as COPMAGUA? How will the movement respond to the backlash fomented by those who resent the international funding of indigenous initiatives generated by the peace accords? How can more effective dialogues and collaboration across the Ladino-Maya divide be fostered? Though small in global terms, indigenous-rights movements provide revealing challenges to prevailing top-down models of "development" and to assimilationist models of nationalism in multicultural settings. They also raise issues for international observers about reading politics and multiculturalism closer to home.

Appendix One

Summary of the Accord on Identity and the
Rights of Indigenous Peoples

THE INDIGENOUS ACCORD is divided into four parts, a sacred number in Maya cosmology. The tone is constructive, and concrete remedies are suggested for grave social problems. The accord provides a vision of a just society and a measure of the substantial structural and cultural changes necessary to achieve this vision. The first part calls for the *formal recognition* of Guatemala's indigenous people, something denied them when non-Maya *mestizos* were conventionally assumed to be the standard of citizenship. Mayas are defined as the descendants of an ancient people who speak historically related indigenous languages and share common culture, self-identification, and a cosmology that sees the earth as a life-giving mother and corn as a sacred cultural axis. Maya identity is conceived of as having a plurality of sociocultural and linguistic expressions, just as indigenous identity also includes the non-Maya indigenous Xinca and the Afro-Guatemalan Garífuna, who also become rights-bearing groups.

The second part of the accords focuses on the struggle against discrimination. Given that racial discrimination must be overcome to achieve the peaceful coexistence of all ethnic groups, the accord urges legislative reform to make discrimination a crime, root out discriminatory laws, promote public education, and secure the active defense of rights by providing legal aid for the poor. The rights of indigenous women who suffer double discrimination on the basis of ethnicity and gender draw special mention. The accord urges congress to make sexual harassment a crime and to promote the UN Convention to Eliminate All Forms of Discrimination against Women. It also calls for a reaffirmation of the International Convention for the Elimination of All Racial Discrimination and the ILO Convention 169 on Indigenous and Tribal Peoples, which after being promulgated in 1989 was sidelined repeatedly in the Guatemalan Congress until its passage in 1995.

The third section of the accord identifies key cultural rights for indigenous communities. It calls for the recognition and support of indigenous people as the authors of their own cultural development through distinctive institutions. Key to these efforts would be the constitutional recognition of indigenous languages in schools, social services, official communications, and court proceedings. Individuals and communities would gain the right to shed hispanicized names, as they wished.

Maya spirituality and spiritual guides would be recognized, the distinct spiritual practices of different indigenous groups constitutionally protected. Of great concern is the conservation of temples, ceremonial centers, and archeological sites of ancient Maya culture as indigenous heritage and national patrimony. The accord asserts that indigenous communities should be involved in the conservation and administration of these centers and archaeological sites. The use of indigenous dress in all arenas would be guaranteed and supported by educational programs.

The accord recognizes the existence and value of Maya scientific and technological knowledge, which, along with the knowledge of other indigenous groups, should be fostered and disseminated through a variety of institutions and media. Increased indigenous access to contemporary knowledge and to opportunities for scientific and technical exchange are to be promoted.

Through the accords, the government commits itself to wide-ranging educational reform, including regional decentralization; the inclusion of families in all areas of local education, including the appointment of teachers; the integration of Maya materials and educational methods; the promotion of indigenous languages and bilingual intercultural education; the promotion of national unity and cultural diversity at all educational levels; the development of bilingual teachers and indigenous administrators; and the expansion of educational funding for programs and students. In addition to programs for Maya education, intercultural education would be supported for all children. The Maya schools movement would be fostered along with the development of a Maya university.

Finally, this section of the accords identifies wider access to mass media, especially the radio, for indigenous programming, broadcasts in indigenous languages, and the dissemination of educational programming for the wider public.

The fourth section of the accord deals with constitutional reforms in civil, political, social, and economic rights to make possible a multi-ethnic, pluricultural, and multilingual vision of national society. Decentralization would be promoted through governmentally funded municipal autonomy, which would involve the recognition of localized customary law and community decision-making powers in issues of education, health, culture, and community development. The accord calls for a reform of municipal codes and a regionalization of government structures along the lines of indigenous language communities to facilitate the participation of local communities in wider decision-making bodies. The importance of institutionalizing indigenous representation at all levels so indigenous interests can be actively pursued means that indigenous representatives should be included in all administrative bodies and communities consulted whenever government actions might affect them.

The accords assert the right of communities to use their customary norms to regulate internal affairs as long as local standards are not incompatible with national law or international human-rights doctrine. Training programs in customary law are mandated for judges and ministry officials. With subsidized access to legal aid and official interpreters, no one would be judged without access to court proceedings in his or her own language.

Regarding the urgent problem of indigenous land rights, the accords argue for the recognition of communal and individual landholdings, the right of communities to administer communal lands according to local norms, and rights to natural resources in benefit of local communities. In view of the historical vulnerability of local communities to land seizures by those with political connections, financial resources, and fluency in the national language (Spanish), the accords call for legislative and administrative reforms to title, protect, defend, and settle land claims; to provide educational, legal, and linguistic assistance so communities can defend their interests; and to compensate communities that have lost lands. The government is urged to distribute state lands to communities without sufficient land as long as this does not hurt small land owners.

The accords designate commissions, composed of representatives from the government and indigenous groups active in the civil assembly, which will be set up over four years to further refine the reform process in each of the areas under discussion.[1] The United Nations Mission to Guatemala is the international organization entrusted with the verification of the peace accords.

Appendix Two _____

Questions from the 1989 Maya Workshop
Directed to Foreign Linguists

THESE QUESTIONS were dictated to Nora England by Mayas in the audience during the discussion. The list was circulated at the Guatemala Scholars Network meetings of the American Anthropological Association in November 1989 and reprinted in the *Guatemala Scholars Newsletter* in February 1990. The categories and translation are mine.

(1) Doubts about researchers' interests, motivations, intentions:

"Why are foreign linguists interested in Maya languages?" "Their roles are diverse: what are their individual motivations?"

"Gringos are interested in Maya culture: out of pity, as a mockery, as a joke?" "Do you really want to help us in Maya linguistics, or do you want to confuse us?"

"Apart from science, what do foreign linguists feel for the Maya people? What are they looking for with the Maya people and what do they want?"

"When did writing Maya in contemporary script begin in Guatemala? Who was the first person to have this idea? Was it the Summer Institute of Linguistics?" "If there are a variety of linguists, foreign as well as Maya, why haven't they done something about real writing; that is to say, writing with its own symbols, like they have with the Maya numeric system?"

"Why does the PLFM [Proyecto Lingüístico Francisco Marroquín] pay for studies of Maya dialects? Does this stem from personal interest or is it benefitting the language communities? Or is it that you simply want to acquire complete knowledge of all Mayas?"

"For whom does the linguist work?" "The work of the linguists is limited solely to research. Or perhaps they are really working for the politics and ideology of their government?" "What goal does research done by foreigners have in their own country?"

(2) Doubts about the benefits of research:

"What concrete support have foreign linguists given to Maya languages?" "Show specific evidence of your activities, projects, and works that have benefited the indigenous Maya nation."

"Why do foreign linguists begin their studies in Guatemala and end by publishing in the United States without giving an account of them in Guatemala?"

"Will the work of foreign linguists be negative for Maya languages or will it benefit all speakers of Maya languages?"

(3) Observations about the continuing political asymmetry of research despite expressed foreign interest in dialogues and assistance:

"How can foreign linguists speak of service and help if they neither respect nor are subject to the interest of the Mayas?"

"Why haven't foreign linguists supported the unification of the alphabet for the Maya languages?"

"Does knowledge of Maya languages contribute to the subordination of the Maya population?" "Is it possible for foreign linguists to contribute to the elimination of the different tentacles of internal and external colonialism that currently affect the Mayas?"

"If speakers of Maya languages come to have power over the destiny of Maya linguistics, would the foreign linguists accept being subject to rules established by the speakers?" "Would you be willing to do work in conjunction with Maya groups or associations, working with them in an equitable manner?"

Glossary

Acronyms, Organizations, and Cultural Terms

ajq'ij — alternatively referred to as a Maya spiritual guide, priest, diviner, shaman, or witch, depending on the politics of the speaker.

ALMG — Academia de Lenguas Mayas de Guatemala (Academy for Maya Languages of Guatemala).

AVANCSO — Asociación para el Avance de las Ciencias Sociales en Guatemala (Association for the Advancement of Social Sciences in Guatemala), a research center that stresses class issues and working-class struggles in the analysis of social change.

ASC — Asemblea de Sociedad Civil (Assembly of Civil Society), which served as the forum for civilian input into the peace process.

CECMA — Centro de Estudios de la Cultura Maya (Center for the Study of Maya Culture), a Pan-Mayanist NGO involved in Mayanist workshops on education and legal issues and the publication of *Iximulew*, circulated as a supplement in the newspaper *Siglo Veintuno*.

CEDIM — Centro de Documentación e Investigación Maya (Center for Maya Documentation and Investigation), the Maya archives and center of educational programing in Guatemala City.

Cholsamaj — the major publisher of Pan-Maya research and school texts.

CIRMA — Centro de Investigaciones Regionales de Mesoamérica (Center for Investigations of Regional Mesoamerica), a library and multipurpose research center located in Antigua.

CNEM — Consejo Nacional de Educación Maya (National Council for Maya Education), a network of Maya educational organizations in cooperation with government entities and national NGOs that promotes educational reform.

COCADI — Coordinadora Cakchiquel de Desarrollo Integral (Coordination for Caqchikel Integral Development), a NGO supportive of Maya agriculture and spirituality and critical of Western development ideology.

COMG — Consejo de Organizaciones Mayas de Guatemala (Council of Maya Organizations of Guatemala), an early umbrella group of Mayanist organizations.

CONAVIGUA — Coordinadora Nacional de Viudas de Guatemala (National Coordinator of Guatemalan Widows), the *popular* movement's grassroots widows' organization for war survivors.

CONIC — Coordinadora Nacional Indígena y Campesina (National Indigenous and Campesino Coordination), a Maya-identified group with strong *popular* roots, which focuses on land issues.

costumbre — local Maya traditions, associated with the civil-religious hierarchy, saints societies, and shaman-priests in rural communities.

CUC — Comité de Unidad Campesina (Committee for Campesino Unity), a grassroots Left organization active in rural affairs.

desaparecidos — the disappeared, those whose fate from the years of the civil war is not known.

encomienda — Spanish land grants that gave awardees special rights over the population living in their jurisdiction.

FAR — Fuerzas Armadas Rebeldes (Rebel Armed Forces), a guerrilla movement active in the western highlands.

FDNG — Frente Democrático para una Nueva Guatemala or El Frente (New Guatemala Democratic Front), the left-leaning political party created in 1995 under the leadership of the *popular* movement and the URNG, which won six seats in Congress.

FLACSO — Facultad Latinoamericana de Ciencias Sociales (Latin American Faculty of Social Sciences), a research center that publishes widely on social issues and the Maya movement.

FRG — Frente Republicano Guatemalteco (Guatemalan Republican Front), a political party on the right associated with former president Efrain Ríos Montt.

GAM — Grupo de Apoyo Mútuo (Mutual Support Group), the urban Left organization of families of the disappeared.

indígena — indigenous, Maya.

k'amöl b'ey — ritual guides and marriage brokers in Maya communities.

kaxlan — non-Maya or foreigner.

ILRL — Instituto de Lingüística (Institute for Linguistics at the Rafael Landívar University), a major producer of textbooks in Maya languages.

Ladinos — nonindigenous Guatemalans.

ladinización — Ladinoization, a theory which holds that social change for Mayas ineviatably involves the assimilation of Ladino culture and identity.

la violencia — the violence, a colloquial term for the civil war.

MINUGUA — Missión de las Naciones Unidas en Guatemala (UN Verification Commission in Guatemala).

MLN — Movimiento de Liberación Nacional (Movement for National Liberation), a conservative political party.

municipio — basic official settlement unit that includes a county seat and surrounding hamlets.

OKMA — Oxlajuuj Keej Maya' Ajtz'iib', a Pan-Maya linguistics research organization.

ORPA — Organización Revolucionaria del Pueblo en Armas (Revolutionary Organization of People in Arms), the wing of the guerrilla movement active in the Sololá-Chimaltenango region.

PACS — *patrullas de autodefensa civil* (civil self-defense patrols), organized by the army in local communities in 1982.

PAN — Partido de Avanzada Nacional (National Advancement Party), a conservative political party that won the presidency and the majority in congress in the 1995 elections.

PLFM — Proyecto Lingüístico Francisco Marroquín (Francisco Marroquín Linguistics Project).

populares — the grassroots Left.

principales — elders in rural communities

PRONADE — Programa Nacional de Autogestión para el Desarrollo Educativo (National Program for Self-Managed Educational Development).

PRONEBI — Programa Nacional de Educación Bilingüe (National Program for Bilingual Education) now called DIGEBI—Dirección General de Educación Bilingüe (National Board for Bilingual Education).

rajaw a'q'a — masters of the night, shape changers in Kaqchikel mythistories.

reducción — Spanish colonial policy of concentrating dispersed populations into communities for missionization.

repartimiento — a forced-labor policy that gave elite colonists the right to request labor, through colonial officials, from indigenous communities.

Saqb'ichil-COPMAGUA — Coordinación de Organizaciones del Pueblo Maya de Guatemala (Coordination of Organizations of the Maya People of Guatemala), a coalition of representatives from indigenous groups, including Pan-Mayanists and the popular movement, which emerged during the peace accord process and is active in the implementation process.

SPEM — Seminario Permanente de Estudios Mayas (Maya Studies Permanent Seminar), a research seminar and lecture series organized by Pan-Maya intellectuals.

Taller Maya — Maya Workshop, an annual Pan-Maya conference on language issues held in different parts of the countryside.

UNICEF — United Nations Children's Fund office in Guatemala, a major source of coordination and support for Maya educational projects.

URNG — Unidad Revolucionaria Nacional Guatemalteca (Guatemalan National Revolutionary Unity), the umbrella guerrilla organization which became active in the peace negotiations and reconstituted itself as a leftist political party.

Notes

Preface

1. On different anthropological definitions, frameworks, and subject positions for studying "Indians," see Field's insightful essay (1994).

2. This overview of the PLFM is based on my own experiences and on a history written by its founders, which to the best of my knowledge remains unpublished. See Froman et al. 1978.

3. Half of the twenty-five volunteers were supported by the Peace Corps. The "volunteer" status of the PLFM personnel created its own problems because international funders did not perceive the staff as stable professionals. Because of their hybrid foreign-Maya model, the PLFM fell between categories for support from sources such as the Ford Foundation and the Interamerican Development Fund. As a result they received only token funding from NGOs and the private sector. Twenty years later—after some of the foreign volunteers had become senior academics, the applied linguists gained professional prominence in Guatemala, and new generations of student linguists began their training with at least some high school if not college—hybrid projects were quite successful in competing for support from European funders.

4. Students pursued their full-time studies in Antigua, where they took six month-long courses over a three-year period. Afterward, they applied what they had learned in their home towns and received seven months of additional training, one week a month. According to plan, 65 percent of their time was spent working in their own communities (see Froman et al. 1978).

5. Community action projects, such as literacy training and the production of reading materials in Maya languages, were generated by the students on their own initiative as part of the program.

6. See Froman et al. (1978, 244–47) for the worries about Maya elites, Fischer (1993) for evidence from Tecpán, and C. Smith (1990c, 1993) for the Totonicapán situation, which contrasts with the Kaqchikel region in patterns of activism and political economy.

7. This decision reflected the philosophy of the PLFM, which looked for students with strong local commitments and fluency in indigenous languages. The fear was that more educated prospects would have already spent years away from home in secondary school, would be less settled in local roles and practicalities, and might see the training as an opportunity for personal advancement rather than as a chance to benefit their communities.

8. Antigua and later Quetzaltenango became bustling centers of Spanish schools for international students, although few others have expressed interest in directing profits toward community projects.

9. By paying competitive wages and offering adequate working conditions, the PLFM Spanish school became a significant though, given the ebb and flow of foreigners, an unstable source of employment for Ladinos with thirteen years of educa-

tion and teaching certificates. An early attempt to unionize the teachers was not successful (Froman et al. 1978, 260, 357–58).

10. For insider accounts, see Chacach (1997), an early participant in the PLFM, and Cojtí Cuxil (1997a), whose account is discussed in the next two chapters. For an early critical history written in solidarity with the Cold War Left, see Falla (1978b). Other Guatemalan accounts have been written by Arias (1990), the Spanish research team Bastos and Camus (1996), and Solares (1993). For excellent recent anthropological accounts, see Fischer (1996) and the Fischer and Brown collection (1996), which includes essays by long-term North American allies such as Nora England, Judith Maxwell, McKenna Brown, and Linda Schele.

11. An orthography is, in effect, a technical linguistic alphabet, attuned to the sound system of a language and particularly to contrasts in pronunciation that make a difference in meaning. When Maya languages are spelled following Spanish conventions, important sounds may not be discriminated and inappropriate writing practices from Spanish are transferred to Maya languages. To escape these dilemmas, early Spanish writers, for example, use "x" to represent the "sh" sound common in Maya languages, as in *ixim* (pronounced eesheem), the word for corn, and linguists now use specialized conventions to represent glottal stops, long vowels, and sounds unique to these languages.

The PLFM attempted to introduce a standardized "rational" orthography to differentiate the representation of Maya languages from Spanish, facilitate the production and publication of materials for wider audiences, and make possible historical and comparative language. The ALMG was successful in formalizing the alphabet, which, for instance, rejects the hispanic *c/qu* spelling for the velar stop [k] and, instead, uses *k* for the velar stop [k] and *q* for the uvular stop [q], a sound common in Maya languages and absent in Spanish. See England (1996, 8) for the details.

12. This continues despite scholarship that demonstrates the historical and contemporary roles that international actors play in creating ranked forms of difference and in polarizing politics. Clearly violent conflict has many causes. See Maybury-Lewis (1997), Malkki (1995), Prunier (1995), and Woodward (1995).

13. See Shobat and Stam (1994) for an interesting discussion of alternative critical modes of consuming culture.

Introduction

1. The works Maya scholars have written in service of the movement are discussed throughout this book. Among the non-Guatemalan cultural anthropologists who have written on Maya nationalism and revitalization are C. Smith (1991, 1992a, 1996), R. Adams (1994), Watanabe (1994), Wilson (1995), Nelson (1999), Richards and Richards (1992, 1996), and contributors to the transnational collections edited by C. Smith (1990a), England and Elliot (1990), and Fischer and Brown (1996). Foreign anthropologists are also represented in the Maya-edited transcultural collection from the *Primer Congreso de Estudios Mayas* (Universidad Rafael Landívar, Instituto de Lingüística 1997). Younger scholars, such as Green (1993), Fabri (1994), E. Fischer (1996), and A. Adams (1998), have produced a new generation of dissertations bearing on culture and politics in Guatemala. Linguists, such as England, Maxwell, and

Brown, and glyph experts, such as Schele, have also written on a range of issues related to cultural revitalization.

2. For a critique of the post-Marxist turn and its fascination with post-modernism and rereadings of Gramsci, see Petras and Morley's condemnation of "the retreat of the intellectuals" (1992). Also see Larsen's (1995) critical maneuver of *Reading North by South*.

3. For more on radical democracy, the contested place of Marxism in this transformation, and the heterogeneity of Marxist approaches themselves, see Laclau and Mouffe (1985), Mouffe (1992, 1993), and Trend (1996).

4. Richard Falk (1997) roots the contemporary tension between international law and anticolonial struggles in the differences between Lenin's concern with decolonization and Woodrow Wilson's concern with self-determination within the integrity of the colonial order at the close of World War I. After 1945, the United States was forced to seriously engage decolonization given emerging great power politics and the Soviet support of liberation movements.

5. See Maybury-Lewis (1997) for a discussion of "indigenous" in contrast to "ethnic" and "political minority." From the anthropological point of view, the contrasts among these terms are historically and politically constructed—and thus situational—rather than essential or structural. In the Americas, contemporary indigenous groups have special status because their community histories of New World occupation antedate the process of European "discovery" and colonization that violently dispossessed them of their territories and governing structures. For the UN definition of indigenous peoples, which makes clear the heterogeneity of the category, see Wilmer (1993, 216).

6. See Wilmer (1993) for additional details on this transnational history.

7. See Halperin and Scheffer (1992) for additional details, a history of international law, and arguments in favor of widening conceptions of self-determination. Danspeckgruber (1997) includes useful comparative case studies and critiques of ethnic paradigms for state politics.

8. See Young (1976), who reconsidered his position in a more recent edited volume (1993). In J. G. Castañeda's urban-focused work, the influential grassroots and indigenous efforts to rethink the state throughout Latin America and the indigenous turn of the Zapatista rebellion in Chiapas, Mexico, remain unanticipated, apparently because they violate the grammar of party politics (see, especially, 1993, 198–201, 232–33).

9. In the Americas, indigenous organizing is not a uniquely post–Cold War phenomena. Charles Hale's (1994a) insightful study of the tensions between the Miskitos and Sandinistas during the socialist regime in Nicaragua is a case in point.

10. For examples of recent studies of indigenous-state relations, see Stern (1987), Díaz Polanco (1997), Smith (1990a), Urban and Sherzer (1991), Stavenhagen (1992), Kicza (1993), Campbell et al. (1993), Wilmen (1993), Van Cott (1994), Collier (1995), J. Nash (1995), Beckett and Mato (1996), Rappaport (1996), Yashar (1996; forthcoming), Maybury-Lewis (1997), Rubin (1997), and Ramos (1998).

11. For example, Stoll (1993) argues against the relevance of ethnicity, and Arias (1990) sees indigenous leadership, which does not reflect agrarian class interests, as a manipulative and confused response of the Indian bourgeoisie. In Guatemala, the *popular*-allied research center AVANCSO has long stressed the class perspective,

though they are sponsoring ethnographic research on ethnicity and class by Matilde González, which will examine the class dimensions and tensions within Maya segments of a biethnic community. FLACSO-Guatemala has produced a series of very important works by Bastos and Camus (1995a, 1995b, 1996) on urban Mayas, the Maya and popular movements, and the peace process. Through FLACSO, the sociologist Amanda Pop is pursuing new lines of research, which deal in innovative ways with class, ethnic, and gender issues.

12. For a postmodernist critique from Peru, see Starn et al. (1995).

13. For revitalization, see Wallace (1972); for the invention of culture, see Hobsbawm and Ranger (1983); for the cultural politics of ethnicity and nationalism, see Fox (1990b), Chatterjee (1993), B. Anderson (1991), Horowitz (1985), and Young (1976, 1993); for social movements, see Escobar and Alvarez (1992), Alvarez, Dagnino, and Escobar (1998), Eckstein (1989), and Touraine (1987); and for anthropologies of the state, see Taussig (1992, 1993), Navaro (1997), and Ferguson (1994).

14. On this history, which has generated important revisionist analysis, see Lutz (1984).

15. See Tzian (1994) on the politics and social history of counting.

16. There is some controversy over how many Maya languages are spoken in Guatemala. If Achi is counted as a dialect of K'ichee', as OKMA advocates on linguistic grounds, the number is twenty, a sacred number of Maya cosmology and calendrics. If Achi is given separate status, as the ALMG has conventionally done in the 1990s, then the number is 21.

17. I realize this is modernist language and will return to this issue later in the book. The Mayas, in fact, use a great deal of this language, though it is infused with distinctive meanings, as becomes clear in chapter eight, for instance, when leaders talk about "modernizing" Kaqchikel culture.

18. Compare Raxché (1989), Cojtí Cuxil (1991a), Otzoy and Sam Colop (1990) with Fischer and Brown (1996) and Cojtí Cuxil (1994). For the theorizing of transcultural flows, see, among many other important works, Appadurai (1991), Gupta and Ferguson (1992), Hall (1990), Hanchard (1992), Prakash (1992a), and Starn et al. (1995).

19. See Koizumi (1997) for a parallel argument for local communities.

20. See Guha and Spivak (1988) and Prakash (1992a; 1992b).

21. See Skinner (1983), Anzaldúa (1990), Rosaldo (1990), Behar (1993), and Fuss (1991).

22. See Hu-Dehart (1991), Okihiro (1991), Mazumdar (1991), Abu-Lughod (1990), Poole and Rénique (1991), and Starn (1991). Other trends that have contributed to this reassessment include the appropriation of orientalist representations by ethnic nationalists for their own purposes and research on nationalism as a discourse (see Bhabha 1990, Chatterjee 1986, Aretxaga 1997, and Navaro 1997).

23. There are additional words for others: *gringo* is common in Guatemala and *alemán* is used in a similar way in Chiapas, according to June Nash (personal communication).

24. See A. Adams (1998) and Nelson (1999) for more on the politically charged character of *gringo*.

25. June Nash pointed out to me that *pueblos originarios* comes from Bolivian

usage and *naciones nativas del continente* from Canadian usage, which only under-scores the transnational character of this discourse.

26. See Warren (1992).

27. See Nelson's insightful postmodern analysis of identity, popular culture, and urban politics at the quincentenary (1989).

28. See Schirmer (1997b) and MINUGUA (1998) for evidence of the tensions in Guatemalan democratization.

29. There are diverse reasons for this situation and one must hasten to add that each Latin American country has its own educational history. The poverty and po-larized class systems of Latin American societies result from their historical insertion into extractive global markets, a hierarchical pattern reduplicated on the provincial level. Ambivalence to making education truly universal, the urban-centrism of school funding, the politicized character of many universities, and neoliberal economic pres-sures to cut state services have influenced policymakers and their allocation of resources.

30. Few of these writers are known in the United States because their works have yet to be translated into English. See Lomnitz-Adler (1992) for a rich analysis of the multiplicity of intellectuals and their articulation with the hierarchical organization of regional spaces in Mexico.

31. See Hall (1990) and Clifford (1988).

32. These expressions range widely. See, for example, the discussions of black power and civil rights protests, funk and charm, and Toni Morrison's *Beloved* in Hanchard (1993; 1994), Aretxaga (1993; 1997), and Wood (1993).

33. See Warren (1993), Carmack (1988b), Stoll (1993), and Taussig (1992).

34. My approach here creates an ethnography of reading and traces its politics. See Boyarin (1993) for the important cross-cultural issues raised by this framing of ethnography.

35. See CECMA (1994), Raxché (1989), and Cojtí Cuxil (1994).

36. See, for example, Escobar and Alvarez (1992).

37. Other examples of work focusing on the cultural mediation of politics in Me-soamerica would include Warren (1978), B. Tedlock (1991), D. Tedlock (1993a), Wilson (1995), and, across the border in Chiapas, Bricker (1981), Gossen (1994), and J. Nash (1967/68; 1995). Clearly this analysis takes issue with explanations that focus on transcultural rational choice (Stoll 1993), psychological needs (Horowitz 1985), or class to the exclusion of cultural issues (Bossen 1984; Wasserstrom 1983).

Chapter One

1. The Primer Encuentro, held in Bogotá, Colombia, in 1989, was the culmination of a series of regional meetings through which the grassroots Left mobilized the antiquincentenary campaign in the Americas. The *popular* movement portrays the Primer Encuentro Continental de Pueblos Indios, held in Quito, Ecuador, as another current of their efforts, although the meeting had a more indigenous-centric agenda.

2. For more on the congress, see the final report (Segundo Encuentro Continental, 1991) and the insightful analyses of C. Smith (1991, 1992a) and Hale (1994b). All three of us attended the meetings. In their writings for public consumption, Pan-

Mayanist intellectuals referred only obliquely to the meetings until Cojtí Cuxil's (1997a) recent history of the Pan-Maya movement.

3. Whether or not there is a unified Left in current political practice—or how current politics relates to the history of the Left's internal divisions—is not the task of these chapters. Congresses, such as the Segundo Encuentro, argued forcefully that the grassroots Left, in all its diversity, needs to share a common international political paradigm. On the Latin American Left, see J. Castañeda (1993).

4. My estimates of the number of participants at the congress come from the Segundo Encuentro's (1991) registration figures. By contrast, the march figures are disputed. C. Smith (1992a) suggests that press reports of thirty thousand marchers were journalistic exaggerations to stimulate the common fear of an indigenous rebellion, and she puts the number at twelve thousand; the Segundo Encuentro (1991) reported the number at an overly optimistic one hundred thousand. By any measure the march was very impressive.

5. These figures are from C. Smith (1992a). The ethnic composition of the Guatemalan *popular* delegation is in dispute. Smith says that half of the delegation was Ladino. The Mayanists I talked to disputed this framing of indigenous representation and declared that many of the supposedly indigenous delegates had no track record of representing Maya cultural issues in their political advocacy or practice.

6. By "social struggle" he means rights framed by the "class struggle" paradigm.

7. See, for example, Materne (1976). In fact, there have been a series of international indigenous meetings in Guatemala, including Rigoberta Menchú's Indigenous Summit in 1993 and CECMA's conference, which resulted in the volume *Derecho Indígena* (CECMA 1994), among many others.

8. Most of my information comes from public events, specialized conferences, and interviews with grassroots leaders, intellectuals, academics, AID officials, development workers, and townspeople in San Andrés. Another source has been the very public airing of these disputes in the Guatemalan press. In some cases members of the international *popular* Left have met with me to explain their views. Mayanists have also shared press clippings and discussed their critics with me in interviews in their offices and in conversations at events such as the Segundo Encuentro and Mayanist congresses and workshops. Guatemalan organizations sympathetic to indigenous issues also circulate clippings internationally. I have decided not to mention individual names from personal discussions. Some critics have moderated their opinions over time; others have intensified their intolerance. Particular lines of criticism continue to travel between Guatemala and the United States along the conference circuit. In contrast to the evasiveness of other foreigners, Levenson-Estrada (1997) and Stoll (1993) have written critiques of Pan-Mayanism from politically opposing points of view.

9. *Sólo cuando un pueblo accepta su historia y asume su identidad, tiene derecho a definir su futuro.*

10. See, for example, ALMG (1992; 1993), CEMCA (1992), Consejo de Educación Maya de Guatemala (1994), Oxlajuuj Keej Maya' Atz'iib' (1993), and England and Elliot (1990).

11. See Sam Colop (1991), Pop Caal (1992), and Racancoj (1994).

12. See Tay Coyoy (1996), CECMA (1992), Ajquijay On and Rodríguez (1992), and Dávila (1992a, 1992b, 1992c, 1993), among many others.

13. See COCADI (1992a, 1992b) and CECMA (1994).

14. See CECMA (1994), COMG (1991), Cojtí Cuxil (1991a; 1994; 1996a; 1997c).

15. See the candidate forum organized by Permanent Seminar for Maya Studies (SPEM), edited by CEDIM (1992), and published by Cholsamaj.

16. For example, funders of projects include the European Economic Community; Norwegian groups such as Redd Barna, Autoridad Noruega para el Desarrollo Internacional (NORAD), Programa Noruego de Pueblos Indígenas (FAFO), and Ayuda Popular de Noruega (APN); the Canadian Center for Human Rights, Development, and Democracy (CIDHDD); and the UN through a variety of programs such as UNICEF and Programa de Naciones Unidas para Desplazados, Refugiados, y Repatriados (PRODERE). U.S. funders include AID, the Plumsock Foundation, and, for scholarly exchanges, the Guatemalan Scholars Network and LASA. University supporters include the Universidad Rafael Landívar through the Instituto de Lingüística and the Universidad Mariano Galvez.

17. See Charles Hale (1996, 1995, and 1996c) for important ethnographic work on Ladino reactions to Maya mobilization.

18. A sustained reply to each of these lines of criticism is a task that belongs to the Pan-Mayanists themselves. However, much of this book deals with the interplay of national and local leadership in indigenous affairs and, in the process, addresses the issues of Maya intellectuals' commitments to rural communities and local responses to the movement.

19. Pan-Mayanists would argue that foreign and national academics have their own agendas in publishing on Guatemala that differ from the research agenda of Maya intellectuals.

20. *Indio* is understood by indigenous Guatemalans as a pejorative term when used by others. Morales also purposefully uses the world *mayista*, instead of the movement's self-ascription *mayanista*.

21. Personal communication, Apr. 23, 1997.

22. Good examples of his work include commentaries in *Siglo Veintiuno* such as "Again the Arrogance of Indianist Racism" (July 29, 1995), "The Globalization of San Lucas Tolimán" (Aug. 10, 1995), "Hybrid and Negotiable Identities" (Jan. 7, 1996), "Not Pan-Mayanism nor Ethnic War but Pure Tourism" (July 8, 1996), "A Minute to Critique Pan-Mayanism" (July 22, 1996), and "'Maya' Culture: A Mestizo Authenticity" (Aug. 5, 1996). See also, Morales (1997a; 1997b)

23. My thanks to Morales for responding to this section of the chapter, for saving me from factual errors (especially those dealing with the history of the clandestine Left), and for checking my translations of his commentaries. The analysis remains my own.

24. The Guatemalan congress formally ratified ILO 169 on March 5, 1995. See Nelson (1999) and the Instituto Centroamericano de Estudios Políticos (1993) for more details on the ILO convention in Guatemala.

25. See Zimmerman (1995a, 1995b) for a fuller account of his literary production, which includes novels in rebellious and revolutionary settings, the translation of Robert Carmack's edited book on the impact of the guerrilla/counterinsurgency war on Maya communities, which he undertook for FLACSO, and work in a hybrid *testimonio/novela* genre. Of Morales's post-1992 work, Zimmerman (1995b, 278) comments, "He raised significant questions about Guatemala's revolutionary past and the

place of Guatemala and the Guatemalan left in a new order where the older left-right categories no longer had meaning."

The Guatemalan leftist intellectual García Escobar (in Zimmerman 1995b, 279) advances the same argument, though clearly in more anxious prose: "It could be that he has to withdraw from his left position to make a critique of the left. But he's also drawing on the frustrations he's had . . . with the *comandante* of the Guatemalan left, and I'm waiting to see where all this will end. . . . It is true that I never expected this; I thought Mario Roberto would be one of the voices of the left, not a voice of the criticism of the left. . . . All Marxists who have survived the worldwide changes are engaged in this process of self-criticism. . . . they're seeking a new configuration of theory that would be Marxist or post-Marxist."

26. For Cojtí Cuxil's analysis and reply to them, see his "Problemas de 'La Identidad Nacional' en Guatemala" (1991a, 41).

27. These writers come from diverse political backgrounds. Carlos Manuel Pellecer, who writes for *La Hora*, is a former leftist from the generation of the 1950s revolution. By contrast, Mario Sandoval, a Pan-Maya critic who contributes to *Prensa Libre*, has been a leading organic intellectual on the Right, associated with the Movement for National Liberation (MLN), a conservative political party.

28. Ladino intellectuals, however, working with groups such as FLACSO-Guatemala have published very important scholarly works on Maya resurgence. See Bastos and Camus (1995a; 1996) and Solares (1993). Zevalos Aguilar of the Instituto Andino de Estudios Culturales in Peru contributed an insightful critique of Morales's essentialism in *La Hora* (Mar. 18, 1995).

29. Cojtí Cuxil has a doctorate in communications from Belgium and works for UNICEF; Sam Colop earned a doctorate in Maya linguistics from SUNY-Buffalo after his Guatemalan law degree and works on legal issues in Maya development. Zapeta, who pursued doctoral studies in anthropology at SUNY-Albany, is currently working as a journalist in Guatemala.

30. Pan-Mayanists have responded more directly over time in other media. They invited Morales to the 1996 and 1997 Congresos de Estudios Mayas, where he gave controversial lectures, in which he took his familiar line and was challenged by the audience. In his books, Cojtí Cuxil (1995; 1997a) has replied to the charge of separatism and Sam Colop (1991) denounced notorious journalists in the national press. For his part, Zapeta has produced critiques of the movement, which echo some of the Ladino language and concerns. In 1997 Zapeta and Morales stepped into the roles their virtual debates in the press had cast for them by publicly meeting twice for highly publicized face-to-face debates.

31. Several caveats are important here. There is no need for cultural capital to represent a *comprehensive* theory of the (commodified) relation of culture and political economy, on the order of hegemony for Gramsci's champions, for example. In my usage, cultural capital raises the ethnographic issues of meaning, context, and the reaffirmation of certain social relations (at the expense of other possibilities), not just the mechanical accumulation of capital or the abstract circulation of commodities. See Himpele (1995) for examples of this meaning-centered approach to what is often reductively read as commodification. I have been delighted to discover the convergence of my formulation with Kearney's work (1996) in this area. His insightful analysis of the transnationalism of Mixtec and Zapotec migrants to California and

critical reappraisal of the category "peasant" provide fascinating counterpoints to the case of Pan-Mayanism.

32. Lewis's unitary framing of culture leaves serious biases intact, not to speak of his implied stereotyped virtues for the middle class and his homophobia. For early critiques, see Leacock (1971).

33. Relevant to any sustained discussion of Guatemala would be larger issues of political economy, such as the country's place in the NAFTA regionalization and the continuation of *maquiladora* production as one national development strategy among others.

34. This is not the first instance of ethnic intensification on either side of the divide. See Brintnall (1979) for an argument that the activities of Catholic Action and Protestant groups in the 1950s and 1960s intensified indigenous identity and anti-Ladino sentiment by bridging cleavages that had subdivided communities.

35. The relative numbers are 21 percent versus 42 percent, according to the AVANCSO (1991, 55), which draws on the Instituto Nacional de Estadística data from its 1989 survey. Statistics by gender show illiteracy rates of 30 percent for Ladina women and 60 percent for Maya women. See Tay Coyoy (1996) for further breakdowns by region and gender according to the 1981 census and Núñez et al. (1991) for Instituto Nacional de Estadística rural-urban and gender statistics from the 1989 survey.

36. There are a variety of important studies that deal with the difficult issue of shifting sources of employment and urban migration. See, for example, Ehlers (1990) and Annis (1987). Another source of employment receiving scholarly attention is the *maquila* industry, centered around Guatemala City.

37. See Charles Hale (1995 and 1996c).

38. See Himpele (1995) for the comparative example that inspired this analysis.

39. They are correct that many foreign professionals come from families with working class and impoverished rural backgrounds and have used education and employment to consolidate comfortable middle-class lives. This writer's background from two generations ago certainly fits the profile.

Chapter Two

1. For the details, see Viteri (1997) and Colmenares (1997).

2. See Manz (1988, 30, 209). The toll of thirty years of war is even higher: more than one hundred thousand dead, forty thousand disappeared, and more than a million driven into exile (Schirmer personal communication). There is a Baudrillard-like aspect to citing one or another set of statistics for the violence in Guatemala. Shifting choices among alternatives may reflect different methods for estimating the terrible slaughter. But the politics of consensus building also means that statistics become a code to represent political allegiances.

From my point of view, shared by former MINUGUA administrator Roger Plant (1997), the longer conflict was not uniform in time or geography, and, thus, something is lost when analysts merge the crisis of 1978–85 into the longer history of insurgency/counterinsurgency conflicts for the country as a whole. This account treats the period when national conflict came to the highlands and centered on Maya communities.

3. He elaborated this point in a presentation on March 14, 1997, at the Woodrow Wilson Center's Conference on Comparative Peace Processes in Latin America.

4. On the indigenous use of the language of human and cultural rights in international forums to advance a rich agenda of issues including cultural recognition, constitutional reform, access to state institutions, land issues, self-administration, and the reconfiguration of national culture and the state, see Stavenhagen (1988, 1992, 1996), Ewen (1994), and the Instituto Centroamericano de Estudios Políticos (1993). On the development of international human rights organizations working in Latin America, see Sikkink (1996) and Cleary (1997) and on rights issues and the discipline of Anthropology, see Messer (1995).

5. Fujimori successfully consolidated power in Peru through a dictatorial takeover of his own government, legitimized in part by the failure of earlier counterinsurgency efforts to stamp out the Shining Path guerrilla movement.

6. See Arnson and Quiñones Amézquita (1997).

7. The process and constellation of participating Mayanist and *popular* groups has a particularly complex history, which has been well documented in studies of social movements and the peace process by Guatemalan-based social scientists such as Aguilera et al. (1996), Bastos and Camus (1995; 1996), and Borrell et al. (1997). For an insightful comparative study of peace processes in Latin America, see Arnson and Quiñones Amézquita (1997).

8. See COMG (1991; 1995).

9. See Nelson (1999) for the history of ILO Convention 169 in Guatemala.

10. See Saqb'ichil-COPMAGUA (1995).

11. Other accords dealt with the global accord on human rights, the resettlement of populations uprooted by the armed confrontation, the establishment of a commission for historical clarification of human rights violations, socioeconomy and the agrarian situation, the strengthening of civil power and the function of the military in a democratic society, constitutional reform and the electoral system, the definitive ceasefire, and the basis for the legal incorporation of the URNG into civil society (see ASIES 1996).

12. This antagonism played out through a discourse of cultural difference in *Rutzijol*'s first-page editorials on Nov. 1–15, 1994; Nov. 16–30, 1994; Mar. 16–31, 1995; and Apr. 16–30, 1995. See also Cojtí Cuxil (1997c) and Serech (1996).

13. On these issues and critiques of the process and substance, see *Rutzijol* (Apr. 16–30), Serech (1995), and Velasco Bitzol (*La República*, May 4, 22, and 29, 1994).

14. See ASIES (1996) for the phasing of all of the accords.

15. Their analysis, which was first published in 1970, drew on a range of others, including Gonzales Casanova, Stavenhagen, Fanon, and Memmi. In 1995, Pan-Mayanists republished the out-of-print Guzmán Böckler and Herbert book in its first Guatemalan edition through the Maya press, Editorial Cholsamaj.

16. For example, compare Jonas and Tobis (1974) with Jonas (1991) and Jonas and Stein (1990).

17. See Serech (1996) on political versus nonpolitical groups working on Maya issues. As a result of these dialogues, for example, the Fundación Rigoberta Menchú, which despite its name was thought of as a Ladino-run institution, will be funding projects in Maya education, and Demetrio Cojtí Cuxil has published with AVANCSO (Asociación para el Avance de las Ciencias Sociales en Guatemala) and FLACSO-

Guatemala (Facultad Latinoamericana de Ciencias Sociales-Guatemala), research centers long associated with *popular* issues, though the latter has been very active in research on the Maya movement.

18. The social and historical reasons for the hegemonic, often intolerant nature of the *popular* movement and its scholars are beyond the scope of this chapter. But the punishing reactions at the 1992 LASA meetings to Carol Smith's (1992b) historical analysis of racism in the work of nationally prominent academics on the Left and to my own early work on the Segundo Encuentro show how difficult it was in the recent past to pursue this history. A social history of the full scope of the Left and its views of other political tendencies might do much to show how this political vision has been reproduced over time.

19. See Laclau and Mouffe (1985), Mouffe (1992; 1993), and Trend (1996).

20. Of course they are not the only movement to do so. Internationally, religious revivalist movements have had similar agendas. See Denoeux (1993).

21. For important recent work on Maya cosmology in Guatemala, see Hill and Monaghan (1987), Wilson (1995), and Watanabe (1990; 1992).

22. That religious revitalization in other situations has been fraught with tensions, however, should not surprise us, given the diversity of theologies and organizational interests in Guatemala (see chapters eight and nine).

23. Chapter nine documents the multiple centers of power/knowledge in rural communities and in the Pan-Maya movement. In so doing, the analysis complicates the pattern of class mobility I discuss here and elaborates my critique of Bourdieu.

Chapter Three

1. See Bourque and Warren (1978; 1981).

2. The historical irony here is that the initial critique of Adams's Ladinoization was an anti-imperialist challenge by the leftist academic establishment in Guatemala. See Flores Alvarado (1983). For another example of academic ethnocide, see Vargas Llosa's portrayal of the future for indigenous populations in Peru (1983, 1990).

3. The following is, obviously, a distilled presentation of the lecture. The point of this presentation was to identify abstract ways identity has been modeled in Mesoamerican studies by North Americans. Clearly each of the works I mention deserves a full reading in its own right as well as the historical contextualization of its contribution. Many of these writers have produced constructionist analyses in their more recent work, so it would be unfair to treat their individual perspectives as fixed or unitary over time.

4. For a discussion of transnationalism and power relations in research, see Mato (1996). For a post-orientalist examination of the changing conventions for ethnographic representation that influence metropolitan and indigenous intellectuals, see Field (1996).

5. Elements of this view are reflected in the important studies of Maya traditionalism by B. Tedlock (1982a), Carmack (1973; 1981), and Hill and Monaghan (1987). A similar range of models can be found in studies of ethnically and racially stratified systems such as the United States.

6. In the colonial period, when *repartimiento* policies displaced the *encomiendas*,

plantation owners had to request indigenous forced labor from governmental authorities. See Sherman (1979).

7. For examples of this very influential view in Mesoamerican scholarship, see Harris (1964), M. Nash (1970), Stavenhagen (1970), Wasserstrom (1983), and Handy (1984).

8. Friedlander (1975) and Carmack (1973) are examples from very different theoretical orientations.

9. For an elegant example of Maya worldview as hegemonic, see Gossen (1984). For an important analysis of Indian subethnicities, see Brintnall (1979).

10. On diversity, see Watanabe (1992), Brintnall (1979), and chapter eight.

11. Migdal (1974) represents the comparative argument; Frank Cancian (1988) offers a case study.

12. Given the dominance in the 1960s and 1970s of historical materialism and dependency theory in social scientific research by Latin Americans and North Americans on Central America, this has been a very influential view. For example, see Stavenhagen's (1970) classical formulation, Jonas and Tobis (1974), and Wasserstrom (1983).

13. See Jonas and Tobis (1974).

14. See Hawkins (1984) for a fully elaborated example of this perspective.

15. There are echoes of Oscar Lewis's (1966) culture of poverty in this mode of thinking.

16. In the lecture, I did not pursue the issue of multiple identities given the tensions around different religious affiliations and the dismissal of gender as a major issue by many, but certainly not all, Maya scholars at that point. My very presence may have raised some of these issues. "Why," asked my Ladina language coach, "would university scholars listen to a woman lecture? It's only that you are a North American that anyone would bother." It never occurred to her that the university audience would be Maya.

17. See R. Adams (1991).

18. See R. Adams (1970) and Grindle (1986).

19. See Hendrickson (1991).

20. See Stoll (1990).

21. See Geertz (1973); Guidieri, Pellizzi, and Tambiah (1988); and Anderson (1991).

22. See Bruner (1986).

23. Both race and ethnicity are constructions, and current scholarship is interrogating accepted distinctions between these phenomena. Even *putative physical difference* as the central organizing principle for race is differentially constructed and contested across cultures, as, for example, Caribbean migrants learn when they come to the United States.

24. *Mestizo* is often taken by foreign scholars literally as a metaphor for mixtures of Spanish and Indian blood. But in practice the term more accurately refers to participants in the Latin American mainstream, with its distinctive hybrid of New World and European cultures.

25. In the mid-1980s migration surged with clashes between the Shining Path guerrilla movement (*Sendero Luminoso*) and the Peruvian military; see Bourque and Warren (1989).

26. See van den Berghe and Primov (1977).

27. On reflection, there are interesting ironies here. My reaction is shaped by a belief in an essential "self," a real and constant Kay Warren, whom others should find accessible. Here I am a native informant (the innocent transparency of my self-construction is part of the message) not the anthropologist (who would question transformations of Kay Warren from one situation to another in her daily life, not to speak of over the time period of this research during which paradigm-defying changes, in fact, did occur in my life). For me, constructionist fluidities are located in the realms of ethnicity, gender, and sexuality. Maya constructions involve an interesting mix of essentialist and constructionist attributions for the self and, for Pan-Mayanists, an essentialized inner core for ethnicity complemented with all sorts of additive constructions.

28. On reflection, the theoretical and comparative language of my talk (as well as my own preferred teaching style) may have contributed to their fears. I wanted to avoid politically charged issues and also to allow Mayas to respond in an open-ended way to the talk. So purposefully there was no closure, no definitive comparison of Peru and Guatemala. In this sense I was evasive, calling for an interactive dialogue. Their public silence and private concerns can be seen as responses to the talk as a veiled language requiring further interpretation and avoidance of comments that would reveal personal politics (cf. chapter four). If talking about Quechua resistance to Peruvian reforms were by chance a veiled commentary on the Guatemala situation, then the audience had to worry about who was listening, especially at CIRMA, where there were many strangers. Implicitly we shared reservations about talking about anything politicized; by convention no one mentioned the violence that had dominated recent Guatemalan (or Peruvian) politics.

29. My thanks to John Watanabe for insights into the local grounding identity for some Pan-Mayanists. See his analysis of place, soul, and ethnicity in a Mam community (1992). In practice my analysis argues for a complex interplay of perspectives, which themselves are both local and transnational.

30. Note that their concerns did not take the variant of skepticism that dismisses anthropology as the study of the anthropologist's own reflection in another culture. Hidden forms of control, not narcissism, was the worry.

31. Evangelicals, for instance, publish in Maya languages with the goal of promoting conversions; the Catholic church has experimented with cultural revitalization and in some cases with religious pluralism to slow the erosion of their official religious monopoly. Of course the tourism industry and North American and European development groups have other stakes and audiences.

32. On the issue of tactical essentialism and relativism, see Ramos (1997). It is a misreading to attribute a singularity or stability to essentialism in this case. Essentialism has become a Mayanist way of reclaiming authority from the assimilationist currents of the state and the economic development community. It is also a way of legitimizing the authoritativeness of new Maya institutions vis-à-vis local communities, which for their own part have not left such assertions uncontested.

33. Including, among others, notable early panels at the 1990 and 1991 American Anthropological Association meetings, the Mesoamerican Conferences at SUNY-Albany, the 1991 Latin American Studies Association meetings, and the 1991 international Segundo Encuentro Continental in Guatemala. In 1996 and 1997, Congresos de

Estudios Mayas were organized by Pan-Mayanists with North American and, after the first year, with broad-based Guatemalan input from progressive research centers.

34. See Lovell (1988).

35. This is not to suggest that foreign research has been insensitive to current political crises or human rights violations. See Carmack (1988b), Manz (1988), Davis (1988b), Lovell (1995), Schirmer (1998), and Carlsen (1997).

36. Personal communication.

Chapter Four

1. "The terror" may be a more apt translation of *la violencia*. In some areas, *la situación* was used to the same effect (Smith and Boyer 1987; Stoll 1993).

2. See Jonas (1991) for details on state politics during this period.

3. For details, see Davis (1988a), Carmack (1988b), Stoll (1993), Ehlers (1990).

4. Filmed in Mexico, this movie offers a powerful portrayal of political refugees' experience fleeing Guatemala through Mexico to California. In my view, however, this representation seriously underplays ethnic tensions as part of a strategy to cast North American imperialism as the primary source of injustice and conflict in Guatemala.

5. The groups included the Fuerzas Armadas Rebeldes (FAR), the Ejército Guerrillero de los Pobres (EGP), the Organización Revolucionaria del Pueblo en Armas (ORPA), and the Partido Guatemalteco del Trabajo (PGT-Núcleo).

6. See Davis (1988b), Smith and Boyer (1987), Fernández (1988), and Menchú and CUC (1992; 1993).

7. After all, some Ladinos are landless laborers and some Mayas own businesses and employ other Mayas on large farms.

8. See Handy (1984); Painter (1987); Sherman (1979); and Stavenhagen (1970).

9. See Menchú (1984), Montejo (1987), and Montejo and Akab' (1992).

10. See McClintock (1985, 65–69) for the details.

11. See T. Anderson (1992).

12. See the citations for these organizations in the bibliography.

13. The implications of this irony are important. Catholic Action's rhetoric was oppositional, whereas in practice their relationship with the civil-religious hierarchy was a complex pattern of negotiation, appropriation, resistance, and reconciliation. A focus on practice (Bourdieu 1977) rather than on sociological group formation explodes some of the scholarly myths about the alien nature of Catholic Action, Maya essentialism, and cultural authenticity.

14. For more violent areas, see Carmack (1988b), Manz (1988), Montejo (1987), Stoll (1993), Falla (1994), and Carlsen (1997).

15. See Hinshaw (1988).

16. President Vinicio Cerezo Arévalo took office in 1986 as the first democratically elected civilian leader since 1970. Although hopes were high for a democratic opening and for reforms, Cerezo was candid about the continued powers and autonomy of the military. He was slow to change structures, unable to pursue human-rights violators, and unsuccessful in taming the serious erosion in the value of the national currency, the *quetzal* (Painter 1987). Rural populations are skeptical of the ability of any president to roll back structures of surveillance and military power from

the past. Selective kidnappings and political assassinations continue to be common in Guatemala. See Americas Watch and the British Parliamentary Human Rights Group (1987) and Americas Watch and Physicians for Human Rights (1991).

17. *"La verdad es que la violencia siempre se mantiene."*

18. *"Aquí no tuvo bastante fuerza la violencia." "No tuvo mayor fuerza."*

19. There were, however, other organizations on the Left, such as the semiclandestine CUC, which focused on mass mobilization.

20. See Bermúdez (1986) and Warren (1989).

21. See Warren (1989) for background on the earlier ethnic division of labor in San Andrés Semetabaj.

22. See Paul and Demarest (1988).

23. See Stoll (1993) for an attempt to do this for the Ixil region.

24. See Friedl, Schele, and Parker (1993) and Art Museum, Princeton University (1995).

25. This is a translation of the Spanish version of the narrative I taped in 1989. The problems of translation in this case, beyond the linguistic limitations of the analyst, have to do with important differences between Maya Spanish and English. Markers of familiarity and hierarchy, which are elaborated in Maya Spanish in pronoun and verb choices, are difficult to maintain in written English. Differences in tacit knowledge are bridged for the non-Maya reader in the anthropological exegesis of the story, which parallels the Maya practice of explaining the significance of the story through a series of summary retellings to conclude the performance. The written version, of course, suffers the restrictions of the medium. In practice, these stories are enacted with highly expressive body language, changes in voice and intonation to represent different characters, and much stylistic repetition. Although I have cut out standardized repetitions of phrases—something that is part of the enjoyable, energetic cadence of the telling—I have maintained the original metaphors and figures of speech. I have kept the word *"rajaw"* or *"dueño"* (which can be translated as "master," "lord," "owner," or "guardian") in the original Kaqchikel to mark the fact that this concept has no easy counterpart in English, especially when talking about shape changers.

26. Steve Gudeman has also suggested to me in personal communication that the story may represent a possible Maya appropriation of a Ladino archetype—the goat—for male philandering. The issue of the historical production of culture is briefly explored in this analysis through the discussion of the *nagual-tonal* complex. Clearly, much remains to be done to document the interplay of Spanish-Ladino and indigenous systems of representation as they influenced what was available for people to reproduce, appropriate, and subvert in local culture (cf. Warren 1989). On the issue of cultural production, identity, and conflict, see Stanley Tambiah's (1986) analysis of the politics of ethnic difference and representation in Sri Lanka.

27. This is not just my construction; rather, it reflects the responses of my colleagues, lecture audiences, friends, and family members in the United States.

28. Unfortunately, I did not have the opportunity to discuss these narratives with women at that time, so other interpretations may well have been muted in this framing of the analysis (cf. Bourque and Warren 1985).

29. In the literature on *naguales* and companion animals, the emphasis has been on animals as representations of social hierarchies, relative powers, lifespans, and personality characteristics (cf. Gossen 1975; Musgrave-Portilla 1982; Pitt-Rivers 1970).

30. Structural functionalist explanations of *naguales* stress social control and the displacement of aggression from other spheres of life on to the transforming individual (Erice 1985).

31. See Musgrave-Portilla (1982), Stratmeyer and Stratmeyer (1979), and Saler (1969) for further background. Watanabe (1989) explores distinctive constructions of the inner "soul" for the county of Santiago Chimaltenango and finds it an important aspect of shared community and ethnicity.

32. For the literature, see Villa Rojas (1947), Vogt (1970), Pitt-Rivers (1970), and Gossen (1975).

33. See Simon's (1987) powerful account.

34. Elsewhere this was not possible, and violence overwhelmed communities, as the next chapter documents (see also Bermúdez 1986 and Simon 1986). In other cases, individuals misused their positions to enhance their own local powers, extort money or sex, and kill personal enemies (Paul and Demarest 1988; Simon 1986).

35. This calls for examinations of the interplay of ethnic, regional, class, gender, cultural, and religious cleavages, identities, and forms of domination.

36. For studies of U.S. policy and involvements, see the important work done by McClintock (1985, 1992) and Americas Watch and the British Parliamentary Human Rights Group (1987).

37. Of course, anthropological accounts are mediated by additional narrative conventions. In this chapter, I found myself compelled to contextualize the analysis and to establish its scholarly scope and significance through the conventions of an introductory overview and the brief historical treatment of the significance of transforming selves in Mesoamerica.

38. In the case of the press, this is a purposeful policy, the result of intimidation, self-censorship, and a sensationalist style (cf. Americas Watch and British Parliamentary Human Rights Group 1987, 59–61).

39. See also Montejo (1987, 107).

Chapter Five

1. From Montejo and Akab' (1992, 3).

2. See Adams (1994).

3. See Zimmerman (1995b) for a useful overview of *testimonio* literature in Latin America and the genre as practiced in Guatemala.

4. For more on *testimonios*, see Stephen (1994) and the excellent collections of articles "Voices of the Voiceless" in *Latin American Perspectives* (1991).

5. That Montejo is fluent in these norms is clear from other works (1993a; n.d.).

6. In other ways, he has had a very different exile experience in the United States. See Hagan (1994) on Guatemalan refugees in Houston, Texas, and Burns (1993) on refugees in Indiantown, Florida.

7. See chapter eight for the argument.

8. Cojtí Cuxil frames his history of the Pan-Maya movement in terms of this suppression (1997, 11).

9. See Zimmerman (1995b) for a very important survey of the critical literature on Menchú and for an insightful reading of Menchú against Sexton's testimonies from Ignacio.

10. See, for example, Zimmerman (1995b, 96) and the Stoll and D'Souza controversies described in the same volume.

11. See Carey-Webb and Benz (1996) for evidence of this hegemony and for the variety of ways the book has been used and read in U.S. classrooms.

12. For examples of human-rights discourse for the Kuchumatans in the early 1980s, see the Americas Watch and Amnesty International citations in the bibliography.

13. In 1976, these covenants entered into force as legally binding for the thirty-five member states that had ratified them. See Donnelly (1993) for the fuller history of international rights and their implementation.

14. In part this goal was achieved when, after congressional hearings, the United States cut direct support of the military. Yet indirect support continued through U.S. programs and military advisers that trained Guatemalan officers in counterinsurgency techniques, through development funds redirected to paramilitary police forces, and through the CIA's hiring of individual military contacts, as has come to light recently.

15. See the Americas Watch Committee publications cited in the bibliography. For a view critical of the human rights community during the war in Guatemala, see Stoll (1993).

16. This is a pseudonym.

17. See Taussig (1992) on terrorism.

18. See, for example, León Portilla (1974; 1984). For more on the history of the Kuchumatans, see Lovell (1992).

19. For detailed reports on the region, see Americas Watch (1984b) and Montejo (1993a).

20. I have made the editorial decision *not* to reproduce excerpts that detail acts of torture or killing—they are too graphic for a short essay where, unlike a contextualized longer work, their shock value displaces other issues and orientalizes the other.

21. As Montejo discusses in an expository mode in his dissertation, military rhetoric "shifted from Indians as savages to Indians as communists who threatened to seize private property and introduce a totalitarian system. . . . Indians were equated with guerrillas, subversives, and instruments of communism (1993a, 59–60).

22. See Clifford (1988), Clifford and Marcus (1986), and Fox (1991) for discussions of ethnographic authority, the diversification of anthropological narrative strategies, the politics of authorship and representation, the representation of the plural contributors to ethnographic knowledge, and the awareness of culturally diverse audiences for ethnography. In dealing with closely related genres of realist representation, documentary films, and fictions, Nichols (1994) reveals that other fields have long grappled with issues that anthropology has discovered only recently.

23. Montejo made a self-conscious decision here, given that he is fluent in North American academic conventions through his graduate work (see Montejo 1993a).

24. These were written at the camp's school under the supervision of the schoolmaster, which most likely accounts for their similarity.

25. That other states exercise powerful forms of coercion on the exiles is clear in Montejo (1993a), Burns (1993), and Hagen (1994).

26. I discontinued work in Peru with the political scientist Susan Bourque when the Shining Path guerrilla movement and the Peruvian army overwhelmed the region

where we had done ethnographic research for eight years. See Bourque and Warren (1989).

27. In a similar vein, Montejo (1993a, 9–11) discusses the sources of refugee reticence toward strangers and research projects in the camps, and deals with the Mexican government's ideological organization of the camps. He decided to conduct interviews in camps outside formal government control.

28. Another issue for activists is the difference between those who stayed and those who lived in exile.

Chapter Six

1. See Stocking (1983).

2. That these titles are multilingual is a measure of Sam Colop's linguistic abilities and, as this essay argues, of the important role of transculturalism in ethnic resurgence. As of 1993, versions of the essays had been published in Spanish, English, and Italian. To further illustrate his argument, he wrote "1992 y El Discurso de Encubrimiento: Five Hundred Years of Guatemalan Maya Resistance: A Dialogue between Mayan and Non-Mayan Scholars" for a collection of indigenous writings in the journal *Global Justice* in 1992. A related essay appears in Fischer and Brown (1996).

3. His terms are *"discurso de encubrimiento," "discurso de invasión," "discurso del indio,"* and *"discurso colonial del siglo XX."*

4. Other indigenous accounts of the invasion are available, as Sam Colop notes in his analysis of *"discurso indio"*: the *Chilam Balam, Anales de los Kaqchikeles, Popol Wuj,* and the *títulos* are important Guatemalan sources. Gananath Obeyesekere (1992) discusses the ways in which European projections onto others reinforced their fears of cannibalism and even lead local populations to dramatize European expectations in the Pacific.

5. For their service to the Crown, Spaniards were rewarded with *encomiendas,* trusteeships that gave them the right to extract tribute and labor from a given regional population.

6. Of course, subsequent history has revealed Germany's ambivalence and reluctance. Moreover, Germany and Russia have been transformed into new entities since 1989. I note this to underscore the volatility of such claims and the reason that, although Mayas use comparative observations to make the case for alternative possibilities, they also look to organizations such as the United Nations for trans-state leverage.

7. See Rajasingham (1993).

8. Maltby finds a striking transformation in the process of translation: "[Las Casas] argued that cruel and barbarous *men* were engaged in the colonization of America and that their worst excesses should be legally curbed. It was his English translator who decided that the Spanish were an exceptionally 'cruel and barbarous *nation*'" (1968, 20, emphasis mine).

9. As a traditionalist historian and apologist for Spain (and for the United States, which he sees in a similar dilemma in the modern world), Maltby argued against polemical exaggeration and continually evaluated the truth-value of different accounts. Evident though not fully explored in his account is the relation between con-

structions of Spanish and English brutality at particular historical moments. In addition, Maltby could have made much more of the changing nature of the legend and the very different readings Las Casas has received over time. Finally, it would be interesting to know more about public opinion to determine which elements of the Black Legend were persuasive and when and who decided to encourage and exploit the English hatred of the Spanish.

10. Oxib' Kej and B'elejeb' Tz'i', the K'ichee' leaders.

11. I use Mackie's English translation because Sam Colop cites it after quoting the Spanish version in Recinos (1952, 75).

12. For current echoes, see Schirmer (1998) and Davis (1992).

13. See Obeyesekere's (1992) critique.

14. As Benjamin observed: "To articulate the past does not mean to recognize it 'the way it really was.' . . . It means to seize hold of a memory as it flashes up at a moment of danger" (1969, 255).

15. Mayas used this strategy in earlier times, when religion became a veiled commentary on ethnic relations (see Warren 1989). Religion was a safe bet since it was not deemed "political" by those in power.

16. For an elaborated version of this argument, see Obeyesekere (1992).

17. See Prakash (1992a, 372) and Spivak (1985, 372–45).

18. See Carmack (1994) for a parallel recognition of the political stakes in historical representations.

19. This has been evident at number of Pan-Maya meetings, most notably at the *Primer Congreso de la Educación Maya* in 1994.

20. See al-'Azm (1991) on the dangers of reverse orientalism.

21. For a critique of Prakash from a Marxist problematic, see O'Hanlon and Washbrook (1992); for his reply, see Prakash (1992b).

22. I am not suggesting the sequences or periodicities of Latin American and South Asian historiography mirror each other. Their colonial histories are distinctive with different regimes of power, patterns of differentiation between the colonized and colonizer, experiences of nationalism, and reactions to internal heterogeneity. In India, nationalism was part of a twentieth-century challenge to European colonizers. By contrast, after five centuries of colonial society in Latin America, the nineteenth-century struggle for independence was waged among political groups with New World cultural, ethnic, and political stakes. Although there was no hegemonic European national/racial group to eject, there were heterogeneous populations constructed as being outside the mainstream of emerging nation-states.

23. See Stoll (1997) for an example of the complexity of these land conflicts.

24. Sam Colop's (*Prensa Libre*, Mar. 20, 1997) condemnation of the Fischer and Brown (1996) volume in his newspaper column shows how ambivalent this collaboration remains.

Chapter Seven

1. Todorov (1984) and Sahlins (1981; 1985; 1995) are drawn to the "other" as radically different in apprehending and representing the world and politically disadvantaged by these categorical, dichotomizing differences. Obeyesekere (1992) takes on this issue to show the mythmaking nature of European society and the self-inter-

ested political nature of Hawaiian politics. The balance is tricky. On the one hand, as long as difference is essentialized and seen as hegemonic, the risk is reverse orientalism instead of an analytically level playing field. Alternatively, when difference is collapsed, the risk is a universalized political rationality. Each of these authors seeks a dynamic model but Prakash (1992a) would argue that none has solved the post-orientalist riddle.

2. Freed from the pressures of their normal work week by Linda Schele's Maya symposium in Austin, Texas, the study group of Kaqchikel-speaking linguists was eager to turn to the chronicle along with Judith Maxwell, professor of linguistics at Tulane, and Helen Rivas, who provided logistical support. Nora England and I sat in on the sessions, and Nik'te' and Saqijix from Oxlajuuj Keej—who were working on the *Rabinal Achi*—frequently dropped by to check on the group's progress. This was a vacation for all of us, so the tone of the study group was celebratory and informal with a great deal of spontaneous discussion and cross-language wordplay. The leadership of the endeavor was collaborative and clearly Maya with Judith Maxwell as a peer.

3. See, for example, Racancoj (1994).

4. Here, of course, one sees why Scott's (1990) structuralism with its emphasis on otherness sometimes misses the mark. The "hidden transcript" here is as much about internal divisions and worries as it is about the oppressor.

5. Along these lines, Galeano (1986, 29–30) writes: "The sacred myths [of the *Popol Wuj*] announce a time of fighting and punishment for those who are arrogant and greedy. They remind the Indians of Guatemala that they are people and have a history, one much longer than the society which uses and despises them, and so they are born again each day."

6. The community was called Tzolola in prehispanic times.

7. Specifically, the group worked on the origins section, which juxtaposes the coming of Q'aq'awitz and Saqtekaw from Tulan to establish the founding Kaqchikel lineages and the creation by Tz'aqol B'itol of the first humans (passages 1–5 in Brinton, Recinos, and Villacorta), the migration of the early Kaqchikels and their wars with neighboring groups (passages 15–16, 37–38), the Iximche' revolt and the participation of women warriors (passages 99–103), the Spanish invasion (passages 144–49), and the demand for tribute and subsequent wars of conquest involving the Kaqchikels, Tz'utujils, and K'ichee's (passages 152–56). On page 188, Brinton comments "I append the [English] translation of the remainder of what I believe to be the original work . . . but as its contents are of little general interest, I omit the [Kaqchikel] text." At that point the group switched to the Villacorta version in Kaqchikel for the Pakal B'alam genealogy (passage "o"), which was, in fact, of great interest.

8. See D. Tedlock (1983, 261–71) for a fascinating argument that these recountings in postinvasion chronicles represent resistance to Christian narratives of singularity.

9. I include illustrative excerpts based on the work of the 1992 study group in Spanish and Kaqchikel to give readers a sense of the text. Passages are numbered following Brinton, Recinos, and Villacorta. I am departing from the group's strategy for Spanish translation by using the Kaqchikel verse structure, which marks the genre of formal speech and prayer. See Sam Colop (1994) on verse structure.

10. This is based on the group's retranscription and translations of Brinton's ver-

sion. One of the ironies of the anthropological process, of course, is that I must provide another level of translation—and thus perpetuate the very problem this group was attempting to remedy—in order to give English readers a sense of the Oxlajuuj Keej texts. My special thanks to Judith Maxwell for reviewing this English version.

In other cases, the issue is easier. Brinton (1885) and Recinos and Goetz (1953) produced English translations, which I draw on when appropriate. Spanish and English translations lose the elaborate language for Maya leadership. In English, I have avoided *chief*, a term common in other English translations, as well as the intolerant language of *pagans* and *idols*, although elsewhere this language becomes the focus of analysis. One unavoidable gap has to do with the levels of meaning in Maya formal discourse. There is no way to represent the simultaneity of meanings and associations in straight narrative, another reason why the discussion of exegesis and translation is conjoined.

11. Obsidian stone.

12. Tz'aqol is, according to D. Tedlock (1983, 267), associated with "mason, builder, construction" and B'itol with "former, shaper, modeler."

13. The leader of the Tuquche' forces.

14. Mayanist histories, such as the Racancoj volume (1994, 34, 36), run the risk of rekindling these tensions when they historically justify women's marginalization in public affairs. In Racancoj's account, the consolidation of a class-free harmonious indigenous civilization based on "men of corn" flowed from men's ancient decision to shift women from their early central role as the primary agriculturalists to the domestic sphere.

15. This is their English translation of Recinos (1950, passage 148): "En verdad infundían miedo cuando llegaron. Sus caras eran extrañas. Los Señores *los tomaron por dioses*" or Villacorta (1934, passage 148) ". . . fué cosa terrible cuando entraron; sus rostros eran extraños y los jefes *los tomaron por dioses.*"

16. The 1992 Oxlajuuj Keej translation reads "Realmente *era aterrorizante cuando llegaron*, no eran conocidos. Los caciques supusieron que *eran seres no naturales.*"

17. D. Tedlock's (1993a) readings of the *Popol Vuh* and *Annals* reaffirm this interpretation. He finds provocative evidence of Spanish torture to exact confession in these indigenous accounts.

18. The Guatemalan Army (Ejército de Guatemala 1963) sponsored a fascinating scholarly evaluation of the Tecún Umán myth. A panel of highly respected Ladino scholars painstakingly evaluated colonial documents and in the process showed their variations and subjectivities as well as problems in translation. In this sense, the project followed procedures similar to those advocated by the Maya study group. However, the concluding paragraphs of the book disavow any indeterminacy. The study claims to have definitively proven, through a weighing of indirect evidence, the occurrence of Tecún Umán's battle with Alvarado and the significance of his death. Thus, the national hero is reaffirmed as an established truth. This study deserves a fuller treatment and contextualization in terms of the State's construction of an encompassing nationalism during an earlier period of unrest.

19. Alternatively, many Mayas adopt calendric names from the 260-day annual count for men and from the 20-day month count for women.

20. The issue of their position as experts who broker and authenticate Maya knowledge is pursued in chapters eight and nine.

21. One might ask if Pan-Mayanists ever use the language of race, even in a masked form.

22. Nongovernmental organization.

23. Until recently this contrasted with the massive funding of religious evangelization by the U.S.-based 700 Club and other conservative religious groups, and the equally massive funding of *popular* movements by international solidarity movements in the United States, Europe, and Latin America. The Guatemalan government's funding of the Academia de Lenguas Mayas de Guatemala, the European Community's announcement of the Fondo Indígena, and the surge of foreign support for peace-accord generated initiatives from European and U.S. sources may well transform the movement into a more bureaucratic form. Some worry that too much funding may hurt the movement.

24. Yet, even this hierarchy is unstable as Mayas finishing Ph.D.s—whether as Guatemalans or as exiles—become professors at U.S. universities.

Chapter Eight

1. Watanabe (1992) and B. Tedlock (1982) base their analyses of Maya worldview on communities where saint societies are not significant. In contrast, saint societies have been central to the social and religious life of many other communities (see, for example, Cancian 1965; Rojas Lima 1988; W. Smith 1977).

2. See Watanabe's (1992) insightful analysis of Maya constructions of commitments to the local.

3. See Rosaldo (1968).

4. This is a translation of the discourses given in Kaqchikel at the Cofradía de María for the celebration of Corpus Cristi in 1972. Dios *ruch'ulew* (the Earth/the World and, more recently, Nature), the saints, and the *rajav juyu* where one's farms are located are also prayed to for pardon.

5.   "Angel señor San Bernadino,"
        xutz'et pe ri mi'er q'ij, ri mi'er "ora."
        Ya k'a la' xtz'eto richin,
        ya k'a la' xkochin richin,
        akuchi' chajin jun b'is,
        akuchi' chajin oq'ej,
        akuchi' chajin jun "alegre contenta,"
        chi ru wach ulew.
        Ya k'a la xekamayin rutz'etik,
        chi ruxe' ri kaj, xe' ri ulew,
        tata "dyos."

        El angel señor San Bernadino,
        vió el día de hoy, la hora de hoy.
        Fué él quien lo vió,
        Fué él quien lo regaló,
        donde hay una tristeza,
        donde hay un llanto,

donde hay una alegría,
sobre la tierra.
Ellos presenciaron de ver,
bajo el cielo, bajo la tierra,
Padre Dios.

6.   ¿ya ri akuchi' nuju' pe ruq'a, raqan
     ri jun qachalal,
     ri jun qate'?
     Niq'ajam pe ri "santas campanas,"
     pa ruwi' ri qasiwan,
     pa ruwi' qatinamit;

     ¿Desde dónde se levanta su mano, su pie,
     aquel nuestro hermano,
     aquella nuestra madre?
     Suenan las santas campanas,
     sobre nuestros barrancos,
     sobre nuestro pueblo.

7. That is, to where they originated.

8. K'a ri', k'a ri', xb'e "dyos" qanima.
    Ai "dyos," ¿achike k'a npe?
    ¿Achike k'a nu tata'?
    achike k'a wachalal?
    yixb'e yixtzolij
    pa ruq'a', pa raqan ri "dyos"?
    "Dyos" k'a katuk'wan,
    "dyos" k'a kachajin,
    "dyos" k'a tub'ana' "perdonar."

    Así, así se irá con Dios nuestro espíritu,
    ¡Ay, Dios! ¿qué es lo que viene?
    ¿Quién es mi padre?
    ¿Quién es mi hermano?
    Se van, regresan para allá.
    a las manos, a los pies de Dios.
    Será Dios quien te llevará,
    Será Dios quien te cuidará,
    Será Dios quien te perdonará.

9. I have purposefully left blanks in the trascription and translations when community members in 1989 could no longer fathom phrases of the ritual language, which was taped in 1972 and fell into disuse in the community after the mid-1970s.

10. Xojalax k'a richin ri chuwa'q,
     Xojalax k'a richin ri kab'ij,
     Xqucha' ta na k'a,

xa jun "qadyos" ri nqaya',
nqasipaj ———,
utz laj "critiano hermanita".
traj xa jun chik ri qaq'ij,
xa jun chik ri qab'anik,
traj xa yojkikot apo chi rij,
trajo' xa ri nqatzaq chik jun itzel tzij,
jun itzel ch'ab'al,
chi rij ri b'enan
ri tzolijen;

Nacimos pues para el mañana,
Nacimos pues para el futuro,
Diríamos,
Solo a un Dios le damos, le regalamos ———,
Nuestro hermano es buen cristiano.
Tal vez ya solo un nuestro día,
Ya solo uno somos,
Tal vez estamos alegre por él,
Tal vez diremos otra mala palabra,
un mal pensamiento,
sobre la ida, sobre el regreso.

11. xa man ya' ta k'a ri nub'an
    "mandar" ri "dyos,"
    xa jun loq'oj tzij
    xa jun ———
    xqucha' ta na k'a
    "pero" xa mani k'achoj ta chik,
    traj xa jun chik ri qaq'ij,
    traj xa jun chik ri qab'anik
    ———xepe wi ri qate',
    ri qati't, ri qamama',
    ojer "tyempo," ojer tzij,
    utz taq tzij k'o pa kina'oj,
    xexuke' chi ruwach ulew.

Eso no es lo que manda Dios.
Solo unas sagradas palabras,
Solo un ———,
Diríamos, pues.
Pero tal vez ya no tiene remedio,
Tal vez ya solo nos queda unos días,
Tal vez ya solo somos de otra forma.
——— vinieron nuestras madres,

nuestras abuelas, nuestros antepasados,
antiguo tiempo, antigua historia.
Buenas palabras, tenían buenos pensamientos,
y se hincaron ante la faz de la naturaleza.

12. Chi ri wi k'a,
xyataj ri kiq'ij,
xyataj ri "kityempa,"
traj xkib'an ri kisamaj chi kamal, oxmal,
chi rupan ri loq'olaj jay "kab'ilda,"
traj xkiban ri kipatan chi kamal chi oxmal
chi rupan ri loq'olaj jay "santa iglesia,"
traj xkiban ri kikisamaj ri kipatan,
chi kamal chi oxmal chi rupan ri loq'olaj jay "cowradiye."

Allí pues,
Les dieron sus días,
les dieron sus tiempos.
Tal vez se esforzaron en su servicio dos, tres veces
en la sagrada casa en el cabildo.
Tal vez se esforzaron en su servicio dos, tres veces
en la sagrada iglesia.
Tal vez se esforzaron en su servicio dos, tres veces
en la sagrada cofradía.

13. Chi ri wi k'a,
xyataj k'a ri kiq'ij,
xyataj k'a ri "kityempo,"
traj xsaqir na k'a kiwi',
xsaqir na k'a kijolon
traj xeb'e yan
traj xeniman,
traj xech'emeyan

Allí pues,
Les dieron sus días,
les dieron sus tiempos.
Tal vez se les blanqueó su cabello,
se les blanqueó su cabeza.
Tal vez ya se fueron,
tal vez obedecieron,
tal vez envejecieron en su servicio.

14. Ya' k'a ri oj,
ri kime'al, oj kajk'wal,
oj kisi'j, oj kijotay,
traj xa ma ya' ta k'a chik
ri nqach'ab'ej
ri jun qate', ri jun qatata',
ri jun saq ruwi', saq rujolon.

Somos nosotros, pues
sus hijas, sus hijos,
sus floreceres, sus retoños.
Tal vez ya no es eso
lo que diremos
a un nuestra madre, a un nuestro padre,
al de cabello blanco, de cabeza blanca.

15. Man atux ta k'a nub'an,
    ri jun qate',
    ri jun qatata',
    wi ta ri qanima,
    wi ta nich'emeyan
    chi rupan ri rub'ey.
    traj xa niqanim,
    traj xa niqachakamayij ta qa k'a.

    No hará nada,
    Aquella nuestra madre,
    Aquello nuestro padre,
    Si nuestra espíritu,
    Si queda una sola parte incompleta
    En su camino, su vida de servicio.
    Tal vez los animamos,
    Tal vez los empujamos.

16. Outside the *costumbre* the parents have celebrated in their lives.

17. Chi ri' wi k'a nimpoqonaj,
    jun qate',
    jun tata',
    jun saq rwi'
    jun saq rujolon.
    "¡Ah dyos!" xa atnumeal,
    xa atwajk'wal,
    xa atnusij
    xa atnujotay,
    kek'ala' nab'an qa chwe,
    ma ri k'o ra' wanin,
    ma ri k'o ra' wochoq'a
    k'o ra'na'oj
    yinanim qa chupan ri nub'ey
    yatiwa achi
    yatiwa awech.

    Allí es cuando me da lástima,
    a una nuestra madre,
    a un nuestro padre,
    a uno de cabello blanco,
    a uno de cabeza blanca.
    Ah, Dios, eres mi hija

eres mi hijo,
eres mi florecer,
eres mi retoño.
Así me haces.
Porque tienes vigor
porque tienes fuerzas,
tienes tu conocimientos,
me quieres sacar del camino de mi vida
tal vez con tu boca,
tal vez con tus ojos.

18. In the east.
19. In the west.
20. Xtib'e q'ij
   xtib'e "tyempa"
   traj xtuya' tzij, ra'woyoxik,
   traj xuke'
   traj xmeje'
   pa rulab'al,
   qajb'al "angel señor San Bernadino"
   chi ri' wi k'a ni q'alataj,
   ri "qatyempa,"
   ni q'alataj k'a ri qa q'ij,
   tril ma tril q'ij,
   tril ma tril "ora,"
   ri qub'e ri qutzolij,
   pa ruq'a,
   pa ruqan, ri "Dyos."

   Se irán los días,
   Se irá el tiempo.
   Tal vez mandó a llamarte
   Tal vez se hincó,
   Tal vez se postró
   en la salida del sol [el este],
   en la puesta del señor San Bernadino [el oeste].
   Allí pueses donde se aclara
   nuestro tiempo,
   donde se descubre nuestros días,
   Si llega o no llega el día,
   Si llega o no llega la hora,
   de nuestra ida, de nuestro regreso,
   en las manos, en los pies de Dios.

21. Xa qach'abal,
   xa qana'oj
   ri qanimo ri quchakamayin,
   traj k'o na k'a ri tzij,
   traj k'o na k'a ri chab'al

peri k'achoj,
ta chik k'a yojch'o,
choch ruch'ulew;

Solo nuestra voz,
solo nuestra inteligencia,
es lo que animamos, empujamos.
Tal vez habrá palabra,
tal vez habrá voz,
pero ya no podremos hablar,
ante Dios mundo.

22. There are many interpretations of the role of the civil-religious hierarchy, and particularly the saint societies, in Maya communities. One can see this as a transformation of pre-Hispanic ideology (Carmack 1981), as a colonial and neocolonial attempt to control Maya populations (W. Smith 1977), or as a social form subverted by local communities to create cultural and political space (Warren 1989).

23. Exchange, appropriate and inappropriate, is another theme in the wider set of narratives that portray the powers of the *rajav juyu*, the master of the mountain.

24. The issue of humans with animal counterparts and beings with the power to transform themselves, an ancient one in Mesoamerica, was reshaped by the interplay of distinctive beliefs at the conquest. See chapter three for the details.

25. The dogs are said to bark because they smell the stench of the *rajav a'q'a*. It is perhaps significant that Ladinos are also believed to have a bad smell and are colloquially referred to as *xex*, "the foul-smelling ones."

26. Catholic confession is seen as a private affair between the priest and the individual. Diviners discover the nature of the problem in dialogue with the individual, his or her body, and divining stones (see B. Tedlock 1982).

27. *No hay que tener confianza ni con su proprio cuerpo.*

28. See B. Tedlock (1982) for a community where divining dominates religious action.

Chapter Nine

1. Examples that come to mind are D. Tedlock (1993b), Tsing (1993), and the Fox collection of experimental ethnographies (1991).

2. This Western frame of reference is hardly static, as Ariès' (1962) classic work demonstrated. We have also witnessed the politicization of certain generations (such as the rebellious 1960s) and the proclivity of advertisers to identify/create new generational markets (the "baby boomers" and "generation x") with varying amounts of success.

3. See, for example, the work of Warren (1989).

4. See Warren (1989) and C. Smith (1993).

5. See, for example, the important work of B. Tedlock (1982), John Watanabe (1992), Robert Carmack (1973), and, across the border in Chiapas, Gary Gossen (1984) and Evon Z. Vogt (1969).

6. See Carmack (1995) for a pathbreaking case study of the interplay of local and

national tensions in indigenous affairs and for the changing and varying experience of domination by different sectors of the indigenous population of Momostenango.

7. In one key drama, enacted at Holy Week, a Ladino-like figure—*xutio*, San Simón, or Judas, as he is alternatively called—takes on local men in rough mock battles through the town. Later he takes effigy form and is given candles and offerings by petitioners in a shrine at the jail. At the end of Holy Week, *xutio* is hung high on the Calvario church's facade. After the resurrection, the figure is lowered, torn apart limb from limb, and burned behind the jail by townspeople. Clearly this figure has an ethnic dimension, and, just as clearly, the polysemy of the symbolism is not exhausted by an ethnic reading. See June Nash (1967–68), E. Michael Mendelson (1958; 1959), and Warren (1989) for analyses of this figure in different communities.

8. This was a common pattern in the highlands; see Brintnall (1979).

9. For details, see Warren (1989).

10. I remember making this decision quite strategically in 1970 as I cut off interviewees eager to discuss *pedidas* in favor of what I saw as more important public rituals and formal institutions. Feminist anthropology made the implications of this selectivity increasingly clear to me. See Bourque and Warren (1981) for a critique of the public/private, formal/informal, male/female dichotomies that muted women's voices in anthropological field research.

11. Early in Pan-Mayanism, the saint societies were rejected as well. They were seen an another instance of Spanish colonialism in contrast to the autochthonous character of shamanism. That the state offered financial incentives for saint society processions and rituals to spur tourism further stigmatized these organizations. More recently, with the goal of revitalizing councils of elders, there has been a reassessment of the contribution of the civil-religious hierarchy (COCADI 1992b; CECMA 1994).

12. Perhaps he, too, sees irony in Alfonso's decision to mark his son's high-school graduation with a Maya ceremony and the traditional graduation mass favored by urban youth.

Conclusions

1. See Falla (1978b), Arias (1990), and de Paz (1993). Falla saw this failure as proof that Mayas would not be able to organize on the basis of ethnic or cultural identity as opposed to revolutionary class identity in solidarity with Ladino workers.

2. Cojtí Cuxil takes this a step further by personalizing the identity crisis as one characteristic of Ladinos (1991a, 4–10). This is a particular kind of reverse orientalism, given that its goal is to deconstruct naturalizations of the Ladino as dominator by showing the volatility of the category in history and lack of persuasiveness of the term for the population in question. If cultural identity involves self-conception and Ladinos resist this, then their control seems much less categorical and given. Cojtí Cuxil argues that there is a particular signature to Ladino cultural domination that flows from their insecurity.

3. On race, see also Cojtí Cuxil (1991a, 6, 17–21, 26–27).

4. Actually, only some existing departmental divisions conform roughly to cultural and linguistic regionality. Despite Tax's (1937) elevation of the *municipio* as the basic unit of cultural identity, there is a great deal of indigenous multiculturalism within

municipal divisions, which undoubtedly has a long history. See Carmack (1995) and Brintnall (1979).

5. In this and other central phrasings, Cojtí Cuxil employs the Maya aesthetic of parallel phrasing, much like the *k'amöl b'ey* does in ritual discourses.

6. This is an ironic choice, given that Lebanon's discord resulted in part from an inclusive but rigid system of ethnic representation.

7. While Anderson's (1983) language is useful, the culturalist analysis represents an important critique of his top-down model.

8. See, for example, Michael Hanchard (1994).

9. A similar point has been made for Latin America by historical materialists, such as Friedlander (1975), who sought to show that many putatively indigenous practices, which appeared authentically indigenous to the twentieth-century eye, were more often than not colonial impositions or practices of a capitalist underclass unable to keep up with market driven changes.

10. For these insights related to this issue, see Ramos (1997).

11. See Warren (1994) for an overview.

Appendix One

1. See Saqb'ichil/COPMAGUA (1995; 1996).

Bibliography

Newspapers and Related Periodicals

Crónica
El Gráfico
La Hora
Iximulew
New York Times
El Periódico
Prensa Libre
El Regional
La República
Rutzijol
Siglo Veintiuno
Tinamit

Reference List

Abu-Lughod, Lila. 1990. "Anthropology's Orient: The Boundaries of Theory on the Arab World." In *From Theory, Politics, and the Arab World*, 81–131. New York: Routledge.

———. 1991. "Writing against Culture." 137–62. In *Recapturing Anthropology: Working in the Present*, ed. Richard Fox, 137–62. Santa Fe: School of American Research.

Adams, Abigail. 1998. "Word, Work, and Worship: Engendering Evangelical Culture in Highland Guatemala and the United States." Ph.D. dissertation, Department of Anthropology, University of Virginia.

———. Forthcoming. "Gringas, Ghouls, and Guatemala: Transnational Kinship and Hypogamy in the Post-NAFTA World." *American Anthropologist*.

Adams, Richard N. 1970. *Crucifixion by Power: Essays on Guatemalan National Social Structure, 1944–1966*. Austin: University of Texas Press.

———. 1991. "Strategies of Ethnic Survival in Central America." In *Nation-States and Indians in Latin America*, ed. Greg Urban and Joel Sherzer, 181–206. Austin: University of Texas Press.

———. 1994. "A Report on the Political Status of the Guatemala Maya." In *Indigenous Peoples and Democracy in Latin America*, ed. Donna Lee Van Cott, 155–86. New York: St. Martin's Press.

———. 1995. *Etnias en Evolución Social: Estudios de Guatemala y Centroamérica*. Mexico: Universidad Autónoma Metropolitana.

———. 1996. "Un Siglo de Geografía Etnica Guatemalteca 1893–1994: Evolución y Dinámica de los Sectores Etnicos durante los Ultimos Cien Años." Guatemala: *Revista USAC*, no. 2, 7–58.

———. 1997. "Acerca del Problema de Identidades entre No Indígenas en Guatemala." Guatemala: *Cultura de Guatemala*, año XVII (May–August), 1:166–94.

Aguilera, Gabriel, Rosalina Bran, and Claudinne Ogaldes. 1996. *Buscando la Paz; El
Bienio 1994–1995*. Debate 32. Guatemala: FLACSO.

Ajquijay On, Adela, and Demetrio Rodríguez. 1992. *Cultura Maya: Pasado y Futuro*.
Guatemala: Instituto de Lingüística, Universidad Rafael Landívar.

al-'Azm, Sadik Jalal. 1991. "Orientalism and Orientalism in Reverse." *Khamsin*, 5–
25.

ALMG (Academia de Lenguas Mayas de Guatemala). 1991. *Ley de la Academia de
las Lenguas Mayas de Guatemala y su Reglamento*. Guatemala: Editorial Maya
Wuj.

———. 1992. *Informe de XIII Taller Maya, 1991*. Guatemala: ALMG.

———. 1993. *Informe de XV Taller de Lingüística Maya, 1993*. Guatemala: ALMG.

———. 1996. *La Planificación Lingüística en Paises Multilingües de Abya Yala*.
Congreso Americano de Lenguas Aborígenes de Abya Yala, September 19–20,
1995. Guatemala: ALMG.

———. 1997. "Propuesta de Modalidad de Oficialización de los Idiomas Indígenas
de Guatemala." Guatemala: Congreso de Oficialización de los Idiomas Indígenas
de Guatemala, August 12–14.

Alvarez, Sonia, Evelina Dagnino, and Arturo Escobar, ed. 1998. *Cultures of Politics/
Politics of Culture: Revisioning Latin American Social Movements*. Boulder: Westview Press.

Americas Watch. 1982. *Human Rights in Guatemala: No Neutrals Allowed*. New
York: Americas Watch Committee.

———. 1984a. *Guatemala: A Nation of Prisoners*. New York: Americas Watch.

———. 1984b. *Guatemalan Refugees in Mexico, 1980–1984*. New York: Americas
Watch Committee.

———. 1985. *Little Hope: Human Rights in Guatemala, January 1984 to January
1985*. New York: Americas Watch Committee.

———. 1986. *Civil Patrols in Guatemala*. New York: Americas Watch Committee.

Americas Watch and the British Parliamentary Human Rights Group. 1987. *Human
Rights in Guatemala during President Cerezo's First Year*. New York: Americas
Watch.

Americas Watch and Physicians for Human Rights. 1991. *Guatemala: Getting Away
with Murder*. New York: Human Rights Watch.

Amnesty International. 1983. *Amnesty International Report 1983*. London: Amnesty
International.

Anderson, Benedict. 1991. *Imagined Communities: Reflections on the Origin and
Spread of Nationalism*. London: Verso.

Anderson, Thomas. 1992. *Matanza*. 2d ed. Willimantic: Curbstone Press.

Annis, Sheldon. 1987. *God and Production in a Guatemalan Town*. Austin: University of Texas Press.

Anzaldúa, Gloria, ed. 1990. *Making Face, Making Soul, Haciendo Caras: Creative
and Critical Perspectives by Feminists of Color*. San Francisco: Aunt Lute Books.

Appadurai, Arjun. 1991. "Global Ethnoscapes: Notes and Queries for a Transnational
Anthropology." In *Recapturing Anthropology*, ed. Richard Fox, 191–210. Santa Fe:
School of American Research.

————. 1996. *Modernity at Large: Cultural Dimensions of Globalization.* Minneapolis: University of Minnesota Press.

Aretxaga, Begoña. 1993. "Striking with Hunger: The Cultural Meanings of Political Violence in Northern Ireland." In *The Violence Within: Cultural and Political Analyses of National Conflicts*, ed. Kay B. Warren, 219–53. Boulder: Westview Press.

————. 1997. *Shattering Silence: Women, Nationalism, and Political Subjectivity in Northern Ireland.* Princeton: Princeton University Press.

Arias, Arturo. 1990. "Changing Indian Identity: Guatemala's Violent Transition to Modernity." In *Guatemalan Indians and the State, 1540–1988*, ed. Carol Smith, 230–57. Austin: University of Texas Press.

Ariès, Philippe. 1962. *Centuries of Childhood: A Social History of Family Life.* New York: Alfred A. Knopf.

Arnson, Cynthia, and Mario Quiñones Amézquita, eds. 1997. *Memoria de la Conferencia: Procesos de Paz Comparados.* Guatemala: Asociación de Investigación y Estudios Sociales (ASIES) and the Latin American Program of the Woodrow Wilson International Center for Scholars.

Art Museum, Princeton University. 1995. *The Olmec World: Ritual and Rulership.* Princeton: Art Museum, Princeton University.

Asad, Talal. 1973. *Anthropology and the Colonial Encounter.* Atlantic Highlands, N.J.: Humanities Press.

ASIES (Asociación de Investigación y Estudios Sociales). 1996. *Acuerdo de Paz Firme y Duradera: Acuerdo sobre Cronograma para la Implementación, Cumplimiento y Verificación de los Acuerdos de Paz.* Guatemala: ASIES.

Asociación de Escritores Mayances de Guatemala. 1988. *Diccionario Kaqchikel.* Guatemala: Asociación de Escritores Mayances de Guatemala.

Asturias, Migel Angel. 1977. *Sociología Guatemalteca: El Problema Social del Indio. Guatemalan Sociology: The Social Problem of the Indian.* Bilingual edition. Translated by Maureen Ahern. Tempe: Arizona State University.

Asturias, Miguel Angel, and J. M. Gonzales de Mendoza. 1937. *Anales de los Xahil de los Indios Cakchiqueles.* Translated from French by Georges Raynaud. 2d rev. ed. Guatemala: Tipografía Nacional.

Asturias de Barrios, Linda, and Sergio Francisco Romero. 1997. "Estudio Aproximativo de la Situación Sociolingüística de las Comunidades y Escuelas de PRONADE en los Departamentos de Chimaltenango, Sololá, Totonicapán, Quiché, Huehuetenango y Suchitepéquez." Unpublished report with the institutional support of PRONADE.

AVANCSO. 1991. "'Vonós a la Capital': Estudio sobre la Emigración en Guatemala." *Cuadernos de Investigación*, no. 7. Guatemala: Asociación para el Avance de las Ciencias Sociales en Guatemala.

Azmitia fsc, Oscar. 1993. *El Instituto Indígena Santiago, Una Alternativa de Educación Media Rural: Sistematización de la Experiencia.* Guatemala: Instituto Indígena Santiago.

Barth, Fredrik, ed. 1969. *Ethnic Groups and Boundaries.* Boston: Litle, Brown.

Bastos, Santiago, and Manuela Camus. 1995a. *Abriendo Caminos: Las Organizaciones Mayas desde el Nobel hasta el Acuerdo de Derechos Indígenas.* Guatemala: FLACSO.

———. 1995b. *Los Mayas de la Capital: Un Estudio sobre Identidad Etnica y Mundo Urbano.* Guatemala: FLACSO.

———. 1996. *Quebrando el Silencio: Organizaciones del Pueblo Maya y sus Demandas, 1986–1992.* Guatemala: FLACSO.

Beckett, Jeremy, and Daniel Mato, eds. 1996. *Identities: Global Studies in Culture and Power* 3, nos. 1–2. Special issue on Indigenous People/Global Terrains.

Behar, Ruth. 1993. *Translated Woman: Crossing the Border with Esperanza's Story.* Boston: Beacon Press.

Benjamin, Walter. 1969. *Illuminations: Essays and Reflections.* Edited and introduced by Hannah Arendt. New York: Schocken Books.

Bermúdez, Fernando. 1986. *Death and Resurrection in Guatemala.* New York: Orbis Books.

Bhabha, Homi K. 1990. *Nation and Narration.* London: Routledge.

Birk, Fridolin, ed. 1997. *Guatemala: ¿Oprimida, Pobre o Princesa Embrujada?* Guatemala: Fundación Friedrich Ebert.

Black, George. 1984. *Garrison Guatemala.* New York: Monthly Review Press.

Bonfil Batalla, Guillermo. 1988. *Utopia y Revolución: El Pensamiento Político Contemporáneo de los Indios en América Latina.* Mexico: Editorial Nueva Imagen.

Boon, James. 1999. *Verging on Extra-Vagance: Anthropology, History, Religion, Literature, Arts . . . Showbiz.* Princeton: Princeton University Press.

Bossen, Laurel. 1984. *The Redivision of Labor: Women and Economic Choice in Four Guatemalan Communities.* Albany: State University of New York Press.

Bourdieu, Pierre. 1977. *Outline of a Theory of Practice.* Cambridge: Harvard University Press.

———. 1984. *Distinction: A Social Critique of the Judgement of Taste.* Cambridge: Harvard University Press.

———. 1986. "The Forms of Capital." In *Handbook of Theory and Research for the Sociology of Education*, ed. John G. Richardson, 241–58. New York: Greenwood Press.

Bourgois, Philippe. 1995. *In Search of Respect: Selling Crack in El Barrio.* New York: Cambridge University Press.

Bourque, Susan C., and Kay B. Warren. 1978. "Denial and Reaffirmation of Ethnic Identities: A Comparative Examination of Guatemalan and Peruvian Communities." Program in Latin American Studies, Occasional Papers no. 8. Amherst: University of Massachusetts.

———. 1981. *Women of the Andes: Patriarchy and Social Change in Two Peruvian Towns.* Ann Arbor: University of Michigan Press.

———. 1985. "Gender, Power, and Communication: Women's Responses to Political Muting in the Andes." In *Women Living Change: Cross-Cultural Perspectives*, ed. Donna Robinson Divine and Susan C. Bourque, 255–86. Philadelphia: Temple University Press.

———. 1989. "Democracy without Peace: The Cultural Politics of Terror in Peru." *Latin American Research Review* 24, no. 1: 7–34.

Boyarin, Jonathan, ed. 1993. *The Ethnography of Reading.* Berkeley: University of California Press.

Brasseur de Bourbourg, Charles Etienne. 1861. *Popol Vuh: Le Livre Sacré et les*

Mythes de l'Antiquité Americaine, avec les Livres Héroiques e Historiques de Quiches. Paris.

Bricker, Victoria. 1981. *Indian Christ, Indian King.* Austin: University of Texas Press.

Brintnall, Douglas E. 1979. *Revolt against the Dead: The Modernization of a Mayan Community in the Highlands of Guatemala.* New York: Gordon and Breach.

Brinton, Daniel G. 1885. *The Annals of the Cakchiqueles.* Brinton's Library of Aboriginal American Literature, no. VI.

Brown, R. McKenna, and Edward Fischer, eds. 1996. *Maya Cultural Activism in Guatemala.* Austin: University of Texas Press.

Bruner, Edward M. 1986. "Ethnography as Narrative." In *The Anthropology of Experience*, ed. Victor W. Turner and Edward M. Bruner, 139–55. Urbana: University of Illinois Press.

Burgos-Debray, Elisabeth, ed. 1984. *I Rigoberta Menchú: An Indian Woman in Guatemala.* London: Verso Editions.

———, ed. 1985. *Me Llamo Rigoberta Menchú y Así Me Nació la Conciencia.* Mexico: Siglo Veintiuno Editores.

Burns, Allan G. 1993. *Maya in Exile: Guatemalans in Florida.* Philadelphia: Temple University Press.

Campbell, Howard, Leigh Binford, Miguel Bartolomé, and Alicia Barabas, eds. 1993. *Zapotec Struggles: Histories, Politics, and Representations from Juchitán, Oaxaca.* Washington, D.C.: Smithsonian Institution Press.

Cancian, Frank. 1965. *Economics and Prestige in a Mayan Community.* Stanford: Stanford University Press.

———. 1988. "State and Church Effects on Community Boundaries of Zinacantan." Paper presented at the American Anthropological Association meetings, Phoenix, offers a case study.

———. 1992. *Decline of Community in Zinacantan.* Stanford: Stanford University Press.

Cardoza y Aragón, Luis. 1965. *Guatemala, las Líneas de su Mano. 2d ed.* Mexico: Fondo de Cultura Económica.

———. 1989. "La Conquista de América." In *Nuestra América Frente al V Centenario: Emancipación e Identidad de América Latina, 1492–1992.* Mexico: Editorial Joaquín Mortiz, Planeta.

Carlsen, Robert S. 1997. *The War for the Heart and Soul of a Highland Maya Town.* Austin: University of Texas Press.

Carlsen, Robert, and Martin Prechtel. 1991. "The Flowering of the Dead: An Interpretation of Highland Mayan Culture." *Man* (N.S.) 26: 23–42.

Carey-Webb, Allen, and Stephen Benz. 1996. *Teaching and Testimony.* Albany: State University of New York Press.

Carmack, Robert. 1973. *Quichean Civilization: The Ethnohistoric, Ethnographic, and Archaeological Sources.* Berkeley: University of California Press.

———. 1981. *The Quiché Mayas of Utatlán.* Norman: University of Oklahoma Press.

———. 1988a. "The Story of Santa Cruz Quiché." In *Harvest of Violence: The Maya Indians and the Guatemalan Crisis*, ed. Robert M. Carmack, 39–69. Norman: University of Oklahoma Press.

————. 1988b. *Harvest of Violence: The Maya Indians and the Guatemalan Crisis.* Norman: University of Oklahoma Press.

————. 1994. "Introducción: Centroamérica Aborigen en su Contexto Histórico y Geográfico." In *Historia Antigua*, vol. 1 of *Historial General de Centroamérica*, ed. Robert Carmack, 15–59. 2d ed. San José, Costa Rica: FLACSO.

————. 1995. *Rebels of Highland Guatemala: The Quiche-Mayas of Momostenango.* Norman: University of Oklahoma.

Casaus Arzú, Marta Elena. 1992. *Guatemala: Linaje y Racismo.* San José: FLACSO.

Castañeda, Jorge G. 1993. *Utopia Unarmed: The Latin America Left after the Cold War.* New York: Knopf.

Castañeda, Quetzil. 1996. *In the Museum of Mayan Culture: Touring Chichén Itzá.* Minneapolis: University of Minnesota Press.

CEDIM (Centro de Documentación e Investigación Maya). 1992. *Foro del Pueblo Maya y los Candidatos a la Presidencia de Guatemala.* Guatemala: Editorial Cholsamaj.

CECMA (Centro de Estudios de la Cultura Maya). 1992. *Hacia una Educación Maya: Encuentro Taller de Escuelas con Programas de Cultura Maya.* Guatemala: Editorial Cholsamaj.

————. 1994. *Derecho Indígena: Sistema Jurídico de los Pueblos Originarios de América.* Guatemala: Serviprensa Centroamericana.

CEM-G (Consejo de Educación Maya de Guatemala). 1994. "Logros y Experiencias de la Educación Bilingüe Intercultural en Guatemala." Guatemala: PRONEBI.

Chacach, Martín. 1997. "El Arte de la Lengua en los Ultimos 20 Años." Guatemala: *Cultura de Guatemala*, año XVII (May–August), 2:13–34.

Chatterjee, Partha. 1986. *Nationalist Thought and the Colonial World—A Derivative Discourse.* London: Zed Books.

————. 1993. *The Nation and Its Fragments: Colonial and Postcolonial Histories.* Princeton: Princeton University Press.

Chávez, Adrián. 1969. *Kí-chè Tzib.* San José, Costa Rica: Instituto Centroamericano de Extensión de la Cultura (ICECU).

Chea, José Luis. 1988. *Guatemala: La Cruz Fragmentada.* San José, Costa Rica: DEI y FLACSO.

Choy, Ricardo. 1992. *La Escuela Bilingüe Intercultural.* Guatemala: Universidad Rafael Landívar.

Churchill, Ward. 1992. "Naming Our Destiny: Toward a Language of Indian Liberation." *Global Justice* 3, nos. 2–3: 22–33.

Cleary, Edward. 1997. *The Struggle for Human Rights in Latin America.* Westport, Conn.: Praeger.

Clifford, James. 1988. *The Predicament of Culture: Twentieth-century Ethnography, Literature, and Art.* Cambridge: Harvard University Press.

————. 1992. "Traveling Cultures." In *Cultural Studies*, ed. Lawrence Grossberg, Cary Nelson, and Paula Treichler, 96–112. New York: Routledge.

Clifford, James, and George Marcus, eds. 1986. *Writing Culture.* Berkeley: University of California Press.

CNEM (Consejo Nacional de Educación Maya). 1996. *Propuesta Maya de Reforma Educativa Nacional.* Guatemala: Editorial Cholsamaj.

COCADI (Coordinadora Cakchiquel de Desarrollo Integral). 1985. *El Idioma, Centro de Nuestra Cultura*. Guatemala: COCADI, Departamento de Investigaciones Culturales.

———. 1988. *Maya Kaqchikel Ajlab'al: Sistema de Numeración Maya Kaqchikel*. Guatemala: COCADI.

———. 1992a. *Agenda 1992*. Guatemala: COCADI y el Consejo Kaqchikel Moloj Ri'il Pa Runik'ajal Tinamit "Kaji' Imox."

———. 1992b. *Conclusiones Generales: Primera Reunión en Consejo de Principales Kaqchikeles*. Guatemala: COCADI y el Consejo Kaqchikel Moloj Ri'il Pa Runik'ajal Tinamit "Kaji' Imox."

Cojtí Cuxil, Demetrio. 1987. "La Educación Bilingüe: Mecanismo para la Uniformidad o para el Pluralismo Lingüístico?" *Boletín de Lingüística* 1, no. 5 (August).

———. 1990. "Lingüística e idiomas Mayas en Guatemala." In *Lecturas sobre la lingüística Maya*, ed. Nora C. England and Stephen R. Elliott, 1–25. Guatemala: CIRMA (Centro de Investigaciones Regionales de Mesoamérica).

———. 1991a. *Configuración del Pensamiento Político del Pueblo Maya*. Quetzaltenango, Guatemala: Asociación de Escritores Mayances de Guatemala.

———. 1991b. "Universidades Guatemaltecas, Universidades Colonialistas." Paper presented at the Latin American Studies Association meetings, Chicago.

———. 1992. *Idiomas y Culturas de Guatemala*. Guatemala: Universidad Rafael Landívar, Instituto de Lingüística, PRODIPMA.

———. 1994. *Políticas para la Reivindicación de los Mayas de Hoy*. Guatemala: Editorial Cholsamaj.

———. (Waqi' Q'anil). 1995. *Ub'aniik Ri Una'ooj Uchomab'aal Ri Maya' Tinamit: Confirguración del Pensamiento Político del Pueblo Maya*. Vol. 2. Guatemala: Seminario Permanente de Estudios Mayas and Editorial Cholsamaj.

———. 1996a. "The Politics of Mayan Revindication." In *Mayan Cultural Activism in Guatemala*, ed. Edward Fischer and R. McKenna Brown, 19–50. Austin: University of Texas Press.

———. 1996b. "Estudio Evaluativo del Cumplimiento del Acuerdo sobre Identidad y Derechos de los Pueblos Indígenas." In *Acuerdos de Paz: Efectos, Lecciones y Perspectivas*, ed. Carlos Aldana, debate 34. Guatemala: FLACSO.

———. (Waqi' Q'anil). 1997a. *Ri Maya' Moloj pa Iximulew: El Movimiento Maya (en Guatemala)*. Guatemala: Editorial Cholsamaj.

———. 1997b. "Heterofobia y Racismo Guatemalteca: Perfil y Estado Actual." Guatemala: *Cultura de Guatemala*, año XVII (May–August), 1:393–424.

———. 1997c. "Unidad del Estado Mestizo y Regiones Autónomas Mayas." In *Guatemala: ¿Oprimida, Pobre o Princesa Embrujada?* ed. Fridolin Birk, 175–89. Guatemala: Fundación Friedrich Ebert.

Cojtí Macario, Narciso. 1988. *Mapa de los Idiomas de Guatemala y Belice*. Guatemala: Piedra Santa.

Collier, George. 1995. *Basta! Land and the Zapatista Rebellion in Chiapas*. Oakland: Food First Books.

Colmenares, Carmen María de. 1997. "La Situación Actual del Proceso de Paz." In *Memoria de la Conferencia: Procesos de Paz Comparados*, ed. Cynthia Arnson and Mario Quiñones Amézquita, 21–33. Guatemala: ASIES and the Latin American Program of the Woodrow Wilson International Center for Scholars.

COMG (Consejo de Organizaciones Mayas de Guatemala). 1991. "Derechos Específicos del Pueblo Maya: Rujunamil Ri Mayab' Amaq.'" Guatemala: Editorial Cholsamaj.

———. 1995. *Construyendo un Futuro para Nuestro Pasado: Derechos del Pueblo Maya y el Proceso de Paz.* Guatemala: Editorial Cholsamaj.

Corradi, Juan E., Patricia Weiss Fagen, and Manuel Antonio Garretón, eds. 1992. *Fear at the Edge.* Berkeley: University of California Press.

Coto, Fray Thomás de. 1983. *Theavrvs Verborv: Vocabulario de la Lengua Cakchiquel V[el] Guatemala.* Mexico: UNAM.

Crisóstomo y Crisóstomo, Luis, ed. 1994. *Uso e Importancia del Idioma Materno en la Educación.* Guatemala: Academia de las Lenguas Mayas de Guatemala.

Curruchich, María Luisa, and Rafael Coyote Tum. 1990. *Nimawa'in.* Quetzaltenango: Asociación de Escritores Mayances de Guatemala.

Curruchiche Gómez, Miguel Angel. 1994. *Discriminación del Pueblo Maya en el Ordenamiento Jurídico de Guatemala.* Guatemala: Editorial Cholsamaj.

Dagnino, Evelina. 1998. "Culture, Citizenship, and Democracy: Changing Discourses and Practices of the Latin American Left." In *Cultures of Politics, Politics of Cultures: Re-visioning Latin American Social Movements,* ed. Sonia Alvarez, Evelina Dagnino, and Arturo Escobar, 2–63. Boulder: Westview Press.

Danspeckgruber, Wolfgang, with Arthur Watts, ed. 1997. *Self-Determination and Self-Administration: A Sourcebook.* Boulder: Lynne Rienner.

Dávila, Amílcar. 1992a. *Educar, No Alienar: Identidad, Etnias y Educación en Guatemala.* Guatemala: Universidad Rafael Landívar.

———. 1992b. *La Escuela Bilingüe Intercultural.* Guatemala: Universidad Rafael Landívar, Instituto de Lingüística/PRODIPMA.

———. 1992c. *Por Qué y Para Qué Educación Bilingüe en Guatemala?* Guatemala: Universidad Rafael Landívar, Instituto de Lingüística/PRODIPMA.

———. 1993. *Ka'i' B'anob'äl, Jun Tijob'äl: Experiencia de la Franja de Lengua y Cultura Maya.* Guatemala: Universidad Rafael Landívar.

Davis, Mary-Ellen, director. 1992. *Guatemala: Devil's Dream.* Video, 58 mins., Cinema Guild.

Davis, Sheldon. 1988a. "Introduction: Sowing the Seeds of Violence." In *Harvest of Violence: The Maya Indians and the Guatemalan Crisis,* ed. Robert M. Carmack, 3–36. Norman: University of Oklahoma Press.

———. 1988b. "Agrarian Structure and Ethnic Resistance: The Indian in Guatemalan and Salvadoran National Politics." In *Ethnicities and Nations: Processes of Interethnic Relations in Latin America, Southeast Asia, and the Pacific,* ed. Remo Guidieri, Francesco Pellizzi, and Stanley J. Tambiah, 76–106. Austin: Rothko Chapel/University of Texas Press.

de Dios Rosales, Juan. 1968. "San Andrés Semetabaj." In *Los Pueblos del Lago de Atitlán,* vol. 23. Guatemala: Seminario de Integración Social Guatemalteca, 159–200.

Denoeux, Guilain. 1993. "Religious Networks and Urban Unrest: Lessons from Iranian and Egyptian Experiences." In *The Violence Within: Cultural and Political Opposition in Divided Nations,* ed. Kay B. Warren, 123–56. Boulder: Westview Press.

de Paz, Marco Antonio. 1993a. *Maya' Amaaq' xuq Junamilaal; Pueblo Maya y De-*

mocracia. Guatemala: Seminario Permanente de Estudios Mayas and Editorial Cholsamaj.

———, ed. 1993b. *Identidad y Derechos de los Pueblos Indígenas: La Cuestión Etnica 500 Años Después.* Guatemala: Instituto Centroamericano de Estudios Políticos.

Díaz del Castillo, Bernal. 1933. *Verdadera y Notable Relación del Descubrimiento y Conquista de la Nueva España y Guatemala.* Guatemala: Biblioteca Goathemala de la Sociedad de Geografía e Historia.

Díaz Polanco, Héctor. 1997. *Indigenous Peoples in Latin America: The Quest for Self-Determination.* Translated by Lucía Rayas. Latin American Perspectives Series, no. 18. Boulder: Westview Press.

Donnelly, Jack. 1993. *International Human Rights.* Boulder: Westview Press.

Early, John. 1982. *The Demographic Structure and Evolution of a Peasant System: The Guatemalan Population.* Boca Raton: Florida Atlantic University.

Eckstein, Susan, ed. 1989. *Power and Popular Protest: Latin American Social Movements.* Berkeley: University of California.

Ehlers, Tracy. 1990. *Silent Looms: Women and Production in a Guatemalan Town.* Boulder: Westview Press.

Ejército de Guatemala. 1963. *La Muerte de Tecún Umán.* Guatemala: Editorial del Ejército.

England, Nora. 1983. *A Grammar of Mam: A Mayan Language.* Austin: University of Texas Press.

———. 1988. *Introducción a la Lingüística: Idiomas Mayas.* Guatemala: Proyecto Lingüístico Francisco Marroquín.

———, compiler. 1990. "Questions for Foreign Linguists: Panel on the Role of Foreign Linguists in Mayan Linguistics." Taller Maya, June 1989, Quetzaltenango, Guatemala. In *Guatemala Scholars Network News*, Marilyn Moors, coordinator, February, p. 3. Washington, D.C.: GSN.

———. 1992a. "Endangered Languages: Doing Mayan Linguistics in Guatemala." *Language* 68: 29–35.

———. 1992b. *Autonomía de los Idiomas Mayas; Historia e Identidad: Rukutamil, Ramaq'il, Rutzijob'al; Ri Mayab' Amaq'.* Guatemala: Editorial Cholsamaj.

———. 1995. "Linguistics and Indigenous American Languages: Mayan Examples." *Journal of Latin American Anthropology* 1, no. 1: 122–49.

———. 1996. "The Role of Language Standardization in Revitalization." In *Mayan Cultural Activism in Guatemala*, ed. Edward Fischer and R. McKenna Brown, 178–94. Austin: University of Texas Press.

England, Nora C., and Stephen R. Elliot, eds. 1990. *Lecturas sobre la Lingüística Maya.* Guatemala: Centro de Investicaciones Regionales de Mesoamérica.

Erice, Ana. 1985. "Reconsideración de las Creencias Mayas en Torno al Nahualismo." *Estudios de Cultura Maya* 16:255–270.

Escobar, Arturo, and Sonia E. Alvarez. 1992. *The Making of Social Movements in Latin America: Identity, Strategy, and Democracy.* Boulder: Westview Press.

Esquit Choy, Alberto, and Víctor Gálvez Borrell. 1997. *The Mayan Movement Today: Issues of Indigenous Culture and Development in Guatemala.* Guatemala: FLACSO.

Esquit Choy, Edgar, and Carlos Ochoa García, eds. 1995. *Yiqalil q'anej, kunimaaj tziij, niman tzij: El respeto a la palabra.* Guatemala: Centro de Estudios de la Cultura Maya.

Ewen, Alex, ed. 1994. *Voices of Indigenous Peoples: Native People Address the United Nations.* Santa Fe: Clear Light.

Fabian, Johannes. 1986. *Language and Colonial Power: The Appropriation of Swahili in the Former Belgian Congo, 1880–1938.* Cambridge: Cambridge University Press.

Fabri, Antonella. 1994. "(Re)Composing the Nation: Politics of Memory and Displacement in Maya Testimonies from Guatemala." Ph.D. dissertation, State University of New York at Albany.

Fahim, Hussein, ed. 1982. *Indigenous Anthropology in Non-Western Countries.* Durham: Carolina Academic Press.

Falk, Richard. 1997. "The Right of Self-Determination under International Law: The Coherence of Doctrine versus the Incoherence of Experience." In *Self-Determination and Self-Administration: A Sourcebook,* ed. Wolfgang Danspeckgruber with Sir Arthur Watts, 47–63. Boulder: Lynne Rienner.

Falla, Ricardo. 1978a. *Quiché Rebelde: Estudio de un Movimento de Conversión Religiosa, Rebelde a las Creencias Tradicionales, en San Antonio Ilotenango, Quiché, 1948–1970.* Guatemala: Editorial Universitaria.

———. 1978b. "El Movimiento Indígena." *Estudios Centroamericanos* 33, nos. 356–57 (Junio-Julio): 437–61.

———. 1994. *Massacres in the Jungle: Ixcán, Guatemala, 1975–1982.* Boulder: Westview Press.

Farriss, Nancy. 1984. *Maya Society under Colonial Rule: The Collective Enterprise of Survival.* Princeton: Princeton University Press.

Feierman, Steven. 1990. *Peasant Intellectuals: Anthropology and History in Tanzania.* Madison: University of Wisconsin Press.

Field, Les. 1994. "Who Are the Indians? Reconceptualizing Indigenous Identity, Resistance, and the Role of Social Science in Latin America." *Latin American Research Review* 29, no. 3: 237–48.

———. 1996. "Mired Positionings: Moving beyond Metropolitan Authority and Indigenous Authenticity." *Identities* 3, no. 102: 137–54.

Ferguson, James. 1994. *The Anti-Politics Machine: "Development," Depoliticization, and Bureaucratic Power in Lesotho.* Minneapolis: University of Minnesota Press.

Fernández, José Manuel. 1988. *El Comité de Unidad Campesina: Origen y Desarrollo.* Cuaderno 2. Guatemala: Centro de Estudios Rurales Centroamericanos.

Figueroa Ibarra, Carlos. *El Recurso del Miedo: Ensayo sobre el Estado y el Terror en Guatemala.* Cost Rica: Editorial Universitaria Centroamericana.

Fischer, Edward. 1993. "The Pan-Maya Movement in Global and Local Context." Ph.D. dissertation, Anthropology Department, Tulane University.

———. 1996. "Induced Culture Change as a Strategy for Socioeconomic Development: The Pan-Maya Movement in Guatemala." In *Mayan Cultural Activism in Guatemala,* ed. Edward Fischer and R. McKenna Brown, 51–73. Austin: University of Texas Press.

Fischer, Edward, and R. McKenna Brown, eds. 1996. *Mayan Cultural Activism in Guatemala.* Austin: University of Texas Press.

Fischer, Michael. 1986. "Ethnicity and the Post-modern Arts of Memory." In *Writing Culture; The Poetics and Politics of Ethnography*, ed. James Clifford and George Marcus, 194–233. Berkeley: University of California Press.

Flores Alvarado, Humberto. 1983. *El Adamcismo*. Guatemala: Piedra Santa.

Foster, George. 1944. "Nagualism in Mexico and Guatemala." *Acta Americana* 2: 85–103.

———. 1967. *Tzintzuntzan: Mexican Peasants in a Changing World*. Boston: Little, Brown.

Foucault, Michel. 1979. *Discipline and Punish: The Birth of the Prison*. Trans. by Alan Sheridan. New York: Vintage.

———. 1983. *Power/Knowledge: Selected Interviews and Other Writings, 1972–1977*. New York: Pantheon.

Fox, John W. 1987. *Maya Postclassic State Formation: Segmentary Lineage Migration in Advancing Frontiers*. Cambridge: Cambridge University Press.

Fox, Richard. 1990a. "Hindu Nationalism in the Making, or the Rise of the Hindian." In *Nationalist Ideologies and the Production of National Cultures, ed. Richard Fox, 68–80*. Washington, D.C.: American Anthropological Association.

———, ed. 1990b. *Nationalist Ideologies and the Production of National Cultures*. American Ethnological Monograph Series, no. 2. Washington, D.C.: American Anthropological Association.

———, ed. 1991. *Recapturing Culture: Working in the Present*. Santa Fe: SAR Press.

Fox, Richard, and Orin Starn. 1997. *Between Resistance and Revolution: Cultural Politics and Social Protest*. New Brunswick, N.J.: Rutgers University Press.

Franco, Leonardo, et al. 1996. *La ONU y el Proceso de Paz en Guatemala*. Debate 33. Guatemala: FLACSO.

Friedl, David, Linda Schele, and Joy Parker. 1993. *Maya Cosmos: Three Thousand Years on the Shaman's Path*. New York: W. Morrow.

Friedlander, Judith. 1975. *Being Indian in Hueyapán: A Study of Forced Identity in Contemporary Mexico*. New York: St. Martin's Press.

Froman, Jo, Bob Gersony, and Tony Jackson. 1978. "A History of the Proyecto Lingüístico Francisco Marroquín." Unpublished manuscript.

Fuss, Diana. 1991. *Inside/Out: Lesbian Theories, Gay Theories*. New York: Routledge.

Galeano, Eduardo. 1973. *The Open Veins of Latin America*. New York: Monthly Review Press.

———. 1986. *El Descubrimiento de América que Todavía No Fue y Otros Escritos*. Barcelona: Editorial Laia.

Gález Borrell, Víctor, coordinator. 1997. *Qué Sociedad Queremos? Una Mirada desde el Movimiento y las Organizaciones Mayas*. Guatemala: FLACSO.

Garzon, Susan, R. McKenna Brown, Julia Becker Richards, and Wuqu' Ajpub'. Forthcoming. *The Life of the Kaqchikel Language: Maintenance, Shift, and Revitalization*. Austin: University of Texas Press.

Gates, Henry Louis, Jr., and Cornell West. 1996. *The Future of the Race*. New York: Alfred Knopf.

Geertz, Clifford. 1973. *The Interpretation of Cultures*. New York: Basic Books.

Gellner, Ernest. 1983. *Nations and Nationalism*. Ithaca: Cornell University Press.

Giddens, Anthony. 1987. *The Nation State and Violence*. Berkeley: University of California Press.

González, Gaspar Pedro. 1992. *La Otra Cara*. Guatemala: Ministerio de Cultura y Deportes, Serie Miguel Angel Asturias (Novela).

———. 1995. *A Mayan Life*. Translated by Elaine Elliot. Rancho Palos Verdes: Yax Te' Press.

———. 1997. *Kotz'ib': Nuestra Literatura Maya*. Rancho Palos Verdes, California: Yax Te' Press.

González Casanova, Pablo. 1969. *La Sociología de la Explotación*. Mexico: Siglo Veintiuno.

Gossen, Gary. 1975. "Animal Souls and Human Destiny in Chamula." *Man* 10, no. 3: 448–61.

———. 1984. *Chamulas in the World of the Sun: Time and Space in Maya Oral Tradition*. Prospect Heights, Ill.: Waveland Press.

———, ed. 1986. *Symbol and Meaning beyond the Closed Corporate Community*. Albany: Institute of Mesoamerican Studies, SUNY.

———. 1994. "From Olmecs to Zapatistas: A Once and Future History of Souls." *American Anthropologist* 96, 3: 553–70.

———. Green, Linda. 1994. "Fear as a Way of Life." *Cultural Anthropology* 9, no. 2: 227–56.

1998. *Fear as a Way of Life: Mayan Widows in Rural Guatemala*. New York: Columbia University Press.

Grindle, Merilee S. 1986. *State and Countryside: Development Policy and Agrarian Politics in Latin America*. Baltimore: Johns Hopkins.

Gugelberger, Georg, ed. 1996. *The Real Thing: Testimonial Discourse and Latin America*. Durham: Duke University Press.

Guha, Ranajit, and Gayatri Chakravorty Spivak, eds. 1988. *Selected Subaltern Studies*. New York: Oxford University Press.

Guidieri, Remo, Francesco Pellizzi, and Stanley J. Tambiah, eds. 1988. *Ethnicities and Nations: Processes of Interethnic Relations in Latin America, Southeast Asia, and the Pacific*. Austin: Rothko Chapel/University of Texas Press.

Gupta, Akhil, and James Ferguson. 1992. "Beyond 'Culture': Space, Identity, and the Politics of Difference." *Cultural Anthropology* 7:6–23.

Guzmán Böckler, Carlos. 1995. *Ri Okel Nqetamaj pa Iximulew: Cuando se Quiebra los Silencios, Lo que Todos Debemos Saber sobre la Historia de Guatemala*. Guatemala: Editorial Cholsamaj.

Guzmán Böckler, Carlos, and Jean-Loup Herbert. 1995. [1970]. *Guatemala: Una Interpretación Histórico-Social*. Guatemala: Editorial Cholsamaj.

Hagen, Jacqueline María. 1994. *Deciding to be Legal: A Maya Community in Houston*. Philadelphia: Temple University Press.

Hale, Charles. 1994a. *Resistance and Contradiction: Miskitu Indians and the Nicaraguan State, 1894–1987*. Stanford: Stanford University Press.

———. 1994b. "Between Che Guevara and the Pachamama: Mestizos, Indians, and Identity Politics in the Anti-quincentenary Campaign." *Critique of Anthropology* 14, no. 2: 9–39.

———. 1995. "El Discurso Ladino del Racismo al Revés en Guatemala." Paper presented at the Latin American Studies Association meetings, Washington, D.C., September.

————. 1996a. "*Mestizaje*, Hybridity, and the Cultural Politics of Difference in Post-revolutionary Central America." *Journal of Latin American Anthropology* 2, no. 1: 34–61.

————, ed. 1996b. *Mestizaje: Journal of Latin American Anthropology* 2, no. 1.

————. 1996c. "Maya Effervescence and the Ladino Imaginary in Guatemala." American Anthropological Association meetings, San Francisco, November 11, 1996.

————. 1997. "Cultural Politics of Identity in Latin America." *Annual Review of Anthropology* 26:567–90.

Hall, Stuart. 1990. "Cultural Identity and Diaspora." In *Identity: Community, Culture and Difference*, ed. Jonathan Rutherford. London: Lawrence and Wishart.

Halperin, Morton, and David Scheffer with Patricia Small. 1992 *Self-Determination in the New World Order*. Washington D.C.: Carnegie Endowment for Peace.

Hanchard, Michael. 1993. "Culturalism versus Cultural Politics: Afro-Brazilian Social Movements since the 1970s." In *The Violence Within: Cultural and Political Analyses of National Conflicts*, ed. Kay B. Warren. Boulder: Westview Press.

————. 1994. *Orpheus and Power: The Movimiento Negro of Rio de Janeiro and São Paulo, 1945–1988*. Princeton: Princeton University Press.

Handy, Jim. 1984. *Gift of the Devil: A History of Guatemala*. Boston: South End Press.

————. 1994. *Revolution in the Countryside: Rural Conflict and Agrarian Reform in Guatemala, 1944–1954*. Chapel Hill: University of North Carolina Press.

Hanke, Lewis. 1965. *The Spanish Struggle for Justice in the Conquest of America*. Boston: Little, Brown.

Hanks, William. 1997. "Converting Words: The Emergence of Colonial Maya Discourse." Paper presented at the Workshop on the Anthropology of Latin America, May 31, University of Chicago.

Haraway, Donna. 1989. *Primate Visions: Gender, Race, and Nature in the World of Modern Science*. New York: Routledge.

Harris, Marvin. 1964. *Patterns of Race in the Americas*. New York: W. W. Norton.

Harrison, Regina. 1989. *Signs, Songs, and Memory in the Andes: Translating Quechua Language and Culture*. Austin: University of Texas Press.

Hawkins, John. 1984. *Inverse Images: The Meaning of Culture, Ethnicity and Family in Postcolonial Guatemala*. Albuquerque: University of New Mexico Press.

Helms, Mary W. 1975. *Middle America: A Cultural History of Heartland and Frontiers*. Englewood Cliffs, N.J.: Prentice-Hall.

Henderson, John. 1994. "El Mundo Maya." In *Historia Antigua*, vol. 1 of *Historia General de Centroamérica*, ed. Robert Carmack, 62–133. 2d ed. San José, Costa Rica: FLACSO.

Hendrickson, Carol. 1991. "Images of the Indian in Guatemala: The Role of Indigenous Dress in Indian and Ladino Constructions." In *Nation-States and Indians in Latin America*, ed. Greg Urban and Joel Sherzer, 287–306. Austin: University of Texas Press.

————. 1995. *Weaving Identities: Construction of Dress and Self in a Highland Guatemalan Town*. Austin: University of Texas Press.

————. 1996. In *Mayan Cultural Activism in Guatemala*, ed. Edward Fischer and R. McKenna Brown, 156–64. Austin: University of Texas Press.

Hernández A. de Mota, Luz Helena. 1992. *Fundamentos de Lingüística para Maestros*. Guatemala: Universidad Rafael Landívar.

Herrera, Guillermina. 1987. *Estado del Arte sobre Educación en Guatemala.* Guatemala: Centro de Información y Documentación Educativa de Guatemala and Universidad Rafael Landívar.

—. 1989. "Las Lenguas Guatemaltecas en la Nueva Constitución: Un Desafío." In *Cultura Maya y Políticas de Desarrollo, Raxché, 89–102.* Guatemala: COCADI.

—. 1990. "Las Lenguas Indígenas de Guatemala: Situación Actual y Futuro." In *Lecturas sobre la Lingüística Maya*, ed. Nora England and Stephen Elliot, 27–50. Guatemala: CIRMA.

—. 1993. *Lengua Franca: Castellano Como Segunda Lengua para Niños Mayahablantes.* Guatemala: Universidad Rafael Landívar, Instituto de Lingüística.

Hill, Robert M., and John Monaghan. 1987. *Continuities in Highland Maya Social Organization: Ethnohistory in Sacapulas, Guatemala.* Philadelphia: University of Pennsylvania Press.

Himpele, Jeffrey. 1995. "Distributing Difference: The Distribution and Displacement of Media, Spectacle and Identity in La Paz, Bolivia." Ph.D. dissertation, Department of Anthropology, Princeton University.

Hinshaw, Robert E. 1988. "Tourist Town Amid the Violence: Panajachel." In *Harvest of Violence: The Maya Indians and the Guatemalan Crisis*, ed. Robert M. Carmack, 195–205. Norman: University of Oklahoma Press.

Hobsbawm, Eric 1990. *Nations and Nationalism since 1780.* Cambridge: Cambridge University Press.

Hobsbawm, Eric, and Terence Ranger, eds. 1983. *The Invention of Tradition.* New York: Cambridge University Press.

Holland, Dorothy, and Jean Lave, eds. 1998. *History in Person: Enduring Struggles and the Practice of Identity.* Santa Fe: SAR Press.

Horowitz, Ronald. 1985. *Ethnic Groups in Conflict.* Berkeley: University of California Press.

Hu-DeHart, Evelyn. 1991. "From Area Studies to Ethnic Studies: The Study of the Chinese Diaspora in Latin America." In *Asian American Studies: Comparative and Global Perspectives*, ed. Shirley Hune et al., 5–44. Pullman: Washington State University.

Huntington, Samuel. 1968. *Political Order in Changing Societies.* New Haven: Yale University Press.

Iglesia, Ramón. 1942. *Cronistas e Historiadores de la Conquista de México.* Mexico: Fondo de Cultura Económica.

Instituto Centroamericano de Estudios Políticos. 1993. *Identidad y Derechos de los Pueblos Indígenas: La Cuestión Etnica 500 Años Después.* Guatemala: INCEP.

Instituto de Estudios Interétnicos. 1993. *Estudios Interétnicos*, año 1, no. 1, Noviembre. Guatemala: Universidad de San Carlos de Guatemala.

Isbell, Billie Jean. 1978. *To Defend Ourselves: Ecology and Ritual in an Andean Village.* Austin: University of Texas Press.

Jacoby, Russell. 1987. *The Last Intellectuals: American Culture in the Age of Academe.* New York: Noonday Press.

Jelin, Elizabeth, and Eric Hershberg, eds. 1996. *Constructing Democracy: Human Rights, Citizenship, and Society in Latin America.* Boulder: Westview Press.

Jonas, Susanne. 1991. *The Battle for Guatemala: Rebels, Death Squads, and U.S. Power.* Boulder: Westview Press.

————. Forthcoming. *Of Centaurs and Doves: Guatemala's Peace Process*. Boulder: Westview Press.

Jonas, Susanne, and Nancy Stein, eds. 1990. *Democracy in Latin America: Visions and Realities*. New York: Bergin and Garvey.

Jonas, Susanne, and David Tobis, eds. 1974. *Guatemala*. Berkeley: North American Congress on Latin America.

Jones, Grant. 1989. *Maya Resistance to Spanish Rule: Time and History on a Colonial Frontier*. Albuquerque: University of New Mexico Press.

Kearney, Michael. 1996. *Reconceptualizing the Peasantry: Anthropology in Global Perspective*. Boulder: Westview Press.

Kicza, John. 1993. *The Indian in Latin American History: Resistance, Resilience, and Acculturation*. Wilmington, Del.: Scholarly Resources.

Klor de Alva, Jorge. n.d. "Aztec Confessions: On the Invention of Colonialism, Anthropology, and Modernity." Unpublished manuscript.

Koizumi, Junji. 1997. "Against Reductionism: Or How to Read the Civil-Religious Hierarchy of Middle America." Paper prepared for "The Past and Future of Social Science Seminar," Institute for Advanced Study, Princeton, May 14.

Kondo, Dorinne. 1997. *About Face: Performing Race in Fashion and Theatre*. New York: Routledge.

Laclau, Ernesto, and Chantal Mouffe, eds. 1985. *Hegemony and Socialist Strategy: Towards a Radical Democratic Politics*. London: Verso.

La Farge II, Oliver, and Douglas Byers. 1997. *El Pueblo del Cargador del Año*. Translated by Victor Montejo and Oscar Velázquez Estrada. Guatemala: Fundación Yax Te' and CIRMA.

Lan, David. 1985. *Guns and Rain: Guerrillas and Spirit Mediums in Zimbabwe*. Berkeley: University of California Press.

Larsen, Neil. 1995. *Reading North by South: On Latin American Literature, Culture and Politics*. Minneapolis: University of Minnesota Press.

Latin American Perspectives. 1991. First of two special issues on Voices of the Voiceless in Testimonial Literature, 18, no 3. (summer).

Las Casas, Bartolomé de. 1951. *Historia de Indias*. Vol. 3. Mexico: Fondo de Cultura Económica.

————. 1974. *The Devastation of the Indes: A Brief Account*. New York: Seabury Press.

————. 1975. *Apologia*. Madrid: Editoral Nacional.

Leacock, Eleanor Burk, ed. 1971. *The Culture of Poverty: A Critique*. New York: Simon and Schuster.

León-Portilla, Miguel, ed. 1962. *The Broken Spears: The Aztec Account of the Conquest of Mexico*. Boston: Beacon Press.

————. 1974. *El Reverso de la Conquista*. Mexico: Editorial Juaoquín Martiz.

————. 1984. *Visión de los Vencidos: Relaciones Indígenas de la Conquista*. Mexico: UNAM.

————. 1988. *Time and Reality in the Thought of the Maya*. Norman: University of Oklahoma Press.

Levine, Daniel. 1981. *Religion and Politics in Latin America: The Catholic Church in Venezuela and Colombia*. Princeton: Princeton University Press.

Levenson-Estrada, Deborah. 1994. *Trade Unionists against Terror: Guatemala City, 1954–85*. Chapel Hill: University of North Carolina Press.

———. 1997. "Commentary." In *Self-Determination and Self-Administration—A Sourcebook*, ed. Wolfgang Danspeckgruber with Sir Arthur Watts, 194–97. New York: Lynne Rienner. Boulder: Westview Press.

Lewis, Oscar. 1966. "The Culture of Poverty." *Scientific American* 215:19–25.

Lima, Ricardo. 1991. *Héroes de la Vida Cotidiana: Personajes Mayas*. Guatemala: Universidad Rafael Landívar.

Lomnitz-Adler, Claudio. 1992. *Exits from the Labyrinth: Culture and Ideology in the Mexican National Space*. Berkeley: University of California Press.

López Raquec, Margarita. 1989. *Acerca de los Alfabetos para Escribir los Idiomas Mayas de Guatemala*. Guatemala: Ministerio de Cultura y Deportes.

Lovell, W. George. 1988. "Surviving Conquest: The Maya of Guatemala in Historical Perspective." *Latin American Research Review* 23, no. 2: 25–58.

———. 1992. *Conquest and Survival in Colonial Guatemala: A Historical Geography of the Cuchumatán Highlands, 1500–1821*. Montreal and Kingston: McGill-Queen's University Press.

———. 1995. *A Beauty that Hurts: Life and Death in Guatemala*. Toronto: Between the Lines.

Lovell, W. George, and Christopher H. Lutz. 1994. "Conquest and Population: Maya Demography in Historical Perspective." *Latin American Research Review* 29, no. 2: 133–40.

Lutz, Christopher. 1984. *Historia Sociodemográfica de Santiago de Guatemala, 1541–1773*. Guatemala: CIRMA.

Lux de Cotí, Otilia. 1997. "La Participación Representativa del Pueblo Maya en una Sociedad Democrática y Pluralista." Guatemala: *Cultura de Guatemala*, año XVII (May–August), 1: 29–38.

Mackie, Sedley J., ed. 1924. *An Account of the Conquest of Guatemala in 1524 by Pedro de Alvarado*. New York: Cortes Society.

Magzul Patal, Hermelina. 1997. "Identidad desde la Perspectiva de Género." Guatemala: *Cultura de Guatemala*, año XVII (May–August), 1:97–105.

Malkki, Liisa. 1995. *Purity and Exile: Violence, Memory, and National Cosmology among Hutu Refugees in Tanzania*. Chicago: Univesity of Chicago Press.

Mallon, Florencia. 1995. *Peasant and Nation: The Making of Postcolonial Mexico and Peru*. Berkeley: University of California Press.

Maltby, William S. 1968. *The Black Legend in England: The Development of Anti-Spanish Sentiment, 1558–1660*. Durham: Duke University Press.

Mannheim, Bruce. 1991. *The Language of the Inka since the European Invasion*. Austin: University of Texas Press.

Manz, Beatriz. 1988. *Refugees of a Hidden War: The Aftermath of Counterinsurgency in Guatemala*. Albany: SUNY Press.

Marcus, George E. 1993. *Perilous States: Conversations on Culture, Politics, and Nation*. Chicago: University of Chicago Press.

Martínez Peláez, Severo. 1985. *La Patria del Criollo: Ensayo de Interpretación de la Realidad Colonial Guatemalteca*. 10th ed. Guatemala: Editorial Universitaria.

Marx, Anthony. 1992. *Lessons of Struggle: South African Internal Opposition, 1960–1990*. New York: Oxford University Press.

Materne, Yves. 1976. *The Indian Awakening in Latin America*. New York: Friendship Press

Mato, Daniel. 1996. "On the Theory, Epistemology, and Politics of the Social Construction of 'Cultural Identities' in the Age of Globalization: Introductory Remarks to Ongoing Debates." *Identities* 3, nos. 1–2: 61–72.

Maxwell, Judith. 1996. "Prescriptive Grammar and Kaqchikel Revitalization." In *Mayan Cultural Activism in Guatemala*, ed. Edward Fischer and R. McKenna Brown, 195–207. Austin: University of Texas Press.

MAYA (Programa de Desarrollo de los Pueblos Mayas). 1995. *Acuerdo sobre Identidad y Derechos de los Pueblos Indígenas y Documentos de Apoyo para su Comprensión*. Guatemala: Cholsamaj.

Maybury-Lewis, David. 1997. *Indigenous Peoples, Ethnic Groups, and the State*. Boston: Allyn and Bacon.

Mazumdar, Sucheta. 1991. "Asian American Studies and Asian Studies: Rethinking Roots." In *Asian American: Comparative and Global Perspectives*, ed. Shirley Hune et al., 29–44. Pullman: Washington State University.

McClintock, Michael. 1985. *The American Connection: State Terror and Popular Resistance in Guatemala*. London: Zed Press.

———. 1992. *Instruments of Statecraft: U.S. Guerrilla Warfare, Counterinsurgency, and Counterterrorism, 1940–1990*. New York: Pantheon.

McDowell, John. 1990. "The Community-building Mission of Kamsá Ritual Language." In *Native Latin American Cultures through their Discourse*, special publications of the Folklore Institute, ed. Ellen Basso, 67–84. Bloomington: Indiana University.

McAdams, Doug, John McCarthy, and Mayer Zald, eds. 1996. *Comparative Perspectives on Social Movements: Political Opportunities, Mobilizing Structures, and Cultural Framings*. New York: Cambridge University Press.

Melucci, Alberto. 1989. *Nomads of the Present: Social Movements and Individual Needs in Contemporary Society*. Edited by John Keane and Paul Mier. London: Hutchinson Radius.

Menchú, Rigoberta, and Comité de Unidad Campesina. 1992. *Trenzando el Futuro: Luchas Campesinas en la Historia Reciente de Guatemala*. Donostia: Tercera Prensa.

———. 1993. *El Clamor de la Tierra: Luchas Campesinas en la Historia Reciente de Guatemala*. Donostia: Tercera Prensa.

Mendelson, E. Michael. 1958. "The King, the Traitor, and the Cross: An Interpretation of a Highland Maya Religious Conflict." *Diogenes* 21:1–10.

———. 1959. "Maximón: An Iconographical Introduction." *Man* 59:57–60.

Messer, Ellen. 1995. "Anthropology and Human Rights in Latin America." *Journal of Latin American Anthropology* 1, no. 1: 48–97.

Migdal, Joel S. 1974. *Peasants, Politics, and Revolution*. Princeton: Princeton University Press.

———. 1988. *Strong Societies and Weak States: State-Society Relations and State Capabilities in the Third World*. Princeton: Princeton University Press.

MINUGUA (United Nations Verification Mission in Guatemala). 1998. "The Situation in Central America: Procedures for the Establishment of a Firm and Lasting Peace and Progress in Fashioning a Region of Peace, Freedom, Democracy and Development." A/52/757. New York: United Nations.

Montejo, Victor. 1984. *El Kanil: Man of Lightning*. Translated by Wallace Kaufman. Carboro, N.C.: Signal Books.

————. 1987. *Testimony: Death of a Guatemalan Village*. Willimantic, Conn.: Curbstone Press.

————. 1992a. *The Bird Who Cleans the World and Other Mayan Fables*. Translated by Wallace Kaufman. Williamantic, Conn.: Curbstone Press.

————. 1992b. *Testimonio: Muerte de una Comunidad Indígena en Guatemala*. Guatemala: Editorial Universitaria, Universidad de San Carlos de Guatemala.

————. 1993a. "The Dynamics of Cultural Resistance and Transformations: The Case of Guatemalan-Mayan Refugees in Mexico." Ph.D. dissertation, Department of Anthropology, University of Connecticut.

————. 1993b. "In the Name of the Pot, the Sun, the Broken Spear, the Rock, the Stick, the Idol, Ad Infinitum & Ad Nauseam: An Exposé of Anglo Anthropologists' Obsessions with and Invention of Mayan Gods." *Red Pencil Review: A Journal of Native American Studies* 9, no. 1 (spring): 12–16.

————. 1995. *Sculpted Stones*. Translated Victor Perera. Williamantic, Conn.: Curbstone Press.

————. n.d. "Elilal: Mayan Exile and Survival." Unpublished manuscript.

Montejo, Victor, and Q'anil Akab'. 1992. *Brevísima Relación Testimonial de la Continua Destrucción del Mayab' (Guatemala)*. Providence, R.I.: Maya Scholars Network.

Moore, Barrington. 1966. *The Social Origins of Dictatorship and Democracy*. Boston: Beacon Press.

Morales, Mario Roberto. 1997a. "Me Llamo Miguel Angel Asturias y Así Me Nació la Conciencia: Dos Procesos Discursivos de Concientización y Autocreación de Sujetos Mestizos." *Cultura de Guatemala*, año XVII (May–August), 3:177–201.

Morales, Mario Roberto. 1997b. "Construyendo la Identidad Ladina." Paper presented at the II Congreso de Estudios Mayas, Rafael Landívar University, August 6–8.

Mouffe, Chantal. 1993. *The Return of the Political*. London: Verso.

————, ed. 1992. *Dimensions of Radical Democracy: Pluralism, Citizenship, Community*. London: Verso.

Mucía Batz, José. *NIK: Filosofía de los Números Mayas; El Resurgir de la Cultura Maya*. Guatemala: CEDIM/SAQB'E.

Musgrave-Portilla, L. Marie. 1982. "The Nahualli or Transforming Wizard in Pre- and Postconquest Mesoamerica." *Journal of Latin American Lore* 8, no. 1: 3–62.

Nash, June C. 1967–68. "The Passion Play in Maya Indian Communities." *Comparative Studies in Society and History* 10:318–27.

————. 1979. *We Eat the Mines and the Mines Eat Us: Dependency and Exploitation in Bolivian Tin Mines*. New York: Columbia University Press.

————. 1989. *From Tank Town to High Tech: The Clash of Community and Industrial Cycles*. Albany: SUNY Press.

————. 1995. "The Reassertion of Indigenous Identity: Mayan Responses to State Intervention in Chiapas." *Latin American Research Review* 30, no. 3: 7–41.

Nash, Manning. 1970. "The Impact of Mid-nineteenth Century Economic Change upon the Indians of Middle America." In *Race and Class in Latin America*, ed. Magnus Morner, 170–83. New York: Columbia University Press.

Navaro, Yael. 1997. "Travesty and Truth: Politics of Culture and Fantasies of the State in Turkey." Ph.D. dissertation, Department of Anthropology, Princeton University.

Nelson, Diane. 1999. *The Finger in the Wound: Ethnicity, Nation, and Gender in the Body Politic of Quincentennial Guatemala*. Berkeley: University of California Press.

Newman, Saul. 1991. "Does Modernization Breed Ethnic Political Conflict?" *World Politics* 43, no. 3: 451–78.

Nichols, Bill. 1994. *Blurred Boundaries: Questions of Meaning in Contemporary Culture*. Bloomington: Indiana University Press.

Nordstrom, Carolyn, and JoAnn Martin, eds. 1992. *Paths to Domination, Resistance, and Terror*. Berkeley: University of California Press.

Núñez, Gabriela, Beatrice Bezmalinovic, Susan Clay et al. 1991. *Primer Encuentro Nacional: Educando a la Niña: Lograremos el Desarrollo de Guatemala*. Guatemala: U.S.-AID.

Obeyesekere, Gananath. 1992. *The Apotheosis of Captain Cook: European Mythmaking in the Pacific*. Princeton: Princeton University Press.

Oficina de Derechos Humanos del Arzobispado, ed. 1997. *Memoria del Taller Internacional, Metodología para una Comisión de la Verdad en Guatemala*. Guatemala: Oficina del Arzobispado.

O'Hanlon, Rosalind, and David Washbrook. 1992. "After Orientalism: Culture, Criticism, and Politics in the Third World." *Comparative Studies of Society and History* 34, no. 1: 141–67.

Okihiro, Gary. 1991. "African and Asian American Studies: A Comparative Analysis and Commentary." In *Asian American: Comparative and Global Perspectives*, Shirley Hune et al., 17–28. Pullman: Washington State University.

Ortner, Sherry. 1995. "Resistance and the Problem of Ethnographic Refusal." *Comparative Studies in Society and History* 137, no. 1 (January): 173–93.

Otzoy, Irma. 1988. "Identity and Higher Education among Mayan Women." M.A. Thesis, Department of Anthropology, University of Iowa.

———. 1996. *Maya' B'anikil Maya' Tzyaqb'äl: Identidad y Vestuario Maya*. Guatemala: Editorial Cholsamaj.

Otzoy, Irma, and Enrique Sam Colop. 1990. "Identidad Etnica y Modernización entre los Mayas de Guatemala." *Mesoamérica* 19 (June): 97–100.

OKMA (Oxlajuuj Keej Maya' Ajtz'iib' [Ajpub', Ixkem, Lolmay, Nik'te', B'alam, Saqijix, and Waykan]). 1993. *Maya' Chii': Los Idiomas Mayas de Guatemala*. Guatemala: Editorial Cholsamaj.

———, trans. 1992. "Anales de los Kaqchikeles." Paper presented at the Maya Hierogliphic Workshop, University of Texas, Austin, March 10–15.

Painter, James. 1987. *Guatemala: False Hope, False Freedom*. London: Catholic Institute for International Relations (CIIR) and Latin America Bureau.

Pastor, Beatriz. 1988. *Discurso Narrativo de la Conquista de América*. Guatemala: Casa de las Americas.

Paul, Benjamin D., and William J. Demarest. 1988. "The Operation of a Death Squad in San Pedro la Laguna." In *Harvest of Violence: The Maya Indians and the Guatemalan Crisis*, ed. Robert M. Carmack. Norman: University of Oklahoma Press, 119–55.

Perera, Victor. 1993. *Unfinished Conquest: The Guatemalan Tragedy*. Berkeley: University of California Press.

Petras, James, and Morris Morley. 1992. *Latin America in the Time of Cholera: Electoral Politics, Market Economics, and Permanent Crisis*. New York: Routledge.

Pitt-Rivers, Julian. 1970. "Spiritual Power in Central America: The Naguals of Chiapas." In *Witchcraft Accusations and Confessions*, ed. Mary Douglas, 183–206. London: Tavistock.

Plant, Roger. 1997. "Indigenous Identity and Rights in the Guatemalan Peace Process." Paper presented at the Conference on Comparative Peace Processes, the Woodrow Wilson Center, Washington, D.C., March 13–14.

Polo Sifontes, Francis. 1986. *Los Cakchiqueles en la Conquista de Guatemala*. Guatemala: CENALTEX.

Poole, Deborah, and Gerardo Rénique. 1991. "The New Chroniclers of Peru: U.S. Scholars and their "Shining Path' of Peasant Rebellion." *Bulletin of Latin American Research* 10, no. 1: 133–91.

Pop Caal, Antonio. 1992. *Li Juliisil Kirisyaanil ut li Minok ib': Judeo Cristianismo y Colonización*. Guatemala: Seminario Permanente de Estudios Mayas and Editorial Cholsamaj.

Prakash, Gyan. 1992a. "Writing Post-orientalist Histories of the Third World: Indian Historiography Is Good to Think." In Nicholas B. Dirks, ed., *Colonialism and Culture*. Ann Arbor: University of Michigan Press, 353–88.

———. 1992b. "Can the 'Subaltern' Ride? A Reply to O'Hanlon and Washbrook." *Comparative Studies of Society and History* 34, no. 1: 168–84.

Pratt, Mary Louise. 1992. *Imperial Eyes: Travel Writing and Transculturation*. London: Routledge.

PRONADE (Programa Nacional de Autogestión para el Desarrollo Educativo). 1997. *Propuesta de Financiamiento*. Guatemala: Ministerio de Educación.

PRONEBI (Programa Nacional de Educación Bilingüe Intercultural). 1994. *Logros y Experiencias de la Educación Bilingüe Intercultural en Guatemala: Documento de Análisis para el Primer Congreso de Educación Maya*. Guatemala: Ministerio de Educación.

Proyecto Lingüístico Francisco Marroquín. 1994. *Rub'is Jun Mayab': Tristeza de un Maya*. Guatemala: PLFM.

Prunier, Gerard. 1995. *The Rwanda Crisis, 1959–1994: History of Genocide*. London: Hurst.

Quintana, Stephen M., and Yetilu de Baessa. 1996. *Autoestima, Preferencia y Conocimiento Etnico de Niños K'iche's*. Guatemala: Editorial Cholsamaj.

Racancoj A., Víctor. 1994. *Socioeconomía Maya Precolonial*. Guatemala: Editorial Cholsamaj.

Rajasingham, Darini. 1993. "The Afterlife of Empire: Immigrants and the Imagination in Post/colonial Britain." Ph.D. dissertation, Department of Anthropology, Princeton University.

Ramírez, Margarita, and Luisa María Mazariegos. 1993. *Tradición y Modernidad: Lecturas sobre la Cultura Maya Actual*. Guatemala: Universidad Rafael Landívar, Instituto de Lingüística.

Ramos, Alcida Rita. 1997. "Indigenous Movements, Sources and Strategies of Self-Representation: A Discussion." Paper presented at the American Anthropological Association Meetings, Washington, D.C., November 19–23.

———. 1998. *Indigenism: Ethnic Politics in Brazil*. Madison: University of Wisconsin Press.

Rappaport, Joanne. 1990. *Politics of Memory: Native Historical Interpretation in the Colombian Andes*. New York: Cambridge University Press.

———. 1994. *Cumbe Reborn: An Andean Ethnography of History*. Chicago: University of Chicago Press.

———, ed. 1996. *Ethnicity Reconfigured: Indigenous Legislators and the Colombian Constitution of 1991*. Special issue of *Journal of Latin American Anthropology*. Vol. 1, no. 2 (spring).

Raxche', Demetrio Rodríguez Guaján. 1989. *Cultura Maya y Políticas de Desarrollo*. Guatemala: COCADI.

———. 1995. *Las ONGs y las Relaciones Interétnicas*. Guatemala: Editorial Cholsamaj.

———. 1996. "Maya Culture and the Politics of Development." In *Mayan Cultural Activism in Guatemala*, ed. Edward Fischer and R. McKenna Brown, 74–88. Austin: University of Texas Press.

Raxche', Demetrio Rodgríguez et al. 1995. *Nab'ey Tzij Pa Ruwi' Ri Maya' K'aslemal: Introducción a la Cultura Maya*. Guatemala: Editorial Cholsamaj.

Recinos, Adrián, trans. 1950. *Memorial de Sololá: Anales de los Cakchiqueles*. Mexico: Fondo de Cultura Económica.

———. 1952. *Pedro de Alvarado, Conquistador de México y Guatemala*. Guatemala: José de Pienda Ibarra.

———. 1984. *Crónicas Indígenas de Guatemala*. Guatemala: Academia de Geografía e Historia de Guatemala.

Recinos, Adrián, and Delia Goetz, trans. 1953. *The Annals of the Cakchiquels: Title of the Lords of Totonicapan*. Norman: University of Oklahoma Press.

Reed, Thomas F., and Karen Brandow. 1996. *The Sky Never Changes: Testimonies from the Guatemalan Labor Movement*. Ithaca: Cornell University Press.

Rénique, José. 1995. "The Latin American Left: Epitaph or New Beginning?" *Latin American Research Review* 30, no. 2: 177–94.

Richards, Julia Becker, and Michael Richards. 1992. *Relaciones Interétnicas*. Guatemala: Universidad Rafael Landívar, Instituto de Lingüística, PRODIPMA.

———. 1996. "Mayan Education: An Historical and Contemporary Analysis of Mayan Language Education Policy." In *Mayan Cultural Activism in Guatemala*, by Edward Fischer and R. McKenna Brown, 208–21. Austin: University of Texas Press.

Rodríguez, Ernest. 1992. "International Organization of Indigenous Resource Development." *Global Justice* 3, nos. 2–3: 39–44.

Rojas Lima, Flavio. 1988. *La Cofradía: Reducto Cultural Indígena*. Guatemala: Seminario de Integracíon Social Guatemalteca.

Rosaldo, Renato. 1968. "Metaphors of Hierarchy in a Mayan Ritual." *American Anthropologist* 70:524–36.

———. 1989. *Culture and Truth: The Remaking of Social Analysis*. Boston: Beacon Press.

Rubin, Jeffrey. 1997. *Decentering the Regime: Ethnicity, Radicalism, and Democracy in Juchitán, Mexico*. Durham: Duke University Press.

Ruthrauff, John. 1997. "The Guatemala Peace Process and the Role of the World Bank and Interamerican Development Bank." Paper presented at the Conference on Democracy and Development, Rafael Landívar University, Guatemala.

Ruthrauff, John, and Teresa Carlson. 1997. *Una Guía al Banco Interamericano de Desarrollo y al Banco Mundial: Estrategias para Guatemala*. Guatemala: Centro para la Educación Democrática.

Saenz de Santa María, Carmelo. 1940. *Diccionario Cakchiquel-Español*. Sociedad de Geografía e Historia de Guatemala.

Sahlins, Marshall. 1981. *Historical Metaphors and Mythical Realities: Structure in the Early History of the Sandwich Islands Kingdom*. Ann Arbor: University of Michigan Press.

———. 1985. *Islands of History*. Chicago: University of Chicago Press.

———. 1995. *How "Natives" Think*. Chicago: University of Chicago Press.

Said, Edward. 1978. *Orientalism*. New York: Random House.

Salazar Tetzagüic, Manuel, et al. 1995. *Universidad Maya de Guatemala: Deseño Curricular (Propuesta)*. Guatemala: Editorial Cholsamaj.

Saler, Benson. 1969. *Nagual, Brujo, and Herichero en un Pueblo Quiché*. Guatemala: Ministerio de Educación.

Sam Colop, Luis Enrique. 1983. "Hacia una Propuesta de Ley de Educación Bilingüe." Thesis for the Licenciatura en Ciencias Jurídicas y Sociales, Universidad Rafael Landívar, Guatemala.

———. 1990. "Foreign Scholars and Mayans: What Are the Issues?" In *Guatemala Scholars Network News*, coordinated by Marilyn Moors, February, p. 2. Washington, D.C.: GSN.

———. 1991. *Jub'aqtun Omay Kuchum K'aslemal: Cinco Siglos de Encubrimiento*. Seminario Permanente de Estudios Mayas, Cuaderno No. 1. Guatemala: Editorial Cholsamaj.

———. 1992. "1991 y El Discurso de Encubrimiento." *Global Justice* 3, nos. 2–3: 33–38.

———. 1994. "Maya Poetics." Ph.D. dissertation, Department of English, SUNY-Buffalo.

———. 1996. "The Discourse of Concealment and 1992." In *Mayan Cultural Activism in Guatemala*, ed. Edward Fischer and R. McKenna Brown, 107–13. Austin: University of Texas Press.

Sam Colop, Luis Enrique, and Irma Otzoy. 1996. *Publicaciones Periódicas Dirigidas a Lectores Mayas*. Guatemala: Cholsamaj.

Sandoval, Franco. 1988. *La Cosmovisión Maya Quiche en el Popol Vuh*. Departamento de Literatura de la Dirección General de Promoción Cultural, Ministerio de Cultura y Deportes de Guatemala. Guatemala: Serviprensa.

———. 1993. *Popol Vuh: Versión Transparente*. Colección Novelas y Leyendas. Guatemala: Artemis-Edinter.

Saqb'ichil/COPMAGUA (Coordinación de Organizaciones del Pueblo Maya de Guatemala). 1995. *Acuerdo sobre Identidad y Derechos de los Pueblos Indígenas*. Punto 3 del Acuerdo de Paz Firme y Duradera. Guatemala: COPMAGUA.

———. 1996. *Acuerdo sobre Identidad y Derechos de los Pueblos Indígenas, Versión Maya Ilustrada*. Guatemala: Editorial Saqb'e.

Saqb'e, Editorial. 1996. *Recopilación de los Acuerdos de Paz*. Guatemala: Editorial Saqb'e.

Scarry, Elaine. 1985. *The Body in Pain: The Making and Unmaking of the World*. New York: Oxford University Press.

Schele, Linda, and David Freidl. 1990. *A Forest of Kings: The Untold Story of the Ancient Maya*. New York: William Morrow.

Schele, Linda, and Nikolai Grube. 1996. "The Workshop for Maya on Hieroglyphic Writing." In *Mayan Cultural Activism in Guatemala*, ed. Edward Fischer and R. McKenna Brown. Austin: University of Texas Press, 131–40.

Schele, Linda, and Mary Ellen Miller. 1986. *The Blood of Kings: Dynasty and Ritual in Maya Art*. New York: George Braziller.

Schele, Linda, with Phil Wanyerka, ed. 1992. *The Proceedings of the Maya Hieroglyphic Workshop*. Austin: University of Texas at Austin.

Schele, Linda, et al. 1992. *Maya Hieroglyphic Workshop in Guatemala*. Translated by Nora England, Lola Spillari de López, Jorge Traviesa, and Jorge Orejel. Austin: University of Texas at Austin.

Schirmer, Jennifer. 1996. "The Looting of Democratic Discourse by the Guatemalan Military: Implications for Human Rights." In *Constructing Democracy: Human Rights, Citizenship, and Society in Latin America*, ed. Elizabeth Jelin and Eric Hershberg, 85–97. Boulder: Westview Press.

———. 1997a. "Universal and Sustainable Human Rights? Special Tribunals in Guatemala." In *Human Rights, Culture and Context: Anthropological Perspectives*, ed. Richard Wilson, 161–86. London: Pluto Press.

———. 1997b. "Prospects for Compliance: The Guatemalan Military and the Peace Accords." Paper presented at the Guatemala after the Peace Accords Conference, Institute of Latin American Studies, University of London, November.

———. 1998. *The Guatemalan Military Project: A Violence Called Democracy*. Philadelphia: University of Pennsylvania Press.

Scott, James C. 1990. *Domination and the Arts of Resistance: Hidden Transcripts*. New Haven: Yale University Press.

Scott, Joan. 1991. "The Evidence of Experience." *Critical Inquiry* 17 (summer): 773–97.

Segundo Encuentro Continental. 1991. *Documentos y Conclusiones*. Guatemala: Secretaria Operativa del Segundo Encuentro Continental.

Serech, José. 1995. "Perspectivas Mayas y Reconstrucción Social Guatemalteca." Paper given at the Nineteenth Congress of the Latin America Studies Association, Washington, D.C.

———. 1996. "Oferta y Aporte de las Culturas Subalternas y Dominadas en el Proceso Hacia una Nueva Sociedad." In *Globalización y Diversidad Cultural*, ed. Antonio Gallo. Guatemala: Textos Ak' Kutan, 109–18.

Sherman, William L. 1979. *Forced Native Labor in Sixteenth-century Central America*. Lincoln: University of Nebraska Press.

Shobat, Ella, and Robert Stam. 1994. *Unthinking Eurocentrism: Multiculturalism and the Media*. New York: Routledge.

Sieder, Rachel. 1997. *Customary Law and Democratic Transition in Guatemala*. London: University of London, Institute of Latin American Studies Research Papers.

Sikkink, Kathryn. 1996. "The Emergence, Evolution, and Effectiveness of the Latin American Human Rights Network." In *Constructing Democracy: Human Rights, Citizenship, and Society in Latin America*, ed. Elizabeth Jelin and Eric Hershberg, 59–84. Boulder: Westview Press.

Simon, Jean-Marie. 1986. *Civil Patrols in Guatemala*. New York: Americas Watch.

————. 1987. *Guatemala: Eternal Spring, Eternal Tyranny*. New York: W. W. Norton.

Simpson, Lesley Byrd, trans. 1964. Francisco López de Gómara, *Cortés, the Life of the Conqueror by His Secretary: Istoria de la Conquista de México*. Berkeley: University of California Press.

Skinner, Elliot. 1983. "Afro-Americas in Search of Africa: The Scholar's Dilemma." In *Transformation and Resiliency in Africa as Seen by Afro-American Scholars*, Pearl T. Robinson and Elliott P. Skinner, 3–26. Washington, D.C.: Howard University.

Smith, Anthony D. 1988. "The Myth of 'Modern Nations' and the Myths of Nations." *Ethnic and Racial Studies* 2:1–26.

Smith, Carol, ed. 1990a. *Guatemalan Indians and the State, 1540–1988*. Austin: University of Texas Press.

————. 1990b. "Origins of the National Question in Guatemala: A Hypothesis." In *Guatemalan Indians and the State, 1540–1988*, ed. Carol Smith, 72–95. Austin: University of Texas Press.

————. 1990c. "Class Position and Class Consciousness in an Indian Community: Totonicapán in the 1970s. In *Guatemalan Indians and the State, 1540–1988*, ed. Carol Smith, 205–29. Austin: University of Texas Press.

————. 1990d. "Conclusions: History and Revolution in Guatemala." In *Guatemalan Indians and the State, 1540–1988*, ed. Carol Smith, 258–85. Austin: University of Texas Press.

————. 1991. "Mayan Nationalism." NACLA *Report on the Americas* 25, no. 3: 29–33.

————. 1992a. "The Second 'Encuentro Continental.'" *Guatemala Scholars Network News*, April, 1–3.

————. 1992b. "Marxists on Class and Culture in Guatemala." Paper presented at LASA, for the session "500 years of Guatemalan Mayan Resistance: A Dialogue between Maya and non-Mayan Scholars." Los Angeles, September.

————. 1993. "Local History in Global Context: Social and Economic Transitions in Western Guatemala." In *Constructing Culture and Power in Latin America*, ed. Daniel H. Levine, 75–118. Ann Arbor: University of Michigan.

————. 1996. "Myths, Intellectuals, and Race/Class/Gender Distinctions in the Formation of Latin American Nations." *Journal of Latin American Anthropology* 2, no. 1: 148–69.

————. 1997. "The Symbolics of Blood: *Mestizaje* in the Americas." *Identities* 3, no. 4 (May): 495–521.

Smith, Carol, and Jeff Boyer. 1987. "Central America since 1979: Part One." *Annual Review of Anthropology* 16:197–221.

Smith, Waldemar R. 1977. *The Fiesta System and Economic Change*. New York: Columbia University Press.

Solares, Jorge, ed. 1993. *Estado y Nación: Las Demandas de los Grupos Etnicos en Guatemala*. Guatemala: FLACSO.

Solares, Jorge. 1995. *Derechos Humanos desde la Perspectiva Indígena en Guatemala*. Debate 29. Guatemala: FLACSO.

Sommer, Doris. 1991. "Rigoberta's Secrets." *Latin American Perspectives*, first of two special issues on "Voices of the Voiceless in Testimonial Literature," 18, no. 3 (summer): 32–50.

———. 1996. "No Secrets." In *The Real Thing: Testimonial Discourse and Latin America*, ed. Georg Gugelberger, 130–57. Durham: Duke University Press.

Son Chonay, Obdulio, and Pakal B'alam José O. Rodríguez. 1994. *Maya' Tz'ib': Introducción a la Escritura Maya*. Guatemala: Editorial Cholsamaj.

Spivak, Gayatri. 1988. "Subaltern Studies: Deconstructing Historiography." In *Selected Subaltern Studies*, ed. Ranajit Guha and Gayatri Chakravorty Spivak, 3–32. New York: Oxford University Press.

Starn, Orin. 1991. "Missing the Revolution: Anthropologists and the War in Peru." *Cultural Anthropology* 6, no. 1: 63–91.

Starn, Orin, Carlos Iván Degregori, and Robin Kirk, eds. 1995. *The Peru Reader: History, Culture, and Politics*. Durham: Duke University.

Stavenhagen, Rodolfo. 1970. "Classes, Colonialism and Acculturation." In *Masses in Latin America*, ed. Irving Louis Horowitz, 235–88. New York: Oxford University Press.

———. 1971. "Decolonizing the Applied Social Sciences." *Human Organization* 30, no. 4 (winter): 333–57.

———. 1988. *Derecho Indígena y Derechos Humanos en América Latina*. México: Colegio de México and Instituto Interamericano de Derechos Humanos.

———. 1992. "Challenging the Nation-State in Latin America." *Journal of International Affairs* 45, no. 2: 421–40.

———. 1996. "Indigenous Rights: Some Conceptual Problems." In *Constructing Democracy: Human Rights, Citizenship, and Society in Latin America*. Boulder: Westview Press, 141–59.

Stavenhagen, Rodolfo, and Diego Iturralde, eds. 1990. *Entre la Ley y la Costumbre: El Derecho Cosuetudinario Indígena en América Latina*. México: Instituto Indigenista Interamericano and Instituto Interamericano de Derechos Humanos.

Stephen, Lynn. 1994. "The Politics and Practice of Testimonial Literature." In *Hear My Testimony: Maria Teresa Tula, Human Rights Activist in El Salvador*, ed. Lynn Stephen, 223–33. Boston: South End Press.

Stern, Steve, ed. 1987. *Resistance, Rebellion, and Consciousness in the Andean Peasant World: 18th to 20th Centuries*. Madison: University of Wisconsin Press.

Stocking, George. 1983. "History of Anthropology: Whence/Whither." In *Observers Observed: Essays on Ethnographic Fieldwork*, ed. George Stocking, 3–12. Madison: University of Wisconsin Press.

Stoll, David. 1990. *Is Latin America Turning Protestant? The Politics of Evangelical Growth*. Berkeley: University of California Press.

———. 1993. *Between Two Armies in the Ixil Towns of Guatemala*. New York: Columbia University Press.

———. 1997. "To Whom Should We Listen? Human Rights Activism in Two Guatemalan Land Disputes." In *Human Rights, Culture and Context: Anthropological Perspectives*, ed. Richard Wilson, 187–215. Chicago: London Press.

Stratmeyer, Dennis, and Jean Stratmeyer. 1979. "El Nawal Jacalteco y el Cargador del Alma en Concepción Huista." *Guatemala Indígena* 14, nos. 3–4: 102–29.

Sturm, Circe. 1996. "Old Writing and New Messages: The Role of Hieroglyphic

Literacy in Maya Cultural Activism." In *Mayan Cultural Activism in Guatemala*, ed. Edward Fischer and R. McKenna Brown, 114–30. Austin: University of Texas Press.

Suarez-Orozco, Marcelo. 1989. *Central American Refugees and U.S. High Schools: A Psychosocial Study of Motivation and Achievement*. Stanford: Stanford University Press.

Tambiah, Stanley. 1986. *Sri Lanka: Ethnic Fratricide and the Dismantling of Democracy*. Chicago: University of Chicago Press.

Taussig, Michael. 1980. *The Devil and Commodity Fetishism in South America*. Chapel Hill: University of North Carolina Press.

———. 1987. *Shamanism, Colonialism, and the Wild Man: A Study in Terror and Healing*. Chicago: University of Chicago Press.

———. 1992. *The Nervous System*. New York: Routledge.

———. 1993. *Mimesis and Alterity: A Particular History of the Senses*. New York: Routledge.

———. 1997. *The Magic of the State*. New York: Routledge.

Tax, Sol. 1937. "The Municipios of the Midwestern Highland of Guatemala." *American Anthropologist* 39: 423–44.

———. 1968. *The Heritage of Conquest*. New York: Cooper Square.

Tay Coyoy, Alfredo. 1996. *Análisis de la Situación de la Educación Maya en Guatemala*. Guatemala: Editorial Cholsamaj.

Tedlock, Barbara. 1982. *Time and the Highland Maya*. Albuquerque: University of New Mexico Press.

———. 1991. "Quiché Maya Dream Interpretation." *Ethos* 9: 313–30.

Tedlock, Dennis. 1983. *The Spoken Word and the Work of Interpretation*. Philadelphia: University of Pennsylvania Press.

———, trans. 1985. *Popol Vuh: The Definitive Edition of the Mayan Book of the Dawn of Life and the Glories of Gods and Kings*. New York: Simon and Schuster.

———. 1993a. "Torture in the Archives: Mayans Meet Europeans." *American Anthropologists* 95, no. 1: 139–52.

———. 1993b. *Breath on the Mirror: Mythic Voices of the Living Maya*. San Francisco: Harper San Francisco.

Thorn, Judith. 1996. *The Lived Horizon of My Being: The Substantiation of the Self and the Discourse of Resistance in Rigoberta Menchú, MM Bakhtin and Víctor Montejo*. Tempe: Arizona State University Press, Center for Latin American Studies.

Todorov, Tzvetan. 1984. *The Conquest of America*. Richard Howard, trans. New York: Harper.

Touraine, Alain. 1987. *Actores Sociales y Sistemas Políticos en América Latina*. Santiago, Chile: PREALC.

Tranfo, Luigi. 1979. "Tono y Nagual." In *Los Huaves de San Mateo del Mar, Oaxaca*, 177–210. Mexico: Instituto Nacional Indigenista, 177–210.

Trend, David. 1996. *Radical Democracy: Identity, Citizenship, and the State*. New York: Routledge.

Trudeau, Robert. 1993. *Guatemalan Politics: The Popular Struggle for Democracy*. Boulder: Lynne Reinner.

Tsing, Anna. 1993. *In the Realm of the Diamond Queen*. Princeton: Princeton University Press.

Tzian, Leopoldo. 1994. *Kajlab'aliil Maya'iib' Xuq Mu'siib': Ri Ub'antajiik Iximuleew—Mayas y Ladinos en Cifras: El Caso de Guatemala.* Guatemala: Editorial Cholsamaj.

Universidad Rafael Landívar, Instituto de Lingüística. 1997. *Cultura de Guatemala: Primer Congreso de Estudios Mayas*, vols. 1–3, Año XVIII (May–August). Guatemala: Universidad Rafael Landívar.

Urban, Greg, and Joel Sherzer. 1991. *Nation-States and Indians in Latin America.* Austin: University of Texas Press.

Van Cott, Donna Lee, ed. 1994. *Indigenous Peoples and Democracy in Latin America.* New York: St. Martin's Press.

van den Berghe, Pierre, and George P. Primov. 1977. *Inequality in the Peruvian Andes: Class and Ethnicity in Cuzco.* Columbia: University of Missouri Press.

Vargas Llosa, Mario. 1983. "Inquest in the Andes." *New York Times Magazine*, July 31, pp. 18.

———. 1990. "Questions of Conquest: What Columbus Wrought, and What He Did Not." *Harper's Magazine*, December 1987, pp. 45–53.

Villacorta C., J. Antonio. 1934. *Memorial de Tecpán-Atitlán por Francisco Hernández Arana Xajilá and Francisco Díaz Gebutá Quej.* Guatemala: Tipografía Nacional.

Villa Rojas, Alfonso. 1947. "Kinship and Nagualism in a Tzeltal Community, Southeastern Mexico." *American Anthropologist* 49:578–87.

Viteri E., Ernesto. 1997. "Cinco Años de Negociaciones." In *Memoria de la Conferencia: Procesos de Paz Comparados*, ed. Cynthia Arnson and Mario Quiñones Amézquita, 9–20. Guatemala: ASIES and the Latin American Program of the Woodrow Wilson International Center for Scholars.

Vogt, Evon Z. 1969. *Zinacantan: A Mayan Community in the Highlands of Chiapas.* Cambridge: Harvard University Press.

———. 1970. "Human Souls and Animal Spirits in Zinacantan." In *Echanges et Communications*, ed. Jean Pouillon and Pierre Maranda, 1148–67. The Hague: Mouton.

Wallace, Anthony F. C. 1956. "Revitalization Movements." *American Anthropologist* 58 (1956): 264–81.

———. 1972. *The Death and Rebirth of the Seneca.* New York: Vintage.

Warren, Kay B. 1989. *The Symbolism of Subordination: Indian Identity in a Guatemalan Town.* Austin: University of Texas Press. Originally published in 1978.

———. 1992. "Transforming Memories and Histories: Meanings of Ethnic Resurgence for Mayan Indians." In *Americas: New Interpretive Essays*, ed. Alfred Stepan, 189–219. Oxford: Oxford University Press.

———. 1993. "Interpreting *la Violencia* in Guatemala: Shapes of Kaqchikel Resistance and Silence." In *The Violence Within: Cultural and Political Opposition in Divided Nations*, ed. Kay B. Warren. Boulder: Westview Press, 25–56.

———. 1994. "Language and the Politics of Self-Expression: Mayan Revitalization in Guatemala." *Cultural Survival Quarterly*, summer–fall, 81–86.

———. 1995. "Each Mind Is a World: Dilemmas of Feeling and Intention in a Kaqchikel Maya Community." In *Other Intentions: Culture and the Attribution of Inner States*, ed. Lawrence Rosen, 47–67. Seattle: University of Washington Press and School of American Research.

———. 1996. "Reading History as Resistance: Mayan Public Intellectuals in Guatemala." In *Mayan Cultural Activism in Guatemala*, ed. Edward Fischer and R. McKenna Brown, 89–106. Austin: University of Texas Press.

———. 1997a. "Identidad Indígena en Guatemala: Una Crítica de Modelos Norteamericanos." Guatemala: *Mesoamérica* 18, no. 33 (June): 73–91.

———. 1997b. "Narrating Cultural Resurgence: Genre and Self-Representation for Pan-Mayan Writers." In *Auto/Ethnography: Rewriting the Self and the Social*, ed. Deborah Reed-Danahay, 21–45. Oxford: Berg.

———. 1997c. "Tensiones Persistentes e Identidades Cambiantes: Luchas de la Familia Maya en Guatemala." In *Primer Congreso de Estudios Mayas*, 271–96. Guatemala: Instituto de Lingüística, Universidad Rafael Landívar and Editorial Cholsamaj.

———. 1997d. "The Indigenous Role in Guatemala Peace." *Cultural Survival Quarterly* 21, no. 2 (summer): 24–27.

———. 1997e. "Mayan Self-Determination and Educational Choice in Guatemala." In *Self-Determination and Self-Administration: A Sourcebook*, ed. Wolfgang Danspeckgruber with Sir Arthur Watts, 179–98. New York: Lynne Rienner.

———. 1998. "Indigenous Movements as a Challenge to a Unified Social Movement Paradigm for Guatemala." In *Cultures of Politics/Politics of Cultures: Re-visioning Latin American Social Movements Revisited*, ed. Sonia E. Alvarez, Evelina Dagnino, and Arturo Escobar, 165–95. Boulder: Westview Press.

———. Forthcoming a. "Enduring Tensions and Changing Identities: Mayan Family Struggles in Guatemala." In *History in Person: Enduring Struggles and the Practice of Identity*, ed. Dorothy Holland and Jean Lave. Santa Fe: SAR Press.

———. Forthcoming b. "Mayan Multiculturalism and the Violence of Memories." In *Violence, Political Agency, and the Self*, ed. Veena Das. Berkeley: University of California Press.

Wasserstrom, Robert. 1983. *Class and Society in Central Chiapas*. Berkeley: University of California Press.

Watanabe, John. 1989. "Elusive Essences: Souls and Social Identity in Two Highland Maya Communities." In *Ethnographic Encounters in Southern Mesoamerica: Essays in Honor of Evon Zartman Vogt, Jr.* Albany: Institute for Mesoamerican Studies, 263–74.

———. 1990. "From Saints to Shibboleths: Image, Structure, and Identity in Maya Religious Syncretism." *American Ethnologist* 17, no. 1: 131–50.

———. 1992. *Maya Saints and Souls in a Changing World*. Austin: University of Texas Press.

———. 1994. "Unimagining the Maya: Anthropologists, Others, and the Inescapable Hubris of Authorship." *Bulletin of Latin American Research* 14, no. 1: 25–45.

———. Forthcoming. "Mayas and Anthropologists in the Highlands of Guatemala since the 1960s." In *Ethnology,* vol. 6 of *Supplement to the Handbook of Middle American Indians*, ed. John Monaghan. Victoria Bricker, gen. ed. Austin: University of Texas Press.

Williams, Raymond. 1977. *Marxism and Literature*. Oxford: Oxford University Press.

Wilmer, Franke. 1993. *The Indigenous Voice in World Politics*. Newbury Park: Sage.

Wilson, Richard. 1991. "Machine Guns and Mountain Spirits: The Cultural Effects of State Repression among the Q'eqchi' of Guatemala." *Critique of Anthropology*, 33–61.

———. 1993. "Anchored Communities: Identity and History of the Maya-Q'eqchi'." *Man* 28, no. 1: 121–38.

———. 1995. *Mayan Resurgence in Guatemala: Q'eqchi' Experiences*. Norman: University of Oklahoma Press.

———. 1997a. *Human Rights, Culture and Context: Anthropological Perspectives*. London: Pluto Press.

———. 1997b. "Representing Human Rights Violations: Social Contexts and Subjectivities." In *Human Rights, Culture and Context: Anthropological Perspectives*, ed. Richard Wilson, 134–60. London: Pluto Press.

Wolf, Eric. 1957. "Closed Corporate Communities in Mesoamerica and Central Java." *Southwestern Journal of Anthropology* 13:1–18.

———. 1968. *Peasant Wars of the Twentieth Century*. New York: Harper and Row.

———. 1986. "The Vicissitudes of the Closed Corporate Peasant Community." *American Ethnologist* 13:325–29.

Wood, Davida. 1993. "Politics of Identity in a Palestinian Village in Israel." In *The Violence Within: Cultural and Political Opposition in Divided Nations*, ed. Kay B. Warren, 87–121. Boulder: Westview Press.

Woodward, Susan. 1995. *Balkan Tragedy: Chaos and Dissolution after the Cold War*. Washington, D.C.: Brookings Institution.

Yashar, Deborah. 1996. "Indigenous Protest and Democracy in Latin America." In *Constructing Democratic Governance: Latin America and the Caribbean in the 1990s, Themes and Issues*, ed. Jorge Domínguez and Abraham Lowenthal, 87–105. Baltimore: Johns Hopkins University Press.

———. 1997. *Demanding Democracy: Reform and Reaction in Costa Rica and Guatemala, 1870s–1950s*. Stanford: Stanford University Press.

———. Forthcoming. "Contesting Citizenship: Indigenous Politics and Democracy in Latin America." *Comparative Politics*.

Young, Crawford. 1976. *The Politics of Cultural Pluralism*. Madison: University of Wisconsin Press.

———. 1993. *The Rising Tide of Cultural Pluralism: The Nation-State at Bay?* Madison: University of Wisconsin Press.

Yúdice, George. 1996. "*Testimonio* and Postmodernism." In *The Real Thing: Testimonial Discourse and Latin America*, ed. Georg Gugelberger, 42–57. Durham: Duke University Press.

Zimmerman, Marc. 1995a. *Theory, History, Fiction, and Poetry*. Vol. 1 of *Literature and Resistance in Guatemala: Textual Modes and Cultural Politics from El Señor Presidente to Rigoberta Menchú*. Athens: Ohio University Center for International Studies.

———. 1995b. *Testimonio and Cultural Politics in the Years of Cerezo and Serrano Elias*. Vol. 2 of *Literature and Resistance in Guatemala: Textual Modes and Cultural Politics from El Señor Presidente to Rigoberta Menchú*. Athens: Ohio University Center for International Studies.

Index